GREEN
BYWAYS

GREEN BYWAYS

Garden Discoveries in the Great Lakes States

Sharon Lappin Lumsden

Lime Tree Publications
Champaign, Illinois

To order additional copies of *Green Byways,* contact your bookseller. Or write to Lime Tree Publications and send $22.00 for one book ($19.95 plus postage and handling); for each additional copy sent to the same address add $21.00 ($19.95 plus $.86 extra postage).

Illinois residents add sales tax of $1.45 *per book*.

Send your check or money order to:
    Lime Tree Publications - GB
    507 South Garfield Avenue
    Champaign IL 61821

Be sure your name and address are clearly written. Allow 4-6 weeks for delivery.

© 1993 Sharon Lappin Lumsden

Lime Tree Publications
507 South Garfield Avenue
Champaign IL 61821

(217) 355-5424

Library of Congress Catalog Card Number 93-78515

Design by André Kuzniarek
Typesetting by IntelliText Corporation

for . . . Bob and Paul and Kenneth and Margaret

Contents

Messages to the Reader / **vii**

Introduction and Acknowledgments / **ix**

Illinois: Northeast
North of Interstate 74 and east of Interstate 39/US Route 51 / **1**

Illinois: Northwest
North of Interstate 72 and west of Interstate 39/US Route 51 / **41**

Illinois: Southeast
South of Interstate 74 and east of US Route 51 / **53**

Illinois: Southwest
South of Interstate 72 and US Route 36 and west of US Route 51 / **61**

Indiana: Northeast
North of Interstate 70 and east of US Route 31 / **73**

Indiana: Northwest
North of Interstate 74 and west of US Route 31 / **87**

Indiana: Southeast
South of Interstate 70 and east of Interstate 65 (includes Indianapolis) / **93**

Indiana: Southwest
South of Interstate 74 and west of Interstate 65 / **105**

Michigan: The Upper Peninsula and northern Lower Peninsula
North of US Route 10 / **113**

Michigan: Southeast
South of US Route 10 and east of US Routes 27 and 127 / **123**

Michigan: Southwest
South of US Route 10 and west of US Routes 27 and 127 / **149**

Minnesota: North
North of US Route 10 and Minnesota Route 210 / **171**

Minnesota: South
South of US Route 10 and Minnesota Route 210 / **177**

Ohio: North
North of Interstate 70 / **199**

Ohio: South
South of Interstate 70 / **251**

Wisconsin: North
North of Wisconsin Route 21, US Route 151 on the east, and Interstate 90 on the west / **279**

Wisconsin: South
South of Wisconsin Route 21 extended / **289**

Index / **308**

Each section of the text begins with a map of the geographic area under discussion. City maps are:

Chicago, Illinois / **2**
Fort Wayne, Indiana / **74**
Detroit, Michigan / **124**
Minneapolis and St Paul, Minnesota / **178**
Cleveland and Columbus, Ohio / **200**
Cincinnati, Ohio / **252**
Madison, Wisconsin / **290**

Messages to the Reader

You'll find *Green Byways* a pleasant traveling companion and a useful guide to gardens. The six featured states are listed alphabetically and divided into manageable sections. Cities and towns within each section are also in alphabetical order, as are sites within a city. The maps will quickly tell you if there's a listed garden in a given area. Icons and information accompany each description to give you a quick impression of the site.

💲 An admission fee is charged (it's usually less than admission to a first-run movie). Specific fees aren't listed because they change from year to year.

♿ *At least some part* of the garden and its facilities are acccessible to the handicapped.

☕ Food is available. It may come from vending machines, a cafeteria, or a genteel tea-room.

Very few of the sites in *Green Byways* require an appointment for your visit. However, before you drive to an out-of-the-way garden, especially one that's part of a small business or an historic site, we suggest that you call to confirm hours, offerings, and the current state of the plantings.

Many of our growers and nurseries offer catalogs for mail orders. Few of these catalogs are free but, again, charges aren't listed because they change. Enclose *at least* two dollars when you request a catalog from any of the *Green Byways* sources. If you've sent too much you'll get a credit towards your order and if you've not sent enough the nursery will let you know. Along the same lines, if you ask one of the smaller businesses for information, include a letter-sized (No. 10) self-addressed stamped envelope to encourage a prompt and complete reply.

A file for the second edition of *Green Byways* already exists; you can contribute. If you find a site significantly different from its description, perhaps because of garden additions, major renovations, or obvious neglect, please let me know.

Also, in spite of the many resources I used to find gardens, I could very well have missed your favorite. Or you might discover a new garden. If you know about a horticultural site that should be included in the next *Green Byways*, please send me as much information as you can, including, if possible: its name and specific location; the name and address of a contact person or the group responsible for the garden, such as a park district, a garden club, or a business; pertinent flyers or brochures; and a description of the features that make the site worth visiting. Some of my favorite places, such as Lake County Nursery and the Japanese Garden at Normandale Community College, were just such word-of-mouth recommendations.

Send your information to Lime Tree Publications, 507 South Garfield, Champaign IL 61821. I'll doubly refund your postage and will be eternally grateful . . . at least for a little while.

Enjoy.

Sharon Lappin Lumsden

Introduction and Acknowledgments

It all began with daylilies in the middle of Kansas. On our way to the neighborhood restaurant with the highly recommended breakfasts, we glimpsed a tiny park filled with glowing daylilies. After this bright beginning to our day, I realized that many pleasing but unheralded gardens are scattered across our area, quietly inviting travelers to stretch their legs and refresh their minds. To me, "garden" can mean a lovely nook, acres of planned verdure, wildflowers tucked into woodlands, plant-filled greenhouses, display beds that are the pride of a small grower, or the habitat houses of a major conservatory. The trick is to find these places.

The states included here were settled by agriculturists and it shows; we love our gardens and all things related. The Great Lakes states are rich in public gardens large and small, commercial display gardens and thriving greenhouses, flower and garden shows, garden-related festivals, and horticultural societies. We support gardens and gardening with our attendance and our dollars; several of our public gardens are undergoing expansion or renovation and new arboretums and botanical gardens are developing. Hundreds of thousands of admirers visit these public gardens each year. Some sources suggest that garden-related businesses are one of the fastest-growing segments of our regional economy. I learned all this, and much, much more, from countless letters and telephone conversations and numerous garden visits (over 175) during the process that produced *Green Byways*.

This book would not exist without the wisdom and moral support of two Bobs. The first is my husband and traveling companion, a non-gardener who loves to travel, who learned to enjoy the gardens and their people, and who has begun to know the plants and to develop his own garden preferences. The second is typesetter and book-birthing midwife Bob Chapdu of IntelliText, a longtime herb society friend whose ideas and enthusiasm, combined with nearly endless patience, have been extremely helpful and are appreciated more than I can say. This treasured individual worked his magic on a file of disks and great piles of paper and turned them into a book. Barbara Cohen, professional indexer extraordinaire, graciously shared her office, her computer, her expertise, and her wit to help build the useful index she believed the book deserved. New friend Keith Crotz, of *The American Botanist, Booksellers*, was an early advocate of the project and has been a lode of worthy suggestions and solid information. André Kuzniarek, besides designing the book and its cover, has helped me begin to learn about creating the physical entity that is a book.

I'm blessed with a number of other friends who know about books and gardens, cronies who are both avid users of books and knowledgable, enthusiastic gardeners. To all these supportive souls, many of whom are fellow members of the Champaign-Urbana Herb Society, my heart-felt thanks for their encouraging words and their interest in the book. Special appreciation goes to Barbara Anderson, Phyllis Brussel, Connie Fairchild, Bette Leach, Aporn Surintramont, and Nancy Works for reading sections of the manuscript for clarity, and to Heather Young, who used her sharp eyes and horticultural expertise to check the manuscript.

Herbarists often mark special occasions with tussy-mussies, which are nosegays of flowers and foliage that have been chosen for their traditional meanings. To each of my helpful friends, a tussy-mussy of bee orchis for your industry, canary grass for your perseverance, and the foliage of an orange tree for your generosity, accompanied by small white bellflowers for my gratitude, garden sage for esteem, and daffodils that symbolize my high regard for you.

In the end, of course, final responsibility for *Green Byways*, its weaknesses as well as its strengths, is mine. From the beginning, the stated aim of the book was ". . . to lead travelers who garden, and gardeners who travel, to the lesser-known horticultural sites and botanical treats in six Great Lakes states." You will decide if the book meets this goal.

I wish you joy in your travels and in your garden discoveries.

Sharon Lappin Lumsden
Champaign Illinois
August 1993

GREEN BYWAYS

Illinois: Northeast

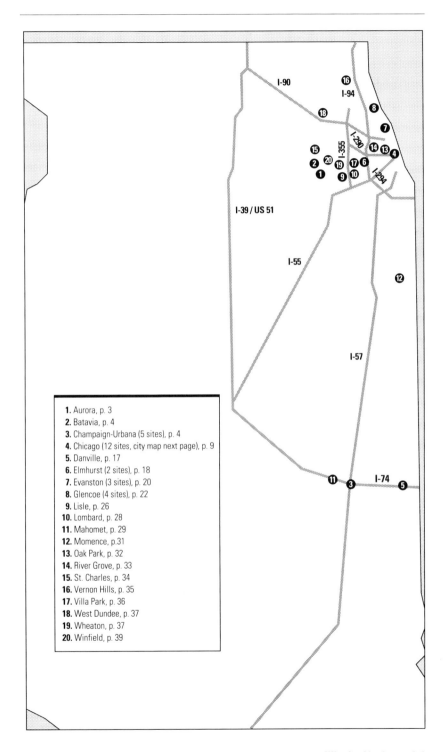

1. Aurora, p. 3
2. Batavia, p. 4
3. Champaign-Urbana (5 sites), p. 4
4. Chicago (12 sites, city map next page), p. 9
5. Danville, p. 17
6. Elmhurst (2 sites), p. 18
7. Evanston (3 sites), p. 20
8. Glencoe (4 sites), p. 22
9. Lisle, p. 26
10. Lombard, p. 28
11. Mahomet, p. 29
12. Momence, p. 31
13. Oak Park, p. 32
14. River Grove, p. 33
15. St. Charles, p. 34
16. Vernon Hills, p. 35
17. Villa Park, p. 36
18. West Dundee, p. 37
19. Wheaton, p. 37
20. Winfield, p. 39

Illinois: Northeast / CHICAGO

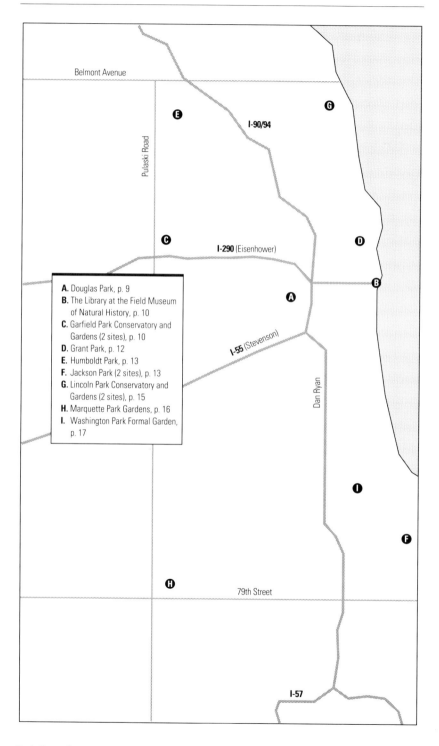

A. Douglas Park, p. 9
B. The Library at the Field Museum of Natural History, p. 10
C. Garfield Park Conservatory and Gardens (2 sites), p. 10
D. Grant Park, p. 12
E. Humboldt Park, p. 13
F. Jackson Park (2 sites), p. 13
G. Lincoln Park Conservatory and Gardens (2 sites), p. 15
H. Marquette Park Gardens, p. 16
I. Washington Park Formal Garden, p. 17

Illinois: Northeast

Those of us who live in east-central Illinois are often chided because our landscape lacks "scenery." True, we have no purple mountains' majesty but on a late summer day, when a high pressure weather system has established itself, life on Illinois highways is a visual delight. Cloud puffs drift in a bright blue sky, ruffles of chicory and Queen Anne's lace edge the highway, and cattails and sedges guard roadside swales. In drier areas, ripening grasses lay a golden haze above small sunflowers and washes of black-eyed Susan and hawkweed. Fences hold trumpet vine in espaliered wildness and an occasional fencepost is claimed by alien morning glory. Torches of pale yellow bring finale to the two-summer life of great mullein. Asters, late-blooming hostas, and ornamental grasses welcome autumn to parks and gardens and it's a fine time to be out and about in Illinois.

Bri-Lea Greenhouses
Box 35, R. 1, Bilter Road
Aurora IL 60504
(708) 851-3480

Commercial grower of African violets. 3,000 sq.ft. greenhouse.

All plants labeled. Plant sales. Intermittent workshops and seminars. Group tours and programs by appointment.
Open Tuesday-Saturday 9am-5pm, Sunday 1pm-5pm. Closed Monday and all holidays.

Many, many, many African violets, in their countless tints and shades, fit into 3,000 square feet. This is Bri-Lea, where graceful sprays of phalaenopsis orchids bring delicious counterpoint to earthbound violets. An information sheet about African violets includes a map that will help you find Bri-Lea and their violets. Additional plant varieties appear at Bri-Lea's annual Open House (on the weekend before Mother's Day); you may be treated to displays of gloxinias, achimenes, Cape primroses (*Streptocarpus* spp.), or other gesneriads. Special events make the greenhouses even more festive than usual but those lovely plants will be hard to resist at any time.

Exit the East-West Tollway (I-88/IL5) at Farnsworth/Kirk Road. Go north a short distance to Bilter Road, then east on Bilter about a mile to Bri-Lea.

Shady Hill Gardens
Geranium Specialists
821 Walnut Street
Batavia IL 60510

At their request, Shady Hill's telephone number is not given. Please *write* for information.

Commercial specialist in geraniums and poinsettias. 53,000 sq.ft. greenhouse.

Catalog. All plants labeled. Plant sales.
Open all year Monday-Saturday 9am-5pm, Sundays in April, May, and June 11am-4pm.

Geraniums are greenhouse fields of jade on this overcast October day. Few of the plants are blooming but the variety of leaf shapes and color patterns is a fine sight. In November, the greenhouses will be filled with poinsettias in assorted colors; that, too, will be impressive.

Just inside the door, tables hold an admirable collection of scented geraniums. Here, too, are succulent geraniums from South Africa whose unusual leaf forms and sturdy stems adapt well to bonsai training. Lush cascades of ivy-leaved geraniums trail from baskets overhead and a few small-leaved scented geraniums are beguiling standards and topiaries.

In summer, the exterior display garden will be a riot of geranium color. The best times to visit Shady Hill, to admire luscious bloom and to purchase plants, are mid-April through summer for geraniums and late November for poinsettias. You may want to acquire Shady Hill's splendid color catalog before you go, to prepare yourself for the abundance here.

Shady Hill Gardens is four blocks west of Batavia Avenue (IL 31) and three blocks south of Batavia's Main Street. Look for the group of large greenhouses on the north side of Walnut Street.

Champaign-Urbana

Klehm's Nursery
Off US Route 150, northwest of Champaign

Commercial producer of peonies and daylilies.

No amenities of any sort.
Open daylight hours.

◄ On a warm, still day in late May, some of these fields glow with blooming peonies and the scent is heavenly. During the hotter days of July and August, the daylily fields are visual extravaganzas. If you're in the Champaign area during peony or daylily season, it's worth a drive on the country roads to give your eyes a feast. In some years, the flower fields can be admired from I-74 west of Champaign.

Although there are no display gardens or retail sales at this field-growing location of Klehm's, there are occasional open houses during peak peony and daylily bloom.

For Open House dates contact Klehm Nursery, Route 5 Box 197, South Barrington IL 60010. (708) 551-3720. Champaign location: (217) 359-2888.

There's no direct access to US Route 150 from I-72 or I-74. Take I-72 to its end at Mattis Avenue and go north on Mattis about two miles to US 150. Go west on US 150 to County Road 900E, the first road that goes north. It doesn't look promising, as there's an immediate dogleg and a bridge over I-74, but the flower fields lie just beyond the bridge.

Lindsay Tennis Center Garden
On Sangamon Street in Centennial Park
Champaign

Two-thirds acre naturalistic plantings.

♿ Plants identified on schematic map in park. Surrounding park offers picnic facilities, public swimming pool, water slide, children's activities.
Open all year during daylight hours.

The perennial tapestry of Lindsay Garden is attractive from early spring through the depth of winter, just as planned. Great crowds of astilbes, yarrows (*Achillea* spp.), and daylilies follow the thousands of daffodils who announce spring. Joe-Pye weed (*Eupatorium purpureum*) and asters add broad cool-color strokes to summer's gold. Autumn brings hazy blue Russian sage (*Perovskia atriplicifolia*) and dense planes of rosy-copper sedum 'Autumn Joy'. Stalwart remnants of all these stand among yuccas and stately grasses for winter texture and color.

This is one of the midwest's few public installations by Oehme, van Sweden and Associates. These east coast landscape designers originated "The New American Garden," a refreshing style that employs washes of texture and color, banks of native or hardy plants, year 'round appeal, and the appearance of low maintenance. This approach seems particularly appropriate here in east-central Illinois, where our skies are wide and our open land may appear to lack interest; even a relatively small installation such as this exudes majesty. I visit this garden at least once a month throughout the year and I always find joy in its richness and diversity.

For information contact the Director, Champaign Park District, 706 Kenwood Road, Champaign IL 61821. (217) 398-2550.

Go east on I-72 to Mattis Avenue then south on Mattis a few blocks to the stoplight at John Street. Go west on John a short distance to Crescent Street and turn south onto Crescent. Go a long block to Sangamon, then west on Sangamon to the garden.

Jaques House Garden
207 West Elm Street
Urbana

Cottage garden and herb garden around an 1870 home.

♿ Brochure in garden. Most plants labeled. Small picnics possible. Spring plant sale. Open daylight hours.

The season of beauty at Jaques House extends from very early crocuses and pasqueflowers through the glory of summer bloom to autumn's display of coneflowers, hardy cyclamens, and heavily perfumed sweet autumn clematis (*Clematis paniculata*). Small-scale and creeping plants inhabit a raised walkside bed; passersby have an intimate view of the flowers and can caress the herbs to provoke their scents. The central lavender garden surrounds a handsome sundial, herbs and climbing roses grow against a handcrafted picket fence, and stately plume poppies (*Macleaya cordata*) stand beside the clematis-covered arbor. A teak bench encourages contemplative relaxation. Employees of nearby businesses often enjoy alfresco lunches in this garden, surrounded by glorious colors and luscious scents.

These plantings, designed and maintained by the Champaign-Urbana Herb Society, are supported by a plant sale held here in early May, amidst the garden's spring exuberance. Hushed moments of summer twilight are lovely here too, as some flowers begin to collect dew and others glow in the evening light. Jaques House Garden is inviting at almost any time.

For details contact the Reference Librarian, Urbana Free Library, 201 South Race, Urbana IL 61801. (217) 367-4405.

▶

◄ *Exit I-74 at Cunningham/US Route 45 and go south. (Cunningham becomes Vine Street at University Avenue/US Route 150.) Continue south past the stoplight at Main Street and go one more block to Elm Street. Go west on Elm about three and a half blocks to the garden, just west of the Urbana Free Library.*

Meadowbrook Herb Garden
Meadowbrook Park
South Race Street
Urbana

40'x40' herb garden with theme gardens.

Brochure in garden. Most plants labeled. Nature trail in adjacent restored prairie. Picnic facilities (limited, no restrooms). Group tours by appointment.
Open daylight hours all year.

Honeysuckle twines along the rail fence that embraces this compact garden and, in the rock garden, early spring pasqueflowers herald summer's herbs, old roses, and scented geraniums (*Pelargonium* spp.). Oriental poppies in the Shakespeare Garden lord it over rue, rosemary, lavender, columbine, and other Elizabethan favorites. Familiar plants and less common individuals inhabit the tea garden; perhaps you'll see the ornate blooms of gas plant (*Dictamnus albus*) or the bank of fragrant daisy-like flowers that is chamomile. Midsummer brings flamboyant color to the dye garden as butterfly weed (*Asclepias tuberosa*) and golden marguerite (*Anthemis tinctoria*) come into their own among a wealth of other dye plants. Stately foxglove (*Digitalis* sp.), a source of heart medication, reigns over the medicinal garden until its floral spikes give way to hot peppers, comfrey, garlic, and other plants of traditional medicine. Alliums (garlics and onions and chives), several varieties of basil, and other favorite kitchen herbs inhabit the culinary border, where a hop vine sprawls along the fence. A thorny old-fashioned rose sits in a corner and treats us to heavily scented flowers or decorative large red rosehips in their season. Plant species that were used in Native American medicine or rituals fill the adjacent border.

Meadowbrook Park also holds public plots for organic gardening; here are some of the most beautiful, most lovingly tended vegetable gardens you'll ever see. Here, too, in a sizable tract of restored prairie, a soft path leads you through flatland prairie, over a wooded creek, and to hillside grasses and forbs. ►

◀ Meadowbrook Herb Garden is planned and maintained by the Champaign-Urbana Herb Society; as a member of that group, I revel in garden fellowship while we tend all the chores a public garden presents. I knew this space as a cattle feed lot and as a graveled parking lot before its garden incarnation. How can I describe it objectively? After my own garden, it's my favorite place in Champaign County. When we work here on summer evenings there's almost always a breeze on the herb garden hill, nighthawks quarter the sky, hawk-moths hover at the nicotianas, and this is where I want to be.

For further information or to arrange a tour, contact the Urbana Park District, 901 North Broadway Avenue, Urbana IL 61801. (217) 367-1536.

Exit I-74 at Cunningham/US Route 45 and go south on Cunningham/Vine over a mile to Florida Avenue. Go west on Florida to Race Street, then south on Race about a mile to Windsor Road. Meadowbrook Park is on Race not far south of Windsor. Park near the vegetable gardens and walk up the slope to the herb garden.
Or, from US 45 south of Champaign, take Windsor Road a few miles east to Race Street, then go south a short distance to the park.

University of Illinois
Urbana

There are a few horticultural installations of interest around the University of Illinois campus: the long walk and allée-to-be that stretches north from the Illini Union to Beckman Center (from Green Street to University Avenue, just east of Wright Street); the Noel Garden of floriferous perennials on the south side of Krannert Art Museum, where spring bulbs bloom, daylilies flourish, and coneflowers are brilliant against the museum's white marble wall; a collection of native and ornamental grasses near the Horticulture Building on South Orchard; the small new conservatory at the Plant Sciences Laboratory on South Dorner. Otherwise, most campus plantings are aggregations of annuals that tend to be either boring or garish. Our "Quad," however, is stunning in the spring, when the abundant ornamental trees and shrubs are in flower.

A major botanical garden and arboretum are under development at the University; initial planting is projected for 1993. The garden will stretch along Lincoln Avenue, from its intersection with Florida Avenue (for many years, the site of AAS Trial Gardens) south to Windsor Road, where the current evergreen plantation will become the core of a full-fledged arboretum. Long-range plans call for a sunken garden, relocated trial gardens, a picnic grove, perennial plantings, education buildings, and other amenities. This will bear watching. ▶

◀ For information on the status of this project contact the UI Arboretum and Hartley Garden, University Office for Capital Programs, 610 South Sixth Street, Champaign IL 61820. (217) 333-3620.

Chicago

Chicago's lakefront offers nearly continuous beaches, bike and jogging trails, well-used parks, and popular museums, amenities that are important to city-dwellers and visitors alike. The Chicago Park District maintains a number of gardens and conservatories that are green and colorful islands amidst the stone and steel. These, plus numerous neighborhood parks and the large holdings of the Cook County Forest Preserve District, mean that Chicagoans and suburbanites are never far from a garden or a natural area. Visitors, too, can always find a park or garden to enjoy.

Under various names, the Chicago Park District has been an entity since the middle of the nineteenth century. Chicago's 1893 Columbian Exposition was a strong incentive for park development and enrichment; some of the most interesting features of today's parks are direct descendents of those projects. The Park District can send you a brochure, *The Chicago Park District OUTDOOR GARDENS*, and pamphlets and schedules for their conservatories. Chicago parks and conservatories are open every day and there is never an admission fee.

The scale of some of these gardens can be daunting: 4,000 rose bushes in 100 varieties, 25,000 bedding plants, 20,000 square feet of greenhouse. As I visit these vast plantings or read about them, I find myself longing for a shady nook, an intimate garden. Perhaps that's why I found the Japanese Garden in Jackson Park (which *isn't* mentioned in the Park District brochure) so appealing.

For brochures and other information contact the Chicago Park District, Department of Public Information, 425 East McFetridge Drive, Chicago IL 60605. (312) 294-2200.

Douglas Park Formal Garden
On Roosevelt Road (1200 south) a few blocks west of Western Avenue (2400 west)
West of downtown Chicago

A water lily pool, a natural lagoon, and a pergola provide lovely backdrop for nearly 20,000 annuals in this formal garden. The pool holds over 60 water lily plants, including a few winter hardy varieties. Their flowers, some of which open at night, include varied reds, amber, yellows, pure white, and shell pink.

The garden is south of Ogden Avenue, which bisects Douglas Park, and east of Sacramento Boulevard, which runs along the west edge of the park.

The Library at the Field Museum of Natural History
Roosevelt Road at Lake Shore Drive
Chicago IL 60605
(312) 922-9410

Large collection of natural history books and publications.

♿ Free access to library (there is a fee for the museum). Ask the guard at the museum's north door for a pass to the library. Call ahead to arrange for handicapped access.
Open Monday-Friday 8:30am-4:30pm.

The Field Museum sits just across Lake Shore Drive from the south end of Grant Park, in a building reclaimed from the Columbian Exposition. The library, founded in 1893, uses a closed stack and call slip system; all books and journals must be used in the Reading Room. Global coverage of natural history is strongest in those areas the museum has traditionally emphasized: the Americas, the Far East, and Oceania. The Mary Runnells Rare Book Room houses 8,000 volumes of early natural science literature, many with hand-colored illustrations. Most of the museum's scientific and popular publications, dating back to 1894, can be purchased in the Reading Room. Wouldn't you welcome a quiet time in the library after visiting the sunny gardens of Grant Park?

Garfield Park Conservatory
300 North Central Park Boulevard
Chicago IL 60624
(312) 533-1282

Major conservatory with 4½ acres of grounds. Eight different collection areas open to public. Habitat houses. Seasonal shows.

♿ Brochure and show schedule. Some plants labeled. Occasional lectures and seminars. Plant clinic.
Open every day 9am-5pm, until 9pm on Friday. Hours may be extended during major shows. ▶

Luscious well-groomed gardens live in this 1893 conservatory, in buildings that are less crowded, and more light and airy, than most other century-old conservatories. A small pool reflects dramatic foliage in the Palm House, ". . . a tropical paradise of graceful palms and many varieties of exotic foliage plants." When I visit the Show House on a late October day, the yearly Chrysanthemum Show is under construction. Compact cushion forms, tall "football game" mums, daisy types, and spider-flowered varieties will join lush flower towers and hanging baskets of trailing mums. Tidy brick pathways wind among the mums and the geometric forms of carefully trimmed boxwoods. All of this plays against free-standing birch clumps and fig hedges of *Ficus retusa* and *F. benjamina*. It's beautiful now and will be even more appealing when everything is in place.

In the Aroid House, aerial roots of extraordinary vines are a delicate veil above the still pool. The subliminal hiss of steam jets explains the enveloping warmth and humidity here. Magenta spires top variegated cocoa-toned leaves of chocolate plant (*Pseuderanthemum alatum*) in tasty combination.

Stapelias reign in the Cactus House today. They boast 8" star-shaped flowers in cream and maroon, 5" burgundy "hairy starfish," and tiny ivory or wine-colored stars, all slightly bizarre and smelling, if they smell at all, of rotting meat, the better to attract their fertilizing flies. A twelve-foot hedge cactus (*Cereus peruvianus*) towers over opuntias large and small while a many-armed euphorbia guards agaves that are nearly 10 feet across. Here, too, you'll find some of the jungle cacti, the ones that *don't* require hot, dry, sunny locations, the cacti that tend to do well in our midwestern climate. Raised beds hold an impressive array of other succulent plants.

In the Warm House, houseplants gone giant join cold-tender figs, eucalypti, and masses of bright crotons. Some of the plants here and in the Economic House produce grapefruit, cacao, cinnamon, cotton, and other familiar products. These are plants that intrigue those not otherwise interested in gardening.

The Fernery may lead you to believe you've discovered an ancient Eden. Lush ferns and handsome cycads thrive in the humid warmth while tropical water lilies embellish a small pool. Pitcher plants, club mosses, and lichens add to the almost prehistoric feel of this garden; one almost expects to see a small dinosaur lurking nearby.

The conservatory holds four seasonal flower shows and a series of educational lectures each year. The Plant Question Answering Service, at (312) 533-1281, will field your questions about houseplants or gardening in general.

◀ There is a wealth of plants and plant information at Garfield Park Conservatory.

Exit the Eisenhower Expressway (I-290) at Independence Boulevard and go north a very short distance to Lake Street. Turn east and go about one block to the fenced conservatory parking lot at the corner of Lake Street and Central Park Boulevard.

Garfield Park Formal Garden
Toward the south end of Garfield Park

Four acres. Annual flower beds. Water lily pools.

No particular amenities.

In this formal garden, vine-covered pergolas provide impressive views of the colorful flower beds that surround two huge pools, where 200 water lily plants (in 50 varieties) bloom in a wide range of colors. The north pool, 160'x90', is billed as the largest pool of tropical water lilies in Illinois.

Grant Park
Between Lake Shore Drive and Michigan Avenue
Due east of downtown Chicago

Very large park. Extensive formal gardens. Substantial rose garden.

 Picnic facilities.
Open daylight hours and summer evenings.

The Grant Park plantings are formal garden designs; in the Rose Garden, near Buckingham Fountain, grass panels contrast with rose beds in Versailles-style plantings. Eight thousand plants of 260 varieties include large groups of 'Chicago Peace Rose' (a dark pink sport developed at Cantigny Farms in Wheaton, Illinois), old-fashioned roses, and some of the newest introductions. Imagine the delight of summer evenings here, with roses glowing in the perfumed twilight and a gentle lake breeze ruffling the fountain's lighted sprays.

Grant Park's Court of Presidents, along Congress Parkway, is a formal arrangement of annuals. Although the original plan was to honor each of our presidents with a statue, only St. Gaudens's well-known "Seated Lincoln" has been installed. Because the Court is not far from the offices and shops of Michigan Avenue, it's a popular place for alfresco lunches.

In many senses, Grant Park is the front door of Chicago. Travelers and residents come by the thousands to visit the nearby museums, the summer band concerts and festivals, "Taste of Chicago," Buckingham Fountain, and the gardens.

Grant Park, between Michigan Avenue and Lake Shore Drive (US Route 41), is easily reached from Lake Shore Drive or from the Eisenhower Expressway/ Congress Parkway. Park on the street or in Grant Park's underground spaces.

Humboldt Park Flower Garden
North and west of downtown Chicago

Its entrance flanked by two life-sized bronze bison, this sunken garden covers a 300-foot circle with paved walkways, grassy areas, and beds of annual flowers.

Humboldt Park lies eight blocks west of Western Avenue (2400 west), between Division Street (1200 north) and North Avenue (1600 north). Sacramento Boulevard/Humboldt Drive (3000 west) runs through the park.

Jackson Park
The Japanese Garden on Wooded Island
Just south of the Museum of Science and Industry, near Lake Michigan
South of downtown Chicago

Half-acre Japanese garden.

Brochure. No other amenities.
Open daylight hours.

A soft path leads me to carefully located viewing spots, past the waterfall and small pond, beneath carefully shaped and sited trees, over the arched bridge, and back up to the pavilion for an overview of the garden. This "Finished Hill Style Stroll Garden" adjoins a larger tree-rimmed lagoon in a symbiotic relationship that provides interesting contrasts in scale. On this windless October day, the curved bridge makes a nearly perfect circle with its reflection, a lovely sight with the larger lagoon beyond. The garden will be stunning again in spring when the azaleas bloom and viburnums and honeysuckles perfume the air.

The original Japanese Pavilion and Garden, gifts of the Japanese government, were placed on this site for the 1893 Columbian Exposition. After many years of neglect, the gardens were expanded and rehabilitated for the 1934 Century of Progress World's Fair. The bamboo tea house, built where the pavilion now stands, must have known hustle and bustle quite different from today's isolated serenity. Fire and vandalism destroyed the buildings and the garden in 1945 but renewed interest arose during the 1970s. It was once again refurbished and was rededicated in 1981. For whatever reason, this garden seems to need renewal about every forty years. I fervently hope its beauty will last longer this time.

The pamphlet that provides garden history and explains the various viewing points and features isn't always available at the site, so write for it. You can certainly savor the garden without it, however.

For the brochure (free) contact the Chicago Park District, Department of Public Information, 425 East McFetridge Drive, Chicago IL 60605. (312) 294-2200.

The garden is near the north end of Wooded Island, south of the Museum of Science and Industry at 57th Street and Lake Shore Drive. Park near the museum or in the lot at 63rd and Cornell Drive, near the south end of Wooded Island. Cross to the island on a footbridge and take the easternmost trail.

Jackson Park Perennial Garden
59th Street and Stony Island

Capacious perennial borders.

No particular amenities.

On this mid-May day, flowering dogwood and crabapple trees, irises, poppies, and masses of cornflowers (*Centaurea montana*) affirm that high spring has arrived. Even the small daisy-like flowers of weedy fleabane (*Erigeron* sp.) ▶

FYI Jackson Park is at the east end of the former Midway Plaisance, yet another feature of the Columbian Exposition. The 12-block esplanade that connected exposition sites in Jackson and Washington parks was "midway" between the two. Here stood many of the less-exalted attractions: "carny" shows, food stalls, and souvenir stands. Soon, every such carnival area was known as a "midway."

seem attractive against the cornflowers. Robins work on their nests, migrating warblers flit through the trees, and traffic speeds by on all sides. Over 180 varieties of perennials and annuals contribute to the allure of this garden, where stone walls and flower beds surround a sunken greensward. There are elaborate floral displays here all season: spring bulbs, flowering trees and shrubs, hundreds of hardy perennials, mass plantings of annuals, and a final burst of color from chrysanthemums, all with the city in the near background.

Park near the Museum of Science and Industry. Walk across South Cornell to the garden, between East 59th and 60th streets.

Lincoln Park Conservatory and Gardens
2400 North Stockton Avenue
Chicago IL 60614
(312) 294-4770

Major conservatory with adjacent outdoor gardens. Climate houses. Seasonal flower shows.

♿ Brochure and show schedule. Some plants labeled. Picnic facilities in park. Conservatory open daily 9am-5pm. Special show hours: Friday 9am-9pm, all other days 10am-6pm.

Blooming orchids and a free-form reflecting pool welcome you to the Palm House and to the conservatory. Among its assortment of economic and ornamental plants the Palm House holds a handsome 50-foot fiddle-leaf fig tree (*Ficus lyrata*), a plant we usually see only in houseplant dimensions. A balcony overlooks the Fernery, a "... jewel-like sunken glade in a tropical setting." Here is a richness of ferns and cycads and a trailing vanilla vine (*Vanilla lutescens* [*V. planifolia*, Hortus III]), an orchid that gives us vanilla beans.

The Cactus House is a piece of southwestern desert in the midwest. All the familiar cacti forms and families stand among euphorbias, gasterias, agaves, aloes, and stapelias. You'll surely make some new plant acquaintances here.

Lincoln Park Conservatory has been consistently popular since it opened in 1892. However, on this perfect October Sunday, the action is outside, at Lincoln Park Zoo or with the crowds watching or running the Chicago Marathon. Noisy helicopters quarter the sky, trying to keep track of 8,000 runners, the conservatory is nearly deserted, and the Palm House jungle is mine alone. When we lived in Chicago, this conservatory was one of our favorite haunts; I vividly remember vast banks of glowing poinsettias that welcomed us in from wind and snow. Now, four major seasonal flower shows salute a different country each year and, in summer, the Show House contains colorful and fancy-leaved foliage plants.

The conservatory complex includes three outdoor gardens, where the Main Garden covers nearly a square block, 296,000 square feet, with lawn and sweeping formal beds of annuals. I compare this with my small garden at home and am nearly overwhelmed. Just east of the Main Garden, the Rock Garden offers an attractive display of alpine plants and appropriate trees.

Grandma's Garden lies across Stockton Drive just west of the conservatory. This friendly pleasance of curvilinear beds and paths, first planted in 1893, may be one of the city's most charming public gardens. On this post-frost day, there is evidence of daylilies, daisies, artemisias, mints, hostas, phlox . . . all the old favorites your grandmother might have planted. Grandma's Garden is a pocket of charm in the middle of the city.

The compact and excellent Lincoln Park Zoo that adjoins the conservatory grounds holds a few interesting plantings. Lincoln Park also offers the Chicago Historical Society, the Chicago Academy of Sciences, protected Lake Michigan beaches, a recreational fieldhouse, and the summer Theater-on-the-Lake. The many-chimneyed Queen Anne-style structure near the southeast corner of the park is the impressive residence of the Archbishop of Chicago. With all it offers, one could spend several long and delightful days in Lincoln Park.

Take Lake Shore Drive to Fullerton Parkway then go west one block to the conservatory. Parking is along Stockton or wherever you can find it. There is often space available on the east side of the zoo and it's a pleasant walk through the zoo to the conservatory.

Marquette Park Rose Garden and Trial Garden
Between Marquette Road (67th Street) and 71st Street, California (2800 west) and Central Park (3600 west)
Southwest of downtown Chicago

Almost two acres of rose, theme, and trial gardens.

Open daylight hours.

◀ Free-form arrangements of rose beds, walks, and pools cover about 40,000 square feet here, in one of the midwest's largest municipal rose gardens. Four thousand rose bushes include hybrid teas, grandifloras, floribundas, and tree roses. A naturalistic border holds 500 plants of shrub and old-fashioned roses, the "roses of legend and romance." Just imagine the heady summer scents and cheerful colors of all these roses.

The new 34,000-square-foot Trial Garden is just west of the Rose Garden. Besides the trial area for new annuals and perennials, there are a cactus and succulent garden, a poolside rock garden, and an herb garden. A special collection holds skillfully shaped topiaries of boxwood, myrtle, and ivy alongside ficus and ilex trained to standards. Over three hundred flowering shrubs and ornamental trees add to the beauty here.

Enter at 67th Street and Kedzie Avenue on the north edge of the park and follow signs to the Rose Garden.

Washington Park Formal Garden
Between Hyde Park Boulevard (5100 south) and 60th Street, Cottage Grove (800 east) and Martin Luther King Drive (400 east)
On the south side of Chicago

Large formal garden.

No particular amenities.

Mass plantings of flowering annuals and huge beds of colored foliage make up this formal garden. You may find coleus and other tropicals in colors you didn't know existed.

Washington Park was the western terminus of the Columbian Exposition's Midway Plaisance; see "Jackson Park Perennial Garden" for details.

The garden is at Cottage Grove Avenue and 55th Street.

Vermilion County Museum
116 North Gilbert
Danville IL 61832
(217) 442-2922

▶

Illinois: Northeast / 17

◀ One-tenth acre. Herb gardens. Medicinal herbs. Fragrance garden.

Small fee to visit house/museum. Museum shop. Some plants labeled. Seasonal plant sales. Grounds open all year during daylight hours.
House/museum open Tuesday-Saturday 10am-5pm, Sunday 1-5pm. Closed Monday.

This small and pretty herb garden contains medicinal herbs, as well as culinary and Biblical herbs, because Dr. William Fithian, first owner of the house that became the museum, was a mid-nineteenth century physician who grew many of the herbs he used in his practice. The rectangular garden, based on a Williamsburg design, has brick paths and is centered on an armillary sphere. Globes of bush basil, glowing green, mark the garden entrance and some of the thriving plants sprawl over the paths.

The Shutt Fragrance Garden, a 4'x10' raised bed at the rear of the house, contains scented geraniums, other strongly scented plants, a variety of textures, and plant labels in braille. Both of these gardens are maintained by the Herb Study Groups of the Danville Garden Club.

On this mid-September day, a huge magnolia tree and the ground beneath it hold hundreds of baroque seedheads that are bursting with shiny orange-red seeds. This tree must have been very pleasing during its summer bloom, with its creamy flowers and glossy dark green foliage.

Most special events here are history-related rather than garden-oriented but herb garden products are sold in the museum's shop.

From I-74 go north on Gilbert Street about 2 miles to the museum, a large brick house on your left. Parking is on the grounds at the side of the house.

Elmhurst College Arboretum
Elmhurst

Campus plantings.

 Brochure. Many trees and shrubs labeled.
Open daily.

Lovely on a rainy October morning, this arboretum is surely charming when its magnolias, pears, dogwoods, and other flowering trees blossom in the spring. The grounds of Elmhurst College are an accredited arboretum; more than 1,000 plants of 270 species and varieties decorate this 24-building campus and many are labeled with botanical and common names. An attractive and informative arboretum brochure is available in the foyer of the college's Buehler Library or by writing to the address below. A walk among these hardy specimens makes an interesting contrast to the tropical plants in the nearby Wilder Park Conservatory.

For information contact the Elmhurst College Arboretum, Physical Plant Office, 190 Prospect, Elmhurst IL 60126. (708) 617-3180 or (708) 617-3032.

From Roosevelt Road (Illinois Route 38), take York Road north to St. Charles Road, then go west two short blocks to Cottage Hill. Go north on Cottage Hill a short distance, then left into Wilder Park. Elmhurst College and Wilder Park are across the street from each other; follow the signs for the college.

Wilder Park Conservatory
225 Prospect
Elmhurst IL 60126
(708) 834-2215

Small conservatory in village park. Adjoining outside gardens.

 Many plants labeled. Picnic facilities in park. Seasonal plant sales. Conservatory open daily 9am-5pm. Outside gardens open daylight hours.

Sturdy tropical plants sit near windows that are fogged with condensation on this cool and misty Sunday. It's a perfect day to visit a warm conservatory whose green growing things and exotic blooms can ignore the non-tropical weather. Outside, at one side of the conservatory, a small formal garden of annuals holds radiant fall color through the rain. Benches under the tall trees are, of course, deserted. I'll come back to enjoy them on a warmer, drier day.

Formally established in 1923, Wilder Conservatory includes a greenhouse that dates from 1868. The buildings are being renovated and the smallish herb, rose, and formal gardens expanded. Every year, Wilder hosts Easter, Autumn, and Christmas flower shows and two plant sales. The conservatory is in a park complex that includes picnic tables, large play areas, flower beds, the Elmhurst Public Library, and the Lizzadro Museum of Lapidary Art.

If you're "doing" the western suburbs, a picnic in the park and a stroll through Wilder Conservatory would be a most pleasant break in your day.

For details and show schedule contact the Chief Horticulturalist, Elmhurst Park District, at the address or phone above.

Ladd Arboretum
Along McCormick Boulevard between Emerson Street/Golf Road and
Green Bay Road
Evanston

Twenty-three acres. Tree collections and native plant gardens on reclaimed land. Ecology Center.

♿ Some plants labeled. Nature trails. Visitor center. Workshops and other educational offerings. Group tours of arboretum or Ecology Center by appointment: (708) 864-5181. Arboretum open all year during daylight hours. Ecology Center open Tuesday-Saturday 9am-4:30pm.

This urban arboretum and bird sanctuary, established in 1959, gives us walking/skiing trails, prairie plantings, meadows, trees in groves and allées, and education. Here, too, are the Rotary International Friendship Garden, several memorial plantings, and an environmental education center.

The Ecology Center, a working demonstration of alternative energy use, offers ongoing programs in environmental education. Plants installed around the center, chosen according to their environmental role and needs, help homeowners plant their landscapes sensibly. Behind the center, native prairie plants provide slope stabilization and season-long color.

Many flowering trees and shrubs inhabit the arboretum. Wouldn't it be fine to meander along the Washington National Cherry Tree Walk during bloomtime, then move on to enjoy the rest of the arboretum? In winter, varied conifers and winding paths provide their own beauty.

For schedules and additional information contact the Assistant Superintendent of Parks, City of Evanston, 2100 Ridge Avenue, Evanston IL 60201, (708) 866-2911, or The Ecology Center, 2024 McCormick Boulevard, Evanston IL 60201. (708) 864-5181.

From Sheridan Road on the Northwestern University campus, go west on Emerson Street across town to McCormick Boulevard and the southwest end of the arboretum. Parking is available further north at the Ecology Center.

Merrick Rose Garden
At Oak and Lake streets
Evanston

◄ 104'x224' rose display and All-American Rose Selection garden.

 Most plants in AARS garden labeled.
Open daylight hours.

Merrick Rose Garden has been lovely and vigorous since its dedication in 1948. 'Peace' roses ornament the entry and welcome you to this tranquil garden, where about 1,000 bushes of nearly 80 varieties furnish season-long color. Comfortable benches invite leisurely appreciation of long-established plants and of recent All-American Rose Selection tests and introductions. You'll enjoy this beauty spot in the middle of Evanston.

For details contact the Assistant Superintendent of Parks, City of Evanston, 2100 Ridge Road, Evanston IL 60201. (708) 866-2911.

From Sheridan Road take Lake Street west to the garden at Oak Street, in the center of town.

The Shakespeare Garden
220 Sheridan Road
Evanston

70'x100' hedge-enclosed garden of Elizabethan plants. Jens Jensen design.

 Many plants labeled.
Open daily dawn to dusk.

You'll feel transported to another time and place within these hedge walls; William Shakespeare would have seen many of these plants in Anne Hathaway's garden. Cottage garden borders hold the traditional plants you know and love and inner beds display tidy knot gardens of compact plants.

On this mid-May afternoon, handsome alliums (*Allium aflatunense*) accent masses of pansies, harebells, and columbines. Sturdy clumps of hardy geraniums (*Geranium endressii* 'Wargrave Pink' and *Geranium sanguineum*) join sculptured leaves of lady's-mantle (*Alchemilla mollis*) and soft, silvery flocks of lamb's ears (*Stachys byzantina*). Sunny double buttercups stand in one corner but perky johnny-jump-ups bloom in *all* the beds, having jumped as is their way. Verdant masses of ferns and sweet woodruff will be attractive all season. In coming weeks, rich green clusters of tiny lily buds will become splendidly colored trumpets. ►

◀ Elegant sweeps of autumn anemones promise that delicate late summer color will join bright yarrow and daylilies and other old favorites. Heritage roses will perfume the garden as their blooms come and go.

The only formal garden known to have been designed by Jens Jensen, the Shakespeare Garden combines Tudor garden ideas with Jensen's use of space and naturalistic forms. Conceived in 1915 by the Garden Club of Evanston, the garden continues to be that club's major project. Summer riches yield to burnished autumn and, when autumn becomes winter, evergreen boxwood and ivy accent skeletal branches of the 70-year-old hawthorn hedge. As with most of Jensen's designs, this garden is attractive in all seasons.

In the course of a year, this hushed "garden within a glen" sees weddings, painting classes, bird-banding projects, club meetings, and many, many visitors who come simply to savor its beauty. Stone benches and a memorial fountain encourage restful contemplation of the garden in any season. Shakespeare would be pleased, I think.

For additional garden information write to the Garden Club of Evanston, 2703 Euclid Park Place, Evanston IL 60201.

The garden is on the campus of Northwestern University, just north of the east end of Garrett Place, between Sheridan Road and Lake Michigan. Look for the Garrett Theological Seminary, then look for a place to park. (Parking can be a problem on class days.) On the east side of a small chapel with a pleasant "wedding garden," follow the bluestone walk to the Shakespeare Garden.

The Chicago Botanic Garden
P. O. Box 400
Glencoe IL 60022
(708) 835-5440 or (708) 835-8213

Total grounds three hundred acres. Several acres of theme gardens, including major rose, English, and Japanese gardens. Greenhouses/conservatories.

💲 ♿ ☕ Many plants labeled. Extensive library. Picnic facilities. Intermittent plant sales. Full schedule of educational activities. Group tours and programs by appointment.
Gardens and greenhouses open daily 8am-sunset. Closed December 25. The Garden Shop open weekdays 10am-3:30pm, weekends noon-3:30pm. Library open Monday-Saturday 9am-4pm.
Food for Thought Café open daily: summer hours 8:30am-4:30pm, fall and winter hours 8:30am-3:30pm.

You can see it all at the Chicago Botanic Garden, where nearly 20 different gardens feature plant collections from all over the world, including our upper midwest. For an especially rich experience, visit the gardens on a cool and misty day in May and share the space with songbirds, ducks and geese, and few people. Espaliers in the under-construction English walled garden wait for apple and pear trees and partially completed brick walks delineate planting beds. Muddy but full of promise now, this space will be lush and colorful in a few weeks, in time for its early autumn dedication.

A gravel path winds past the joyful waterfall garden, where water streams among spring green perennials and showy blue camas (*Camassia cusickii*), cascades enthusiastically down the hillside, and rushes to a placid lake. If ever one would lust after a garden, this is the one. In the misty near-distance, carefully groomed islands display majestic examples of Japanese tree pruning and training techniques. A closer look reveals elegant stone lanterns among vigorous broad-leaved evergreens and imaginative ground covers.

Several months later, a cold March day finds me at the garden again. Canada geese chat and call through the fog as I walk to the Education Center, and the entry-way sculpture, a bronze group of flying geese, seems especially appropriate. The greenhouses provide welcome refuge on this damp day. In a house filled with flowering plants for the home, azaleas brighten corners while clivias, hydrangeas, and anthuriums bloom above rampant ground covers. In a large Wardian case, pitcher plants wait to be fed and fancy sundews grasp jewels of moisture. Nearby are stuffed topiary forms like you've never seen: a nearly life-sized prancing pony, a camel, a crane, a giant green man. Tricolored strawberry geranium (*Saxifraga stolonifera* var.), creeping fig (*Ficus reptans*), a tiny dark green liriope, and small draecenas bring these creations to verdant life.

Deep pink bougainvillea and a tree festooned with blooming orchids dominate the tropical/economic greenhouse. Puzzling whiffs of sweetness lead me to gardenia bushes and a miniature grove of flowering citrus trees. The tiny green kumquats, hiding among their porcelain flowers and deep green leaves, are particularly captivating. A small waterfall in the bog area pours past streamside irises and the dramatic corkscrew spathes of "curly anthurium."

In the Cactus House, a stately hundred-year-old jade tree is quietly radiant with soft pink flowers. More raucous blooms adorn nearby aloes, euphorbias, rhipsalids, crassulas, agaves, and cacti.

The outside gardens lie mostly dormant today but tiny rosettes of the sedum 'Autumn Joy', signs of life among remnants of last year's verdure, peek through damp soil in the English Walled Garden. Sculpture and fountains and an invigorating view of the lagoon enrich this spacious new formal garden. The cottage garden is ". . . a cheerful jumble of flowers, herbs, fruits, and vegetables." ▶

◄ Prairie and woodland plants comprise the Naturalistic Garden, where one plot features plants particularly attractive to birds and butterflies. The Landscape Garden holds ideas for *your* landscape: a small herb garden, ornamental grasses, deciduous and evergreen shrubs, and other suggestions. It's a good time to see what remains attractive through a northern Illinois winter.

Several plant societies hold seasonal shows here, specialty plant sales often accompany these shows, and there is a full schedule of lectures, exhibits, family activities, and garden tours. If you reach sensory overload from all of this, visit the Botanic Garden Library and surround yourself with horticulture books, seed catalogs, and how-to-garden books. If the hour is right, refresh yourself at the Food for Thought Café or visit the Garden Shop, where you'll find a broad selection of garden-related gifts and books.

From mid-April through October, free narrated tram tours provide an overview of the gardens. Or, bring your bike and enjoy the gardens from the bike path, which connects with the Cook County Forest Preserve District network. Here, at any time of year, you'll find much to please your senses, to arouse your curiosity, and to answer your questions. Be sure to allow plenty of time or be prepared to deal with the frustration that comes with leaving treasures unseen. Just as when you visit a large museum, the best plan may be to choose one or two areas for full enjoyment and to leave the rest for "next time."

Exit I-294 or Edens Expressway (US 41) at Lake-Cook Road (County Line Road). Go east to the garden; it's 6 miles from I-294, a mile or so from Edens Expressway. Entry to the garden is on the south side of Lake-Cook Road.

Glencoe downtown parks

1,000 sq.ft. rose garden. Perennial and annual plantings.

 All parks open daylight hours.

Small parks brighten downtown Glencoe, near the intersection of Glencoe Road (Green Bay Road) and Park Street. Look for the flagpole in the center of the Memorial Park Rose Garden, then let your nose guide you to the shrub roses, damasks, and other "good smellers" here. Just across Park Street, you'll see Kalk Park's colorful plantings. Here, where annuals and perennials join forces for all-season color, comfortable benches and an attractive gazebo encourage lengthy visits.

Other gardens are developing in Glencoe. Continue east on Park Street to Lakefront Park, where a lush combination of annuals, perennials, and tender summer-blooming bulbs border tennis courts. Nearby, beachside bluff restoration employs hardy grasses, shrubs, and perennials and provides a pleasant overlook that allows sweeping views of Lake Michigan. Evergreen Garden is being installed at the corner of Tudor Court and Glencoe Road. This 20'x150' plot will display dwarf and mid-sized conifers in a living reference for do-it-yourself landscapers.

For information contact the Superintendent of Parks, Glencoe Park District, 999 Green Bay Road, Glencoe IL 60022. (708) 835-4648 or (708) 835-3030.

Plantlife Resources Project
Glencoe

Municipal greenhouses. Community-wide plantings.

Seasonal plant sales. Greenhouse or site tours by prior arrangement.
Open every day 9am-4pm.

Wherever you go in Glencoe, if the season is right, you'll notice appealing installations of perennials and annuals. Much of this beauty owes its existence to the Plantlife Resources Project, the brainchild and ambitious undertaking of Glencoe resident Dr. Ingrid J. Rosenfeld. Through the years, she had seen the community landscape deteriorate due to population pressure and diminishing park district funds. Her solution was to donate three greenhouses to the Park District; the result is an increasingly attractive Glencoe.

Volunteers raise thousands and thousands of plants in the greenhouses every year. Most of these go into public plantings around Glencoe and the remainder are sold to private individuals for beautifying their own property. The advantage to the homeowner is that these plants are locally raised and have been chosen for their good performance in the Glencoe area. The Plantlife Project also includes "a tree and shrub program to replace aging or damaged individuals, green restoration and erosion control of Lake Michigan bluffs, wildflower preservation and restoration, acclimatization and natural disease and insect control of rugosa roses, and emphasis on perennials for all locations, particularly for shade." Another challenging project is the establishment of a "green wall" that will beautify and reduce maintenance along a narrow railroad right-of-way.

You will have noticed that relatively few sites in this book suggest or require an appointment for your visit. I've made an exception for this interesting and valuable program.

◀ For specific information or to arrange a tour, contact the Glencoe Park District at the address and phone numbers above. For directions to sites, ask at the Plantlife greenhouses or call (708) 835-8410. After 6pm or to leave a message: (708) 835-1985.

From I-94 or Edens Expressway (US 41) take Dundee Road (IL 68) east to Green Bay Road and go north to 999, the Glencoe Community House. Park here and walk across the playing fields behind the Community House to the greenhouses. Or go a little further on Green Bay Road to the stone pillars at 1015 and follow the arrows to the greenhouses. If you've taken another route, note that you can reach Green Bay Road via either Lake-Cook Road or Glencoe's Park Avenue. The Community House and the greenhouses are between these two roads.

The Morton Arboretum
Route 53
Lisle IL 60532
(708) 719-2400 or (708) 968-0074

1,500 acres. Tree, shrub, and plant collections.

💲♿⚙ Gift shop/bookstore. Many plants labeled. Wide range of educational offerings. Library. Hiking trails. Plant clinic.
Grounds open daily: Daylight Savings Time 9am-dusk but no later than 7pm, Standard Time 9am-5pm. Library open Monday-Friday 9am-5pm, Saturday 10am-4pm. Hours for other buildings and facilities change seasonally.

These 1,500 acres contain enough plants and other features to satisfy a variety of botanical interests. The arboretum's 76 cultivated plant collections are generally of four types: botanical groups of related plants, i.e. the Maple Collection or the Rose Garden; landscape groups of plants with similar uses, such as the Hedge Garden; geographic groups of plants with a common place of origin; special habitat groups. For instance, the Sand Beds Garden, a collection of plants in modified soil, may teach you how to handle a special plant or situation. Upland woods, riverine woods, and prairie areas provide stunning wildflower displays in season; you may find the arboretum particularly crowded on spring and fall weekends. This variety of habitats makes the arboretum a popular place for birdwatching, especially during migration periods.

The pleasant Visitor Center, where you'll most likely begin your visit, is actually three buildings. The ground level of the Information Building provides exhibits, maps, and publications; the lower level holds the Ginkgo Shop and its fine assortment of books and nature-related gifts. The Theater presents an audio-visual introduction to the arboretum. In The Ginkgo Restaurant and the Coffee Shop, you can fortify yourself for the arboretum-viewing to come or relax and review the wonders just seen.

A short walk from the Visitor Center takes you to the Administration Building and the Sterling Morton Library. Here, for your pleasure and research, are over 23,000 horticultural and botany books, copies of over 400 journals, and hundreds of government publications. Three thousand volumes in the rare book collection, including a small group of Linnaean works, date from the fifteenth to the twentieth century. A 1482 edition of Pliny's *Natural History* is the oldest volume in the library. There is also a sizable collection of prints and drawings, mostly plant studies. Here, too, are the papers and archives of landscape ▶

FYI As you visit gardens around the midwest and in this book, you'll come across the name and work of Jens Jensen (1860-1951). A contemporary and kindred spirit of Frank Lloyd Wright, Jensen was known for the "Prairie Spirit" in landscape design, a naturalistic style which emphasized local native plants. Jensen worked in Chicago's West Parks System from 1886 to 1900 and again from 1905 to 1920; he also aided in the development of the Cook County Forest Preserve District. He began his private practice in 1900 and in 1935 moved to Ellison Bay, Wisconsin, to start The Clearing, an enterprise patterned after the arts and ecology programs of Danish folk schools. Today much of Jensen's landscape work has virtually disappeared, partly because too little is known about managing designed naturalistic landscapes. Some examples (in varying condition) that are open to the public include:

Illinois:
    Evanston: The Evanston Art Center (formerly the Harley Clarke estate), partially restored, and the Shakespeare Garden on the Northwestern University campus, restored.*
    Highland Park: Rosewood Park, the former Julius Rosenwald estate.
    Kenilworth: Mahoney Park, partially restored.
    Lombard: Lilacia Park, maintained.*
    Springfield: Abraham Lincoln Memorial Garden, partially restored.*

Michigan:
    Dearborn: Fair Lane, the Henry Ford estate, under restoration by the University of Michigan.*
    Grosse Pointe Shores: Gaukler Point, the Edsel Ford estate, partially restored.*

Wisconsin:
    Ellison Bay: The Clearing, partially restored.*
    Madison: The Kenneth Jensen Wheeler Memorial Council Ring at the University of Wisconsin Arboretum, restored,* and Glenwood Children's Park.

*Sites discussed elsewhere in *Green Byways*.

architect Jens Jensen and of naturalist/author May Theilgaard Watts. If it's a fine day, take a book outside to the Watts Reading Garden, which is planted with flowers and shrubs significant in botanical history; a plant list for this garden is available at the Reference Desk. The library itself would justify a visit to Morton Arboretum. If you've been out on the roads and trails, relaxing time in the library may be just what you need.

An auto tour of the grounds takes about an hour, assuming you don't often leave the car "to get a closer look." But to know the arboretum better try one of the foot trails, which range from a half mile to three miles in length. During spring and fall, take a guided tour on the open-air bus.

The arboretum grounds, formerly Joy Morton's "Thornhill" estate, include relatively undisturbed woodlands, land once used for agriculture, and cultivated areas. Morton, founder of the Morton Salt Company, probably developed his love of trees under his father's influence; J. Sterling Morton was the Nebraska statesman who originated Arbor Day. A perfect day at this arboretum would be, I think, a morning trail walk, lunch at the Ginkgo Restaurant, an hour or two in the library or the Reading Garden, back to the Ginkgo for mid-afternoon tea, and then another trail walk. Your visit to Morton Arboretum may be one of the most enjoyable days you've ever known.

The arboretum is on Illinois Route 53, just north of its bridge over the East-West Tollway (I-88). Exit the tollway for IL 53 north.

Lilacia Park
Between Maple and Parkside streets
Lombard

8½ acres. Lilac collection. Perennials. Jens Jensen design.

 Fee and plant sales during Lilac Time only.
Open daylight hours.

On this gray autumn day, when a few begonias persist in sheltered nooks, naked lilac bushes of all shapes and sizes hold fat buds as promises for next spring. Plump yellow crabapples garnish the flowering crab allée, evidence of a glorious spring past. Prairie plants border the small garden room where a life-sized bronze deer watches over ironweed, rattlesnake-master (*Eryngium yuccifolium*), coneflowers and sunflowers and remnants of prairie blazing star

(*Liatris* sp.). Juncos are busy in the mist, gleaning seeds under the shrubs; they'll have good winter cover here. A particularly handsome weeping mulberry hangs over the walk, weeping condensed fog today. The array of comfortable benches would invite leisurely garden viewing on a drier day.

In raised beds against the Park District building, summer-blooming perennials supplied color when the lilacs were done. A few monarda (beebalm) and coneflower blooms remain, protected from frost by the building. Sprawling sages, mints, and tarragon, sturdy rue and costmary, and random clumps of chives are the herb garden; there were perhaps tender annuals here earlier. My taste-test proves the tarragon to be the true French variety, not the common but tasteless impostor. This elevated area allows a fine overview of mature conifers and hardwoods scattered among the park's sweeping lawns and flower beds.

Lombard is known for Lilac Time, the annual spring festival that includes a Lilac Queen and her court, concerts, the Lilac Ball, the Lilac Parade, and the sale of lilac bushes. Even the Park District's *Lilac Time News* is printed in purple. In spite of the emphasis on lilacs, I saw no labels on any of the park's 1,000 + lilac bushes. What is the homeowner to do if he wants to get "one like that" for his garden?

During Lilac Time, over 35,000 tulips and numerous early-flowering trees and shrubs add to the glory of Lilacia Park, making it well worth the nominal fee charged during that two-week celebration. The plantings on this slightly rolling land were originally designed by Jens Jensen. As with most of his designs, Lilacia Park's array of trees, flowers, and fruit-, berry-, or seed-producing plants is appealing any time of year.

For Lilac Time information contact the Lombard Park District, 150 South Park Avenue, Lombard IL 60148, (708) 627-1281, or the Lombard Chamber of Commerce, 315 West St. Charles Road, Lombard IL 60148, (708) 627-5040.

From Roosevelt Road (Illinois Route 38), turn north onto Lombard's Main Street. (Several of the western suburbs have a Main Street that crosses Roosevelt Road. Be sure you're in Lombard.) At either Maple or Parkside, turn west and go one block to the park. The park's main entry is at the southeast corner, near the Park District building. However, there are steep steps there; an easier walkway is near the park's northwest corner.

Early American Museum and Garden
Mahomet

◀ 6-acre botanical garden in large county park. Greenhouse. Herb garden. Prairie plot.

💲♿ Fee covers museum and gardens. Museum gift shop. Many plants labeled. Gravel paths. Picnic facilities. Special seasonal events.
Open daily June-August 10am-5pm, weekends May and September.

Brilliant chrysanthemums, stately clumps of maiden grass (*Miscanthus sinensis* 'Gracillimus'), and jewel-toned sedums line the brick walk to the greenhouse today. A few tardy lavender blooms join the reds and yellows of coreopsis, blanket flower (*Gaillardia* sp.), and false sunflower (*Heliopsis* sp.). Prim white metal chairs in the greenhouse classroom face immense hanging ferns and fancy-leaved begonias, lush vines cascade from ceiling to gravel-covered floor, and assorted succulents and dormant orchids fill a table. Window walls have been removed from the Show House and butterflies drift above ornate, almost garish, beds of primary-colored annuals. Brilliant lantanas in their baskets seem pastel by comparison. Water gurgles and trickles from rock to rock in the mossy fountain and the chubby goldfish think I'm going to feed them.

Near the greenhouse, 12-foot stalks of giant reed grass (*Arundo donax* L.) sway and chatter in the wind, their feathery seed heads garnet against the autumn sky. Neighboring hawthorns hold an abundant crop of glossy red berries. Masses of flowering crabapples added their own beauty to the spring here.

Conifers in various sizes, shapes, and colors contrast with graceful daylily leaves in a hillside planting. Japanese maples and a clump of willows adorn the waterfall pond. Pond margins are filled with iris seedheads, further evidence of spring's ample bloom. Today the herb garden shows rampant thymes, artemisias, mints, comfrey . . . and holes from which tender perennials have been lifted. Near the Education Building, the Prairie Sampler holds goldenrod and asters, luscious rosy-gold little bluestem and taller grasses, remnants of coneflowers and rosinweed (*Silphium integrifolium*), and a hundred other native treasures. There's room to wander in these gardens, to enjoy the scattered benches, shade structures, and garden overlooks.

As with many midwestern gardens, this one is being renewed under the guidance of a master plan. But today, clear yellow ash leaves crunch underfoot, it was a good year for the garden, and we're looking toward the pleasures of another growing season.

For information contact the Early American Museum and Garden, P. O. Drawer 669, Mahomet IL 61853. (217) 586-2612. Park Office: (217) 586-3360.   ▶

◀ *From I-74 take Illinois Route 47 north about a mile to the park entrance and the museum.*

Van Drunen Farm
300 West Sixth Street
Momence IL 60954
(815) 472-3100

Over 100 acres. Commercial chive farm. Freeze-dry factory.

Handicapped-accessible by car.
Chive fields can be visited during daylight hours. Processing factory open Monday-Friday 9am-5pm.

Acres and acres of violet flowers and a gentle scent of chives . . . this is the Van Drunen farm on a warm day in late spring. In these quantities, chives are no longer a mundane kitchen plant. A chive-cutting machine is working in a far field, releasing a strong aroma that's so dissipated by distance it only makes me think of fresh green salads. Chives are harvested throughout the growing season here and the freeze-dry factory sits at the far edge of the fields, awaiting drop-in visitors. The scent of chives is *not* gentle inside the factory; after a visit there, you may not need onions on your lunchtime burger.

The main crop at Van Drunen, the second largest chive farm in the country (as you might guess, the largest is in California), is *Allium schoenoprasum*. Rows of taller, darker, flat-leaved garlic chives (*A. tuberosum*) break up the expanse of lavender flowers and will add their attractive white blooms in August. Small quantities of basil, parsley, and other herbs are also grown here to supply regional restaurants.

In late summer and early fall, when hundreds of acres of gladiolus bloom around Momence and nearby St. Anne, their brilliant flowers can be admired from the country roads and the area is Gladarine Heaven. The Annual Momence Gladiolus Festival (early August) features flower-covered floats, antique cars, drum and bugle corps, and other basic festival fare.

For Gladiolus Festival information call 1-800-74-RIVER (1-800-747-4837).

From I-57 take Illinois Route 17 east about 13 miles to IL 1, then go north about 5 miles to Momence and continue across the Kankakee River to Second Street. Go west on Second to the school complex at the edge of town. Chive fields are on both sides of the road just beyond the schools.

The Oak Park Conservatory
617 Garfield Street
Oak Park IL 60304
(708) 386-4700

8,000 sq.ft. conservatory. Outdoor gardens.

 Most plants labeled. Education center. Seasonal plant sales. Open daily 10am-4pm. Closed Monday.

Do you know the Finger of God, the Lacquered Wine Cup, or the Painted Drop Tongue? Have you seen Mexican Horncone, the Giant's Watch Chain, or a Never-never Plant? They're all waiting for you at the Oak Park Conservatory. In the Desert, Tropic, and Fern houses, those treasuries of flowers, fruits, and foliage, you'll find plants you've never seen before as well as some familiar faces. And in the Curiosity Corner you're encouraged to touch and smell the plants, to really get to know them.

The conservatory's outdoor Perennial Garden features herbaceous plants that do particularly well in the Chicago area. Plant material in the Prairie Garden, provided by the Save the Prairie Society, represents a unique gene pool and introduces these hardy beauties to city dwellers. Herb Garden plants taste good, smell good, dye fabric, ease pain, or just generally make life more pleasant.

This is the third largest conservatory in the metropolitan area, after those in Chicago's Lincoln Park and Garfield Park. Completed in 1929, it fell on hard times through the years and, in 1970, was slated to give up its life for a parking lot. Fortunately, concerned individuals mobilized to preserve and enhance the conservatory and now it flourishes as part of the Park District of Oak Park. People of all ages enjoy a wide variety of educational programs in the Earth Shelter and specialized plant societies often meet at the conservatory. You can bring your ailing plant to the weekly plant and garden clinic (Monday 2-4pm). With the help of many, many volunteers, the Oak Park Conservatory has become a thriving regional asset that is well worth a visit at any season.

FYI Finger-of-God is the bromeliad *Aechmea orlandiana*, Lacquered Wine Cup is *Aechmea* X Cv. 'Foster's Favorite', and Painted Drop Tongue is *Aglaonema crispum* (Syn *Schismatoglottis roebelinii*). You may know Mexican Horncone as the cycad *Ceratozamia mexicana*, the Giant's Watch Chain as *Crassula* x *imperialis*, and Never-never Plant as *Ctenanthe oppenheimiana* Cv. 'Tricolor'.

◀ The conservatory is just south of I-290 (Eisenhower Expressway) and just east of Oak Park Avenue. Exit the expressway at Oak Park Avenue or Harlem Avenue and turn south. Almost immediately, turn east onto Garfield Avenue and go a short distance to the conservatory.

Triton College Botanical Garden
2000 Fifth Avenue
River Grove IL 60171
(708) 456-0300

College grounds. Display and theme gardens. Shakespeare Garden. All-America Selections garden.

♿ Gift/flower shop. Many plants labeled. Seasonal plant sales.
Garden open daylight hours. Greenhouse and Flower Shop open Monday-Friday 9am-4pm. Hours vary during summer and holiday vacations.

Varied gardens decorate the grounds at Triton College. You can investigate the garden of medicinal plants, visit some of the plants mentioned by Shakespeare, and learn more about the relatively new field of horticultural therapy. There's an All-America Selections garden and a garden for cut flowers; your souvenir bouquet is waiting at the Flower Shop. You'll find a nursery, experimental gardens, and an educational greenhouse in this exciting array of garden offerings.

These gardens and other features are planned and maintained by the Triton Horticulture Club, horticulture or landscape students, and interested volunteers. The Senior Garden Club, a group of older people who enjoy all aspects ▶

FYI You may want to visit the Oak Park Visitor Center in conjunction with your trip to the Oak Park Conservatory. The village of Oak Park contains a splendid group of Frank Lloyd Wright buildings and a fine collection of Victorian structures. Maps for self-guided walking tours or auto routes are available at the Visitor Center or at the Wright Home and Studio. Both facilities are open daily 10am-5pm.

For brochures and other information contact the Oak Park Visitor Center, 158 Forest Avenue, Oak Park IL 60302, (708) 848-1500, or The Frank Lloyd Wright Home and Studio, 951 Chicago Avenue, Oak Park IL 60302, (708) 848-1978.

Exit I-290 (Eisenhower Expressway) at Harlem Avenue North. Go north 6 or 7 blocks, under the train tracks, and immediately turn east onto North Boulevard. At Forest Avenue, turn north to Lake Street and the Center. The Home and Studio is at the corner of Forest and Chicago avenues, just a short distance from the Visitor Center.

◀ of gardening, is responsible for the Senior Center Patio Garden. The Horticulture Club offers a variety of lectures and other events throughout the year. Write to the Horticulture Club Faculty Advisor at the school for a schedule that will surely include something to interest you.

River Grove is north of North Avenue (Illinois Route 64) and is bisected by First Avenue. Take North Avenue to Fifth Avenue, turn north and go about a half mile to the college.

The Natural Garden
38 W 443 Highway 64
St. Charles IL 60175
(708) 584-0150

Commercial grower of native plants. Several acres display gardens and sales area.

Catalog. Garden shop. Plants in sales lot labeled. Off-site workshops and seminars. Open January-March Monday-Friday; April-June every day; July-Thanksgiving Monday-Saturday; Thanksgiving-Christmas every day. Hours always 9am-5pm, with possible seasonal extensions. Closed major holidays.

Prairie grasses and forbs near the parking area show late season tenacity on this October afternoon and, unless heavy autumn rains knock them down, they'll be handsome all winter. A delightful woodland garden meanders under mature trees, its ferns shining in today's rain. It will be even more charming here in spring and summer; today, many of the plants are comfortably dormant. These woodland and prairie gardens contain common ornamentals and some native plants rarely found elsewhere. Guided garden tours are possible in the spring; May and June are the best months for bloom and for plant selection. Plants in the gardens aren't labeled but their counterparts in the sales area are clearly marked.

The sales lots are an education; over 1,000 varieties of prairie or woodland plants are sorted according to their requirements for sun and moisture. Labels indicate bloom time, mature size, botanical and common names, and cultural needs. Similar information is given for each plant in The Natural Garden's excellent catalog. You should have few surprises from these plants.

The shop is cozy on this wet day, the wood stove radiating nicely. Everlastings and dried prairie grasses hang from the ceiling or just stand around in containers, relaxing after last summer's busy growth. Globe amaranth and globe thistle, big bluestem and little bluestem sit surrounded by spring-flowering bulbs, herb and rock garden books, and other garden treasures.

We find the combination of sturdy plants, naturalistic garden design, and helpful information irresistible. Graceful maiden grass and little bluestem, silvery leadplant (*Amorpha canescens*), and assertive rattlesnake-master (*Eryngium yuccifolium*) will be dramatic against our fence, thriving in *our* natural garden.

The Natural Garden is on North Avenue (Illinois Route 64), 1½ miles west of its intersection with Randall Road. The entrance is the second driveway west of Oakwood Drive, on the south side of the road.

The Cuneo Museum and Gardens
1350 North Milwaukee Avenue
Vernon Hills IL 60061
General information: (708) 362-2025, Director (708) 362-3042, Greenhouse (708) 362-4495

75-acre estate grounds. Over 2 acres of gardens. Formal gardens. Rose garden. 80'x120' greenhouse/conservatory. Deer park.

💲♿☕ Brochure and event schedule. Turf paths. Conservatory plants labeled. Grounds-only admission gives access to the grounds and gardens, the deer park, and the conservatory. Full admission includes museum (house) tour. Group tours by prior arrangement.
Museum and gardens open Tuesday-Sunday 10am-5pm. Closed Monday. Last museum tour 4pm. Garden Pavillion Restaurant open Tuesday-Saturday 11:30am-3pm, Sunday brunch 11:30am-2:30pm. Brunch reservations requested.

This lovely estate holds formal gardens, courtyards, and antique statuary, lakes, fountains, and pools . . . gracious elements that form delightful surroundings for today's visitors. In spring, the flowers of 37,000 bulbs embellish the grounds, making winter worth the wait. Summer's formal gardens are bright with thousands of annuals, most of them raised from seed here at Cuneo. Roses and roses and roses, over 1,500 bushes in many varieties, fill the rose garden with heady scents and rich hues. In the conservatory, fat and colorful koi lounge below the waterfall and a "river" winds through tropical vegetation that's spiced with orchids.

A pleasant lunch or afternoon tea in the Garden Pavillion Restaurant may add the perfect touch to your visit, whether you've come for the gardens or for one of Cuneo's special events, such as an art or antique exhibit or a flower show. For a special treat, come to Cuneo on a summer evening to enjoy a performance by the Lake Forest Symphony (reservations required).

If you lived in the Chicago area in the mid-twentieth century, you knew of Hawthorn-Mellody Farms, a commercial dairy; this estate was part of those farms. The 32-room mansion was designed in 1914 for Samuel Insull, a partner of Thomas Edison and a founder of Commonwealth Edison. John F. Cuneo, founder of the Cuneo Press, the dairy, and other businesses, purchased it in 1937 and his family lived here until 1990. Now, for a nominal fee, it's ours to enjoy.

From I-94 go west a mile or so on Illinois Route 60 to Milwaukee Avenue (IL 21). Go north on Milwaukee a half mile to the Cuneo Museum entrance.

Orchids by Hausserman
2N134 Addison Road
Villa Park IL 60181
(708) 543-6855

Commercial. Four acres of orchid greenhouses. Showrooms and plant production houses.

Catalog. Plants labeled. Plant sales.
Open Monday-Friday 8am-4:30pm, Saturday 9am-4:30pm, Sunday 11am-3pm.

Orchids are always blooming at Hausserman's, orchids in all their colors and shapes and occasional scents. On this early March day, one greenhouse offers thousands of splendid phaelanopsis sprays. Ivory, peach, and other almost irresistible tints vie for attention. How could one possibly choose among them? Adjoining houses hold cattleyas, dendrobiums, cymbidiums, paphiopedilums, and myriads of other species, some plants in bloom, others resting.

Less common orchids, if any orchid can be considered common, fill tables in a small show area. Today there are greenish orchids with wispy, twining sepals, flat-faced ones in flaming orange, scented orchids, and mossy boxes of cypripediums, the lady's-slippers of woodland lore. You'll also find a few primroses, African violets, and miniature roses among the orchids but their blooms seem pedestrian by comparison.

Orchids by Hausserman is a short distance north of Illinois Route 64 (North Avenue). Some maps indicate that Addison Road intersects Roosevelt Ave-

nue; it does not. Exit I-355 at North Avenue and go east to Addison Road, then north on Addison. Or take I-294 to I-290 north, exit at North Avenue, and go west to Addison Road.

Oak Hill Gardens
37 W 550 Binnie Road
West Dundee IL
(708) 428-8500

Commercial orchid grower. 20,000 sq.ft. of greenhouses.

Catalog. Plants labeled. Plant sales. Shop.
Open Monday-Saturday 8am-6pm. (Remember, in winter it will be dark in the greenhouses before 6pm.) Closed Sundays and holidays.

Imagine large greenhouses filled with the rainbow hues of orchids in all shapes and sizes, from minute seedlings to full-flowering adults. Imagine these orchids joined by bromeliads, anthuriums, bougainvilleas, and an assortment of haworthias and other succulents. Baskets of unusual plants, including two types of jasmine and an assortment of epiphytic cacti, hang overhead. Add Holly, the mellow watchdog, and a large black rabbit who does morning patrol in the greenhouses. That's Oak Hill, a luscious bit of the tropics in northern Illinois.

If you have the tiniest bit of technical aptitude, you'll be interested in the Oak Hill water collection system. Rainwater that falls on the greenhouses is piped to an underground cistern. In the winter, interior condensation collects in drip gutters and is drained into the same cistern. This "distilled" water is then available for the plants. You'll hear the pumps working as you roam through the lush greenhouses, trying to decide which orchid is most attractive and which plants want to go home with you.

For a catalog, write Oak Hill Gardens, P. O. Box 25, West Dundee IL 60118-0025.

From I-90/290 (Northwest Tollway) go north on Illinois Route 31 to IL 72, then west on IL 72 to Randall Road. Go north on Randall to Binnie Road, then west a short distance to the greenhouses.

Cantigny Gardens
1S151 Winfield Road
Wheaton IL 60187
(708) 688-5161

◀ 500-acre grounds. 10 acres of gardens. Rose garden. Military museum.

 Fee for some special events. Some plants labeled. Picnic facilities.
Grounds and gardens open every day during daylight hours. Museum open Tuesday-Sunday 10am-5pm during summer, 10am-4pm the rest of the year. Closed Mondays and the month of January.

Here are large semi-formal gardens and more personal informal gardens. Sweeps of immaculate lawn, approached by firm gravel paths, contrast with richly planted flower beds, mature specimen trees, and woods. The Rock Garden contains a particularly interesting collection of conifers. On this cool and misty October day, berries on some of the deciduous shrubs shine like holiday ornaments. Vertical accents of handsome ornamental grasses are scattered throughout the gardens. Near the small lake, a riot of tuberous begonias, loving the cool and damp, brightens a vine-covered shade structure but the celosia collection looks like a flock of grumpy chickens in the rain. Heavy-budded mums trail down gray steps in a beautiful carpet-to-come. Mums in hanging planters are 4-foot globes of greenery that will be stunning in bloom, if a hard freeze doesn't get them first. Sturdy cotoneaster standards guard the vigorous clematis collection.

Wherever you wander here, through a garden of silver plants, a rose garden, a euonymus collection, or a stand of alders and birches, you're always surrounded by an array of healthy and well-tended plants. When you've had enough wandering, enjoy one of the many benches that are strategically placed for pleasant views.

Cantigny hosts a full schedule of indoor and outdoor concerts, garden lectures, and other events. Many activities require reservations, a few entail a fee; call for details and a schedule.

Cantigny, once a farm called "Red Oaks," was the estate of publisher Joseph Medill, the *Chicago Tribune* editor who was a founder of the Republican party and who helped elect Abraham Lincoln. Medill's grandson, Col. Robert R. McCormick, renamed the estate "Cantigny" after the small French village that was, in World War I, the site of America's first army offensive in Europe. Col. McCormick established the museum as a memorial to the First Armored Division and its role in America's wars. Near the museum today, children are happily, noisily climbing on Army tanks. Their parents may be in the museum, watching old newsreels or activating the push-button dioramas. The tanks and films and gardens are, for me, a chilling combination so I concentrate on the inviting gardens. ▶

◀ *From the East-West Tollway/Eisenhower Expressway, exit at Naperville Road. Go a half mile north to Warrenville Road, then west on Warrenville three miles to Winfield Road. Go north on Winfield about 2 miles to Cantigny. From Roosevelt Road (IL 38) on the west side of Wheaton, go south on Winfield Road a few hundred yards to the Cantigny entrance.*

The Planter's Palette
28 W 571 Roosevelt Road
Winfield IL 60190
(708) 293-1040

Commercial. Sizable gardens. Display beds of unusual perennials.

♿ Catalog. Garden shop. Plant sales. Workshops. Woodchip paths may make access difficult for some.
Open April 15-October 16 and November 24-December 23. Specific hours change with the seasons but always open Monday-Saturday 10am-5pm and Sunday noon-5pm.

You know you've found a good place when the parking lot holds lavishly planted raised islands. It's a fine introduction to the rich variety of plants and other treasures you'll find here. Shade-loving plants and sample gardens spread beneath tall trees and invite you to roam.

In the retail sales area near the shop, an amazing variety of healthy and clearly labeled plants fills an expanse of tables. On this misty day, the ferns and hostas are particularly handsome. Fifteen or twenty different mints, assorted eucalypti, scented geraniums, and fancy sages are only part of the ample herb collection. Here are gallon pots of striking grasses and delightful succulent ground covers. The pleasing assortment of less common shade plants includes 3 different lungworts (*Pulmonaria* spp.), delicately blooming variegated toad lily (*Tricyrtis horta* 'variegata'), and robust specimens of Japanese burnet (*Sanguisorba obtusa*). Miniature hollyhocks (false mallow, *Sidalcea* sp.) are blooming bravely in pots, standing up to today's cold and wet as reminders of warmer, drier days.

The shop holds an especially pleasing selection of small-scale garden statuary, unusual cards, a fine group of gardening books, splendid English and Swiss garden tools, and an intriguing assortment of garden gadgets that you're sure to need. In autumn, thousands of spring-blooming bulbs await your choosing. ▶

◀ The Planter's Palette calendar includes seasonal open houses, other special events, and seminars on herbs and perennials. Plants and seminars and a well-stocked shop . . . choices are difficult at Planter's Palette.

Planter's Palette is on the south side of Roosevelt Road (Illinois Route 38), about a mile west of Winfield Road and a mile east of IL 59. Their sign isn't large so look for attractive plantings by a driveway that disappears into the woods. Planter's Palette is very near Cantigny Gardens.

Illinois: Northwest

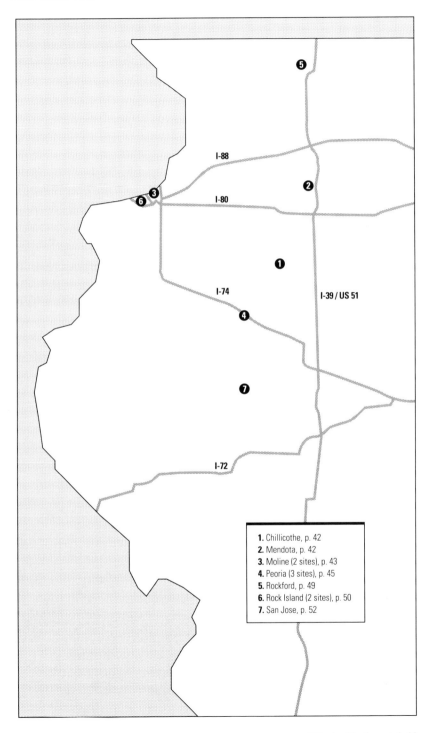

1. Chillicothe, p. 42
2. Mendota, p. 42
3. Moline (2 sites), p. 43
4. Peoria (3 sites), p. 45
5. Rockford, p. 49
6. Rock Island (2 sites), p. 50
7. San Jose, p. 52

The American Botanist, Booksellers
1103 West Truitt Avenue (or P. O. Box 532)
Chillicothe IL 61523
(309) 274-5254

Commercial. Rare and out-of-print books on agriculture, horticulture, and the history of gardening.

Periodic catalogs. Always call before visiting.
Open Monday-Saturday 10am-5pm.

The gardens you'll see here are those in rare books, out-of-print books, or current issues. Out-of-prints alone usually number about 3,000 titles. This is the place to find that tome you've been searching for; if the Botanist doesn't have it, he'll try hard to find it for you. Savor beautiful rare botanicals and herbals, browse through the stacks, or settle in a chair with a recent issue. You'll no doubt find an irresistible volume or two that deals with your special garden interest . . . be aware that the treasures here may awaken *new* interests.

The current catalog will list between 350 and 700 available titles; order it ($2.00) if you can't visit the Botanist.

From I-74 take Illinois Route 29 north to Chillicothe. In Chillicothe, turn west onto Truitt and go a quarter mile (look for the junior high school). Slow down and look for the American Botanist sign at the fourth house on the right.

Smith's Greenhouse and Supply
P. O. Box 218
603 14th Street
Mendota IL 61342
(800) 255-4906

Commercial. Field and greenhouse gardens.

Catalog. Plants labeled.
Open Monday-Saturday 9am-5pm.

Although Smith's is solely a wholesale operation, visitors are welcome to their fields and greenhouses, where pansies are the specialty . . . imagine those bright pansy faces arrayed by the thousands. Assorted perennials can be seen here too, along with demonstrations of organic growing and biological pest control.

▶

From I-39 north of LaSalle, take US Route 34 four miles west to Mendota. It's not a large city; you'll have no trouble finding 14th Street.

Butterworth Center
1105 Eighth Street
Moline IL 61265
(309) 765-7970

Two acres semi-formal gardens. Historic home.

 Brochure. Some plants labeled.
Gardens at the following two sites are open during daylight hours every day. Except for seasonal open houses, the houses are open by appointment only.

The Butterworth gardens are rowdy today, rambunctious with all the yellows and golds of midsummer bloom. Gaillardias, rudbeckias, coreopsis, daisies, daylilies, and potentillas stand and sprawl and nearly overwhelm the glaucous foliage and pastel blooms of lisianthus. An aged lantana, trimmed to display its handsome trunk and sturdy branches, provides an almost Oriental touch in this very midwestern garden. The comely pergola, bedecked with vines and hanging plants, offers welcome shade on this July day. Nearby, pots of lush ferns hang from trees and a stately bald cypress overlooks the brick and tile gazebo, an attractive structure built for viewing lawn bowling in the pitch beyond. Miniature roses are thriving in this summer's heat and drought while mature lilacs and other flowering trees and shrubs promise beauty for the cooler days of spring. Sturdy benches throughout the garden offer relaxation among the flowers. Or, you can sit in comfy chairs on the shady green-tiled porch, admire the view, and pretend it's all your own.

Butterworth Center, originally "Hillcrest," was built in 1892 as a wedding gift for Katherine Deere Butterworth. The widely traveled Butterworths kept very much up-to-date with changing styles and technology. Through the years, the house was extensively remodeled and redecorated; even the hardware on doors and windows was updated from time to time. The gardens, too, have evolved with changing tastes and horticultural introductions. Today, "old-fashioned" plants bloom beside some of the newest varieties.

Butterworth Center hosts nearly a thousand scheduled meetings and events each year and holds two annual open houses. The Christmas Open House, on the first Sunday in December, features Butterworth Center, Deere-Wiman House, and the nearby County Historical Society. The houses are also open without fee on the third Sunday in June, when the gardens are at their late-spring best.

Deere-Wiman House
On Eleventh Avenue between 8th and 10th streets
Moline
(309) 765-7970

Seven-acre grounds. 100'x100' terraced Victorian-style garden. Small rose gardens around historic home.

 Brochure. Some plants labeled.

The terraced perennial garden behind "Overlook," the Deere-Wiman House, is a medley of lavenders, pinks, and purples today, where hosts of garden phlox, lisianthus, roses, and liatris (prairie gayfeather) are accented by ebullient warm-colored clumps of daylilies and blanket flower (*Gaillardia* sp.). Spiky gray-green rattlesnake-master (*Eryngium yuccifolium*) hovers above resting peonies. Feathery celosias and magnificent dahlia-flowered zinnias, in deep reds and flaming scarlets, warm their little piece of hillside. Just beyond these, someone's sense of humor has come into play; a shady "Nature Trail" winds through pots of ferns and columbines. In spite of today's heat, roses manage to perfume the air and hostas and impatiens thrive beneath mature trees.

Walk the grounds of Deere-Wiman, where massive lilac bushes will join peonies and abundant irises in a glorious springtime treat for the eyes and nose. An impressive stone lantern guards a hosta colony that merges with hillside daylilies. Stroll to the bluff's edge for a view across the Mississippi River to the Iowa heights.

This home, extensively remodeled several times since it was built in the early 1870s, was continuously occupied by Deere family members until 1976. The gardens at Deere-Wiman House and at Butterworth Center are quite different in character and in detail, even though the two properties are less than a block apart, are supported by the same trust fund, and are maintained by the same staff. You'll be glad you took time to enjoy both of them.

To both sites: From I-74 through Moline, take 7th Avenue west to its end at 12th Street. Turn left and go about halfway up a long hill to 11th Avenue, then turn ▶

FYI It's fairly easy to find your way around Moline and Rock Island; avenues run east-west and streets go north-south.

◀ *west onto 11th. Deere-Wiman House will be on the right about 3 blocks after you turn and Butterworth Center will be on the left a half block further west. There's ample off-street parking in the lot that serves both sites.*

D. A. Hoerr and Sons
8020 North Shade Tree Drive (Illinois Route 91)
Peoria IL 61615
(309) 691-4561

Commercial nursery. Twenty acres include arboretum, display gardens, and sales area. Emphasis on perennial plants.

♿ Complete garden shop. Nearly all plants labeled. Workshops and seminars.
Open all year Monday-Saturday 8am-5:30pm.

Lovely specimen trees and a blazing display of daylilies call to us as we whiz by on the highway; a quick turn-around brings us back to D. A. Hoerr and a parking lot that is deserted on this July evening. We wander about, admiring a rock garden here, pots and pots of good-looking perennials there. Killdeer swoop and cry, complaining of our intrusion.

This nursery assumes a degree of gardening expertise on the part of its customers. Perennial plants in the sales area are arranged alphabetically by botanical family, rather than by common name, color, habitat preference, or price. The system works particularly well for those less-frequently used plants that tend not to have widely known common names. If, like many of us, you simply shop for plants whose looks and habits appeal to you, you're sure to find them here.

Flowering trees and shrubs make this nursery as attractive in spring as it is today at the height of daylily season. Clearly labeled mature specimens of appealing trees and shrubs are scattered across the grounds; if you buy one of these varieties, you'll know what to expect as it grows. I'm impressed with a nursery that permanently beautifies its grounds in an attempt to educate its public.

Our autumn return to Hoerr finds the gardens dormant. All the action is on the tree and shrub lots and in the intriguing shop. Well-stocked book shelves promise a winter of delightful garden reading, dreaming, and planning. Would you like a Japanese touch for your garden? Do you nurture a very small garden? Whatever your garden interest or needs, you'll find help here. Container gardeners will love Hoerr's trove of terra cotta planters, where fluted rectangles and hanging wall baskets, columns, animal forms, and tubs wait to be filled with lush greenery and bright blossoms. A piece from Hoerr's collection of graceful furniture and irresistible sculpture will complete your garden nicely.

Hoerr offers a range of gardening seminars, workshops, and demonstrations during the year. I'll come back to enjoy their gardens in another season, perhaps to learn in a seminar, and to select special plants for my own garden.

Shade Tree Drive is also Illinois Route 91, on the northwest side of Peoria. Take I-74 or I-474 to Illinois Route 6 and go north on IL 6 to US Route 150. Turn west on US 150 and you'll almost immediately see IL 91. Go north about ½ mile to Hoerr, on the east side of the road.

George A. Luthy Memorial Botanical Garden
Glen Oak Park
2218 North Prospect
Peoria IL 61603
(309) 682-1200

Four acres landscaped grounds. 2,000 sq.ft. conservatory. All-American Rose Selection garden.

Small gift/souvenir shop. Many plants labeled. Picnic facilities in Glen Oak Park. On-going and seasonal plant sales. Education center.
Grounds open daily 8am-dusk. Conservatory open daily 8am-4pm. Shop hours same as conservatory except 10am-4pm weekends.

The sweet spice of roses, the perfume of Luthy's large rose garden, fills the hot, humid July air today. Meandering turf walkways lead to pockets of interest and beauty where trees, shrubs, and smaller plants blend in attractive harmony. Near the greenhouse, an unusual yellow and gray border is especially appealing. Lemon-yellow daylilies, pale yellow coreopsis 'Moonbeam', and a variegated grass highlight crisp dusty miller, furry lamb's-ears (*Stachys byzantina*), old woman wormwood (*Artemisia stellerana*), and a carpet of snow-in-summer (*Cerastium tomentosum*). Large bronzy-plum leaves of *Prunus virginiana* 'Shubert', a chokecherry, are elegant against these pastel hues.

In the conservatory "wedding space," a tiny but noisy waterfall hides among cattleya orchids, bougainvillea, asparagus ferns, and true ferns. Hanging blooms of a dendrobium orchid are like strings of white and lavender butter- ▶

FYI Hoerr is pronounced "hare."

flies. The conservatory's second room holds masses of gerbera daisies and a bank of banana trees, all loving the heat. Comfortable teak benches invite us to "sit a spell" in the middle of this lovely scene but the conservatory temperature is nearing 125 degrees on this July day. It actually feels cool, ever so briefly, when we return to the 97° weather outside.

The conservatory gift shop offers, in addition to a small selection of books, an amazing assortment of trinkets with botany or zoology themes (there is a small zoo near the garden). You may be more interested in the adjacent plant sale room, where bonsai kits hold tiny juniper trees that are trimmed, potted, and accompanied by care and culture directions, or you might find an orchid plant on the shelves filled with more common houseplants. Today, the selection of succulents includes some rarely seen euphorbias and a peculiar-looking succulent artemisia. These shelves offer variety that echoes the gardens outside, less-common plants among familiar plants and all of them attractive.

Luthy hosts a varied schedule of events. Spring brings lily, orchid, and bonsai shows and a sale of perennial plants. Summer offers Rose Sunday and band concerts. In fall and winter, you can take a candlelight tour or see the Mum and Poinsettia shows. The Bio Center is home to many shows and classes, demonstrations, and group meetings. There's always something beautiful and/or interesting at Luthy.

From I-74 take the Knoxville Exit and go north to Nebraska or McClure Street, then east to Glen Oak/Prospect, and turn north again to the park. The gardens are at the north end of Glen Oak Park, north of the large parking lot across from the zoo.

Stone Well Herbs (Home, studio, and gardens)
2320 West Moss Avenue
Peoria IL 61604
(309) 674-1781

Commercial. One acre of herb theme gardens. Mature landscaping around century-old home.

♿ Catalog. Most plants labeled. Workshops and classes.
The gardens are "open" most days but, since this is also a private home, courtesy requires a call ahead and a knock on the door to announce your presence when you arrive.

Stone Well at the Walnut Street Warehouse (Retail shop)
100 Walnut
Peoria IL 61604

▶

◀ ♿ Shop of herb products and garden-related accessories. Snacks available in the Warehouse complex.
Open Wednesday-Saturday 10am-5pm.

The owner of Stone Well Herbs loves to design theme gardens; her enthusiasm and expertise are apparent in the varied and thriving gardens on Moss Avenue. You may even spy the Witches' Garden tucked away in a corner, a nook that includes plants associated with both "good" witches and "bad" witches. (Did you know that parsley supposedly grows better for witches than for anyone else?) Besides beauty, these intimate cottage-style plantings supply material for dried arrangements, potpourri, herbal topiaries, and many other projects.

At Stone Well, you can take classes in a wide range of botanical crafts as well as in garden planning and harvesting. The annual Spring Herb Festival, held on the first weekend in May, features fresh herbs and flowers, craft demonstrations, music, garden tours, and appetizing refreshments. On the last weekend of September, the Fall Harvest Festival focuses on garden harvests, drying and using plant material, and, again, appropriate music and tasty food. A good time will be had by all at either festival.

The Walnut Street shop features "herbal delights" from the Stone Well gardens and unusual items from other sources. A rich selection of garden-related books is accompanied by the standard assortment of everlastings, aprons, herb blends, and small garden sculptures. You'll also find not-so-standard items like herb designs in stencil or needlework kits, handsome silver posy-holders for your lapel, and several sizes of graceful bentwood trellises to support and enhance your house or garden plants. A visit to Stone Well's gardens or shop will be a fine addition to your time in Peoria.

To the gardens on Moss Avenue: From I-74 take the University Street exit and go south several blocks to Moss Avenue at the edge of the riverine bluffs. Go west on Moss through an attractive neighborhood of lovingly maintained or restored older homes, including a Frank Lloyd Wright house, through a slight jog north at Western, then about three blocks beyond Western to Stone Well, a large house set well back, on the south side of the street. The gardens are behind the house. (You can just take Western Avenue south to Moss but the drive is not nearly so pleasant.)

To the Walnut Street Warehouse: From I-74 take Washington Street south a few blocks to the Warehouse, at the corner of Washington and Market. The Stone Well Shop is just inside the main Warehouse entrance.

Sinnissippi Greenhouse and Gardens
1300 North Second Street (Route 251)
In Sinnissippi Park, along the Rock River in Rockford

Rose Garden 200'x100'. Greenhouses. Demonstration gardens.

♿ Many plants labeled. Trails and picnic facilities in park. Occasional workshops in greenhouses.
Gardens open daily sunrise to sunset. Greenhouses open daily 9am-4pm. Closed Christmas Day.

On this June afternoon, the gorgeous rose garden at Sinnissippi is a special treat; it smells just as roses should smell. Several members of the Mens' Garden Club (who plan, plant, and maintain the rose garden) are sprucing up the plants in preparation for this evening's Wives' Party. The tent is pitched, a cool breeze is blowing, the roses are at their prime, and the party will surely be a romantic success.

Sinnissippi Park has two distinct sections: a large tract of mature trees on rolling land and, across the road, gardens on the riverside flood plain. Demonstration areas near the greenhouses include raised beds, a cover crop demo, and herb, space-saving, and container gardens. These containers, where vegetables and annual flowers are growing happily, range from terra cotta pots to bushel baskets and plastic bags. The greenhouses, which hold sizable collections of orchids, gloxinias, and fancy begonias, host two seasonal flower shows. Here, too, you can pick up leaflets and brochures on horticultural activities in the area.

Walk beyond the greenhouses and past the lagoon's flock of begging mallards to the handsome floral clock and the admirable rose garden. Then, stroll along the fine jogging/walking trail that edges the Rock River. The Park District trolley makes a brief stop at Sinnissippi so passengers can explore the gardens. This park is worth exploring.

For park or garden information contact the Rockford Park District, 1330 North Second Street, Rockford IL 61107. (815) 987-8858.
For trolley ride or river cruise information contact the Park District office at 324 North Madison Street, Rockford IL 61107. (815) 987-8894.

▶

FYI Botanic gardens, an educational center, and the Carl and Lois Klehm Arboretum are under development at 2715 South Main Street in Rockford, on land formerly held by the Winnebago Forest Preserve District. For information on these projects and their progress contact the Northern Illinois Botanical Society, P. O. Box 8101, Rockford IL 61126.

◀ *From I-90 take Business Route US 20 west to Illinois Route 251 North. This becomes North Second Street. The park is at North Second Street and Ethel Avenue; turn toward the river for the gardens.*

Hauberg Civic Center
1300 24th Street
Rock Island IL 61201
(309) 788-2132

Small estate grounds. Two acres shade and woodland gardens. Rose garden.

♿ Library in house. Nature trail and picnic facilities on adjacent grounds.
Grounds open daylight hours all year. Hours for the house and the library are quite variable. Call ahead or inquire at the Park District Office.

These shady gardens were carefully designed for consistency with the house, an early Prairie-Style home that was built in 1909 for Susanne Denkman Hauberg. The house and gardens embrace a partially wooded site where native species and horticultural varieties are carefully combined. Stately rhododendrons promise spring drama and hardwoods will glow in the autumn. Shade gardens behind the house gradually merge into a wooded hillside of native plants; toward the foot of the hill, native plants predominate.

In the shade gardens, you'll see at least two plants not commonly seen in public plantings. Today, in early July, sturdy clumps of native celandine poppy (*Stylophorum diphyllum*) still offer a few bits of clear yellow bloom above their lobed glaucous leaves. Bronzy-wine perilla (*Perilla frutescens*), a freely reseeding annual, adds unexpected richness to the garden's green edges.

If you look carefully, you'll see stylized tulip motifs both inside and outside the house, including a tulip-shaped fountain on the terrace. Tulips were the favorite flower of Susanne Hauberg, and spring's abundant tulips and other bulb flowers are organized in beds and naturalized in lawns and woodlands.

There are roses around the house and in a small garden between the main house and the carriage house. A special collection of heritage roses honors deceased members of the Rock Island Women's Club, Garden Department. Near the rose garden you can enter the Arboretum Walk, a short trail down the hill and into the woods, along which you'll find at least 40 varieties of native trees and many wildflower and understory species. This variety of plants and the combination of designed and natural areas makes Hauberg Civic Center attractive and inviting any time of year. ▶

◀ *From I-280, just before you reach the Mississippi River, take Illinois Route 92 to 18th Avenue. Go east on 18th Avenue about two miles to 25th Street and turn north on 24th. You'll see signs for the Park District Administrative Office, which is adjacent to Hauberg Civic Center.*

Longview Park and Gardens
18th Avenue and 17th Street
Rock Island

300'x40' gardens within large park. Small greenhouse. Small conservatory.

♿ Conservatory and greenhouse plants labeled. Picnic facilities in surrounding park. Park and gardens open daylight hours. Greenhouse and conservatory open "business hours."

As with many public gardens across the midwest, those at Longview are under renovation; an expansive "four seasons" garden is replacing small, old planting beds. Today, garden workers in golden yellow shirts are pruning plants, weeding, and installing the masses of annuals that will provide sweeps of color in weeks to come. Numerous variations of lush caladiums edge the newly built shade house and, nearby, a small arched bridge and a collection of dwarf conifers suggest a Japanese garden. The "pond" under the new bridge will be a pool of rich blue ageratum. Soon, prickly pears (*Opuntia* sp.) will present silken blooms in the small cactus garden and ornamental grasses will sport graceful plumes and tassels. Near the park drive, lollipops of tiny flames are brilliant lantanas that have been trained into handsome 5-foot standards.

Many parks and gardens have floral clocks; few have a floral *calendar*. Longview's calendar faces southeast at the entrance corner of the park and you may miss it if you approach the park from the west. Within a design of floral letters and motifs, interchangeable redwood boxes each contain one letter or numeral formed of tightly clipped plants. The month and date is spelled out in plants simply by changing the appropriate boxes. Today's "5" will be replaced early tomorrow morning by the requisite "6" and, at the end of the month, the letters for "August" will supplant those for "July." This quietly ornate feature reminds us of these gardens' Victorian beginnings.

Today, the public greenhouse holds only a mélange of houseplants; its more interesting residents are summering outside. The small Victorian conservatory is also relatively empty but in winter and spring it is alive with seasonal flower shows. ▶

◀ Impressive gold-painted lions greet you at the entry to this park. Further along the park drive, the "long view" is through tall trees and across the Mississippi to towns and heights on the Iowa side. Along the way, between the lions and the river bluffs, you'll see comely gardens designed for all seasons.

For information contact the Rock Island Park District Administrative Office, 1300 24th Street, Rock Island IL 61201. (309) 788-2132.

From I-280 take Illinois Route 92 north to 18th Avenue. Turn right on 18th, go up a hill or two and, after several blocks, the park will be on your left at 17th Street. Look for the golden lions.

Clark's Greenhouse and Herbal Country
R. R. 1 Box 15B
San Jose IL 62682
(309) 247-3679

Commercial herb grower. Over 1 acre of gardens.

Shop of herbal products. Most plants labeled. Seasonal plant sales. Workshops and classes. Open spring through fall, flexible hours. Closed Sunday.

Here at Clark's, a west-facing, sun-catching slope holds tall trees, theme gardens, and cutting beds for fresh-cut herb sales. You'll see herbs used for medicine, those that particularly attract bees, and some old favorites from your kitchen. There are plants that yield pleasant herb teas (tisanes), plants mentioned in the Bible, or those treasured for their fragrance. Some are purported to be special favorites of witches and some yield natural dyestuffs. Mints, thymes, sages, and scented geraniums each have their separate beds. Nearby, a handsome gazebo provides seating and shade for restful enjoyment of the gardens and countryside. On a clear day, you probably *can* see forever from this hillside.

You'll find much to tempt you here. The shop holds fresh herb wreathes and tussy mussies (nosegays) and an assortment of everlasting arrangements. Herb seasonings, teas, and vinegars are joined by a selection of "country" items. In the spring, Clark's offers herb, bedding, and vegetable plants. Throughout the year, a variety of workshops and classes are added attractions in this pleasant country setting.

Take Illinois Route 136 toward San Jose (we call it San Joe's, *not* ho-zay*). About a mile east of San Jose, go south on the road towards New Holland. About 1½ miles south of IL 136, you'll see Clark's on the east side of this road.*

Illinois: Southeast

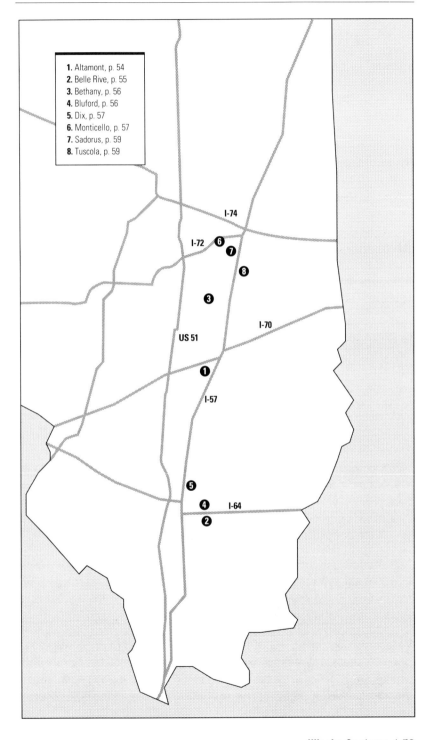

1. Altamont, p. 54
2. Belle Rive, p. 55
3. Bethany, p. 56
4. Bluford, p. 56
5. Dix, p. 57
6. Monticello, p. 57
7. Sadorus, p. 59
8. Tuscola, p. 59

Illinois: Southeast

Much of southeastern Illinois is sparsely populated; it contains the Illinois Ozarks, the vast tracts of Shawnee National Forest, and thousands of acres of marginal farmland. There are few public gardens of any kind but the area has spawned a number of herb-related enterprises. Many of these small businesses have limited hours or seasons *and* inviting display gardens or production fields. Due to the nature and size of these operations, most of them request that you call before planning a visit.

The Illinois Herb Association coordinates at least two annual herb festivals in the late winter and early spring. For information on these contact the Illinois Herb Association, I. S. G. A., 1701 Towanda Avenue, Bloomington IL 61701, or the Mount Vernon Convention and Visitors Bureau, (800) 252-5464.

Alwerdt's Pheasant Farm and Gardens
Rt. 1 Box 152A
Altamont IL 62411
(618) 483-5798

Commercial. Four acres display and production gardens.

♿ Dirt or turf paths. Catalog and calendar. Shop. Most plants labeled. Plant sales. Workshops and festivals. Group tours by appointment (small fee).
Open all year Monday-Saturday 10am-5pm, Sunday 1-4pm. Extended winter holiday hours.

Alwerdt's lush gardens are glowing in today's gentle rain and happy clumps of bamboo stand near the parking lot. Elegant cleomes and shorter, stouter celosias stand fresh and bright in the rainy gardens. The new "rest and relaxation" pavilion provides a lovely view across misty gardens to rolling land and deep woods beyond. For exercise in a particularly pleasant setting, you can stroll the many paths that wind through herbs and flowers.

Seasonal festivals and occasional seminars and workshops make good use of these bountiful plantings. To make your garden look like this (even if you don't have four acres to spare), you can buy plants on site or through Alwerdt's catalog.

Wreathes, swags, bouquets, vine baskets, and bunches of dry flowers adorn Alwerdt's shops. These floral creations (perhaps most attractive I've seen anywhere), are evidence of the owner's background in painting and sculpture. His unique plant-drying method preserves almost all color in the flowers. Blues, those particularly fugitive hues, remain as vivid as on the living plants; pastels stay delicate, luscious, and lively. Here are dried herbs and flowers at their very best.

There are many plans to extend and improve these grounds. A pond, a water garden, and more trails will appear beyond the gardens. If these projects come off with the expertise and the eye for beauty apparent in the existing gardens, they'll be wonderful indeed. Today looks and feels like an all-day rain but, operating on the principle that it occasionally rains on even the most fortunate of travelers, we decided to visit Alwerdt's. It was the right decision.

From I-70 a few miles west of Effingham, take Exit 82, Illinois Route 128. Go south a mile or so and turn left at Alwerdt's sign, then left again in less than a quarter mile.

The Enchanted Crest
Route 1 Box 216
Belle Rive IL 62810
(618) 736-2647

Commercial. 4-acre grounds. Victorian-style herb garden. Rose garden. Pear and pecan orchards. Bed and breakfast establishment.

Gift shop. Hiking trails. Workshops and special events. Group tours and other visits by appointment only. Call for information.

You may indeed find enchantment in the varied gardens that surround this 1881 mansion and its unique barn. Admire over 400 varieties of herbs, perennials, and everlastings in 20 different gardens or, in the rose garden, truly stop to smell the roses. Enjoy walks through pear and pecan orchards or on a nature trail. Listen to the pines that whisper around the 2-acre lake. Come for a pleasant overnight stay surrounded by a large display of antique quilts. Or come with a few friends for a special day that may include a garden tour, basketry classes, the tasty lunch buffet, the lavish Country Victorian Tea, or a ten-course gourmet dinner.

The gardens at Enchanted Crest aren't open to the drop-in public but their other offerings and the scenic rural location may entice you to gather from 5 to 50 friends and make reservations . . . or to give yourself a personal holiday in the country. No directions are given because appointments must be made for any visit to Enchanted Crest.

Bonds Herb Farm
52 Cardinal Drive
Bethany IL 61914
(217) 665-3233

Commercial. Two and a half acres. Gardens and production fields. Greenhouse. Rose garden.

♿ Shop. Plants labeled. Seasonal plant sales. Workshops. Group tours by appointment.
Open Monday-Friday 10am-5pm, Saturday 10am-4pm. Other hours by appointment. Closed Sunday.
Rose Festival: Call for dates and times.

If it has to do with herbs or everlastings it probably grows in the fields, greenhouse, or colonial-style herb garden at Bonds. If it can be dried you'll probably find it in the drying barns or as bundles and attractive arrangements in Bonds' spacious shop. The Bethany Heritage Rose Garden, a collection of over 160 rose varieties, adds perfume and color to all these herbs. This is the site of the mid-May Rose Festival, an event that includes craft displays and demonstrations. In spring, you can buy roses, herbs, everlastings, and perennials for your own garden. At Bonds, there is always *something* that looks good or smells good.

Bonds Herb Farm is at the corner of Main Street and Illinois Route 121 in Bethany.

Oakdale Herb Farm
R. R. 1 Box 46A
Bluford IL 62814-9801
(618) 755-9751

Commercial. Two and a half acre grounds. Nearly 5,000 sq.ft. gardens. 6,000 sq.ft. greenhouse.

Most plants labeled. Plant sales. Classes and workshops. Always best to call ahead. Group tours by appointment.
Open April 15-June 15 Wednesday-Saturday 9am-5pm, Sunday 2pm-5pm. June 16-October 31 by appointment only.

Enjoy the scenic drive from Mt. Vernon to Oakdale Herb Farm, where cottage-style gardens, a large formal herb garden, and a specimen garden wait. You'll find herbs and bedding plants, appealing perennials, heirloom vegetables, native wildflowers, scented geraniums, and an intriguing variety of less common plants in the gardens and for sale here. Come for a Saturday morning garden tour or register for a Tuesday morning class to take advantage of all that Oakdale offers.

From I-57 take Exit 95 (Illinois Route 15) and go east, through Mt. Vernon, about 6 or 7 miles to County Road 2125 E. Turn north on CR 2125 E and go about 2½ miles to CR 1750, then east a half mile to Oakdale Herb Farm.

Windy Pines Natural Farm
R. 1 Box 245
Dix IL 62830
(618) 266-7351

Commercial, wholesale only. Grower and forager of medicinal native plants. "Living Library."

💲 Nominal fee for garden tours. Plants labeled. Workshops. Visits and garden tours by appointment only.

Most of southern Illinois is "garden" for the owners of Windy Pines. Here are the woods, meadows, and fields where they are permitted to gather unsprayed plants for their medicinal botanicals. The home location near Dix offers small plots of mints and culinary herbs but the treasure is the "Living Library" around the house, a plant library that's used for teaching and for plant identification. A 3-acre show and tour garden will soon join this collection of native plants. An informative tour of these plantings, accompanied by pleasant herb tea, can be arranged. Before you visit Windy Pines, a phone call or letter is imperative because this is very much a working farm and because the owners are often away on gathering expeditions. The best time to call is early morning or late evening.

Robert Allerton Park and Conference Center
R. R. 2 Box 135
Monticello IL 61856
(217) 762-2721 or (217) 244-1035

Wooded estate grounds. Formal gardens.

♿ Brochures and trail maps. Vending machine snacks and small selection of books at Visitor Center. Picnic facilities. Hiking trails. ▶

◀ Park and gardens open daily sunrise to sunset. Visitor Center always open between 10am and 4:30pm, earlier or later hours depend on the day and the time of year.

Early in the twentieth century, Robert Allerton developed these Sangamon River flood plains into a "gentleman's country estate"; the European-style landscape presents intriguing contrasts with riverine woods. Walled gardens near the Visitor Center were once Robert Allerton's vegetable garden. Now they hold sculpture, a hedge maze, espaliered roses and pears, and drifts of astilbe. In the nearby woods, wild monkshood (*Aconitum uncinatum*) blooms and catches shafts of sunlight on this October day.

No visit to Allerton Park is complete without a stroll down the Fu Dog allée, a lane of mature white firs that's accented by twenty-two rich blue Chinese dog sculptures. Although it's near the main parking lot, it seems like another world. Elsewhere in the woods, you'll find the Sunken Garden, a popular lawn for weddings and concerts. In a far meadow an impressive sculpture, "The Sunsinger," lifts his arms in praise of sunrise. Other sculptures are scattered through the woods, although several have been removed to the protection of Krannert Art Museum at the University of Illinois.

Allerton Park Visitor Center is one of few places in central Illinois where bougainvillea blooms; this tropical touch is particularly appealing in winter, of course, when the Allerton grounds and gardens are either brown or snow-covered. The Visitor Center also offers snacks, maps, books and booklets, a small greenhouse, and a very informative wildflower bloom schedule. Here, too, are photographic exhibits and an introductory videotape that will help you decide which part of Allerton you want to enjoy first. You may come to Allerton Park for the formal gardens, the bougainvillea, or the spring wildflower riot but you're sure to find other pleasant surprises here.

From I-72 take Exit 61 toward Monticello. At the first intersection turn west and go a little over a mile to the small Allerton Park sign, then turn left and follow signs to the park. At the "Y" at the top of the hill, go left between brick columns, into the woods, past Allerton Farms, and on into the park. The Visitor Center is straight ahead on the left.

FYI Allerton Park is owned by the University of Illinois. Georgian-style Allerton House, built in 1900, overlooks a small lake and a fine vista of rolling meadows edged by native woods. The house is now a conference center, so it's not open to casual visitors, but anyone can stand on the terrace, enjoy the view, and pretend to be an English country squire.

Herbs of Grace Garden
US Route 45 North
Tuscola IL 61953
(217) 253-3777

Two and a half acres. Gardens and cutting fields of herbs and everlastings.

Commercial. Seasonal festivals.
Open daylight hours.

Lamb's-ears (*Stachys byzantina*), lavenders, and blue flax form orderly borders in this garden that's a mother-daughter enterprise, a garden that is a "root division" of Herbs of Grace near Sadorus. Today, workers are readying the garden for tomorrow's Harvest Festival, sprucing up the perennials and removing tender plants blackened by an unusually early frost. I'm sad that most of the basils have collapsed and the brilliant "zinnia wheels" are gone but the globe amaranth (*Gomphrena globosa*) has been shocked into pleasing pastel tones.

About two acres of cutting fields lie adjacent to the display garden. Here are rows and rows of statice, lavender, salvia, opal basil, and other plants whose flowers or foliage keep their color and/or fragrance when they're dried. These fields supply plant material for workshops and for sale at the Sadorus Herbs of Grace.

You'll find no shop or sales at this garden except during seasonal festivals. You *will* find comfortable benches, thousands of attractive flowers, and a myriad of textures and scents in this prairie beauty spot.

From I-57 take the Pesotum/Route 45 exit and go south about 5 miles. The garden is on the west side of the highway, not far south of Douglas County Road 1250 N and about 1½ miles north of Tuscola.

Herbs of Grace Workshop
150 B County Road 400 E
Sadorus IL 61872
(217) 598-2542

Commercial. Herb theme gardens.

♿ Shop. Most plants labeled. Seasonal plant sales. Many workshops and special events. Usually open April 1-June 1 daily 10am-5pm, June 2-December 6 Tuesday-Saturday 10am-5pm. ▶

◀ The Herbs of Grace barn is often filled with dried plant materials, good smells, and an industrious party of workshop participants. Air-dried herbs and everlastings festoon tables, chairs, and ceiling; part of the good smell is the delicious always-ready blackberry tea. Outside, white wicker furniture invites a leisurely appreciation of the attractive Silver Garden; I'd love to see this in full moonlight.

The shop offers a lovely assortment of wreaths, swags, topiaries and other arrangements, herbal cards, and large baskets for gathering your garden's bounty. Herbs of Grace jams, jellies, toppings, and relishes fill a handsome antique cupboard. Faded antique quilts blend with pastel dried arrangements. Small, well-executed cross-stitch depictions of herbs and flowers join colorful flower-decorated hats on walls and tables. And I'm sure my garden would welcome a small ceramic garden saint from the windowsill congregation.

In some years, production fields of everlastings and flowers surround the workshop; in other years, these fields hold corn. On this prime early autumn day, golden corn rustles and rattles in the breeze. And, as gardeners will, the folks at Herbs of Grace are already planning next year's improvements. I'll have an excuse for another delightful road trip.

Note: The Herbs of Grace gardens and workshop have been in flux due to family illnesses and other obstacles. A phone call would be in order before you visit.

From US Route 45 south of Champaign and Tolono, go west on the Sadorus Road, through Sadorus and 2 miles beyond to a large sign for the Sadorus Sportsmen's Club (and, below it, a small sign for Herbs of Grace). Turn south here, go 3½ miles to the next Sportsmen's Club sign, then turn east. The main herb production fields are sometimes at this corner and the workshop barn is just ahead.

Illinois: Southwest

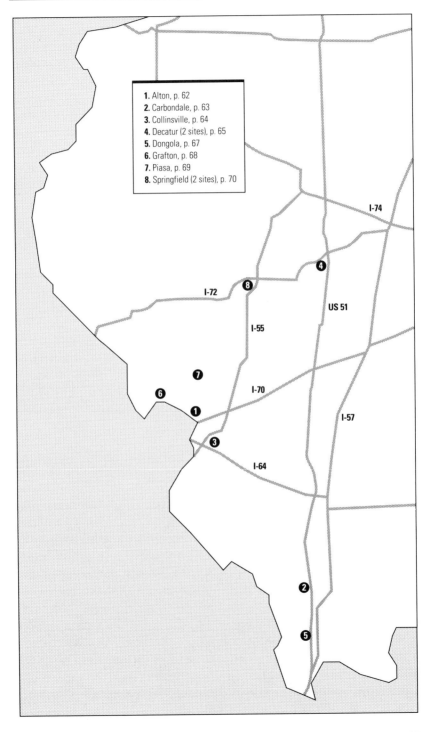

1. Alton, p. 62
2. Carbondale, p. 63
3. Collinsville, p. 64
4. Decatur (2 sites), p. 65
5. Dongola, p. 67
6. Grafton, p. 68
7. Piasa, p. 69
8. Springfield (2 sites), p. 70

Illinois: Southwest

In the late spring of southern Illinois, those scattered fields of joyous yellow might be fallow areas claimed by insidious wild mustard . . . or they could be experimental plantings of canola (*Brassica napus* L.), a genetically improved mustard. *B. napus* is the most commonly planted form of the several brassicas that yield desirable vegetable oil. Canola crop production practices and schedules, similar to those used for wheat, don't fit into the corn/soybean rotation that is dominant further north in Illinois. There is some canola production south of Effingham but present markets don't justify replacing soybeans with canola even though the technology is similar. The market may improve because canola oil is currently considered one of the most healthful vegetable oils. When that happens, if growers switch to canola, spring will bring us additional acres of singing yellow.

For more information on canola as a crop contact Ameri-Can Pedigreed Seed Company, (800) 322-6652.

The Nan Elliott Memorial Rose Garden
Gordon F. Moore Community Park
Alton

Over 1,500 rose bushes of 125 varieties. Large Oriental stroll garden.

 Many plants labeled. Nature trails. Picnic facilities in park.
Open daylight hours all year.
Sunday carillon concerts May-September 5-5:30pm.

Here are roses wonderfully fresh and fragrant, deep green bushes laden with blooms and buds on this cool, clear, and breezy day. I expect a rose garden to look like this in June, but not today, in August, near the end of summer. Almost all the beautiful rose colors and color combinations are in splendid display. I don't see the green or lavender cultivars but it would be easy to miss them in this riot of lush shrub roses and delicate miniatures, tea roses and old-fashioned cabbage roses, tidy bushes and energetic ramblers. The various molds and fungi that attack roses are rare in this dry, dry summer and, somehow, insects have been kept at bay. Chipping sparrows are mining the deep mulch, doing their bit to keep the insect population down. A pleasant pergola provides an impressive rose panorama and a gazebo at the back of the garden invites submersion in rose sights and aromas. Visitors come and go, a positive sign that this garden is appreciated by its public. It is indeed a treasure. ▶

◀ An "Oriental garden" lies near the end of the main park road, not far beyond the rose garden. This is a large, open area with Oriental touches, rather than the intensively planted setting we might expect. A small torii (symbolic gateway) leads to a pond that holds a modest waterfall and freestanding stones. Heavy ropes along the path alert sight-impaired visitors to braille signs that describe plants in the immediate area and that point out other features, such as benches or path intersections. A raised "garden for the blind" holds herbs to be touched and smelled and an adjacent planting is flamboyant with magenta petunias, red-orange zinnias, wine-colored hibiscus, and orange-coral gladiolus.

Azaleas and an entry trellis surround a small contemplation garden and, elsewhere, a shaded deck overlooks the small lake. Large clumps of sumac will flaunt their brilliant fall color; dogwoods and flowering shrubs will dominate the spring. Today, elegant Chinese scholar trees or pagoda trees (*Sophora japonica*) hold clusters of creamy pea-like blooms against their dark foliage.

Moore Community Park is relatively new, the Oriental garden newer yet. It's already a delightful place for a leisurely excursion and will be better and better as the plantings mature.

For details contact the Director of Parks and Recreation, Alton Park and Recreation Department, 1211 Henry Street, Alton IL 62002. (618) 463-3580.

From I-55 take Illinois Route 140 about 15 miles west toward Alton. Moore Community Park is on the south side of IL 140, about a half mile west of the stoplight at Powder Mill Road.
From I-270 take IL 3 north to IL 140 in Alton, then go east on IL 140 to the park.

William Marberry Arboretum
East Pleasant Hill Road and South Wall Street
Carbondale

Twenty-four acre arboretum with lake and swamp.

Many plants labeled. Nature trails.
Open daylight hours all year.

White forsythia to dusty zenobia, *Abeliophyllum distichum* to *Zenobia pulverulenta*, and hundreds of varieties in between wait for you at Marberry Arboretum. Springtime in southern Illinois is enchanting; it must be breathtaking at the arboretum, when 17 varieties of flowering dogwoods, 12 of magnolias, and 8 different rhododendrons join spireas, weigelas, andromedas, and forsythias in vivid display. Summer's exotic Rose-of-Sharon (*Hibiscus syriacus*) and crape myrtle (*Lagerstroemia indica*) accent quiet greens. Ten different Japanese maples (*Acer palmatum* var.) display their intricate foliage and sometimes-contorted branches. In winter, after autumn's flamboyance of hardwood trees, the landscape is dominated by the deep tones and rich textures of coniferous and broad-leaved evergreens, including nearly 40 varieties of American holly.

In addition to native trees, Marberry embraces a vast range of exotic species, many of which were collected by William Marberry during Oriental and European travels. His arboretum harbors one of Illinois' largest collections of exotics, second only to the Morton Arboretum in Lisle. Mr. Marberry planted the trees in consideration of their cultural requirements *and* with an eye to the overall aesthetic effect. There are no flower beds or formal gardens here but you'll find the arboretum a peaceful and beautiful haven.

For further information contact the Carbondale Park District, 1115 West Sycamore, Carbondale IL 62901. (618) 529-4147.

From I-57 take Illinois Route 13 west to US Route 51 in Carbondale. Go south on US 51 through downtown Carbondale, past the Southern Illinois University athletic complex, to a 4-way stoplight. At the light, turn east onto Pleasant Hill Road. (Note that Pleasant Hill has a different name on the west side of US 51.) Go east on Pleasant Hill to the arboretum.

Annual International Horseradish Festival
Woodland Park
Collinsville

Horseradish-theme souvenirs. Picnic facilities in park. Handicapped-accessible shuttle buses.
Festival held the first Saturday in May 10:30am-9pm.

The thought of a festival in honor of homely horseradish (*Armoracia rusticana*) makes me smile and salivate. Even its name reflects the herb's humble origins.

Festival events include the ordinary, such as stage shows and a display of small animals, and the extraordinary; the horseradish root toss, a recipe contest, the Little Miss Horseradish competition, and the horseradish-eating contest are favorites. How many hot dogs covered with freshly ground horseradish could *you* eat in 30 seconds? New events and vendors, each with a horseradish theme, are added each year.

◀ Horseradish, with its long history of medicinal, aphrodisiac, and culinary use, was brought to this country by early colonists. Explorers and settlers soon discovered the suitability of this area's riverine soil for "mare-radish" (from the German "Meerrettich"). Sixty-percent of this country's horseradish is grown in the American Bottoms, an area of fertile floodplain and suitable climate near East St. Louis.

If your sinuses need clearing in early May, come to the wooded hills of Woodland Park for all the horseradish and good fun you can handle.

For details and schedule contact the International Horseradish Festival, Collinsville Chamber of Commerce, 221 West Main Street, Collinsville IL 62234. (618) 344-2884.

From I-55 and I-170 take Exit 5 (Vandalia Avenue/Illinois Route 159) for Collinsville. Go south on Vandalia a short distance to Beltline, then east on Beltline to Woodland Park. There will be route signs for the festival and supplementary parking with free shuttle service.

Mari-Mann Herb Company
R. R. 4 Box 7
Decatur IL 62521-9404
(217) 429-1555
Gingerbread House (gift shop) (217) 429-1404

Commercial herb grower. 100'x100' formal garden. Over 2½ acres herb gardens.

🍲 Shop. Most plants labeled. Plant sales. Workshops and other special events. Walking trails. Open Monday-Saturday 9am-5pm, Sunday noon-5pm. Closed major holidays.

At Mari-Mann, one of the largest herb gardens in the midwest, herbs in all their many forms surround you. Display gardens feature plant combinations that will inspire your own herb gardening efforts and you'll find the plants you need in the greenhouses.

The Gingerbread House holds all Mari-Mann's herbal products: seasoning blends, dry or simmer-type potpourris, jams and jellies, vinegars, and dried everlastings. Here, too, are soup mixes, books, wreaths . . . everything your herbal heart could desire. You may see some old friends here, since Mari-Mann ships their various products to many states and a few foreign countries. But isn't it fun to see them at their source? ▶

◀ The calendar here is filled with classes in plant crafts, cooking with herbs, and a wide range of gardening techniques. Special seasons bring special teas and other culinary experiences. There is almost always something interesting in these gardens and in the workshops. Your favorite "thing" in this country setting might just be quiet time in the herb garden gazebo.

From US Route 48 on the southwest side of Decatur, go west on Rock Springs Road a short distance to St. Louis Bridge Road, then northeast on St. Louis Bridge Road to Mari-Mann.

Scovill Park Gardens
East side of Lake Decatur
Decatur

Two acres. Oriental garden. Small rose collection.

♿ Shop and snack bar at zoo (which has admission charge). Picnic facilities in park. Open daily April 1-November 1 8am-8pm. Oriental garden closes earlier. All hours subject to weather and seasonal changes.

A sophisticated Fu Dog guards the entrance to Scovill's Japanese Garden but, during my late May visit, his dignity is diminished by the denim jacket a workman has hung on his rump. In this intimate garden of Japanese and Chinese elements, a recirculating stream flows over the waterfall and beneath a grassy moon bridge to the shining pool. When the "waterfall" is turned off it becomes a handsome wall of stone above a cobbled streambed. Today, blooming irises, rhododendrons, and azaleas accent dwarf conifers, spreads of ground cover, and winding paths. Workers are installing benches that will encourage quiet meditation . . . or allow respite if you've been to the nearby Children's Zoo.

Near the Oriental Garden, formal beds of annuals and perennials, concentric around a charming redwood gazebo, make a totally different kind of garden. Here are iris, peony, and rose beds, petunias and coleus and a varied mass of dahlias. Perky ornamental peppers, their fruits glowing like candles above compact plants, join ranks of decorative kale and cabbage to march across the hill.

When I visit these gardens again in a different month and a different year, children are in school, the zoo is closed, and the gardens are very, very quiet. The pool in the Oriental Garden reflects decorative grasses and the crisp autumn sky. The brightest of marigolds, petunias, and salvias have replaced last year's cabbages and kales and burnished red fruits on small crabapple trees speak of spring's flaming beauty. These gardens, delightful in spring flower or on this perfect October day, will be equally pleasing during summer's richness.

For information contact the Horticulture Department, Decatur Park District, P. O. Box 1136, Decatur IL 62525. (217) 422-5911.

From I-72 take Business Route US 51 or Illinois Route 48 south to IL 36. Turn east and follow IL 36 across Lake Decatur to Country Club Road, just beyond the bridge. Turn right onto Country Club, then go right again at the Y, to Scovill Park. The gardens are on the north side of the parking lot.

Fragrant Fields
Cross Street
Dongola IL 62926
(618) 827-3677 or (800) 635-0282

Commercial herb grower. Shop complex includes greenhouse and large herb display garden. Farm location: 15 greenhouses, several acres production fields.

Catalog and calendar. Many plants labeled. Seasonal plant sales. Tearoom. Best to telephone ahead. Group tours by appointment.
Shop open Monday-Saturday 10am-5pm.

Over 150 herb and perennial flower varieties live in Fragrant Fields' sizable display garden. Here are herbs for nearly every use, including some new varieties you may find totally irresistible.

Fragrant Fields' shop and tearoom occupies a century-old mule barn and offers dried flower arrangements, potpourri, culinary herbs and herb teas, and other treasures whose components originated at the Fragrant Fields farm. Here, too, are books, essential oils, topiaries, herb plant seeds, and a thousand other things you need.

You may want to visit Fragrant Fields on the first weekend of May to immerse yourself in the Renaissance of Herbs Festival and Garden Party, an annual event that includes herbal taste treats, plant sales, and a full schedule of workshops. What more could one want?

For information write Fragrant Fields, Box 160, Dongola IL 62926.

◀ *From I-57 take Exit 24 and go a half mile west. Fragrant Fields shop is just off the main street of Dongola. To visit the farm and greenhouses, ask for directions at the shop.*

Wildflower Farm
Mason Hollow Road
Grafton

Commercial. One acre wildflower and herb display gardens. Shade house.

♿ Shop. Most plants labeled. Intermittent workshops. Adjacent bed-and-breakfast establishment.
Open April-October Wednesday-Saturday 10am-4pm.

Sunny gardens and untamed meadows fill this enchanting opening in the woods. The woods' edge is shaggy with wildflowers and on this August day the gardens are a little shaggy, too. Wildflower's owners have spent the summer developing their bed-and-breakfast home, creating a new greenhouse, and renovating the shop. In spite of a little neglect and a summer of drought, the farm's hardy herbs and summer wildflowers are thriving.

The shade house hums on this warm afternoon; it's busy with bees visiting gaillardia, balloonflowers, beebalm, foxglove, and coneflowers. Scented geraniums are surrounded by everlastings, herbs, and ornamentals both annual and perennial. I'm particularly taken with the tubular magenta blooms of moss campion (*Silene* sp. 'Schaffa'), which now resides in my garden.

The flamboyant hibiscus at the shop's door is a sample of the visual feast within. Silvery artemisias, brilliant celosias, and globe amaranth, white through apricot to magenta, festoon rafters and walls. You can buy wreathes, culinary herb products, or a good-looking Wildflower Farm T-shirt. If you need gardening books, supplies, or dried plant materials, they are here. You can get help in garden design or landscaping, attend a gardening or cooking workshop, or take part in a garden walk or tour. Perhaps you want to visit the April or October herb festivals. You'll enjoy whatever you choose to do in this delightful setting.

For details and calendar contact Wildflower Farm, P. O. Box 31, Grafton IL 62037. (618) 465-3719.

Illinois Route 100 (The Great River Road) becomes Main Street in Grafton. On the east side of town, look for a street sign that says "890 E/Springfield"; this is also Mason Hollow Road. Turn north and go a half mile or so through a residential area, then through woods to Wildflower Farm.

The Cottage Garden
R. R. 1 Box 12A (Rts. 67-111)
Piasa IL 62079
(618) 729-4324 or (618) 729-4160

Commercial. One acre gardens, greenhouses, and display areas. Herb and ivy topiaries.

♿ Plant list but no mail orders. Most plants labeled.
Open March 15-October 31 and Thanksgiving-Christmas Eve, Monday-Saturday 9am-5pm, Sunday 10am-5pm.

Tall shade trees and fields of corn surround these sunny gardens that, on this August morning, are alive with highly decorative butterflies and wasps dining at the butterfly bush and loosestrife, the blue spirea (*Caryopteris* sp.), and a wealth of other late summer flowers. The shade houses and plant display areas offer a wide variety of hostas, scented geraniums (*Pelargonium* spp.), varieties of bleeding heart, and a collection of "grasses" that includes two tidy and especially attractive sedges, one cream with green edges, the other green with cream edges. Rosemary and ivy topiaries are developing nicely and will be fragrant, lush winter decorations. Luxuriant climbing roses surround the door to the greenhouse, where goldenrods are at their brilliant golden best today.

The small and beautiful gardens and well-maintained plant houses of this young establishment are the work of two caring and energetic gardeners who take pride in offering unusual and hard-to-find plants in addition to the standard favorites. In season, you'll find heritage and shrub roses and daylilies in ▶

FYI Keep your eyes open for unexpected horticultural sights in this part of Illinois. Small rosebushes against a cornfield delighted us, their sun-drenched blooms the ultimate scarlet against dark green corn plants. Come in the spring, when the peach and apple orchards of Calhoun County are clouds of blossoms, or come in the late summer/early fall for the peaches and apples. Near Grafton, a free ferry crosses the Illinois River to Calhoun County.

FYI If you take IL 16 west from Litchfield, look for the 8-mile-long prairie restoration along the south side of IL 16. In August it holds the richly varied textures and greens of sunflowers, black-eyed Susans, milkweeds, willows, and sumacs, all in stunning contrast to the burned-out alien grasses along I-55.

bloom and for sale here. Soon, newly broken ground will become an extensive herb garden that features rare and unusual herb varieties. The Cottage Garden is a business but the emphasis is on the gardens; buying beautiful and healthy plants to carry home is an extra treat.

From I-55 take Illinois Route 16 west from Litchfield and turn south at US 67/IL 111. Go a few miles to the driveway entry just south of a roadside inn.
Or, take US 67/IL 111 north from Alton. The Cottage Garden is about 3 miles north of Brighton, on the west side of the road.

Abraham Lincoln Memorial Garden
2301 East Lake Drive
Springfield IL 62707
(217) 529-1111

77-acre "natural garden." Jens Jensen design.

Handicapped-access to Nature Center only. Picnic facilities. Seasonal plant sales. Hiking trails. Grounds open daily sunrise-sunset. Nature Center open Tuesday-Saturday 10am-4pm, Sunday 1-4pm. Closed Christmas Day through New Year's Day.

Spring wildflower walks and autumn color treks are special treats in this "woodland garden" designed by Jens Jensen (of Chicago Park District and The Clearing fame). Now a project of the Garden Club of Illinois, the area was designated a memorial to Lincoln in 1923, when Lake Springfield was developed. These lakeside acres are planted with trees, shrubs, and wildflowers native to Illinois, Indiana, and Kentucky, the states where Lincoln lived and matured. Tall oaks around the Nature Center grew from acorns collected around Lincoln's birthplace in Henderson KY; a 1936 photo shows proud Girl Scouts planting the seedlings. As with many of Jensen's naturalistic designs, this "garden" looks very much like natural woods; bear in mind that, until the advent of Lake Springfield, this land was very likely cultivated. Today, it resembles woodlands Lincoln might have known and is the home of the Illinois Native Plant Society and other groups interested in the natural environment.

The Nature Center holds an intriguing array of historic regional photos. Here, too, are classrooms and the Split Rail Shop, where you'll find tourist trinkets, a small assortment of nature-oriented books, and a variety of items made from dried plant materials.

◀ If you come here to see manicured gardens or velvet lawns, you'll be surprised; come, instead, to relish a woods that was, once upon a time, a drawing on Jensen's design board. Take time to enjoy the hiking trails and the many benches that encourage further appreciation of your surroundings.

From I-55 take Exit 88 and go three miles east, through a hilly residential area. The route to the garden is well marked.

Washington Park Botanical Garden
Fayette and Chatham Roads
Springfield

3,000-plant All-American Rose Selection garden. Small conservatory. Roman garden. Perennial beds.

♿ Small gift/book shop. Most plants labeled. Library. Picnic facilities in park. Intermittent plant sales.
Gardens open daylight hours. Conservatory open Monday-Friday noon-4pm, Saturday and Sunday noon-5pm. Closed Christmas Day.

I never saw a Roman Garden and never expected to see one . . . but here's one, serene in its simplicity, right in the middle of Springfield. The paved Roman Cultural Garden, built with the guidance of the Springfield Roman Cultural Society, combines tall pillars, a lighted pool, a formal plant arrangement, and screening conifers. At noon on this summer day, sunlight glares and shadows have little depth but this gracious space will be lovely in the late afternoon or early evening, those times when Classical Romans (like contemporary Americans) were most likely to relax and enjoy their gardens.

Washington Park Botanical Garden exemplifies cooperation between a park board, local plant societies, and horticultural businesses. The hillside iris, peony, and daylily gardens are supported by commercial donors and developed by Region 9 of the American Iris Society. The AARS garden, 3,000 rose bushes near the Rees Memorial Carillon, is maintained by the Central Illinois Rose Society. In June, when the roses here are at their peak, the annual International Carillon Festival attracts both music lovers and rose lovers.

Washington Park's small conservatory is divided into "continents" and special attention is given to economic plants; today, the cacao has fruits and the coffee berries are ripening. A variety of exhibits, workshops, lectures, plant sales, and plant shows take place here; seasonal and specialty shows often spill over into the lobby and nearby greenhouses. ▶

◀ The Washington Park Master Plan involves increased plant labeling, additions to buildings, and the development of additional outdoor gardens. It will be interesting to see what comes about on this rolling land, what will be done to make Washington Park even more pleasant.

For details or to check on the status of expansion, contact the Washington Park Botanical Garden, P. O. Box 5052, Springfield IL 62705. (217) 787-2540.

From I-55 take Exit 96 (South Grand). Go west on Grand 4 or 5 miles to Washington Park, on your right. Follow signs for the Conservatory or the Rose Garden.

Indiana: Northeast

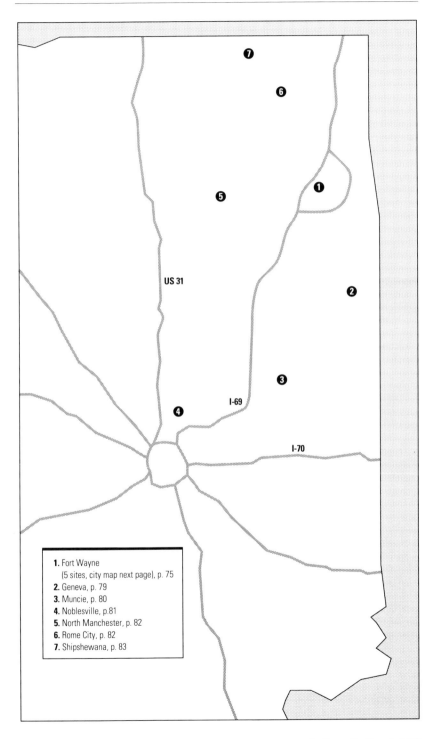

1. Fort Wayne
   (5 sites, city map next page), p. 75
2. Geneva, p. 79
3. Muncie, p. 80
4. Noblesville, p.81
5. North Manchester, p. 82
6. Rome City, p. 82
7. Shipshewana, p. 83

Indiana: Northeast / **FT. WAYNE**

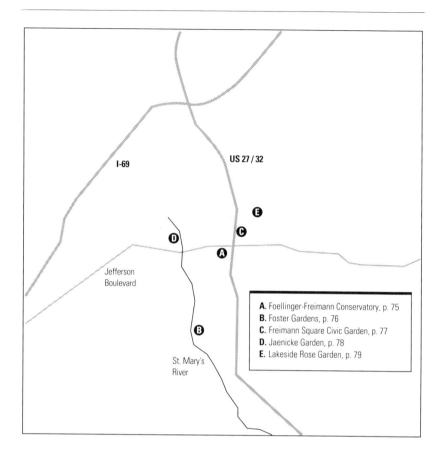

Fort Wayne

Fort Wayne offers a variety of horticultural treats that are under several different jurisdictions. For information on any or all of these, contact the Fort Wayne Visitor Information Center, 1021 Calhoun Street, Fort Wayne IN 46802, (219) 424-3700. Or call (between 7am and 2pm Eastern Time) Fort Wayne Parks and Recreation at (219) 427-1253 and ask for the Greenhouses, then for the Garden Superintendent.

Foellinger-Freimann Botanical Conservatory
1100 South Calhoun Street
Fort Wayne IN 46802
(219) 427-1267

24,500 sq.ft. conservatory. Showcase, Tropical, and Arid houses.

💲 ♿ Brochure. Gift shop. Many plants labeled. Intermittent plant sales.
Open Monday-Saturday 10am-5pm, Sunday noon-4pm. Closed Christmas Day.

These solar-heated pyramids hold a wealth of plants, not the golden trinkets of a pharaoh . . . but a pharaoh would treasure these gardens. Today, the main showhouse holds "A Scented Garden," artfully arranged masses of plants with strongly scented foliage or blooms. We're encouraged to *touch* these plants to better enjoy their scents and textures; such encouragement is not a common conservatory practice. Broad sweeps of herbs, especially basils and scented geraniums (*Pelargonium* spp.), cover slopes and swales. Twelve small bushes of "Old-fashioned Rose" scented geraniums are more effective than just one bush, sixteen lemon eucalypti more emphatic than a single specimen. Lemon mint (*Monarda citriodora*) will soon sport its Siamese-temple blooms, lavender-green flower stacked upon lavender-green flower, and luxuriant oregano will cover the ground and bloom with enthusiasm.

Follow the tunnel to the Tropic House and the cantilevered waterfall that feeds streams and pools in this lush habitat. For an overview of the tropics, climb to the waterfall's top, past the dramatic blooms of red powderpuff (*Calliandria haematocephala*). Then walk to the lower level, past a noisy cage of peach-faced lovebirds, to an orchid-filled tree and a sumptuous variety of begonias and ferns, palms, euphorbias, and tropical cacti. Glossy fan-shaped leaves of mistletoe fig (*Ficus deltoidea*) arch near the exotic coral flowers of a vining variegated hibiscus. Fuzzy feltbush (*Kalanchoe beharensis*) faces green and white snowbush (*Breynia disticha* 'Roseo-picta'), a Pacific island shrub that appears to have been brushed with snow.

▶

◀ Delicate feather bush (*Lyslioma thornberi*) hovers over the shade ramada that welcomes you to the Arid House. This naturalistic arrangement of Sonoran plants is far more satisfying than the usual accumulation of cacti and succulents from all over the world. Prickly pear and cholla (*Opuntia* spp.), hedgehog cacti (*Echinocereus* sp.), and the requisite desiccated cow skull are scattered among aloes, agaves, deciduous trees and shrubs, and succulent ground covers. You'll see a grandly spiked desert spoon (*Dasylion wheeleri*) and the striking curly white filaments of *Yucca elata*, the soap-tree yucca. You'll see turpentine bush (*Happiopapus lancifolius*), acacias, foothill palo verde (*Cerdicium microphyllum*), and ironwood (*Olneya tesota*), all with the tiny blue-green leaves that conserve moisture. *Berberis harrisonia*, a barberry that looks like holly, and creosote bush (*Larrea tridentata*), move in a fan-driven "gentle desert breeze." It's said that harmless Sonoran insects, reptiles, and small mammals live here but, being desert species, they're probably nocturnal and they aren't out and about this afternoon.

Outside, vinca-covered berms echo the pyramidal form of the buildings. Vinca color and texture play against the glass and concrete of this superbly functional "sculpture." Foellinger-Freimann, a relatively new complex and the largest passive solar conservatory in the midwest, hosts diverse activities and functions. Six imaginative theme shows are followed by sales of "Slightly Used Plants." There are plant society displays, jazz concerts on the terrace, and the Bridal Bazaar. Holiday concerts and an exhibit and sale of wreaths enliven winter holidays. You might enjoy Lunch Under Glass, catered luncheons that include visits to the conservatory, and The Tulip Tree Gift Shop, where "botanically inspired" items are featured. With or without lunch, you'll treasure your time at Foellinger-Freimann.

The conservatory is at the south edge of downtown Fort Wayne, on Calhoun just south of Jefferson Boulevard, a one-way street that goes east.

Foster Gardens in Foster Park
Along the St. Mary's River
Fort Wayne

Several acres. Annuals and perennials. Bridal Glen.

♿ Rivergreenway access (Rivergreenway is Park Drive in Foster Park). Many plants labeled.
Hiking trails. Picnic facilities.
Open daylight hours.

▶

Fort Wayne loves cannas, red grasses, elephant ear plants, and Mexican sunflower (*Tithonia rotundifolia*). Foster Gardens' island beds hold these and many other plants in abundance. Colored foliage is used well here: red barberry, copper leaf (*Alternantha* sp.), deep red maples, and red grasses play handsomely against green foliage and a range of flower colors, notably the gorgeous zinnia 'Red Sun'. The hibiscus collection, with flowers large and small, adds an exotic touch to this splendor in late summer. In spring, the lilacs and flowering crabs will make their contribution.

Walk through a heart-shaped arbor to the Bridal Glen and enter a room of reds, whites, and pinks. Caladiums, wax begonias, red barberry, and petunias anchor a color scheme that is enlivened by the pink shrub rose 'Bonica', 'Pink Orbit' geranium, and 'Pink Castle' celosia. The Glen is indeed a stunning wedding site, a jewel within attractive larger gardens.

Foster Park is along the St. Mary's River, southwest of downtown Fort Wayne. From West Jefferson Boulevard (US Route 24/Indiana Route 14, one-way going east), turn south onto Broadway. Go several blocks, across Rudisill Boulevard, and onto Hartman Road. Entrance to the gardens will soon appear on your right.

Freimann Square Civic Garden
In Freimann Park
Downtown Fort Wayne

1,000 sq.ft. Informal beds of annuals.

♿ Picnic facilities.
Open daylight hours all year.

Unusual and attractive color combinations enrich this small plaza in a downtown park, a park that's graced by an equestrian statue of General Wayne himself. These flower beds add a corner of color and texture to the otherwise green and shady park. This year, a sturdy clump of red fountain grass (*Pennisetum* sp.) gives height and texture to a brilliant mass of coleus. Another bed glows with cerise moss rose (*Portulaca* sp.), soft and feathery orange celosia, tall red-leaved canna and an orange-red-flowered canna, Mexican sunflower and red feather grass (*Calamagrostis* sp.). A different viewpoint ▶

FYI The Rivergreenway, green land and public biking-hiking trails, follows the rivers of Fort Wayne. It's usually an independent pathway but sometimes follows existing park roads. Currently about 80% complete, the finished trail will link many of the city's parks and recreation areas and may be extended to neighboring towns.

reveals black-eyed Susans, orange-red cannas, and red grasses singing along with tall lavender-blue ageratum. Elsewhere, gleaming balls of magenta globe amaranth hover above a carpet of soft pink petunias. Flashes of pale lemon-yellow marigolds accent all these reds while weathered bricks and teak benches soften and unify the nearly-garish color scheme. Nearby, zinnias, marigolds and salvias, and tall cannas echo the bright red-orange of welded steel sculpture.

Ornamental flowering trees, oaks, maples, and assorted conifers supply all-season beauty but the large reflecting pool and its spray fountains are especially attractive on this late July day. On fine days this popular corner is filled with brown-bagging workers from nearby offices. It's a delightful place for reprieve from ringing telephones and dreary computer screens . . . or too many hours in the car.

Freimann Square is in downtown Fort Wayne, between Main Street on the south and Superior on the north, Clinton on the west and Lafayette on the east. The garden, Freimann Square, is near Main Street, just west of the Performing Arts Center and the Fort Wayne Art Museum.

Jaenicke Garden in West Swinney Park
Fort Wayne

Small garden of annuals and spring-flowering trees and bushes.

Access to Rivergreenway. Picnic facilities.
Open daylight hours.

Stately autumn amaryllis (*Lycoris squamigera*) and clumps of annuals brighten this corner of a park that is mostly athletic fields and picnic grounds. A small peony bed, large flowering crabapple trees, and mature rhododendrons suggest that this spot will be spectacular in spring.

FYI Folk hero Johnny Appleseed is buried in Ft. Wayne's Johnny Appleseed Park, which is along the St. Joseph River on the north side of town, between Coliseum Boulevard and Parnell Avenue. "Johnny Appleseed" was John Chapman (ca. 1774-1845), a ragged visionary who roamed the midwest for 40 years, his pack filled with apple seeds and Swedenborgian religious tracts. Chapman freely distributed seeds and religion to anyone who would take them and planted seeds wherever he could. It's for the seeds we remember him; many midwestern apple trees and orchards are said to descend from his largesse. An autumn festival in "his" park honors the fact and legend of Johnny Appleseed.

◀ *From downtown Ft. Wayne, go west on Washington Boulevard. Just across the St. Mary's River, turn north onto the park road and follow that to the gardens.*

Lakeside Rose Garden
East Lake Avenue
Fort Wayne

Three acres. Formal gardens. All-American Rose Selection gardens.

♿ Many plants labeled. Picnic facilities in park.
Open daylight hours all year.

The roses are fresh and full of blooms in the morning's cool breeze; perhaps, in this summer of drought, they've had ample water from the nearby lake. This is more than a rose garden. Rose bushes are mixed with perennial flowers and accented with annuals, roses climb on pergola pillars, roses crouch among rhododendrons, neatly clipped yews, and weathered rail fences. Rose beds around the long reflecting pool are edged with low gray santolina and accented with ornamental grasses. The scene is enhanced by the rose-covered pergola and the low serpentine hedges of red barberry that surround other groups of roses. Lovely hybrid tea roses, including the especially attractive 'White Queen' and apricot-colored 'Brandy', join the impressive coral grandiflora rose 'Shreveport'. The mix of plant forms and varieties here guarantees that Lakeside will be attractive almost any time of year.

Lakeside Park is on Lake Avenue west of Anthony Boulevard. From US Route 24/30 (Coliseum Boulevard) on the east side of the city, take Indiana Route 14 east to Anthony Boulevard. Go north on Anthony a few blocks to Lake Avenue, then west a short distance to the park on your right.

Limberlost State Historic Site
P. O. Box 356
Geneva IN 46740
(219) 368-7428

Several acres. 12'x15' conservatory/greenhouse. Orchards. Perennial gardens.

Gift shop. Group tours by appointment.
Open Wednesday-Saturday 9am-5pm (closed 12-1pm), Tuesday and Sunday 1-5pm. Closed Monday and some holidays.   ▶

◀ In summer, lush perennial gardens surround this log house that was, from 1895 to 1913, the home of author Gene Stratton Porter and her family. Although Porter's best-known work is *Girl of the Limberlost*, a novel, she published several other nature-related books as well as numerous articles, short stories, poems, and photographs. Porter was an inveterate collector and student of plants whose imaginative writings and meticulous natural history studies earned national acclaim.

Until 1913, this area was Limberlost Swamp, 25,000 acres of ". . . treacherous swamp and quagmire, filled with every plant, animal, and human danger known." (Supposedly, Limber Jim Corbus went hunting in the swamp but never returned; thus, "Limber's lost.") The swamp was Porter's science laboratory and the inspiration for her writing and photography. The Porters lived here until the swamp was drained in 1913, at which time they moved to a wooded site on Sylvan Lake near Rome City, Indiana. Today, Gene Porter's gardens and orchards thrive again and, in the tiny conservatory attached to the house she left behind, tender plants fill sturdy shelves. Many of us have read one or another of Porter's books and it's gratifying to touch base with her here.

The Limberlost site is two blocks south of the intersection of US Route 27 and Indiana Route 116 in Geneva. Look for the big red sign.

Christy Woods
At the corner of Tillotson Avenue and Riverside Drive
Ball State University
Muncie

Formal gardens, each 10'x20', in 5 acres of lawn. 18 acres woods. 4,200 sq.ft. greenhouse. Wheeler Orchid Collection.

Many plants labeled. Woodland trails (guide available in greenhouse). Picnic facilities. Gardens and arboretum open daylight hours. Greenhouse is a teaching/research facility; accessibility may vary with class demands but usually open 10am-4pm Monday-Saturday all year plus Sunday afternoons during the growing season. Closed Sundays October-April.

Scattered free-form planting beds are united by common design elements in this spacious woods-edge garden; each bed of annuals and perennials features at least one woody plant. Cotoneaster branches are a living tracery across rock garden pebbles while, nearby, rich blue-green creeping juniper contrasts with glowing marigolds and spiky variegated yucca. Yet another bed plays dark weeping beech against pale gray cobblestones. These gardens hold an interesting assortment of dwarf and weeping trees but few have labels to help you know what you're enjoying. ▶

◀ Beyond the main room of the greenhouse and its fairly common houseplants, lies a jewel, the Wheeler Orchid Collection and Species Bank. Here, in one of the nation's larger assortments of cattleya orchids, you are surrounded by blooming orchids and dormant orchids, orchids on tables and shelves, and orchids in trees. Sprays of vanda orchids arch overhead, bamboos reach to the ceiling, arums, bromeliads, and ferns flourish, and a tiny pond shelters lazy goldfish and lush water plants. Today, in early autumn, migrating monarch butterflies drift through open windows and float among lush surroundings reminiscent of their winter home in Mexico. Like them, you'll find this small greenhouse most inviting.

For further information contact the Director of Christy Woods Arboretum, Department of Biology, Ball State University, Muncie IN 47306. (317) 285-8839.

From I-69 west of Muncie or US Route 35 on the east side, take Indiana Route 332 to Tillotson Avenue. Go south on Tillotson about a mile and a half to Riverside. Follow the signs for Ball State University and Christy Woods. Pedestrian entrance to the woods is on Riverside. Park on Riverside or continue south on Tillotson to just beyond the gardens, then turn left and park near the greenhouse.

Hamilton County Master Gardener Association
2003 East Pleasant Street
Noblesville IN 46060

Small display gardens. All-America Selections Trial Gardens.

♿ Plants labeled. Seasonal plant sales.
Open daylight hours during the growing season.

The purpose of these young gardens is to demonstrate production of better quality plants and increased harvests in a "chemically safe" environment. During the growing season, the AAS trial gardens display vegetables and annual and perennial flowers. The gardens are on 4-H grounds and much of their financial support comes from plant sales at the 4-H Fair in late July.

From Indiana Route 37 in Noblesville, take Pleasant Street one block west to the gardens.

The Summer House
R. R. 4 Box 134
North Manchester IN 46962
(219) 982-4707

Commercial. One-quarter acre herb and perennial gardens.

Gift shop. Holiday open houses. Some plants labeled. Seasonal plant sales. Group tours and programs by reservation (fee).
Open daily April 20-December 24 1-6pm. Holiday Open House the weekend before Thanksgiving. Special holiday hours between Thanksgiving and Christmas.

The Summer House gardens, although not large, provide pleasant strolls and little surprises to keep you from taking it all too seriously; "Unattended children will be turned into toads!" according to one sign. For the Little People who dance in the knot garden on moonlit nights, there are tiny wicker chairs and a carpet of thyme for them to rest upon. You may spot other unexpected delights. These perennial and herb gardens, blooming happily on this mid-June day, are obviously tended with love and imagination. A new pond, larger gardens at the foot of the hill, and a path to reach them are being developed.

The small footbridge, embellished with lively clematis, carries you over a tiny pool to the shop and its treasures. Here are rich Williamsburg wreaths made from homegrown everlastings, interesting ceramics, a good selection of books, intriguing small antiques, Amish quilts, and lots of other good things. Hanging bunches of dried everlastings ornament the herb-drying room, where the floor is painted in a traditional local style.

The Summer House was once part of the farm next door. A few years ago, just before it was going to be bull-dozed and burned, today's owners bought the building and an acre of land to put it on. Many labor-filled hours later, the building was moved, restored, and given its current charm. Now, surrounded by delightful cottage gardens, it's a special place.

The Summer House is 3 miles west of Manchester (between Fort Wayne and Logansport), at the intersection of Indiana Route 114 and County Road 300 West. Turn north on CR 300 West to the parking lot.

Gene Stratton Porter State Historic Site
"Wildflower Woods" just south of Rome City

◄ Several acres woods and orchards. Small formal garden with pergola. House museum.

Fee for house tours. Gift shop. Picnic facilities.
Grounds open daylight hours. House and shop open Wednesday-Saturday 9am-4:30pm (closed 11:30am-1pm), Tuesday and Sunday 1-4:30pm.

Gene Stratton Porter, one of Indiana's best-known nature writers, made her home and gardens in Wildflower Woods, a pleasant spot with a small orchard, a stone-floored arbor with tricky footing, and a charming garden. Perennials and annuals in symmetrical beds, shade-lovers and sun-lovers alike, keep close, happy, casual company. Like many of us, Mrs. Porter was a tireless plant collector who could always find room for just one more plant.

Beyond the arbor and gardens, the Porter's 14-room "cabin" overlooks Sylvan Lake. Rockhounds may be particularly interested in the "puddin'stone" fireplace and other stone elements here. The house also holds an assortment of personal memorabilia from Mrs. Stratton's writing career.

Near a small spring at the lake's edge, giant glossy skunk cabbage leaves glisten in the shade and coltsfoot runs vigorously along the ground. On this June day, a noisy weed-eating barge is clearing the neighbor's beach. This interesting but discordant operation takes place only every year or two, so you'll probably enjoy the woods and garden as it sounded (or *didn't* sound) in Mrs. Porter's day.

For details contact the Curator, Gene Stratton Porter State Historic Site, Box 639, Rome City IN 46784. (219) 854-3790.

Northwest of Fort Wayne, take US Route 6 five miles west of Kendalville to Indiana Route 9. Go north on IN 9 three miles to the south edge of Rome City. Turn east at the sign for Limberlost Country Club. Follow this road past the golf course and a little farther to the Gene Stratton Porter State Historic Site.

Greenfield Herb Garden
Corner of Depot and Harrison streets
P. O. Box 437
Shipshewana IN 46565
(219) 768-7110

Commercial. 50'x100' propagation/cutting garden. Small theme gardens. Greenhouse. ►

◀ ♿ Catalog. Three shops. Many plants labeled. Plant sales. Workshops.
Open March-December Monday-Saturday 9am-5pm; January and February Wednesday-Saturday 9am-5pm.

On this mid-summer day the Greenfield greenhouse still holds a wide selection of common and uncommon plants. Cutting gardens sit quietly at one side, having already endured one or two harvests. The large square bed of lavender is recovering from a shearing and a lone globe thistle flower (*Echinops ritro*) has escaped the shears to stand above a wide bed of prickly leaves. Everlastings of many sorts are thriving in this dry summer. Silver-leaved plants fill raised beds and, near the shop, charming hoop fences surround compact and tidy herb theme gardens.

The Greenfield shops offer nearly everything you ever wanted that has to do with gardening. One wall holds a splendid array of seed packets for herbs, everlastings, and native plants. Dried arrangements and a tempting assortment of cards, sculpture, and other miscellanies fill cupboards, shelves, and tables. The bookstore upstairs, where sturdy shelves and inviting volumes surround an old library table, is the library I'd love to have. Quick figuring indicates at least 300 different titles, whose topics range from herb-growing and period gardens to potpourri-making and the medicinal uses of plants. The room is comfortable with quilts and dried arrangements, gentle dulcimer music is in the air, and I don't want to leave.

Greenfield hosts a number of workshops and seasonal festivals during the year. Seeds, books, and potpourri materials can be ordered by mail but plants are sold only on-site. The gardens and shops are worth the trip, whether you want to buy plants or not.

From I-80/I-90 take Exit 107 for Indiana Route 13. Go south on IN 13 a mile or so to IN 120, then east 6 or 7 miles on IN 120 to IN 5. Take IN 5 south about 4 miles to Shipshewana. Look for Depot Street and turn east to Greenfield Herb Garden.

FYI Shipshewana is a tourist-oriented town that accents its Amish and Mennonite heritage *and* an active everyday trade center for the surrounding area. You'll find gift, craft, and antique shops cheek-by-jowl with suppliers of more mundane items. The Shipshewana Flea Market is supposedly the largest in the country.

If you're spending time in the "Shipshe" area, don't miss the Menno-Hof Visitor Center at the south edge of town. A one-hour guided tour of the farmstead-style Center tells the Amish and Mennonite stories. Today, in the Center's small farm garden, a zinnia riot contrasts with pale gold cantaloupes and beautiful glaucous cabbages. ▶

◀ Take a drive through the rolling countryside, past handsome farms with large houses, large barns, and large horses. You'll see vegetable gardens so lush you can almost taste the sweet corn. Blazing flower gardens hold the brightest of celosias, balsam, and marigolds, the most flamboyant petunias and zinnias . . . there are few pastels or somber tones in these gardens. The Shipshewana area offers a variety of garden experiences, whether you have an hour or a day to spend here.

For further information contact the Menno-Hof Visitor Center, Box 701, Shipshewana IN 46565. (219) 768-4117.

♿ ☕ Brochures. Fee for Visitor Center tour.
Visitor Center open Monday-Saturday 10am-5pm.

Indiana: Northwest

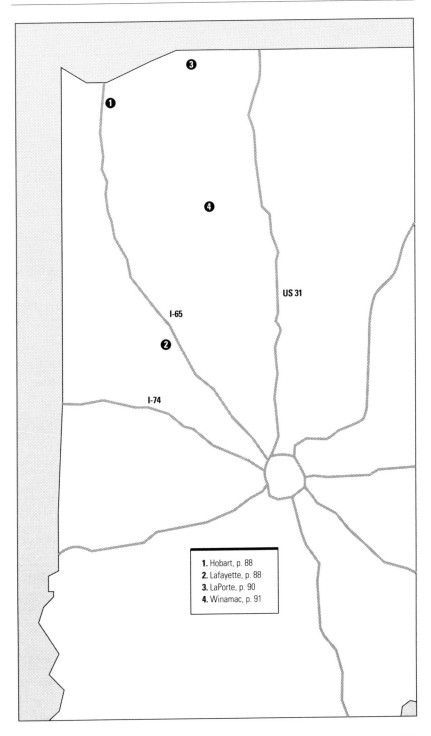

1. Hobart, p. 88
2. Lafayette, p. 88
3. LaPorte, p. 90
4. Winamac, p. 91

Deep River County Park
9410 Old Lincoln Highway
Hobart IN 46342
(219) 769-9030

Half-acre Victorian garden in large park. Restored grist mill.

 Brochure. Shop. Hiking trails. Picnic facilities. Occasional workshops.
Open daylight hours all year.

Nicotianas, begonias, and snapdragons make this gentle garden and its sunny, plant-bedecked gazebo a most inviting place to "sit a spell." On this late July afternoon, fat white ducks are working their way through beds of hostas and impatiens in search of juicy tidbits. Heavily mulched peonies and azaleas appear to be recent installations; the plants are small, with room to grow for luxuriant spring bloom.

The small herb garden in front of Woods Old Mill has become a tangle of thymes and lamb's-ears (*Stachys byzantina*) in this dry, dry summer. The Visitor Center shop offers books and nature-oriented objects . . . and corn meal ground at the mill, which dates from around 1838 and was the first industry in Lake County.

Deep River hosts several festivals, workshops, and wildflower walks during the year, so you can satisfy many of your botanical interests in this attractive park.

From I-65 take US 30 east to Indiana Route 51, then go north on IN 51 to the stop sign at IN 330, the Old Lincoln Highway (there's no sign for the park at this corner). Turn east on Old Lincoln Highway and go 2½ miles to the park, at the intersection of IN 330 and Lake-Porter County Line Road.

Purdue Horticulture Gardens
Lafayette

Two-thirds acre of annuals and perennials. All-America Selections displays. Private horticultural collections. Vegetable display.

 Garden guide. Most plants labeled.
Open daylight hours.

Sprinklers are drenching the gardens on this day in the middle of a very dry summer. The colors of the season shine through rainbows and I'll play sprinkler tag to enjoy marigolds and zinnias, celosias and gaillardias, and all the other mid-summer bloomers here. Zinnias in salmon, pale yellow, and deep pink are particularly fetching against clear yellow coreopsis. The glowing orange flowers of Mexican sunflower (*Tithonia rotundifolia*) dominate one island bed. Purple coneflowers and silvery blue globe thistle are a lovely combination against the leathery leaves of a bayberry hedge.

A small shade house, sheltered by sweet autumn clematis and a spreading beech tree, provides welcome respite from the July heat. Coleus, impatiens, and assorted ivies add quiet color to the shade. Here you can pick up a most helpful publication, the *Guide to the Gardens*, that tells you where specific plants are, who donated them, and where you can expect to buy them.

Beyond the shade house and the main greenhouse, a small vegetable garden holds heritage strains and experimental varieties of various vegetables. Assorted sunflowers, tall and short, dark and light, are lively with bees today. The tiny herb garden proves that even a very limited space can provide a handy selection of culinary herbs.

Individuals have given their collections of daylilies, Siberian and bearded irises, peonies, and daffodils to these gardens; you may want to time your visits for those blooms. All seeds and plants for these gardens are donated by companies and individuals; all annuals are started in the greenhouse by the garden's chief caretaker. The gardens are a project of the Consumer Horticulture Extension Program of Purdue University and much of the seasonal work is done by the Tippecanoe County Master Gardeners.

Under development since 1980, the gardens' progress is guided by a long-range plan. Annual plants and bed designs change from year to year, the collection of ornamental grasses will increase, and more perennials will be added. There will be a parking area, additional paved paths, and lights to encourage evening visits. For now, at the end of its first decade, this is a very pleasant pocket, a charming refuge on a busy campus.

For more information contact the Consumer Horticulture Specialist and Horticulture Gardens Coordinator, Purdue University Cooperative Extension Service, Horticulture Building, West Lafayette IN 47909. (317) 494-1296.

From I-65 or Indiana state highways, follow the signs for Purdue University. These will bring you near Stewart Center, the "front door" of the campus, on State Street (IN 26 W). The gardens are about two blocks south of Stewart Center, on Marstellar Street between Wood and Harrison streets, near the Horticulture Building.

Quail Ridge Farm
3382 E County Road 1000 N
LaPorte IN 46350
(219) 778-2194

Commercial. Two and a half acres of theme gardens. 1,500 sq.ft. greenhouse.

♿ Garden/gift/antique shop. Many plants labeled. Plant sales. Workshops. Cooking classes. Open April 15-November 1 Tuesday-Sunday 9am-5pm. Closed Monday. Garden design consultation all year by appointment.

A shady country road brings you to these lush hillside gardens, gardens that are surrounded by sunny lawn and open fields. Roam along the woodchip paths, past a garden of mints or through the Shakespeare garden. Admire the butterfly garden, the beds of edible flowers, or any of several other theme gardens. Here, showy hibiscus adds a tropical flavor to old garden favorites and there, a bronze armillary sphere gleams among the coneflowers. St. Fiacre blesses the gardens and their workers while other small sculptures lurk among the plants or along the paths. Bold and bristly cardoon (*Cynara cardunculus*) adds its touch of sky-blue to this late summer day and jubilant blackberry lilies (*Bellacamda chinensis*) augur autumn seedpods as black and shiny as their namesakes. An ambitious Japanese garden is developing on the hillside between the greenhouse and the shop, its waterfall and stream dry now but showing promise.

The shop's wide and breezy porch invites you to relax and enjoy the view or to marshall your energy for choosing plants from the greenhouse and treasures from the shop, where you'll find Quail Ridge's own special herb blends and dried plant material for arrangements. An excellent collection of herb books and cookbooks reflects the history of Quail Ridge and the success of their culinary workshops. The select group of small antiques and collectibles is, as my husband observed, "all kinds of good old stuff."

This parcel of land has always been used for farming of one sort or another; the 1833 house and its lovely tall trees are remnants of the first farm in the area and the Quail Ridge shop was built with old barn timbers. The current owner, after years in the Far East and in Chicago, felt the need to return to his Indiana farm roots. Quail Ridge began as an apple farm but the apples were gradually replaced by "weird and odd vegetables from all over the world" and increasing public interest in ethnic foods brought herbs into these gardens. Over 380 herb varieties and 400-plus perennials (including a vast assortment of ground covers) grow at Quail Ridge today.

◀ This area feels, in some ways, like a little piece of the past, but Quail Ridge isn't "backward" in any sense. A visit here is a treat for any gardener.

From I-94 take Exit 1, just north of the Indiana/Michigan state line. Go back south a few miles, toward LaPorte, on the road that becomes IN 39. You'll soon see a large steam engine on the east side of the road and a sign for the Hesston Steam Museum. Turn east here and go four or five miles to Quail Ridge.

Iris Acres
R. R. 4
Winamac IN 46996
(219) 946-4197

Commercial iris grower. Three-quarter acre display and production fields.

 Price list. Plants labeled.
Open daylight hours during bloom season.

Come to Iris Acres in late May or in June and surround yourself with the colors and scents of over 1,000 varieties of tall, dwarf, intermediate, and border irises. Among these are "Space Age" irises, those varieties introduced in the 1950s whose beards end in dramatic horn or spoon shapes. Or you can visit in the fall to admire the scattered flowers of unusual autumn-blooming irises. There are surely plants and flowers here that will be happy in your garden.

Winamac is on Indiana Route 14 northeast of Lafayette, southeast of Valparaiso, and due west of Rochester. From Winamac, take IN 35 north to County Road 700 N. Turn west and go a little over 2 miles to the railroad right-of-way. Iris Acres is the first place on the left beyond the railroad.

Indiana: Southeast

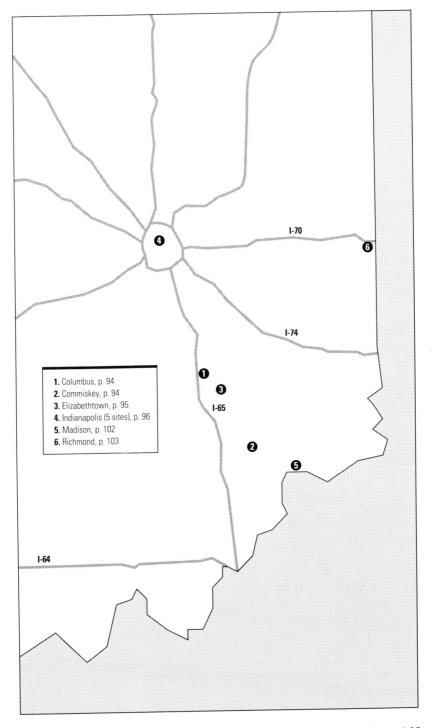

1. Columbus, p. 94
2. Commiskey, p. 94
3. Elizabethtown, p. 95
4. Indianapolis (5 sites), p. 96
5. Madison, p. 102
6. Richmond, p. 103

Columbus

On I-65 about 40 miles south of Indianapolis.

Columbus, Indiana, with its population of less than 40,000, probably boasts more examples of outstanding contemporary architecture than any other town of its size. Over 40 buildings designed by world-renowned contemporary architects share this community with handsome nineteenth-century structures and tasteful renovations. The town is a learning laboratory for students of architecture from all across the middle part of the country. Small public and private plantings make it a treat for gardeners, too. There are no major public gardens here but tours of private gardens, such as the Herbal Garden Tour in early June, are occasionally organized by individuals or community groups. For information on these contact Columbus Area Visitor Information, 825 Washington Street, Columbus IN 47201. (812) 378-2622 or (812) 372-1954.

Irwin Gardens and Greenhouse
605 Sixth Street
Columbus IN 47201
(812) 392-3685

Semi-private estate gardens. Large herbal knot garden.

Many plants labeled.
Open during growing season weekends only, 8am-4pm.

These spacious Italianate gardens feature, among other attractions, a large knot garden that's comprised of more than 100 herb varieties. Public hours for the gardens are quite limited but they are well-known in their locale; mention "Columbus, Indiana" to an area gardener and he will assure you that a visit to the Irwin gardens is worth an adjustment in your schedule.

The gardens, in the 600 block of Fifth Street between Lafayette and Pearl streets, are easily found.

Stream Cliff Herb Farm
R. R. 1 Box 378
Commiskey IN 47227
(812) 346-5859

Commercial. Over an acre. Herb theme gardens.

♦ ♿ Shops. Many plants labeled. Plant sales. Workshops and seminars.
Open May-mid-July, Saturday 10am-5pm, Sunday 1-5pm. Mid-October-Christmas, same days and hours. Strongly suggested that you call ahead if you're coming from a distance.

Stream Cliff's Colonial atmosphere and quilt-based herb garden designs reflect the five generations of the same family who have nurtured this farm. The rich texture and varied hues of lush perennials, sturdy herbs, and colorful annuals fill gardens whose designs are based on traditional quilt patterns, such as Grandmother's Fan, Log Cabin, and Dresden Plate. That favorite old pattern, Nine-Patch, has become a dandy shade garden. Nearby, you'll find a thyme garden and plantings designed specifically to attract butterflies. Warm red bricks in walks and patios, weathered fences, natural stone, and gentle fountains all add to the ambiance here.

The "stream" of Stream Cliff fronts one of the rustic buildings that house studios and shops. Dried herbs and other plants from the gardens have made their way into the shops as arrangements and other plant crafts. Here, too, you'll find family-made traditional crafts and metal items forged by the owner/blacksmith. Workshops and seminars at Stream Cliff are based on such topics as culinary herbs, traditional and herb crafts, and gardening. This historic site was raided during the Civil War; you'll want to raid it for plants, pleasure, and knowledge.

From I-65 take the Uniontown exit and go east on Indiana Route 250 to IN 3. Turn north on IN 3 and go to Commiskey Road, then turn east again and go a half mile to the farm (about 15 miles from I-65).

Nichols and Dimes Antiques and Herbs
Elizabethtown IN 47232
(812) 579-5267

Commercial. Small herb garden.

Gift/garden/antique shop. Many plants labeled. Plant sales. Workshops and other events. Group tours by appointment.
Open daily "by chance or appointment"; best to call before you visit.

During the growing season, the emphasis here is on herbs. You may savor the herb garden in privacy or share the experience with friends in an arranged tour. You can relish the varied scents of herbal potpourri, select a few herb plants to carry home, and, perhaps, enjoy a cup or a glass of herb tea. Here, too, you'll find fleece for the textile crafts, a tempting assortment of antiques and collectibles, and an inviting schedule of workshops. At Nichols and Dimes, you can visit the garden then satisfy your other avocational urges.

Elizabethtown is on Indiana Route 7, about 6 miles southeast of Columbus. Take IN 7 into town, turn north at the 4-way stop, then turn east just beyond the church.

Indianapolis

Indianapolis means auto racing and the Indy 500 to many people. Although the city is also home to several major educational and cultural facilities, Indianapolis has recently promoted itself as a sports hub for the heart of the country. Major sports venues, athletic games and trials, major and minor league sports teams, and countless other events and facilities all claim allegiance and dollars from central Indiana Hoosiers. This may explain why, for an area of its size (over 1,200,000 population in 1988), metropolitan Indianapolis has relatively few municipal gardens; public loyalties and funds are channeled to athletics. There's no question that reasonably popular athletic events will generate more dollars than even the most attractive gardens. The two Indianapolis gardens that I found most pleasing are supported by private foundations or trusts and by volunteer activities.

Garfield Park Conservatory and Formal Garden
2450 Shelby Street
Indianapolis IN 46203
(317) 784-3044

10,000 sq.ft. conservatory. 40,000 sq.ft. formal garden.

💲♿ Tiny fee for conservatory. Some plants labeled. Picnic facilities. Intermittent plant sales. Workshops and lectures.
Garden open daylight hours. Conservatory open Tuesday-Saturday 10am-5pm, Sunday noon-5pm. Special hours for seasonal shows and programs. Closed major holidays.

The first thing we saw upon entering the conservatory was a charming white wedding gazebo surrounded by tropical plants and tiny lights. Waterfall sounds, filtered through the foliage of 500-plus plant varieties, came from another room. An evening wedding in this spot would be a lovely way to begin a marriage.

Two other conservatory rooms contain the waterfall, a limited collection of cacti, and a good variety of scented geraniums (*Pelargonium* spp.), all playing against tropical foliage. Palms of many kinds and sizes arch over the walkways and sit among handsome ferns and bromeliads; imposing rubber tree plants hover over the waterfall.

The "wedding room" is also the site of the yearly Bulb, Chrysanthemum, and Poinsettia shows and sales. The conservatory offers children's events, occasional tropical plant sales, open houses, guided tours, and the "Tropical Talks" lecture series.

The formal garden, as viewed from the conservatory terrace, appears to be mostly clipped conifer hedges and borders of blooming red spirea. A closer look reveals tiny early-season coleus and New Guinea impatiens in the large tile-adorned concrete planters. On this mid-May day, the large reflecting pond, still empty and reflecting nothing, is edged with the lovely blue flower spikes of false indigo (*Baptisia australis*). Someone in Indianapolis loves this good-looking plant; Garfield Park and Holcomb Gardens are the only places I've ever seen it used in such emphatic masses. There will be fine stands of daylilies, coneflowers, and black-eyed Susans later in the season.

Attractive walks of rose-red bricks in herringbone and basketweave patterns surround the formal flower beds. The large concrete planters along these walks will be out of scale even when their coleus and impatiens reach maturity. Perhaps they once held trees; acorns and oak leaves decorate the comely ceramic tiles set into their sides.

This is a garden I will visit again later in the season, when the daylilies and their companions bloom, when the coleus have attained some size and strong color, and when, perhaps, the reflecting pool will echo a summer sky.

The conservatory and garden are part of the Indianapolis Department of Parks and Recreation but information can be obtained from the address above.

Take I-65 south to the Raymond Street exit, then go west on Raymond to Shelby Street. On Shelby, go 5 blocks south to the park entrance. The Conservatory is the newer building by the greenhouses and its entrance is at the far end from the parking lot.

Hillsdale Gardens
7800 Shadeland Avenue
Indianapolis
(317) 849-2810

Commercial. 100'x100' garden of roses and perennials.

◀ Open during "business hours."

This garden, behind an attractive stone home, seems like a private garden but both house and garden are owned by Hillsdale Landscape Company. It will be hot and humid later in this day but for now the garden is dewy, cool, and rose-scented. Opulent poppies and peonies visually overpower beds of small blooming roses, a tall deep purple allium guards the garden house patio, and Japanese irises thrive near the small pool. Slender goldfish, not yet fat on the year's mosquito larvae, dawdle at one end of the pool. In other seasons, the garden features lilacs, spring bulbs, flowering trees, or chrysanthemums.

A slightly lower lawn holds 4 triangular rose beds, each 20 feet on the long side. Climbing roses on trellises border the edges of this grassy area where a larger garden once held 5,000 rose bushes.

Hillsdale seems to be a business in transition. Although still lovely, the rose collection is considerably smaller than in earlier years and the shade structures are empty. You may want to make a phone call before you plan a visit.

The office and mailing address for Hillsdale is Hillsdale Landscape Company, 7845 Johnson Road, Indianapolis IN 46250. (317) 849-2810.

From I-465 on the east side of Indianapolis, take the 56th Street/Shadeland Avenue exit and go north toward Castleton or take the Indiana Route 37 South exit. At the 75th Street stoplight, turn east to Shadeland Avenue, then go north. Look for Hillsdale's large sign on the west side of the road, across from the north end of a large apartment complex. Park in the nursery parking lot and walk a few yards to the garden behind the house.

The New Indianapolis Zoo
1200 West Washington Street
Indianapolis IN 46222
(317) 638-8072

64 acres. Botanical collections that approximate the animals' home habitat. 80-foot diameter conservatory.

💲♿☕ Shops. Many plants labeled. Food at zoo concessions. Library. Special events. Zoo open every day, weather permitting. Gates open at 9am and close at 4pm during winter, at 5pm in spring and fall, and at 6pm in summer. Library open Monday-Friday 8am-6pm, Saturday 8am-5pm, Sunday hours vary.   ▶

◀ African plains, mountain woods, and tropical forest are all here, just a few blocks west of downtown Indianapolis. Botanical collections are still developing in this major zoo that first opened in 1988. In the conservatory, you'll find tropical and desert environments complete with free-flying birds and small (harmless) reptiles. Outside, other colorful and interesting plants ornament the general grounds of the zoo.

As you might expect, the Zoo Library (open to all zoo visitors) houses a book collection whose emphasis is on zoology and botany. A reservoir of information on national and regional zoos and botanical gardens will help you plan other excursions.

In the midst of all these plants and animals, the zoo hosts many special events and functions during the year. Wouldn't a visit at one of those times add a special note to your zoo visit?

For a recorded message about seasonal hours, special events, and other timely information call (317) 630-2030.

The zoo is a mile west of the intersection of West and Washington streets, major streets that can be reached easily from any of the surrounding Interstate highways. Use the Indianapolis inset on your road map.

James Irving Holcomb Woods and Botanical Garden
Butler University
4600 Sunset Avenue
Indianapolis IN 46208

Several acres. Woods and formal gardens.

 Hiking trails. Picnic facilities.
Open daylight hours.

These acres hold enchanting contrasts. Woods and fountains play against gardens, lawn, and the sluggish White River Canal. At the Forest Entrance to Holcomb Woods, you're greeted by a mid-pond geyser fountain, the gift of the Class of 1990. Tiny waterfalls feed and empty the pond and a pleasant terrace overlooks the pond, woods, and a carillon tower. Today, late spring wildflowers edge the dirt and gravel paths.

The gardens are near the canal, on a lower level beyond the woods; a short walk or drive from the pond will get you there. Here, capacious flower beds are surrounded by trimmed yew hedges and vast lawn. The head groundsman tells me that the central flowering crab allée was "breath-taking" earlier in the spring. Today, those trees are clad in more subdued grays and greens but they're lively with nest-building robins and grackles. Cottonwood fluff drifts across the lawn and mallards wing by on their way to the canal, where a song sparrow sings in an overhanging bush. Poppies glow here and there, heavy-headed peonies have sagged in the rains, and a myriad of irises do their best to stand straight and tall. Most of the lilac collection is past bloom but Japanese tree lilacs bloom later and their scent blends with that of nearby mock orange. Broad stands of daylilies promise summer color. One planting bed is anchored by a huge clump of blue star (*Amsonia tabernaemontana*), its pale aqua flowers just coming into their prime. Across the lawn in another bed, a small forest of false indigo (*Baptisia australis*) waves its blue flower spikes and tiny new seedpods. Beyond a small reflecting pool, plum-colored smoke bushes (*Cotinus coggygria* 'Purpureus') are rich against glaucous new blue spruce growth and the fresh green of new deciduous leaves. Persephone, goddess of fertility and vegetation, stands in the pool, having returned from Hades yet one more time so the earth may bloom. These woods and gardens show their gratitude.

Technically, this is not at the moment a "botanical garden." Financial vicissitudes have not allowed maintenance of plant labels. Nor, until recently, have there been funds for replacement of large perennials as they die out; there are more masses of annuals than you might expect. A long-term program is under way to install more perennials and to restore labels, so these gardens will become even lovelier and more informative than they are now.

From I-465 on the north side of Indianapolis, exit at Indiana Route 31 South (Meridian Street). Go south six or seven miles to 46th Street, then west a few blocks to Sunset Avenue and Butler University. Forty-sixth Street ends at the university so you must approach from the east. Turn right at Sunset. Beyond a large parking lot, turn left at the Forest Entrance. Park here and walk down to the pond. Or follow this road a short way into the campus, turning right at the Holcomb Observatory and Planetarium and right again between the marked stone pillars, to the gardens.

FYI Butler University is also home to Friesner Herbarium, a collection of 100,000 dried plants preserved on individual sheets and labeled as to genus, species, and place of collection. A valuable resource for plant identification, the Friesner collection is available to the informed public in Room 72 of the Gallahue Science Building. An early fall Open House demonstrates the work and purpose of an herbarium and features a guest lecturer.

For specific directions and to make an appointment call (317) 283-1143.

Herbarium available September through May during class hours.

Eli Lilly Botanical Gardens

Indianapolis Museum of Art
1200 West 38th Street
Indianapolis IN 46208-4196
(317) 923-1331, Extensions 235 or 295

152-acre grounds. Perennial beds. Woods. Greenhouses. Rock garden.

♿ ☕ Brochures. Fee for museum. Shops. Many plants labeled. Library. Plant sales. Workshops and other special events.
Grounds open daily 6am-6pm. Greenhouse open Tuesday-Sunday 9am-5pm. Museum open weekdays and Saturday 10am-5pm, Thursday until 8:30pm, Sunday noon-5pm. Garden on the Green Restaurant open Tuesday-Sunday 11am-1:45pm (Reservations suggested: [317] 926-2628). Horticultural library open to the public on Wednesday and Saturday afternoons. Shops open later than the museum and close at 5pm. All facilities are closed Monday and major holidays.

The Lilly Botanical Gardens, an agreeable mix of perennials and annuals, lawn and gentle woods, surround the Indianapolis Museum of Art. Occasional benches invite you to rest but winding paths encourage you to stroll through sun and shade. Showy perennials are scattered across the lawns and stand at the woods' edge, and native or naturalized plants fill shady ravines. There's something pleasing here wherever you look.

At the edge of the greenhouse parking lot, a border of pink showy primroses (*Oenothera speciosa*) overlooks a lovely rock garden that descends the hillside. An admirable collection of dwarf conifers crowns a small knoll and, today, irises and perennial cornflowers (*Centaurea montana*) accent the slopes.

Five greenhouse/conservatory buildings house the museum's 500-plant orchid collection and a wide variety of plants that are for sale but, on this May day, herb plants have overflowed to an outdoor sales area. The shade houses offer a good assortment of plants and I decide my garden needs cornflowers and pansies.

In 1967, the J. K. Lilly family donated their estate to the Art Association of Indianapolis as the site of a new art museum. The museum has recently completed a 36.5 million dollar expansion and renovation but the grounds, with their winding paths, pocket gardens, sculpture, and elegant buildings, maintain an aura of privacy.

You may want to time your visit for lunch at Garden on the Green or for shopping at the Better Than New Shop or the Alliance Museum Shop. Perhaps you want to see the museum's particularly strong decorative arts collection or an appealing short-term exhibit. It's easy to spend a few minutes in the greenhouses and rock garden . . . or a whole day enjoying the entire grounds, the museum, and the shops.

For fact sheets on the gardens, other IMA offerings, or an exhibit calendar, contact the Director of Marketing and Communications at the address or phone number above.

From I-465 on the west side of Indianapolis, exit for 38th Street east. Go east about 5 miles to the museum, just east of the White River, and turn left into the museum grounds. To reach the greenhouses and rock garden, follow the signs for "Other Buildings."

Madison in Bloom
Madison

Annual tour of public and private gardens in nineteenth-century Ohio River town. Related events.

Fee for some festival events. Plant sales. Visitor center. Wide range of festival activities. Festival the last two weekends of April. Public gardens open daylight hours during growing season.

A visit to Madison is a treat for garden-lovers and history buffs at any time . . . a visit during Madison in Bloom is particularly rewarding because you can visit private gardens that have been chosen for their distinctive appeal, gardens that aren't available to visitors the rest of the year. Special attention is paid to selected public areas, too, such as the Lanier Mansion State Historic Site, an imposing 1840s estate whose well-groomed grounds sweep downward to the Ohio River. Other public gardens include the Schofield House Herb Garden and the Talbot-Hyatt Pioneer Garden; check at the Visitor Center on the status of these and other gardens. In various years, the festival may include an art exhibit, lectures and seminars, plant sales, or a garden party. Dates often coincide with a Wildflower Weekend at nearby Clifty Falls State Park. There is always plenty to do and see, and ample opportunities to admire flowers and gardens, in Madison.

For festival schedules and other information contact the Jefferson County Historical Society, Madison in Bloom, 615 West First Street, Madison IN 47250, (812) 265-2335; the Madison Area Visitors Center, Main and Jefferson Streets, Madison IN 47250, (812) 265-2956; or Historic Southern Indiana, 405 Carpenter Street, Evansville IN 47708, (812) 428-7592.

◀ Madison is 15 miles east of I-65 on Indiana Route 256, about 40 miles northeast of Louisville KY "as the crow flies." Visitor Center and Festival Headquarters are on the main street downtown.

Hayes Regional Arboretum
801 Elks Road
Richmond IN 47374
(317) 962-3745

355-acre estate grounds. Arboretum of native woody plants. All-American Rose Selection garden. Nature center.

Brochure, trail guides, and wildflower seed list. Shop. Many plants labeled. Foot trails (4.5 miles total) and auto trail. Picnic facilities. Workshops and other events.
Open all year Tuesday-Saturday 9am-5pm, Sunday 1-5pm. Closed Monday.

The barn-like Hayes Nature Center, entry to the arboretum, is cool, shadowy, and relatively empty today. We've arrived on a hot mid-June afternoon, a day or two before Richmond's annual Rose Festival, and slow-moving traffic made us eager to get to the promised shade of the arboretum. It was worth the wait. The Nature Center features, among several intriguing educational exhibits, the Tree-Saver computer program that was developed by the staff at Hayes. The shop offers gardening books, nature guides, nature-related gifts, and a group of attractive watercolor cards by local artists that are truly "suitable for framing."

Hayes Arboretum, a former estate, includes many acres of mature beech-maple forest. Life on the 3½ mile auto tour route, which enters the woods immediately beyond the Nature Center, is delightfully unlike life on Interstate 70. Wildflowers bloom, birds sing, a light breeze blows, and all is well with the world. We park the car and walk to the Fern Garden, its hillsides dense with ferns, wild ginger, and other native shade-lovers. The lush stand of maidenhair fern (*Adiantum pedatum* L.) would shame the few such plants in my home garden. To enhance *our* gardens, the arboretum sells wildflower seeds each year, usually in March; contact the arboretum horticulturist for information and a seed list.

Manicured lawns around the house seem painfully bright compared to the shady woods but the view from inside the house must be lovely; its long lawn contains a sizable rose garden and carefully placed, well-labeled native plants. Paths in the Native Woody Plant Reserve near the house are designed for pleasant strolling among varieties of trees, shrubs, and vines that were familiar to the area's early settlers.

Have you ever wanted to drive on a racetrack? When Stanley W. Hayes, railway equipment inventor, began acquiring this land around 1915, one of his purchases included a former country fairground and its small horse-racing track. That race track, now surrounded by flowering trees, is part of the auto tour route; genteel surroundings suggest a more leisurely pace that allows us to enjoy all that is here at Hayes.

From I-70 exit for US Route 40 West. Go 2½ miles to Elks Road, then turn north and go a half mile to the arboretum's main entrance.

FYI Not far west of the arboretum, on US 40, you'll find the E. G. Hill Memorial Rose Garden/All-America City Rose Garden and Glen Miller Park, with its celebrated sculpture, "Madonna of the Trail." If you love roses, Richmond is the place to be in late June. The annual Rose Festival includes community events, house and garden tours, and tours of Hill's Roses, a commercial rose nursery. For information on the Festival and the city parks, contact the Richmond-Wayne County Convention and Tourism Bureau, 600 Promenade, Richmond IN 47374. (317) 935-8687.

Indiana: Southwest

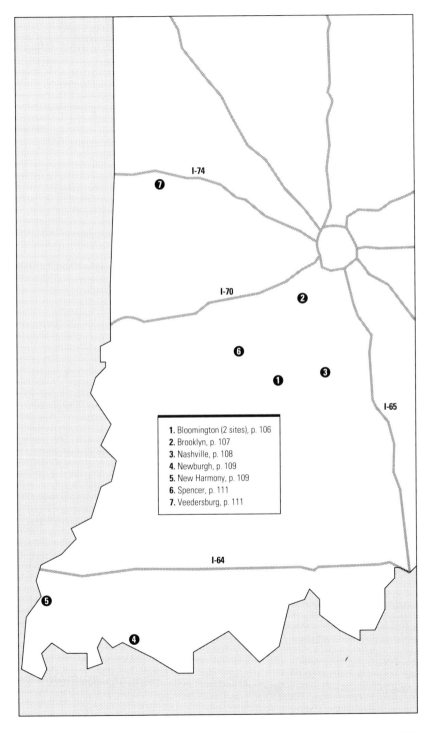

Indiana: Southwest

The Indiana Department of Natural Resources holds spring Wildflower Forays in several of the state's parks. These include guided wildflower walks, evening slide presentations by informed naturalists, and general wildflower information. Five state parks in southern Indiana offer lodges that are delightful bases for your wildflower excursions: Brown Country, Clifty Falls, McCormick's Creek, Spring Mill, and Turkey Run.

For dates and locations of Wildflower Forays, contact the Indiana Department of Natural Resources, Division of State Parks, 100 North Senate Avenue, 616 State Office Building, Indianapolis IN 46204-2216. (317) 232-4124.

Hilltop Garden and Nature Center
Department of Recreation and Park Administration
Indiana University
Bloomington IN 47405
(812) 855-7642

Five acres. Youth garden plots. Garden center. All-America Selections test/display gardens.

♿ Many plants labeled. Seasonal plant sales. Visitor center. Workshops and other events. Open June 1-August 15 weekdays 9am-3pm, other days and times for special events. Annual Spring Garden Festival and Plant Sale the last weekend of April, noon-5pm each day.

On a warm spring day, Hilltop seethes with youngsters who are planning, planting, and tending their vegetable and flower plots, the gardens they maintain in partnership with Indiana University horticulture and recreation students. These beautiful and active acres are home to one of the country's oldest youth gardening programs but adults, too, can take part in garden-related classes and nature-oriented workshops. Landscaped gardens, designed to inspire the home gardener and to encourage community beautification, emphasize plants that thrive in this part of Indiana.

Daffodil fans will rejoice in the mid-April daffodil show and in the fall bulb sale. *Any* gardener will relish April's Spring Garden Festival and Plant Sale, held when the gardens hold their special spring beauty. Daylily and dwarf iris collections, surrounded by a richness of flowers and vegetables, flaunt their baroque forms and colors in season. Delightful Hilltop is a place to savor and to learn. ▶

Hilltop is on the northeast side of Bloomington. From Indiana Route 46 turn west onto 10th Street, then turn right at the first drive on the north side of the street. Go straight up the hill to . . . Hilltop.

University Greenhouses
Room139 A Jordan Hall
Third Street
Indiana University
Bloomington IN 47401
(812) 855-7717 (Greenhouses)
(812) 855-3402 or (812) 855-6283 (Office)

Large research and propagation greenhouses.

Many plants labeled. Group tours by appointment.
Open weekdays 8am-4pm.

Their specific plant occupants change with the semesters, the seasons, and the years but these greenhouses are well-known for their continuous beauty and fascinating diversity. You may see specialized plant collections, horticultural research projects, perennials and bedding plants under production for the coming season, and a range of other projects . . . and there's almost always someone available to show you around and to answer questions.

From Indiana Route 45/46 on the northeast side of Bloomington, take Third Street west to the IU campus and look for Jordan Hall, the entry to the greenhouses.

Link Memorial Daffodil Garden
P. O. Box 84
Brooklyn IN 46111
(317) 831-3283

Seventeen acres. Naturalized daffodils and other spring flowers. Small greenhouse.

Open daylight hours during daffodil season *only,* usually April.

You'll be haunted by every daffodil poem you've ever read as you roam these gardens. Daffodils by the thousands, the flowers of over 2,000 different cultivars, shine above the grassy hillsides, nestle in secluded nooks, and wave boldly in the display garden. Some of these blooms come from 50-year-old bulbs, remainders of the Links' first bulbs-by-the-bushel purchases. Mrs. Link, who admits she is terribly infected with "yellow fever," has hybridized and registered several cultivars of her own. We can only be grateful that she shares her private garden with us at its most joyous time.

From Indiana Route 67 in Brooklyn (which is 20-25 miles southwest of downtown Indianapolis), turn north onto Observatory Road and go about a mile and a half to the garden.

T. C. Steele State Historic Site
R. R. 1 Box 256
Nashville IN 47448
(812) 988-2785

Total 211 acres. 15 acres under garden restoration. 90-acre State Nature Preserve. Historic home.

♿ Shop. Many plants labeled. Nature/hiking trails. Visitor center. Workshops, festivals, and other events. Group tours by appointment.
Open March-December Monday-Saturday 9am-5pm, Sunday 1-5pm. January-February Wednesday-Saturday 9am-5pm, Tuesday and Sunday 1-5pm, closed Monday.

Here are gardens that will bear watching.

In 1907, T. C. Steele, a noted Hoosier impressionist painter, built his home in this inspriational Brown County setting. Mrs. Steele planned her gardens to beautify the grounds *and* to provide subject matter for her husband's paintings. A few of her original plantings remain, such as sweeps of native wildflowers, thousands of daffodils, and the sturdy peonies that brighten late spring. Accurate restoration of the cutting and display gardens is based on Steele's paintings; some of these painted garden records are displayed in the house. Additional renovation will include rebuilt wooden arbors and rejuvenated lily ponds. Guided tours and pamphlets are being developed to aid garden interpretation and enjoyment.

The Steeles frequently opened their home to friends and colleagues so it's appropriate that the site now hosts flower festivals, wildflower forays, art contests, and open houses. This part of Indiana is always lovely; in the not-too-distant future this home and its grounds will look much as they did when the Steeles were in residence and the gardens were in their prime. In the meantime, there is much here that is pleasing.

▶

The Steele site is a mile and a half south of Indiana Route 46 at Belmont, which is midway between Bloomington and Nashville IN.

Newburgh Country Store
224 West Jennings
Newburgh IN 47630
(812) 853-3071

Commercial. Herb festival.

♿ Plant list and seminar information. Fee for seminars. Plants labeled. Plant sales. Workshops. Herb Festival on the last three weekends of April, 8am-6pm each day.

In this small town along the Ohio River, April allows you to submerge yourself in herbs. Established gardens here are minimal but you'll find healthy plants by the thousands in the sales lot and a wealth of information about herbs, their cultivation, and their uses. The festival includes a full schedule of Saturday seminars that may include such topics as landscaping with herbs, country cooking, growing and using old roses, herb condiments, and a myriad of other intriguing subjects. There is a very nominal fee for most of the seminars and reservations are required.

Over 60,000 plants fill the sales lot with variety that is almost overwhelming; the nearly endless array includes over 40 antique roses, more than 70 hardy perennials, and nearly 200 herbs that include 23 different scented geraniums, 18 varieties of thyme, and 14 flavors of mint. (These numbers were taken from the 1990 plant list.) If herbs are new to you, be prepared to fall in love with them; if you're already an herbarist, you're sure to find appealing new varieties here.

Exit I-164 at Indiana Route 662 on the southeast side of Evansville. Go east 7 or 8 miles to Newburgh; it's a small town, so you shouldn't have any trouble finding the festival.

New Harmony

Restored 19th-century utopian community. Varied gardens. 900 sq.ft. greenhouse. ▶

◀ ♿ ☕ Shops. Many plants labeled. Library. Limited plant sales. Visitor center. Workshops and other events.
Gardens open daylight hours. Variable hours for shops, library, and other amenities.

Pockets of botanical interest are scattered across New Harmony, where the grounds of several restored buildings contain small and historically accurate gardens. Here is where I first saw lusty vining hops, not a common sight in the midwest. You'll see and smell old-fashioned roses, heritage apple trees, tidy herb gardens, and lush flower gardens.

Plantings around the New Harmony Inn hold a diversity of plant groups, all of them thriving. Vegetables grow among the flowers and landscape plants as examples of New Harmony's bio-dynamic approach to gardening, ". . . a non-chemical method that enriches the soil and works in cooperation with nature's forces." Because the plant's health and productivity are the prime concern, each plant is put exactly where it will grow best, *wherever* that may be.

Orchids grow happily in the Inn's greenhouse, content among large tender plants that spend their summers on patios and terraces. From this greenhouse, too, come the unusual annuals, perennials, and vegetables that fill the gardens.

Offspring of special New Harmony hybrid peonies may be sold in the future. Although there are currently no on-going plant sales, seeds from some of the Inn's unusual annuals are occasionally available. The Red Geranium Bookstore offers a wide selection of distinctive gardening books. The Bio-dynamics Lending Library (under development) will contain a complete selection of books and pamphlets about bio-dynamic farming and gardening.

New Harmony was founded in 1814 by a small group of German Separatists. In 1825, the entire community was purchased by Scotland's Robert Owen for an experiment in utopian living and, for several decades, it was a center of scientific and intellectual activities. New Harmony knew several incarnations prior to 1937, when the State of Indiana created the first New Harmony Memorial Commission to allow the purchase and protection of key properties. Additional commissions and trusts have followed. Today's New Harmony provides an enjoyable mix of gardens, historic and contemporary architecture, and social history.

For information on the gardens, inn, or restaurant contact Red Geranium Enterprises, P. O. Box 581, New Harmony IN 47631, (812) 682-4431. For general New Harmony information contact Historic New Harmony, P. O. Box 579, New Harmony IN 47631, (812) 464-9595 or (812) 682-4488. ▶

New Harmony is 30 miles west of Evansville, along I-64. It's a relatively small site and all locations are easy to find. Maps are available at the Athenaeum/Visitor Center at North and Arthur streets.

New Hope Herb Farm
Rt. 1 Box 660
Spencer IN 47460
(812) 829-6086

Commercial. Total grounds 40 acres. 6 acres display/theme gardens.

♿ Catalog. Fee for festivals. Plants labeled. Workshops. Group tours, demonstrations, and workshops by appointment.
Open May and June Sundays only, 10am-5pm. Other days and months by appointment. Call in advance *after dark*. Festivals on the second Sundays of July and September 10am-5pm.

Imagine a garden that is at its best in the moonlight . . . or one that features the many varieties of salvia . . . or plantings especially designed to attract butterflies and hummingbirds. They're all here at New Hope, alongside the Biblical Garden, a woodland shade display, a fragrance garden, masses of culinary herbs, and banks of unusual, hard-to-find plants. Doesn't this sound inviting?

New Hope is very much a working farm, where organic farming methods encourage the production of over 400 plant varieties. Because hours for public visits are quite limited, the best way to enjoy New Hope may be at their July and September festivals. These events offer everything required for a delightful day: music and dancers, catered refreshments, plant and book sales, garden tours, and demonstrations. You'll be glad you made the scenic drive to New Hope.

Spencer is on Indiana Route 67, about 50 miles southwest of Indianapolis and 14 miles northwest of Bloomington. Take IN 67 south from Spencer to Freedom (about 8 miles), then turn east on IN 48 and follow the New Hope signs about 4 miles to the farm.

Leigh's Bloomers
R. R. 1 Box 25
Veedersburg IN 47987
(317) 798-3611

◀ Commercial. Semi-formal 40'x80' herb garden.

Many plants labeled. Seasonal plant sales.
Regular "open" hours during May only, Monday-Saturday 10am-4pm, Sunday 2pm-6pm. Call ahead at all other times or be prepared to deal with the resident watchdog.

St. Fiacre, the patron saint of gardeners, stands beneath a rose-of-Sharon bush, surveying raised beds that nearly overflow with basils and comfrey and other fragrant, tasty, and attractive plants. An arbor seat and other garden amenities make these plantings an oasis of color and texture in a desert of cornfields and sweeping lawns. In May, Leigh's sells perennials, roses, herbs, planted hanging baskets, and bedding plants. The public season is short at Leigh's but a phone call will let you enjoy this garden any time during the growing season.

Exit I-74 at US Route 41 (Attica-Veedersburg Road) and go south. Leigh's is six miles south of Veedersburg on US 41.

Michigan: North

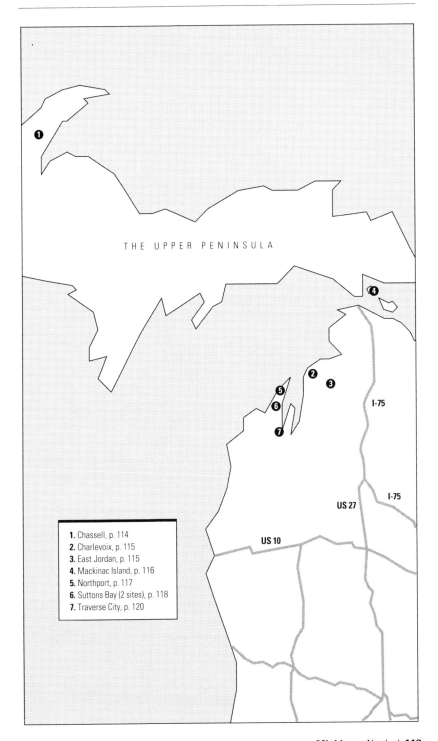

1. Chassell, p. 114
2. Charlevoix, p. 115
3. East Jordan, p. 115
4. Mackinac Island, p. 116
5. Northport, p. 117
6. Suttons Bay (2 sites), p. 118
7. Traverse City, p. 120

Michigan: The Upper Peninsula

About one-third of Michigan's Upper Peninsula ("the U. P.") is occupied by national or state forests, Indian reservations, national lakeshore, state parks, or military reservations. Much of it is heavily forested, most towns are relatively small, and gardens to visit are few . . . but in one sense the entire area is a garden. Wildflowers are abundant and can be spectacular in forests and meadows, on the roadsides, and around the lakes and bogs.

Einerlei
P. O. Box 679
422 Willson Memorial Drive
Chassell MI 49916
(906) 523-4612

Commercial. 50'x50' herb and perennial cottage-type garden. 300 sq.ft. greenhouse.

Calendar and plant list. Shop. Many plants labeled. Workshops (fee) and special events. Open January-April Monday-Saturday 10am-5pm, Sunday noon-5pm. May-December Monday-Saturday 10am-6pm, Sunday noon-5pm.

Einerlei will feel like a garden oasis if you've spent too many days on the lakes or in the forest. The main garden, some of it in raised beds, lies behind the handsome shingled shop. Perch a while on the deck and enjoy a scene where lush and fragrant culinary herbs, hardy perennials, scented geraniums (*Pelargonium* spp.), and ornamentals fill every bit of garden space. Or walk the grassy paths for more intimate views of the plants. In early summer, the greenhouse nearly overflows with an impressive array of herbs (nearly 100 varieties) and a multitude of other appealing plants. In the Einerlei shop, herbs and herbal products join other gardening and cooking "necessities."

If a workshop fits into your vacation plans, this is where you want to be. Recent topics ranged from "Planning and Planting Your Herb Garden" to "An Herb-Woven Basket" and "Harvesting and Drying Herbs." Other sessions dealt with such activities as painting a canvas hat and collecting and preserving vintage clothing. Preregistration is required for all workshops; write for the schedule. The Chassell Strawberry Festival and the Annual Einerlei Quilt Show may draw you to Chassell in early July but once you've found Einerlei, *any* time is good for visiting this corner of the U. P.

Willson Memorial Drive is the same as US Route 41, the route you'll probably take into Chassell. Einerlei is in the center of this small town.

Michigan: The Northern Lower Peninsula

Wintergreen Herbs and Potpourri
R. R. 3, 10970 Burnett Road
Charlevoix MI 49720
(616) 347-7399

Commercial. Four acres. Herb theme gardens.

Catalog. Fee for tour groups. Shop. Many plants labeled. Seasonal plant sales. Workshops and special events.
Open May-December Monday-Friday 9am-5pm, Saturday 9am-4pm. Arts N'Herb Renaissance Festival early August. Scents of Christmas Open House the first weekend of November.

Herbs mentioned in the Bible, plants used in traditional medicine, herbs used for cooking, flowers familiar to Shakespeare, colorful everlastings . . . all these flourish in the Wintergreen gardens. A cottage garden, plants that prefer shade, and a sunny wall garden also thrive here in Charlevoix's cool summers.

The yield of these gardens and plots, transformed into fragrant blends and striking dried arrangements, fills the Wintergreen shop. You'll find herb and ornamental plants in their season and the books that tell you how to grow and use them. Gift items, just the thing for the neighbor who waters the garden while you're gone, will catch your eye. You may want to join one of Wintergreen's how-to-do-it classes or perhaps you'd like to visit one of their annual festivals. Potpourri, built almost entirely from the good things grown at Wintergreen, is a house specialty; you can be sure of appealing scents whenever you visit.

Take US Route 31 a mile north of Petoskey, past Bay Shore Village, turn left onto Murray Road, then make an immediate right turn onto Old US 31. Go a quarter mile to Burnett Road and turn left to Wintergreen at the top of the hill.

Circle Herb Farm
R. R. 1 Box 247 Hejhal Road
East Jordan MI 49727
(616) 536-2729

Commercial herb grower. Sizable demonstration garden.

Catalog. Gift/garden shop. Many plants labeled. Plant sales.
Open May 1-October 31 Monday-Saturday 9am-5pm, Sunday 11am-4pm.

◀ The raised garden at Circle displays the herbs and edible flowers they sell so you can see what your plants will be when they grow up. Herb and culinary items, herb books, and over 125 plant varieties fill the shop. You'll see fresh-cut Circle Farm herbs in area grocery stores, just what you want if tonight's salad needs a few fresh leaves of something tasty. Circle's early July Herb Festival is free; the early June Herb Luncheons, for which you'll need reservations, are not. Summer workshops delve into the cultivation and use of culinary and decorative herbs. Wouldn't workshop activity, surrounded by lovely plants, be the ideal counterpoint to long days of traveling or lounging on the beach?

From I-75 take the Gaylord/Michigan Route 32 exit. Go about 21 miles west on MI 32 to Circle Herb Farm. Or, from East Jordan, go 8 to 10 miles east on MI 32.

The Grand Hotel
Mackinac Island

Spacious grounds around Victorian-era resort hotel. Rose Walk. Theme gardens. Greenhouse.

♿ Brochures and garden information. Shops. Hiking trails. Five restaurants/three lounges. Workshops and special events. For the day-tripping public, there is a fee to visit the hotels, shops, and restaurants and the much-photographed porch.
Hotel open mid-May to late October. Gardens open daylight hours during this period.

Imagine crystalline blue skies above the historic dark waters of Lake Huron and the Straits of Mackinac. Picture an imposing Victorian hotel that gleams white amidst rich lawn, luscious flowers, and stately trees. This is Grand Hotel and her gardens.

The welcoming Entrance Gardens are flowery profusions of Victorian-era favorites, many of which are raised here from heritage seeds. The Rose Walk is dominated by cerise-pink 'Carefree Beauty', a rose hardy enough to withstand the island's harsh winters. Roses perfume the Wedding Garden too, where 'Carefree Beauty' joins pink, white, and yellow roses in a pastel lode that's enriched by lambent blue bellfowers and airy Russian sage (*Perovskia atriplicifolia*). Most Grand Hotel gardens incorporate charming specimens of antique roses and winter-hardy shrub roses.

Come to the Pool Gardens in June, when the Grand Hotel lilacs bloom on bushes brought from Paris and Quebec long ago. A Lilac Festival features this durable species that thrives all across the island. Late June finds an awesome array of bush and tree peonies blooming in the Pool Gardens. Nearby, a fine hosta collection accents the arboretum and wildflower garden.

Are you yearning to visit the Grand Hotel yet? Perhaps you'll be seduced by the Tea Garden, whose plants are chosen to be as light and airy as this garden's central fountain; Russian sage, threadleaf coreopsis, and baby's-breath stabilize the changing parade of annuals. Maybe you're intrigued by the Grand Ladies Garden, where stately ginkgoes guard an elegant collection of bulbs and annuals. You may want to explore the Tennis Court Gardens, the Eyebrow Gardens (named for the shape of their yew plantings), or the Grand Hotel Greenhouse. There are gardens enough here to entertain you for several hours but you must allow time to luxuriate on the famous Grand Hotel porch, honing your people-watching skills and savoring the contrast of lush gardens with the rugged beauty of the Straits.

Several theme weekends enliven the late season at Grand Hotel. Earliest is usually the late-summer Flower and Garden Package: three days of garden tours, wildflower hikes, and workshops that, in a recent year, included such topics as garden photography, designing with old roses, garden architecture, and flower arranging. You may want to return for jazz on Labor Day, the Victorian weekend, or a few days of sleuthing at the Murder Mystery event. Special themes vary from year to year. No matter when you come to the Grand Hotel, you'll be enchanted by the gardens, the history, and the ambiance.

Summer address for information: Grand Hotel, Vice President for Marketing, Mackinac Island MI 49757, (906) 847-3331. Winter address: Grand Hotel, Vice President for Marketing, 116 West Ottawa Street, Lansing MI 48933, (517) 487-1800.

Drive to Mackinaw City or St. Ignace, then take the ferry to Mackinac Island. Cars aren't allowed on Mackinac Island so you'll walk, bicycle, or take a horsedrawn cab to the hotel and its gardens.

Woodland Herbs
7741 North Manitou Trail, West (Michigan Route 22)
Northport MI 49670
(616) 386-5081

Commercial. Sizable herb garden.

Catalog. Shop. Many plants labeled. Seasonal plant sales.
Open May-October Monday-Saturday 11am-5pm. Closed Sunday. Christmas Open House on Friday and Saturday after Thanksgiving.

◀ Burnished cattails and gleaming lilypads, a copper fountain in its sunny pool, accent the variety of herbs that thrive in this lush garden. Tall hedges enclose and protect over 100 hardy herbs that, like the peninsula's human inhabitants, endure long winters and luxuriate in lake-cooled summers. The paved garden walkway leads to a sun-drenched bench that offers a garden overview, a chance to relish these plantings *in toto*.

In May and June, two greenhouses at Woodland are filled with potted herbs for *your* garden, including some of the less common scented geraniums (*Pelargonium* spp.). The folks at Woodland consider themselves "a culinary herb shop"; I read their mail order list and salivate. Stop at the cozy herb-bedecked shop for apricot vinegar . . . raspberry creamed honey . . . zippy horseradish jelly . . . wild leek dip mix . . . wild, wild rice . . . dilled pesto blend. If you can resist this array of tasty creations you're stronger than I am. Would your pet enjoy an herbal treat, such as a catnip mouse or herbal doggie donuts? They're here, alongside herb wreaths, a selection of those handcrafted copper fountains, packaged scents and potpourris, herb books, and other inviting objects. Your time on the Leelanau Peninsula will become even more delightful with a visit to Woodland Herbs.

Woodland Herbs is on Michigan Route 22, between Leland and Northport, about 3½ miles southwest of Northport.

Bellwether Garden
Route 2 Box 210
Suttons Bay MI 49682
(616) 271-3004

Commercial. One acre. Display and production gardens.

♿ Fee for workshops. Shop. Many plants labeled. Plant sales. Workshops and special events. Open May 15-August 31 Tuesday-Saturday 10am-5pm, September 1-December 15 Tuesday-Saturday 1-5pm.

Green life fills the Bellwether gardens and killdeer cry above the hillside but the shop is closed on this day after Labor Day. Terraced gardens, new in 1990, are filling in nicely and the potting shed holds signs of recent activity. When the shop reopens, dried flowers and herbs will adorn ceiling and walls and shelves will overflow with treasures "from and for the garden or the gardener." ▶

◀ A garden bench and a small arbor encourage leisurely enjoyment of the display gardens; in season, you can pick a fresh bouquet from these gardens. Garden statuary nestles among lusty plants on the terrace and in cozy gardens behind the house.

You can take workshops on garden design, "plant crafts," and other topics at Bellwether, where visitors are "very, very welcome." A guided garden tour is yours for the asking and, with luck and good timing, you may join an impromptu garden party. If you're in the area on Saturday morning but can't stop by the gardens, look for Bellwether's colorful display at the Traverse City Farmers' Market.

From Traverse City take MI 22 north. Eight miles north of Tom's Shopping Center, go west a third of a mile on Shady Lane. Look for the large wooden sheep (Bellwether) sign at the corner of Shady Lane and Elm Valley Road, across from a large stone barn.

Busha's Brae
Route 1 Box 232 M
Setterbo Road
Suttons Bay MI 49682
(616) 271-6284

Commercial. Two acres. Herb theme and production gardens.

Fee for teas and luncheons. Newsletter. Shop. Many plants labeled. Picnic facilities. Workshops and special events. Group tours by prior arrangement. Reservations required for teas and luncheons.
Open May 15-October 15 Monday-Saturday noon-5pm. Actual hours are rather flexible; the motto is "If you're here, we're open."

Colorful gardens, well-researched and well-tended, meld with a hillside farmhouse, an inviting shop, and tall trees to become Busha's Brae. Delightful theme gardens include the handsome Shakespeare Garden, the thought-provoking Biblical Garden, and Kent's Garden, a cottage garden lush with bloom and foliage. Stone walls, remnants of a barn, shelter the developing monastery garden, a greenery that will be dedicated to Chad, a medieval Bishop of Lichfield. All theme gardens are attractively labeled with plant names, ▶

FYI A "wether" is a neutered ram sheep who is docile, perhaps timid, and is likely to stay with the flock. When he wears a bell, the shepherd can easily find the flock. Thus, bell(ed) wether.

appropriate quotations, and other useful information. These two acres of lovely and productive gardens, the enchanting site of summer teas and luncheons, are testimony to family cooperation and the owner's abundant enthusiasm. The sky is clear and breezy, birds are singing, and I can't think of a nicer place to be at the moment, except possibly in my own garden.

Sunny slopes and intensively planted production beds supply herbs for the vinegars and seasoning blends produced in Busha's "Ag Kitchen" and sold in many of the region's specialty shops. This kitchen, licensed and regularly inspected by the Michigan Agriculture Department, can't be used for anything else; no whipping up a pizza for the family here.

The small cottage/shop, nestled into the Shakespeare and Biblical gardens, houses attractive displays of seasonings, vinegars, wreaths, and dried plant materials. A self-guided garden tour booklet can be purchased here for a nominal fee. Write for the current Busha's Brae newsletter, which is a compendium of schedules, book reviews, recipes, and anecdotes that is *almost* as good as a summer visit to the gardens.

From Traverse City, take Michigan Route 22 north to Setterbo Road, about 1½ miles beyond Suttons Bay and just *past a left-hand curve in MI 22. Go west on Setterbo a little over two miles to Busha's Brae.*
From the west side of the peninsula, take MI 204 east to Suttons Bay, then MI 22 as above.

Belnap Creek Herb Farm
6989 Fouch Road
County Road 614
Traverse City MI 49684
(616) 947-4206

Commercial herb grower. Display garden and production plots.

♿ Shop. Many plants labeled. Seasonal plant sales.
Open May-December Monday-Saturday 10am-6pm. By appointment January-late April.

FYI So who's Busha and what's a brae? "Busha," says the owner, is one form of "grandmother" in Slavic languages and a "brae" is a Scottish hillside or meadow; in combination they reflect this family's heritage. I later saw an area restaurant, "José's Babushka," that proclaimed another melting-pot combination.

120 / Green Byways

◄ Herbs, annual and perennial flowers, and roses greet you from the garden in front of Belnap Creek Herb Farm. In the spring, you can buy herb plants here; in summer, choose pungent herbs freshly cut from the garden. At any season, the Belnap Creek shop offers herb seasoning blends, fruit and herb vinegars, jams, herb teas, potpourri, and other plant-derived products. Belnap Creek is a Certified Organic Farm whose salt-free herb blends and sugar-free jams reflect their interest in healthful products. On Saturday mornings from mid-May to mid-October, BCHF sells herbs and other goodies at the Farmers' Market in Traverse City. Stop by for some fresh herbs to perk up your culinary efforts.

From Traverse City take Michigan Route 22 north a short distance to Cherry Bend Road. Turn left and go 6½ miles to a yellow house with brown trim on the right side of the road.

Michigan: Southeast

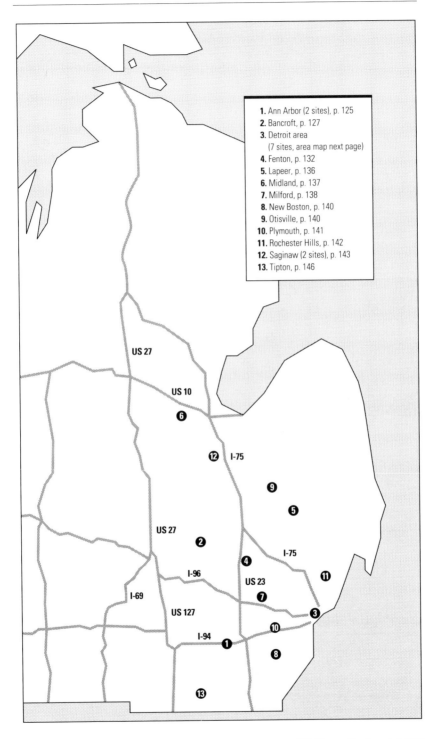

1. Ann Arbor (2 sites), p. 125
2. Bancroft, p. 127
3. Detroit area (7 sites, area map next page)
4. Fenton, p. 132
5. Lapeer, p. 136
6. Midland, p. 137
7. Milford, p. 138
8. New Boston, p. 140
9. Otisville, p. 140
10. Plymouth, p. 141
11. Rochester Hills, p. 142
12. Saginaw (2 sites), p. 143
13. Tipton, p. 146

Michigan: Southeast / DETROIT

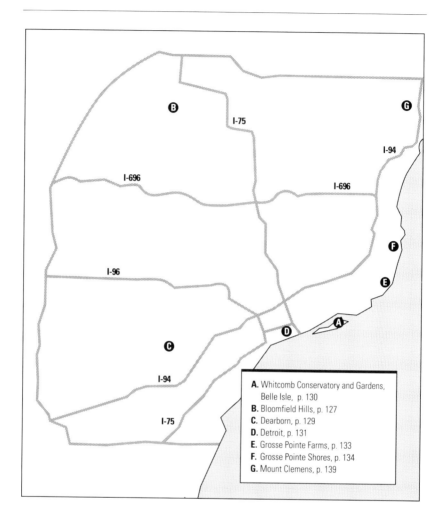

A. Whitcomb Conservatory and Gardens, Belle Isle, p. 130
B. Bloomfield Hills, p. 127
C. Dearborn, p. 129
D. Detroit, p. 131
E. Grosse Pointe Farms, p. 133
F. Grosse Pointe Shores, p. 134
G. Mount Clemens, p. 139

Michigan: Southeast

We enjoy Michigan at any time of year but I especially recommend a visit to southeastern Michigan in early June. Black locust trees, in elegant full bloom, are cumulus drifts against darker woods, above rolling fields and meadows, and along roadsides. In woodlands and natural gardens, wild phlox shines and azaleas and rhododendrons are at their prime. This is truly a perfect time to be here, when all the countryside is a garden.

Matthei Botanical Gardens
1800 Dixboro Road
Ann Arbor MI 48105-9741
(313) 763-7060 or University of Michigan Campus Information (313) 764-1817

250-acre site. 2 acres in theme gardens and conservatory. Natural habitat.

♿ Brochure. Fee for conservatory. Shop. Many plants labeled. Trails. Workshops and other events.
Outdoor grounds open daylight hours every day. Conservatory and gift shop open 10am-4pm. All closed Thanksgiving, Christmas, and New Year's days.

The herbal knot garden is full of promise on this early June evening; tidy brick paths and borders of lavender surround still-small herb plants. Violet-flowered chives and the chartreuse mist of lady's-mantle are bright tonight and by summer these beds will overflow with a richness of herbs. In the nearby rock garden, sea thrift (*Armeria* sp.), Iceland poppies, and a tiny, tiny blue columbine bloom among succulent sedums and echeverias.

An awkward turtle labors at her nest near the nature trail while we share the twilight gardens with birds, rabbits, and a woodchuck. Banks of wild phlox and anemone, celandine and buttercups border mowed grass paths along Fleming Creek, where tall ferns and glossy skunk cabbage fill boggy spots. In the woodland garden, Jacob's-ladder (*Polemonium van-bruntiae*) and wild columbine bloom above lady's slippers, twinleaf (*Jeffersonia diphylla*), and other subtle beauties. Bright rose rhododendrons against the main building seem rowdy by comparison.

We return to Matthei early in the morning a few days later. Behind the conservatory, bearded irises, rose-colored lupines, and salvia 'East Friesland' are brilliant in the early sunlight; the dew-covered yarrows, ornamental grasses, and miniature roses will be even more attractive as the season progresses. The knot garden and rock garden are still inviting . . . but the ground near the nature trail is littered with leathery egg shells and raccoon footprints. The raccoon has feasted on turtle eggs and, although turtles are notoriously neglectful parents, I feel sad.

The large Matthei conservatory features plants of botanical and economic interest and some that are just plain beautiful. You may see orchids or cacti blooming alongside citrus trees and coffee bushes. Call Matthei if you need information on poisonous or medicinal plants; their medicinal garden may supply some answers. The Garden offers a full range of classes and special events and sponsors the annual Ann Arbor Flower and Garden Show, an aesthetic and educational haven for gardeners.

A hissing Canada goose tried to keep us out of "her" gardens and away from her awkward half-downy young. We stayed away from her children but allowed ourselves to thoroughly enjoy the woods, ponds, and gardens that are Matthei.

From US Route 23 on the east side of Ann Arbor, take Exit 38, Geddes Road. Go east on Geddes a short distance to the stoplight at Dixboro Road, then north on Dixboro a little less than 1½ miles to the garden, on the east side of the road.

Nichols Arboretum
The University of Michigan East Medical Campus
Ann Arbor

123 acres of native and exotic woody plants.

Many plants labeled. Trails.
Open all year, sunrise to sunset.

In this lovely landscape you'll find native woodland, mature collections of ornamental trees, and sizable collections of maples, cypress, elms, and pines. Magnolias and cotoneaster join other flowering trees and shrubs in a spring profusion that's punctuated by the blooms of 234 different peony cultivars. You can admire grasses and wildflowers in the Prairie Restoration Project, meet the Korean quassi-bark tree (*Picrasma quassinoides*), and appreciate the stately cedars of Lebanon. Although there are no cultivated "gardens" at Nichols, there's much to see, especially in the spring.

For details contact the Nichols Arboretum, The University of Michigan, School of Natural Resources, Dana Building, 430 East University, Ann Arbor MI 48109-1115. (313) 764-1817 (U. of M. Campus Information).

▶

From US Route 23 on the east side of Ann Arbor, take Exit 37, Washtenaw Avenue. Go west on Washtenaw to East Medical Campus Drive. Turn right to Hospital Lot M-29, where public parking is available on weekends only. Weekday parking is wherever you can find it.

Grand Oak Herb Farm
2877 Miller Road
Bancroft MI 48414
(517) 634-5331

Commercial. 5 acres herb theme gardens and production fields.

Shop. Many plants labeled. Seasonal plant sales. Workshops and other events. Open April 15-December 20 Tuesday-Saturday 9am-5pm. Special holiday hours October 30-December 20.

Nearly twenty different theme gardens wait for you at Grand Oak, including one of old roses and edible flowers, Grandmother's Kitchen Garden, the Lemon Pie Garden redolent with lemon-scented or lemon-flavored herbs, and one planting that's replete with scented geraniums (*Pelargonium* spp.). Here are herbs and everlastings, annuals and perennials, and all manner of flowers and foliage. *Twenty thousand* bundles of these spend time in the drying barn before becoming the custom-blended potpourri or dried wreaths that will be sold in the well-stocked Grand Oak shop.

A Spring Herb Festival, a Holiday Open House, and workshops from early spring to late fall help fill the calendar here. You'll always find something that interests you at Grand Oak.

From I-69 east of Lansing, exit for Michigan Route 52 south. Almost immediately, turn east toward Bancroft on the Lansing Road. Miller Road is a short distance west of Bancroft; go south on Miller Road to Grand Oak.

Cranbrook House and Gardens
Bloomfield Hills

Forty-acre estate. Several acres formal or naturalistic gardens.

💲 Brochure. Trails. Semi-annual plant sales. Workshops and other events. House open for public tours at limited times. Guided group tours of house and/or gardens by appointment.

◀ Open daily May-August 10am-5pm, Sunday 11am-5pm. September daily 1-5pm, Sunday 11am-5pm. October, weekends only, noon-4pm. Closed November-April.

It's hard to know what to admire first here; Cranbrook has it all. We have the gardens to ourselves on this misty June morning, so we pretend it's all ours as we wander about. However, it's the estate of the late George and Ellen Scripps Booth of publishing fame. They were strong supporters of the Arts and Crafts Movement and founders of the Cranbrook Educational Community; their enthusiasm and good taste are apparent here. We suspect that treats lie ahead as we walk down the hemlock-shaded path and through The Pillars into woods shining with rhododendrons. Pinks, purples, and mauves, the favorite colors of Ellen Booth, are abundant in these woods today.

The sunken garden is an orderly riot of blue and white, a visual feast highlighted by false indigo (*Baptisia australis*), icy snow-in-summer (*Cerastium tomentosum*), and a lovely purple-throated white poppy. Bright blue doors in the garden's stone walls echo today's blue flowers but they would be pleasing even in winter. One doorway leads to the woodland garden, where deep pink phlox and yellow lady's slippers bloom among the lush greens of other wildlings.

The houseside herb garden, ruled by a Greek earth goddess, is gray, green, and lavender against red patio bricks. On the other side of the house, there will soon be an incredible peony display at the elegant reflecting pool, a pool surrounded today by crisp Siberian irises, relaxed daisies, silvery artemisias, and vigorous clumps of blue bachelor's buttons (*Centaurea montana*). Starry Oriental dogwoods (*Cornus kousa*) twinkle against the gray stone wall and dust the mounds of hosta at their feet with fallen petals. Summer will bring dramatic reflections of hibiscus and other heat-lovers to the pool.

At Cranbrook, there are gardens wherever you look. In spring, the Golden Glade is alight with daffodils, wildflowers, and flowering trees and the lakeside Henry Booth garden overflows with rhododendrons. The Bog Garden is particularly attractive in spring (when wildflowers bloom and before mosquitoes hatch) while the island Oriental Garden is at its best in summer. The terraces, lawns, and paths of Cranbrook offer exquisite vistas and cozy corners in a designed landscape that is never boring or over-formal.

For information contact the Cranbrook House and Gardens Auxiliary, 380 Lone Pine Road, Box 801, Bloomfield Hills MI 48303-0801. (313) 645-3149.

From Detroit or I-696 take Telegraph Road/US Route 24 north, or Woodward Avenue/Michigan Route 1 northwest, to Lone Pine Road. The estate is on the north side of Lone Pine, east of Telegraph and west of Woodward. There's parking on the grounds, with additional space available across Lone Pine in the Christ Church Cranbrook parking lot. (Don't miss the masses of rhododendrons, banks of daylilies, and other plantings around the church.)

Fair Lane, the Henry Ford estate
Dearborn

Extensive estate grounds. About 2 acres in rose, perennial, herb, and peony gardens. Jens Jensen landscape design.

Fee for house tours. Many plants labeled. Trails. Picnic facilities. Shop (in house). Workshops and other events. Group tours by appointment all year.
Grounds open daylight hours all year, although access may be limited in spring and fall due to university events. Closed Easter, Thanksgiving, Christmas, and New Year's days. Estate Walks April-October Tuesday and Wednesday 12:30 from the Visitor Center. Restaurant open all year Monday-Friday 11am-2pm, closed holidays and Friday after Thanksgiving.

On a walled terrace above the Rouge River, roses in early June bud promise later splendor. Today's shady borders are filled with lush ferns and the sky-blue flowers of Siberian bugloss (*Brunnera macrophylla*) and I can hear the river cascade that Jens Jensen designed. Every garden should have a waterfall in the background. The roses here and those nearer the house are merely a reminder of 10,000 roses that were tended by 20 full-time gardeners when the Fords lived at Fair Lane. A terrace near the house is blue today with the flowers of spiderwort, false indigo (*Baptisia australis*), Siberian and bearded irises, and elegant lupine. In the small herb garden, stately lovage (*Levisticum officinale*) towers above thymes, sages, and others of their ilk.

On a peony-bordered terrace that was designed for evening relaxation, a circular bed that once was a fountain holds miniature roses, begonias, and geraniums. The view from this airy space, through a Jensen allée of native species and across a meadow that still contains its Ford-designed watering system, ends at a wood's-edge pond that was sited to reflect summer sunsets. Undulating allée borders hold shrubs, sub-trees, tall conifers, and sturdy vines, including a healthy growth of poison ivy that *will* be colorful in autumn. Not far away, a most impressive weeping beech has grown from a stripling planted in 1938 to honor the Ford's golden wedding anniversary.

On weekdays you can lunch in the Pool Restaurant, an eatery built in the original swimming pool room, where the Poland water and soybeans of Mr. Ford's diet are still on the menu. Winter holidays bring exquisite decorations and a number of special events to the estate.

◀ Henry Ford spent many hours walking his meadow and river paths with presidents and princes, inventors (Thomas Edison was a favorite), folk heroes, and just plain folks. Mrs. Ford, president of the Women's National Farm and Garden Association for several years, delighted in leading guests through the gardens and grounds of Fair Lane. We can take a tour or wander on our own to relish the treasure they built.

For information contact The University of Michigan-Dearborn, Henry Ford Estate, Dearborn MI 48128-1491. (313) 593-5590.

From US Route 12, Michigan Avenue, exit for Evergreen north and follow signs for the Henry Ford Estate. Fair Lane is near Ford World Headquarters, the Henry Ford Museum, and Greenfield Village.

Anna Scripps Whitcomb Conservatory and Gardens
Belle Isle
Detroit MI 48207
(313) 267-7133

16,000 sq.ft. conservatory. 10 acres gardens and conservatory grounds on 985-acre island.

Brochure and maps. Many plants labeled. Trails. Picnic facilities. Group tours of conservatory by appointment.
Island and gardens open daylight hours every day. Conservatory open every day 9am-6pm. Floriculture greenhouses not open to the public.

The brochure says "There's always a flower show at Belle Isle" . . . and indeed there is. A huge floral clock welcomes you to the island (unless you arrive by boat) and offers a hint of the sights to come. Formal gardens and the conservatory grounds hold trimmed hedges, native Michigan trees, flowering bulbs, a broad array of annuals and perennials, and, for early autumn color, thousands of dahlias. Waterlilies and reflections of the conservatory dome enliven the Lily Pool's still waters.

Beneath that conservatory dome, tropical growth surrounds 60-foot palms as they reach toward the 85-foot-high ceiling. In the Tropical Room, a bit of jungle in the middle of the Detroit River, bananas and other tropical fruits grow among orchids, waxy stephanotis, and brilliant bougainvillea. Other rooms will beckon you: the Show House, site of the year's six seasonal flower shows; the Cactus Room, with its wide variety of plants from the American Southwest; and the Fernery, which contains a worldwide collection of ferns and their relatives. In 20 greenhouses associated with the conservatory, Detroit's Floriculture Unit raises countless plants (including 3,000 or more for the floral clock) to decorate the city's public areas. The Unit also offers a variety of printed materials on gardening and landscaping and will try to answer garden questions over the telephone.

Belle Isle has been a popular retreat since earliest colonial times, even while local farmers kept their hogs there. After the City of Detroit bought it in 1879, the parkscape was designed by Frederick Law Olmstead, architect of New York's Central Park. Today it's the most popular park in Detroit, a place of busy spots and restful corners, home of water, flowers, and woods . . . beauty for every taste.

For information contact the Detroit Recreation Department, Room 1707 Water Board Building, 735 Randolph Street, Detroit MI 48226. (313) 224-0112.

MacArthur Bridge carries the only road to Belle Isle; it's at the corner of East Grand Boulevard and East Jefferson, about three miles northeast of downtown Detroit. There are many ways to reach this point from the freeways and Interstate highways; use the Detroit city map on your Michigan road map.

Detroit Garden Center
Moross House
1460 East Jefferson
Detroit MI 48207
(313) 259-6363

Old-fashioned gardens around historic house on 33'x200' city lot.

Fee for house tours and some special events. Shop. Many plants labeled. Library. Picnic facilities. Seasonal plant sales. Workshops and special events. Group tours by appointment. Open all year Tuesday-Thursday 9:30am-3:30pm.

Intimate gardens and a wisteria-covered pergola decorate the grounds of Moross House, the oldest brick home in Detroit (1840s). On this land that was once part of a French "ribbon" farm, you'll see a small herb garden, a planting of wildflowers, shade beds, old-fashioned perennials, and a "dry" garden that requires little water. Inside Moross House, the Upstairs Shop offers garden-oriented items, "country" objects, Victorian decorative pieces, and antique linens and needlework. Murphy Memorial Library, also in the house, is home to a rare book collection and a broad range of horticultural reference materials. ▶

◀ You may want to attend the annual Open House on the First Saturday of May, when herb and perennial plants and used gardening books fill sale tables.

These walled gardens are a green oasis not far from the offices, hotels, and noise of downtown Detroit. Pick up a carry-out lunch and give yourself a quiet picnic treat here.

Exit I-375 at East Jefferson and go a quarter mile east to Moross House.

Heavenly Scent Herb Farm
13730 White Lake Road
Fenton MI 48430
(313) 629-9208

Commercial. One acre theme gardens. Large greenhouse. Production fields.

Catalog. Shop. Many plants labeled. Picnic facilities. Plant sales. Workshops and other special events.
Open April-December Tuesday-Saturday 10am-5pm. Open Sundays in December. Other hours by appointment.
Herbal Summer Fair the last weekend of August, Saturday 10am-5pm, Sunday 11am-5pm.

You'll know you've come to an extraordinary place when you enter Heavenly Scent's picket-fenced Friendship Garden. Today, in early June, deep purple lupines and irises of lavender and lively mauve are accented by masses of dainty coral bells and vigorous lemon yellow daylilies. Lavender bushes and sprawling lamb's-ears (*Stachys byzantina*) hint at attractive purple and magenta borders to come.

The hillside culinary garden is home to the largest tarragon plant I've ever seen, a fresh green wonder 4 feet in diameter that's surrounded by a variety of edible flowers. Persian star, the ornamental *Allium christophii*, joins lively chive blossoms and a range of garlics and uncommon onions in the allium bed. Stately lovage dominates another border, where deceptively delicate-looking bronze fennel asserts itself above lacy caraway and chervil. This garden and the adjacent picnic area overlook a spacious valley that, at this moment, contains a singing oriole.

Valerian (*V. officinalis*) will soon perfume the Fragrance Garden, where irises and scented geraniums are blooming and bees are mining lavender catmint flowers (*Nepeta* sp.). The nearby greenhouse shelters healthy plants and an impressive array of topiaries grown from rue (*Ruta graveolens*), rosemary, and scented geraniums. Captivating woodsy baskets are planted with low-growing herbs and minute rose plants.

Comfy benches, the sound of gentle fountains, stunning artemisia topiaries, cool breezes . . . all these are on the shady porch of the Heavenly Scent shop. It's *soooo* inviting, you'll find it hard to pull away and investigate the shop. Force yourself. Above a fine collection of books and baskets you'll see rafters hung with dried herbs and flowers, including pastel long-stemmed roses. Here, too, are culinary and gardening supplies and a myriad of other items you need. The Wedding Room holds unusual wreath forms, straw sculptures, and attractive items for herbal weddings.

In Heavenly Scent workshops you can learn a number of useful things, such as how to make herbal jewelry or how to start your own "Silver King Tree." Perhaps you'll visit the Herbal Summer Fair, an August event that includes demonstrations of 30 different herbal skills. No matter when or why you come to Heavenly Scent, you'll be glad you came.

From I-75 take Exit 101, Grange Hall Road. Take Grange Hall west to Fish Lake Road, then go south 2 miles to Fenton Road. Go west on Fenton one mile to Hickory Ridge, then south 2½ miles to Rose Center Road and west a mile to Heavenly Scent, on the left side of the road.
From US Route 23 (a much easier approach), use Exit 77 and go east on White Lake Road 4½ miles to Heavenly Scent. Be aware that White Lake becomes a sand and gravel road at its angular intersection with Fenton Road.

Grosse Pointe Garden Center, Inc.
32 Lake Shore Road
Grosse Pointe Farms MI 48236
(313) 881-4594

One-half acre. Trial beds. Herb garden. Rock garden.

Brochure. Many plants labeled. Library. Workshops and special events.
Gardens open daylight hours all year. Garden Center office and library open Tuesday-Thursday 10am-4pm. Closed August and December.

The lake breezes are refreshing and the shady hillside rock garden is deliciously cool on this otherwise sultry June day. Stately Siberian irises and the delicate pink blooms of low cotoneaster have replaced early spring flowers. Gentle hardy geraniums, small rose bushes, and crisp sedums add to the riches on this hill.

◀ Level ground holds the sunny trial/display garden, where 13 separate sections are designed and maintained by various local garden clubs. Unity is supplied from year to year and from section to section by ivy borders, low yew hedges, and familiar floral favorites. This year, most plantings contain geometric patterns or flowing ribbons of annuals but the "wren house" of white impatiens and burgundy ajuga and the snapdragon "bouquet" tied with a bow of low ageratum are designs reminiscent of more complex nineteenth-century mosaiculture, wherein pictures or geometric designs were "drawn" with closely set flowering plants and colorful foliage.

An ancient millstone in the center of the garden is surrounded by herbal theme beds. The Sacred Garden offers the lovely contrast of lady's-mantle (*Alchemilla mollis*), purple sage, and love-in-a-mist (*Nigella* sp.); the Culinary Garden boasts glorious chives and sunny calendula; and sweet, sweet irises tower over pungent catmint (*Nepeta* sp.), acrid santolina, and spicy clove pinks in the Fragrance Garden. Perennial borders beyond the hedge, lush with late spring flowers and foliage, will be charming all season.

Garden Center offices are in the Grosse Pointe War Memorial Center, formerly the Alger mansion and now a community arts and social center; the gardens are at the northeast corner of the building. At the building's *southwest* corner, the formal garden is possibly at its most beautiful today. Graceful wisteria vines, trained and twisted into sturdy flat-topped trees, drape the courtyard with creamy-white blossoms and eclipse the hedge mazes, attractive reflecting pool, and rose standards. It's a stunning sight that's a bonus to our Garden Center visit.

From downtown Detroit, go north on Jefferson East; it becomes Lake Shore Drive when it leaves Detroit.
From I-94 take Exit 225 and go east on Vernier Road to Lake Shore Drive, then south about three miles.
The War Memorial Center is on the east side of Lake Shore; look for the signs. Parking will be limited if there is an event at the Memorial but there's usually space at the church next door.

Edsel and Eleanor Ford House
1100 Lake Shore Road
Grosse Pointe Shores MI 48236
(313) 884-4222

Eighty-acre estate. One acre in rose garden, perennial allée, cutting garden. Jens Jensen landscape design. ▶

◀ 💲♿☕ Brochure. Special events. Group tours by appointment. Guided public tours Wednesday-Sunday afternoons.
Open all year except major holidays. Grounds generally open 11:30am-5pm, specific hours vary with the season. Tea Room open Wednesday-Saturday 11:30am-2pm.

How delightful it is to walk these nearly flawless lawns and gardens early on a misty June morning . . . now, if ever, a perfect day. Our visit begins at the Activities Center, where a hospitable pavilion overlooks the current cutting garden, a garden that represents the vegetable and flower gardens and the orchards that once stood here. Cutting garden flowers are the varieties and colors favored by Mrs. Ford, although those colors aren't yet apparent today.

Our ticket is for the grounds only, so we aren't invited aboard the shuttle bus that house tourers ride (the mansion is about a quarter mile from the Activities Center). In spite of the intermittent drizzle, I want to walk in this landscape where heavily blooming hawthorns stand in lawns and glorious rhododendrons sing in wooded spots. The central meadow/lawn and its plantings were carefully designed by Jensen to be most beautiful at sunrise and sunset. We are here long after sunrise but these spaces are, nevertheless, eminently satisfying.

Across the meadow lies the swimming pool of which we all dream, a large free-form pool crystalline blue and surrounded by rhododendrons and birch trees, hemlocks and pines, all underplanted with ferns, hostas, and wildflowers. Daffodils have bloomed in masses around this woodland delight. It's clearly an impractical pool, one that requires a staff just to keep it clear of pine needles, leaves, and spent petals. But if you can have this pool you'll have the staff.

Soon, two thousand white and yellow hybrid tea roses, accented by forget-me-nots and other blue flowers, will fill the rose garden's wagon-wheel design. Climbing roses explore the surrounding wall where, today, a golden rain tree supplies the only bright color in the garden. The roses are still in bud but in a few weeks that wall will contain and concentrate their lovely scents and cheerful colors.

The New Garden, built where the Ford children used to play, is a cheerful allée of flowering trees and shrubs and masses of old-fashioned perennials. Hordes of bluebells (*Mertensia virginica*) have bloomed below the trees and shrubs. The allée will be inviting all season and into winter, when seedheads, mature berries, and skeletal trees become the display.

The lucky traveler will visit here late in the week, when the tea room, an airy inside garden, is open. The Ford House hosts a full schedule of exhibits, childrens' programs, performances, tours, and other special events. ▶

◀ As we waited for the entry gates to open, a foreign visitor looked around and pronounced, "This is every American's dream." Actually, few of us can expect to own beauty on this scale and we're thankful that we can enjoy it here for a comparative pittance.

From I-94 take Exit 225 Vernier Road. Go east on Vernier to Lake Shore Road, then north about a mile to the Ford House, on the east side of the road.

Hunter's Creek Perennial Gardens
2555 South Lapeer Road
Lapeer MI 48446
(313) 667-3891 or (313) 667-0635

Commercial. Over an acre of greenhouses and shadehouses. 1½ acres display gardens and lily ponds. 2 acres production fields.

♿ Catalog. Most plants labeled. Plant sales. Workshops and special events.
Open every day April-December. Spring 8am-8pm, summer and autumn 8am-5pm.

Extensive sale yards, inviting greenhouses, pleasing display gardens, and lush container plantings are among the attractions at Hunter's Creek. Shady plant-filled porches and a small farmyard menagerie are part of the picture too... but organically grown perennial plants are the featured attractions here. You'll see all your old favorites as well as more recent introductions and a few of the less common old-timers. Ornamental grasses wave above an array of succulent ground covers that looks like an expansive (and expensive) Oriental carpet. These plants and others are used to good advantage in the waterfall garden, the conifer/grass garden, and the rock garden, where we are attracted to a stunning low allium whose name no one seems to remember. Nearby, a weathered half-barrel is topped by an impressive sprawl of angular *Euphorbia myrsinites*.

The greenhouses here are like gardens, beautifully arranged and full of luxuriant plants. An irresistible variety of Oriental and Iceland poppies fills most of one house. Brilliant bougainvillea and leather-leaved, pink-flowered mandevilla bring exotic color to the clematis house where, on this early June day, few of the clematis are blooming. Walking through these buildings feels like a treasure hunt because nearly every one of them holds botanical treats. We couldn't possibly carry home all the plants that appeal to us here.

Perhaps you'll come to Hunter Creek in August or September, when you can buy dahlia flowers by the armsful. Also in September, the bounty of two acres of everlastings and flowers fills the barn and there are workshops on growing perennials and classes in using dried flowers. A more extensive gift shop will be added in 1993 but Hunter's Creek seems nearly perfect now.

From I-69 take Exit 156. Go south on Michigan Route 24 about 3½ miles to the large red barn that marks Hunter's Creek Perennial Gardens.

Dow Gardens
Midland

Over 60 acres. Display gardens and naturalistic landscape.

$ ♿ Brochure. Shop. Many plants labeled. Library. Trails. Seasonal plant sales. Special events. Specialized or group tours by prior arrangement.
Open every day except Thanksgiving, Christmas Eve and Day, and New Year's Eve and Day 10am-sunset.

Dow has been called "a truly American garden" because it was developed literally from the ground up, every plant and tree and shrub carefully selected and precisely sited for the best effect. That sounds rather calculated and sterile but Dow is more than that. It's a place to wander along a stream or study reflections in a placid pool, a place to admire vermilion bridges in the snow, a place for marveling at witchhazel's crepe flowers in February. Dow has contoured flower beds, casual plantings of herbs and wildflowers, meadows, copses, waterfalls, specimen trees, and thousands of species of green growing things.

It's easy to forget that, in the midst of all this, the Dow Gardens fulfill a major educational mission. Adult education opportunities cover a wide range of horticultural topics, children can choose from a number of activities designed for them, and internships involve collegiate professionals-in-training. Even the casual visitor may learn a little something because nearly all plants in the garden are identified with common and botanical names.

Come to Dow in spring for the bulbs and flowering trees or in summer for the All-America Selections gardens. Perhaps you'll visit Dow for the peak of the fall color or in the depth of snowy winter. Whenever you spend time at Dow Gardens, you'll find it a most satisfying experience.

For details contact Dow Gardens, 1018 West Main Street, Midland MI 48640. (517) 631-2677.

◀ *From I-75 go west on US Route 10 about 15 miles to Eastman Road, then south about 2 miles to the garden entrance at the intersection of Eastman and St. Andrews roads.*

Sunshine Farm and Garden
2460 North Wixom Road
Milford MI 48042
(313) 685-2204

Commercial. Over 4 acres. Theme gardens, production fields, 2 greenhouses.

♿ Catalog. Fee for Herb Fair. Shop. Many plants labeled. Picnic facilities. Plant sales. Workshops and other special events. Group tours and activities by prior arrangement. Open April-December Wednesday-Sunday 10am-5pm.

Imagine feathery *Artemisia arborescens* gone giant . . . these are the 8-foot topiaries that guard Sunshine's summer herb gardens. I usually consider artemisias invasive garden thugs but I could make an exception for these beauties. Sunshine's other theme gardens are equally satisfying; pieces of slate carry Shakespeare's words, Biblical references are inscribed on wooden shakes, and all the gardens are well-planted and thriving. An early June burst of purples and reds draws us to the extensive rockery, where deep purple columbines and violet phlox mingle with poppies, dianthus, and brilliant coral bells (actually, *scarlet* bells) and a life-sized wooden great blue heron peers at lively goldfish in the small pool.

In the greenhouse, scented geraniums of many perfumes are surrounded by a fine selection of herb plants, including some rarely seen varieties: peppery watercress (*Nasturtium officinale*), indigo (*Indigofera tinctoria*), and, for your poison garden, the handsome serrated leaves and wine-veined flowers of henbane (*Hyoscyamus niger*) and the dusty wine cups of *Atropa belladonna*. Here, too, are cheerful miniature roses and elegant topiaries made from rosemary and myrtle.

Caged peafowl preen and scream in their peacocky way, gentle Morgan horses roam the adjacent pasture, and, near the shop, cast "stone" critters share space with picnic tables. The shop holds all the good things you expect *and* some appealing less common items. Perhaps your garden needs a bee skep, a handsome sundial, or a mellow wind chime. Recipe cards feature edible flowers and the seeds with which to grow them. Corked glass bottles and jars will preserve your herbal products while showing them to best advantage. I'm entranced by the array of teapots and teacups, any of which would surely make my teas and tisanes taste even better. ▶

◀ Spring and fall at Sunshine bring a full schedule of classes and workshops and there's always the September Country Herb Fair to visit. Obviously, your time at Sunshine Farm can be more than a simple herbal experience.

From I-96 take Exit 159 for Wixom. Follow Wixom Road about 5 miles north, then west, to Sunshine Farm on the north side of the road.

The Bonsai Center
101 North Groesbeck Highway
Mt. Clemens MI 48043
(313) 465-9555

Commercial. Large greenhouse, shade, and display areas.

♿ Catalog. Shop. Most plants labeled. Plant sales. Workshops and other events. Open Monday-Thursday and Saturday 10am-5pm, Friday 10am-7pm, Sunday 11am-3pm. Closed Friday evening in winter.

Imagine yourself in a forest of diminutive trees and shrubs. The Bonsai Center's sale yard and shadehouse offer over 2,000 potted specimens that are well on their way to maturity. If you want to control your bonsai almost from the beginning, you can choose from over 5,000 "starter" plants, each personally selected by the Center's owner. Inspiration will come to you in the exhibit area, where a 135-year-old white spruce is the patriarch among 50 or more museum-quality bonsai specimens.

There are other unique perennials here. You'll find alpines and dwarf conifers for rock or miniature gardens, hardy garden bamboos, and, in the greenhouse, unusual tropical houseplants. The shop holds a fine selection of pottery and tools, rocks and soils, and beautiful books and magazines, all with the emphasis on bonsai. For our gardenscapes, there are imported hand-carved stone lanterns and an assortment of bamboo fencings.

Guest artists from around the world join the Center's owner to conduct the ongoing schedule of classes, lectures, and demonstrations. I feel cumbersome in the presence of bonsai but I find them absolutely enchanting; it would be a treat to take a class, surrounded by bonsai, and to start my own treasured tree here.

The Bonsai Center is at the intersection of Groesbeck Highway (Michigan Route 97) and Cass Avenue in Mt. Clemens. Both roads are probably shown on the Detroit area enlargement of your road map.

Grass Roots Nursery
24765 Bell Road
New Boston MI 48164
(313) 654-2405 or (313) 753-9200

Commercial. Specialists in water gardens. Over 5½ acres gardens. 10 acres production fields.

 Shop. Many plants labeled. Workshops.
Open February 16-December 24 Monday-Saturday 9am-5pm, Sunday noon-5pm. Summer hours until 6pm Monday-Friday. Closed December 24-February 15.

Bog plants and water lilies, fish and other pond critters, all kinds of wetland plants and animals flourish here at Grass Roots. The gardens and greenhouses also offer general nursery stock, bonsai specimens, plants for shady spots, herbs, and selected plant rarities. Exotic birds add lively color and occasional song to the nursery's visual treats.

In Grass Roots' shop you'll find supplies for your water garden (including the pond forms themselves) as well as dried flowers, gifts, garden statuary, and general gardening supplies. Periodic workshops will teach you to use dried flowers and plants in arrangements. But it will be the shining ponds and their gardens that entrance you.

You can see Grass Roots Nursery from I-275. To get there, take Exit 11 (South Huron Road) and go west a short distance to Bell Road. Go south on Bell a mile to the nursery.

The Gathered Herb
12114 North State Road
Otisville MI 48463
(313) 631-6572

Commercial. Over an acre. Specimen, display, and production gardens. 20'x48' greenhouse.

Catalog. Shop. Many plants labeled. Plant sales. Workshops and other events.
Open April-mid-December Tuesday-Saturday 10am-6pm. Open every day in May. Spring open house in late May, winter open house late November.

◄ An impressive stand of statuesque angelica (*Angelica archangelica*) welcomes us to these attractive hillside gardens. Spreads of cheery golden oregano and ferny yarrow accent terraced plantings of dwarf conifers, heathers, and sturdy herbs. A throaty bullfrog calls from the shallow pond and a shaded bench invites us to pause and admire the view.

Handsome brass sundials mark the entry to The Gathered Herb's tasteful shop, where particularly lovely dried flowers hang above herbal cosmetics and treatments, books, essential oils, and the bronze faucet figures I'm lusting after.

Herbs of many varieties, including scented geraniums and other plants you won't find at your neighborhood garden center, fill sales benches and the greenhouse. Red-veined lyre-leaved sage (*Salvia lyrata*) sits among wild ginger and other native wildflowers. Patchouli (*Pogostemon patchouli*) and several unusual eucalypti release their exotic scents to a gentle touch. In one greenhouse corner, delicate mini-roses contrast with tall and lusty rosemary bushes and equally robust scented geraniums.

Life is especially festive here during the May and November open houses, when herbal comestibles and special items and activities are featured. But you can increase your herbal knowledge in a workshop, peruse the shop and the greenhouse, or relax and enjoy the landscape and the gardens at The Gathered Herb at almost any time.

From I-69 take Exit 145 for Davison (Michigan Route 15). Go north on MI 15 (State Road) about 15 miles to The Gathered Herb.
From I-75 use Exit 131 for Clio and go east on MI 57 (Vienna Road) about 10 miles to its end at MI 15/State Road. The Gathered Herb is about 600 feet north of this "T."

Brookville Gardens
7885 Brookville Road
Plymouth MI 48170
(313) 455-8602

Commercial. Two acres display gardens and production fields.

♿ Catalog. Shop. Many plants labeled. Plant sales. Workshops and other events. Open April 1-June 27 Wednesday-Sunday 10am-5pm. July 1-December 19 Wednesday-Saturday 10am-5pm, closed Sunday. ▶

◀ These attractive houseside gardens began as private landscaping; they're now the Brookville display gardens, where customers can see how the plants will look in *their* yards. Silver-lace vine (*Polygonum aubertii*) climbs the house chimney to make a beacon for visitors, a lovely announcement that "the gardens are here." Rhododendrons are flamboyant against the house and decks on this day in early June. Perennial borders, full of irises, beebalms (*Monarda* sp.), and other traditional favorites, lie below trees and along fences. I'm particularly charmed by the lavenders, blues, and pinks of appealing meadow sage (*Salvia pratensis*).

A circular herb demonstration garden, bordered today by lively magenta soapwort (*Saponaria ocymoides*), sits in front of the house. Here are culinary herbs, dye plants, sages, plants for herb teas, and a special assortment of green things reputed to have magical properties.

The Brookville shop offers an especially good selection of useful books and booklets as well as wreaths and baskets, essential oils, and dried plant materials. Plants for herbs (over 250 varieties) and ornamentals fill a small shade house and sunny shelves. You can learn almost anything you want about gardening, herbs, and herbcrafts at Brookville; the calendar holds one or two workshops nearly every week from April through mid-December. Open houses commemorate Arbor Day, Columbus Day, Halloween, and almost any other "day" that deserves a party. The new greenhouse and expanded shop space will increase the attractions at Brookville but there's ample fun to be had and gardens to be enjoyed now.

From Michigan Route 14 between Plymouth and Ann Arbor, take Exit 15, Gotfredson Road. Go north on Gotfredson until it turns and joins Brookville Road. Go west on Brookville to Curtis Road. The gardens are on the northwest corner of Brookville and Curtis.
From the Plymouth-Ann Arbor Road, go north on Curtis to Brookville Road.

Herbal Endeavors
3618 South Emmons Avenue
Rochester Hills MI 48063
(313) 852-0796

Commercial. Four gardens, emphasis on fragrant plants.

Catalog. Shop. Many plants labeled. Workshops. Strongly suggested that you call before visiting. Open by appointment or by chance. ▶

Medieval folks planted houseleeks (*Sempervivens* spp.) on their roofs to ward off lightning; today, houseleeks, tansy, mugwort, and other useful plants fill Herbal Endeavors' attractive Medieval Garden. Nearby, the Early English Cottage Garden boasts traditional scented plants, selected British favorites that thrive in this part of Michigan. These lush gardens are a source for the scented oils and herbal products made by their owner, a teaching resource for her, and a relaxing treat for visitors. Periodic open houses feature garden tours, herbal goodies, and aromatic fresh-cut bouquets.

The shop at Herbal Endeavors offers herb-centered books, herbal gifts, personal care products, "one of the finest collections of essential oils and perfume-making supplies available anywhere," and the popular Aromatherapy for Beginners Kit. Classes here cover such topics as gardening with herbs, making perfumes, building pomanders, and include an herbal work-study program. Because the owner does a great deal of teaching, she's often not at the site but, if you call, a recording will direct you to the gardens and let you know her schedule. Be persistent . . . it will be worth the effort.

From I-75 use Exit 77 (Michigan Route 59) and go east on MI 59 for 10 or 12 miles to Dequindre Road. Go north about a mile on Dequindre to Auburn Road, then west on Auburn about a half mile to Emmons Avenue. Go south on Emmons to Herbal Endeavors, the last house on the right.

Saginaw Art Museum
126 North Michigan Avenue
Saginaw MI 48602
(517) 754-2491

Two-acre site. 1905 house/art museum. Period gardens under restoration.

Brochure and garden guide. Special events.
Museum and gardens open Tuesday-Saturday 10am-5pm, Sunday 1-5pm. Closed Monday and holidays.

Luscious scent, the perfume of a stunning peony allée, drifts across the museum's gardens in late spring. In this Italianate setting you'll find a formal ▶

> **FYI** "Aromatherapy," a term seen frequently in current gardening and herb journals, is ". . . the use of pure, high quality essential oils to enhance the quality of life." It may mean placing a bowl of spicy potpourri near your favorite chair, choosing scented bath oils according to your mood or needs, or having a unique perfume blended to reflect your personality. The origins of these practices are lost in time; only the name is recently devised.

layout of planting beds, a handsome pergola, and a pedimented tool shed that speaks of classic Rome, an unusual tool shed indeed. By today's garden standards, formal Italian gardens can seem rather stilted but *these* garden beds hold exuberant mixed plantings in turn-of-the-century American style. Siberian irises and tall delphiniums, in all their blues and whites and purples, guard beds where coreopsis, sundrops (*Oenothera* spp.), and hollyhocks will shine later in the season. Garden phlox, that sweet essence of late summer, and heady nicotianas will be followed by the utter charm of silvery-pink fall-blooming anemones. These gardens, with all their sweetly scented flowers, please the nose as well as the eyes and, in autumn, pungent, brilliant chrysanthemums end the garden's season with a flourish.

The museum possesses the landscape blueprint of the gardens that originally surrounded this handsome villa. The exact plant varieties that were installed in 1905 are cited on the plan and, with the help of a recent grant, the museum is replacing newer cultivars, lovely as they may be, with historically correct varieties. The restoration is a gradual process and you may never notice disturbance of the garden's beauty. There are garden-related lectures at the museum and, to the joy of all concerned, an occasional garden party. Imagine the pleasures of a genteel celebration in these lush and colorful surroundings. But, even without a planned event, your visit to these admirable gardens will be a special occasion.

From I-75 take I-675 toward downtown Saginaw. Exit I-675 at Davenport on the west side of the river, then turn left onto Hill Street. Stay on Hill to its T intersection with Congress. Turn left and take Congress to the next stop sign, at Michigan Avenue. Turn right onto Michigan, drive past 2 hospitals and a stoplight, and look for the fieldstone church on your left. The museum's driveway is just past the church. If you reach the intersection of Michigan and Remington, you've gone too far.

Saginaw-Tokushima Friendship Garden
Japanese Cultural Center and Tea House
Ezra Rust Drive and Washington Avenue
Saginaw

3½ acre Japanese garden within large city park. 5,000 sq.ft. perennial garden nearby.

♿ Fee for some teahouse functions. Shop. Special events. Group tours and formal tea ceremony by appointment. Trails and picnic facilities in park.
Garden open during summer Tuesday-Sunday 9am-6pm. Teahouse hours by arrangement.

◀ This garden of greenery, stones, and water is young by Japanese standards. The oldest plantings are only little over 20 years old but stone lanterns, winding paths, and thriving plants provide quiet refuge. Gentle watersounds enhance the wind's piney murmur and sunlight sparkles on the manmade stream. Flowering plum trees and thousands of daffodils bring spring exuberance but the vermilion bridge, arching above the stream, brings good fortune to the garden and its viewers in all seasons. Here is a place to stroll through beauty, to pause and think, to refresh your mind and body.

The intimate *roji* ("mountain path") garden leads you to Awa Saginaw An, reputed to be one of the western world's most authentic Japanese teahouses. It was designed by a Japanese architect, built of traditional materials by local and Japanese craftsmen, and stands on land formally deeded to Tokushima, Saginaw's Japanese Sister City. Tours of the teahouse, classes in several aspects of Japanese culture, and several special events are offered here.

A Japanese garden of this style is a treasure of greens, a drama of texture and scale, a fund of sunlight and shadow . . . and home to few dramatic floral displays. The nearby formal garden supplies season-long color through its wealth of roses and perennials. Some of the roses and other features here are transplants from the Saginaw Rose Garden, a now-defunct installation. That garden, a project of local rose societies and Saginaw's Park Department, was planted above the city's freshwater reservoir in only 30 inches of soil. When possible chemical leaching and the weight of maintenance equipment became a concern, the garden was dismantled and its best specimens moved to the formal garden.

Saginaw has been a major garden center and a city that, at one time, had large greenhouses and a 15-man horticultural staff. Regional economic vicissitudes have greatly reduced those but these gardens near Lake Linton will make you glad you came to Saginaw.

For more information contact the Japanese Cultural Center, 1315 South Washington, Saginaw MI 48601, (517) 759-1648, or the Saginaw Parks Department, 1574 South Washington, Saginaw MI 48601, (517) 753-5411.

From I-75/US Route 23 take Michigan Route 46 west to Washington Avenue. Go north a short distance to Ezra Rust Drive. The gardens are near the northwest corner of this intersection.

Hidden Lake Gardens
Michigan Route 50
Tipton MI 49287
(517) 431-2060

◀ 670-acre arboretum. 9,000 sq.ft. conservatory. All-America Selections garden.

💲♿ Brochure. Shop. Many plants labeled. Library. Trails. Picnic facilities. Workshops and special events. Group tours by reservation.
Grounds and conservatory open every day April-October 8am-dusk, November-March 8am-4pm. Visitor Center open April-October weekdays 8am-4:30pm, weekends and holidays noon-6pm, November-March weekdays 8am-4pm.

Specimen trees stud the rolling meadows that greet you at Hidden Lake, where six miles of picturesque auto roads wind through woods, past glacial bogs and moraines, to secluded copses or grand vistas, and across wildflower meadows and mowed expanses to woody plant collections and habitat demonstrations. Over 5 miles of hiking trails lead you to the more remote meadows, lakes, and woods.

All roads lead to the conservatory, where nearly everything in the temperate house is blooming on this early June day; about the only plant *not* in lively color is the Christmas cactus. Fuchsias, orchids, gesneriads, and hibiscus are arranged according to the heat and light they need to be successful houseplants. The adjacent lath house holds a fine array of fancy-leaved begonias, unusual ferns, and splendid bonsais. Among the bonsais, a miniature grove of crisp 15-year-old Japanese hornbeams is young compared to the 75-year-old white cedar and its contorted 2-foot height. A littleleaf linden (*Tilia cordata*) stands alone in 3-foot splendor, its 20 years of controlled growth covered with winged bud clusters.

The conservatory's tropical dome harbors mature palms and other "houseplants" as well as plants of economic value that are grouped by use. Among these sources of gums, flavors, and tropical fruits I met the exotic producer of toothsome macadamia nuts. In the desert house, euphorbias in many forms stand near clusters of gasterias and haworthias while cacti and echeverias are neighbors to agaves and crassulas. Spikes of the soft orange tubes that are *Aloe vera* flowers rise above the aloe collection. Behind the conservatory, handsome dwarf conifers climb a sunny hillside and the nearby picnic area suggests shaded relaxation.

The Visitor Center holds a well-stocked shop and ecology exhibits that explain the botany and geology of the area, the Irish Hills. Horticulture books and natural science field guides fill shelves among assorted small gift items and an attractive selection of T-shirts whose printed designs range from flamboyant hibiscus to the swans of Hidden Lake. The Center hosts several adult non-credit courses and other special events throughout the year. Not far from the Visitor Center, small demonstration/AAS gardens hold irises, a few perennials, and a colorful array of annuals.

In spring and summer these rolling acres sing with flowering trees and shrubs and thousands of wildflowers and naturalized bulbs; in autumn, hardwood trees blaze on the hills. There are beautiful and interesting things to be seen in every direction, at every time of year, at Hidden Lake.

Hidden Lake Garden is on the north side of Michigan Route 50 a short distance west of Tipton.

Michigan: Southwest

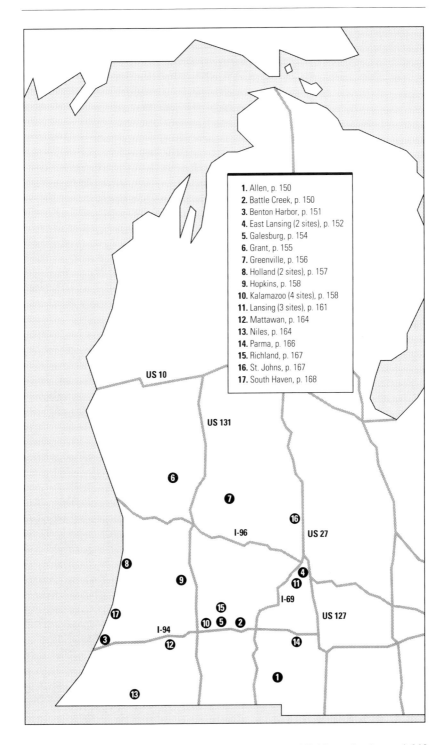

1. Allen, p. 150
2. Battle Creek, p. 150
3. Benton Harbor, p. 151
4. East Lansing (2 sites), p. 152
5. Galesburg, p. 154
6. Grant, p. 155
7. Greenville, p. 156
8. Holland (2 sites), p. 157
9. Hopkins, p. 158
10. Kalamazoo (4 sites), p. 158
11. Lansing (3 sites), p. 161
12. Mattawan, p. 164
13. Niles, p. 164
14. Parma, p. 166
15. Richland, p. 167
16. St. Johns, p. 167
17. South Haven, p. 168

The Little Farm Herb Shop
146 West Chicago Road (US Route 12)
Allen MI 49227
(517) 869-2822

Commercial. Small display gardens of traditional flowers and herbs.

♿ Catalog. Shop. Many plants labeled. Seasonal plant sales. Workshops and special events. Open mid-March-December 22 Monday-Saturday 11am-5pm.

Delectable scents escape through open windows to greet us as we approach the Little Farm shop on a warm June day. This hundred-year-old building, a former chicken coop, surely has never smelled so good before. Here are potpourri, and the supplies with which to make it, and a fine assortment of teas and seasonings, including Shaker herbs from Sabbathday Lake. Here, too, are sun dials and garden sculpture, an excellent collection of garden-oriented books and stationery, and lots of other good things the garden-lover needs. The nearby carriage house is becoming additional sales space, a site for herb and garden workshops, and display space for garden sculpture and furniture.

Sturdy herbs and charming "cottage garden" flowers will soon fill the space between Little Farm's two buildings, the revitalized chicken coop and the renovated carriage house. You'll feel right at home in this cozy enclosure that contains a fragrant garden of lavenders, thymes, and silvery lisianthus, a basil collection, and colorful borders. Over 250 different herbs and old-fashioned plants inhabit the garden's sales tables during spring and early summer.

Allen calls itself "the antique capital of Michigan"; take a break from "old stuff" and refresh yourself at this shop and its gardens. Better yet, treat yourself to Little Farm *first*.

US Route 12 is Chicago Road, the central street of Allen. The Little Farm is on the north side of Chicago Road, between South Allen Road and Michigan Route 149.

Leila Arboretum
Battle Creek

Seventy-two acres. Arboretum/park under restoration.

♿ Trails. Picnic facilities. Seasonal plant sales.
Open daylight hours all year.

▶

◀ On this early September evening, the arboretum is a cool and peaceful haven. Tall trees stand on rolling hillsides and shade-loving plants have spread themselves in the Hemlock Garden. Walkers, bicyclists, and joggers are enjoying the smooth, paved trail that winds through the park.

Leila Arboretum is a botanical asset that's under restoration and revitalization. Once the site of the Battle Creek Country Club, it was a flourishing botanical garden in the 1920s. But the Depression, World War II, and post-war financial difficulties led to its deterioration. In 1982, Leila Arboretum Society was formed to begin restoration and redevelopment. Current plans include a greenhouse, a conservatory, research areas, an amphitheater, a wetlands area, and extended gardens. The Kingman Museum of Natural History and The Pioneer Homestead, an authentic 1850s log cabin, are already here; future developments will complement their offerings. It's a very pleasant park right now, a fine place for a picnic or a walk. It will be interesting to watch it evolve back into a full-fledged arboretum with gardens.

For information on development of the arboretum contact the Leila Arboretum Society, 20th at West Michigan, Battle Creek MI 49017. (616) 969-0270.

From I-94 take Exit 95 (Helmer Road) north to Business Route US 94, then go east on BR 94 about a mile to 20th Street. Go north on 20th about a mile and a half to West Michigan (MI 89) and turn east. The Arboretum entrance is on your left in the middle of the first block.

The Herb Barn
1955 Greenley Avenue
Benton Harbor MI 49022
(616) 927-2044

Commercial. Four acres. Herb theme gardens.

♿ Some gravel paths. Catalog. Shop. Many plants labeled. Plant sales. Workshops and other special events.
Open Monday-Friday 10am-5pm, Saturday 10am-4pm. May-December, summer Sundays and holidays noon-4pm. Closed December 22-January 22, Easter Sunday, and Thanksgiving Day.

Herb-named garden cats may welcome you to the Herb Barn . . . or they may choose to lie under the artemisias and watch you enjoy the gardens. The theme gardens entertain us and provide many ideas for our own gardens;

today, jugs of herb vinegar are tucked away among the plants to brew in the late-August heat. We particularly enjoy the circular Pizza Garden, where wedge-shaped beds of oreganos, basils, peppers, tomatoes, and onions bring on thoughts of lunch. The Tussy-Mussy Garden, concentric rings of small flowers and everlastings, is a giant nosegay. Common and less common plants, such as cardoon (*Cynara cardunculus*), heliotrope, and a fancy oregano (*Origanum pulchella*) inhabit the greenhouse. Goats and rabbits and play equipment in the nearby "Nature Area" provide entertainment for those who want something more active than garden-viewing.

In the shade of the shop's grape arbor, we admire succulent grapes and an appealing menagerie of terra cotta animals. The shop tempts us with luscious aromas and a fine selection of dried plant materials, including tiny rosebuds that still smell like roses. Here are soaps and scents, seeds and seasonings, herb and gardening books, and particularly attractive stationery. Freshly cut herbs are often available in late summer and early autumn.

The Herb Barn's seasonal herb festivals include demonstrations, displays, and delicious herb-based refreshments. Their full schedule of workshops covers a wide variety of herb-related topics. Festivals, workshops, gardens, and shop . . . there's something to enjoy at the Herb Barn almost any time of the year.

From I-94 take Exit 29 to Meadowbrook, which is near the entrance ramp on the east side of I-94. Follow Meadowbrook a mile or so to Greenley. Turn left onto Greenley and go just a short distance to The Herb Barn.

Beal Botanical Garden
Michigan State University, North Campus
Between the MSU Library and the Intramural Sports Center on West Circle Drive
East Lansing

Five acres. Theme gardens and horticultural collections.

(For barrier-free access, use the walkway from Kalamazoo Street.) Many plants labeled. Food usually available at Kellogg Center.
Open daylight hours.

Beautiful Beal Botanical Garden, the oldest continuously operated botanical garden in the US, is a teaching garden, a project of the Botany and Grounds Department of Michigan State University. Consequently, it's well-organized into theme gardens and almost all plants are identified. In addition to the aggregations you might expect, you'll find plantings of woodland food plants, injurious plants (those that cause rashes, have thorns, or are somehow poisonous), nectar plants for honeybees, oil-producing plants, and more and more. Here is the only labeled *weed* collection I've ever seen but if you're faced with a persistent green pest it's good to know what you're fighting.

On this warm September afternoon, plants near the buildings quiver but there's no breeze; beneath the ferns and impatiens, ground squirrels dash about burying acorns. An impressive collection of ferns, ground covers, and small shrubs fills the space between the walk and the buildings. Wedding celebrants in a garden alcove are enjoying open skies and natural beauty beyond the florist's capabilities. Beal Garden contains no statuary, no artful flower beds, no fountains or waterfalls. It has, however, tidy, healthy plant collections among mature trees, and the Red Cedar River in the background.

Kellogg Center, a well-known conference center, stands among handsome perennials and tall evergreens just across Kalamazoo Street from the garden. Most of the MSU north campus is attractively planted, a garden in itself.

For information contact the Director, Beal Garden, B-110A Plant and Soil Science Building, Michigan State University, East Lansing MI 48824. (517) 355-0348.

From I-496 take the Trowbridge exit to Harrison, then Harrison north through the MSU campus to Kalamazoo Street. Turn right onto Kalamazoo and cross the Red Cedar River to the north campus. Beal Garden is on your right, between the river and the buildings. Kellogg Center is on your left. Well-marked Visitor Parking is available ahead on the West Circle. Or, go when classes aren't in session and have access to ample parking. You might also enjoy a visit to the MSU Library at the far end of the garden.

Michigan State University Horticultural Demonstration Gardens
Plant and Soil Science Building
North campus, off Bogue Street
East Lansing

Seven acres (when complete in 1993). Children's Garden. All-American Rose Selection garden. Annual and perennial gardens.

♿ Small fee for parking. Many plants labeled. When complete the gardens will host a full schedule of special events. Group tours will be available by prior arrangement.
Open April 1-November 1 during daylight hours.

◀ This Children's Garden is designed to appeal to children, not maintained by children; it includes a pizza garden, a plant maze, a garden for story-telling, and a dancing chime. Other installations are the rose garden, an informal perennial garden, and a formal garden of annuals around a fountain and reflecting pool. These new plantings are a result of the Horticultural Department's move to the Plant and Soil Sciences Building.

For information contact the Director, Horticultural Gardens, B-110A Plant and Soil Science Building, Michigan State University, East Lansing MI 48824. (517) 355-0348.

From I-496 take the Trowbridge Road exit and turn right onto Harrison. Follow Harrison across the first set of railroad tracks and turn left onto Service Road. Go across Farm Lane to Bogue Street, then turn left across another set of railroad tracks and you'll see the parking lot on your left. There is a small fee for parking. These gardens are about a 20-minute walk from Beal Garden.

Ensata Gardens
9823 East Michigan Avenue
Galesburg MI 49053
(616) 665-7500

Commercial grower of Japanese and Siberian iris. One-quarter acre display gardens. 80 acres production fields.

♿ Turf paths. Catalog. Many plants labeled. Suggested you call before a visit.
Open June and July *only*, by appointment or by chance.

Irises, irises, symbol of the Greek rainbow goddess, fitting messengers of the gods, graceful Siberian irises, stately Japanese irises, truly a rainbow of colors . . . these are the specialty at Ensata, whose gardens surround a handsome nineteenth-century brick home and an ancient dairy barn. Visit Ensata in June for the symphony of Siberian irises (*I. siberica*) and in early July for the glory of the Japanese irises (*I. ensata*, formerly *I. kaempferi* Hort.). The latter are particularly beautiful in their Japanese garden setting, where they're surrounded by hostas, dwarf conifers, and shining pools. In another especially attractive display, ribbons of crisp variegated grass wind among elegant clumps of Siberian iris.

These lovely gardens have hosted meetings of the national Japanese Iris and Siberian Iris societies. Ensata is exclusively a mail order business (no sales on-site) and the iris flowering season is short but you'll be glad you made the effort for a timely visit. ▶

From I-94 take Exit 85 for Galesburg. Go north a short distance to Michigan Route 96/East Michigan Avenue and turn west. There is no sign for Ensata; look for their mailbox number 9823 on the south side of the road about a half mile west of Galesburg. The gardens are at the end of the driveway on the north side of the road.

Maple Spring
135 East 120th Street
Grant MI 49327
(616) 834-5481

Commercial. Two acres. Herbs, edible flowers, gourmet vegetables.

 Grass paths.
Open May 1-September 30 Monday-Friday 9am-5pm. Closed Saturday, Sunday, and all holidays.

The "gardens" at Maple Spring are beautiful production fields, an acre of herbs and edible flowers and an acre of gourmet vegetables, whose yield goes to many fine Michigan restaurants. Here is your chance to see rows and rows of happy and healthy purple basil, silvery lavender, and luscious green herbs, all organically grown, free of chemical herbicides, pesticides, or fertilizers. Late in the season, from mid-summer on, it may be possible to choose and cut the mature herbs you need for herbcraft projects. For those of us who grow two basil plants and half a dozen calendulas, these fields are a revelation.

From Grand Rapids take Michigan Route 37 north to Grant. Go east on 120th Street/State Road a little over a half mile to the yellow brick ranch-style house on the north side of the road.

FYI The West Michigan Botanic Garden in Grand Rapids is an appetizer, a teaser, so to speak, for a major botanical complex that, as of 1991, existed only on paper and in the vision of its sponsors. But there are plans, oh yes, there are plans for a world-class establishment that will include natural beauty and cultivated gardens, a full-scale conservatory, an arboretum, greenhouses, a learning center, an exhibit hall, and a research area, all completely barrier-free. It will be exciting to watch the growth (no pun intended) of this facility.

For information on the status of this project or to make a contribution, contact the West Michigan Horticultural Society, P. O. Box 2345, Grand Rapids MI 49501. (616) 957-1580.

The Sassafras Hutch
11880 Sandy Bottom N. E.
Greenville MI 48838
(616) 754-9759

Commercial. One and a half acres. Herb theme gardens.

Shop. Many plants labeled. Seasonal plant sales.
Open May-December Wednesday-Saturday 11am-5pm.

Over 250 herb varieties flourish and bloom in the Sassafras Hutch gardens, in spite of occasional depredations by deer from the surrounding woods. Small gardens are shaped to reflect their themes; the dye garden is shaped like an artist's palette, the Biblical garden is cruciform. This may be a bit precious for some tastes but I like the tussy-mussy garden, a circular mass of "the language of flowers" plants. In the patio garden, paving blocks alternate with green patches of compact herb plants, an attractive idea that could be used by many gardeners. The Sassafras Hutch greenhouse supplies most of the plants for the gardens and for spring sales that offer herb plants, gourmet vegetables, and plants with edible flowers.

A basket filled with verdant sweet woodruff (*Galium odoratum*) hangs just outside the shop door. Inside, where a sign warns that "Lost Children Will Be Sold," there are many things you *need*. Cornhusk dolls and herbal angels, animal-shaped topiary forms, unusual cookie molds and cutters, and supplies for herbal weddings are just a few of the treasures here.

Sassafras Hutch offers lectures, workshops, contests, and seasonal festivals. You may want to come for the colorful Kent County Harvest Tours in autumn, when the herbs are drying, the cider is fresh-pressed, and the doughnuts are fresh and warm . . . but any season is rewarding at Sassafras Hutch.

For Harvest Tours information contact The Sassafras Hutch or call Klackle Orchards at (616) 754-8632.

From US Route 131 north of Grand Rapids, take Exit 101, Michigan Route 57 (14 Mile Road). Go east on MI 57 about 10 miles to Heintzelman Road and turn north. Note that Heintzelman, a gravel road, is not very well marked along MI 57. Follow Heintzelman to Sandy Bottom and turn left. Sassafras Hutch is on your left just a little way down Sandy Bottom.

Veldheer/DeKlomp Tulip Gardens
12755 Quincy Street and US 31
Holland MI 49424
(616) 399-1900

Commercial. Several acres. Bulb and perennial gardens.

♿☕ Catalog. Fee in spring only. Shops. Many plants labeled. Picnic facilities. Bulb sales. Group tours by appointment.
Open Monday-Friday 8am-6pm, Saturday and Sunday 9am-5pm.

For total immersion in parrot tulips, lily-flowered tulips, cottage tulips, *Tulipa* in all the possible hues and forms, visit Holland in April or May. At Veldheer, windmills, drawbridges, and canals accent millions of tulips and daffodils that are clearly labeled to help you identify the varieties you want for your own garden. Bulbs can be purchased on site July through October or can be ordered for later shipment. In summer, the bulbs are dug and summer-blooming annuals and perennials are planted.

You can tour a Delftware factory and a wooden shoe factory here, too. I still have the wooden shoes my folks bought in Holland when I was five years old, now with pebbles firmly embedded in their soles. I wore them a lot that summer, klomping around the neighborhood, letting everyone know where I was, sneaking up on no one. Now I need to go back to Holland for larger shoes and for the tulips and daffodils.

From I-196 take Exit 55 to Michigan Route 21 southwest. Follow MI 21 to US 31 then go north on US 31 to Veldheer/DeKlomp.

Windmill Island Municipal Park
Corner of 7th and Lincoln streets in downtown Holland

Commercial "park." Several acres.

$ ♿ ☕ Brochure. Shops. Picnic facilities. Group tour discount (25 or more). Group tickets available by mail for Tulip Time Festival.
Open daily late April through October: mid-season hours 9am-6pm, early-and late-season hours 11:30am-5pm.

On Windmill Island, green lawns, tidy walkways, and thousands and thousands of tulips and other flowers in their season surround "De Zwann," the only operating Dutch windmill in the US. You can view a short film about windmills before touring "The Swan" in the company of costumed guides.

For details contact Windmill Island, Holland MI 49423. (616) 396-5433.

From US Route 31 or Business Route I-196, take BR 31 into downtown Holland.

Englearth Gardens
2461 22nd Street, Route 2
Hopkins MI 49328
(616) 793-7196

Commercial specialist in daylilies, irises, and hostas. 45 acres production fields. 7 shadehouses. Over 1 acre display gardens.

 Catalog. Many plants labeled. Plant sales.
Open April through September or October, depending on the weather. Weekdays 9am-5pm, Saturday 9am-3pm, closed Sunday.

Imagine the summer glory of production fields that hold over 450 named varieties of daylilies and you're seeing Englearth Gardens. Earlier in the season, elegant Japanese and Siberian irises reigned. For more subtle beauty, visit the blues and greens and variegations of nearly 200 different hostas in the shadehouses or renew your acquaintance with other favorite perennials. Anytime during the season, you'll find admirable gardens and plants at Englearth.

Take the Hopkins-Bradley exit from US Route 131 (between Kalamazoo and Grand Rapids) to 128th Street. Go west on 128th to Clark Street/22nd Street, then turn south and go 1½ miles to Englearth Gardens on the east side of the road. Look for the gray shingle house.

Kalamazoo

Kalamazoo County is home to an extensive bedding plant industry. *Flowerfest*, a county-wide beautification project that salutes the Kalamazoo Valley Plant Growers Co-op, sponsors spring gardening seminars and a five-day festival in late July. Bronson Park is the focal point for many festival programs and activities that include bus tours, seminars and concerts, and flower shows at various sites around the county.

▶

◀ For information and schedules contact Flowerfest, Inc. or the Kalamazoo County Visitors Bureau, both at 128 North Kalamazoo Mall, Kalamazoo MI 49007. (616) 381-4003.

Bronson Park

Downtown city park. Three or four acres.

♿ Fee for some festival events. Many plants labeled. Picnic facilities. Food available during festival. Workshops and other events at Flowerfest. Group tours for Flowerfest available by appointment.
Bronson Park and other community plantings open daylight hours. Flowerfest hours for Bronson Park and other events are 9am-9pm.

Have you ever seen petunia trees? They grow in Bronson Park. That is, they were petunia trees in 1990; they're potted plants on tiered metal structures, so they could just as easily be marigold or snapdragon trees. This pleasant mid-city park is made of tall (real) trees, shady benches, an uncommonly attractive sculpture fountain, and masses of annual flowers that include beds of varicolored lantana, a pleasing and imaginative choice. In some years, a topiary peacock, exotic and a little campy with his flowering 12-foot tail, guards the west end of Bronson Park.

While you're at Bronson Park, consider visiting the nearby downtown mall (about two blocks east) to admire the lush planters and flower beds there. As you drive around Kalamazoo you'll see attractive plantings in some likely and some unlikely places; chances are, they're entered in community beautification contests. You can enjoy Bronson Park and the scattered gardens any time but to make your visit to K'zoo complete, take advantage of the Flowerfest seminars and classes.

From I-94 take Exit 76-B, Westnedge north. It will shift to Park Street, one-way north. Bronson Park is along Park Street, just west of the downtown mall.

Crane Park
2001 South Westnedge

11-acre city park with gardens. Perennial borders. Small rose garden.

♿ Turf paths. Many plants labeled.
Open daylight hours.

◀ These abundant gardens, blue and white with early June bloom, are truly beautiful in today's mist and fog. Low ageratum glows, echoing the rich blues and violets of bachelor's button (*Centaurea montana*) and classy Siberian irises, sturdy garden sage and delicate forget-me-nots. Cheerful buttercups rise above lush foliage to add a touch of sun. Starry Japanese dogwood (*Cornus kousa*) shines against the wooded background where drifts of wild phlox gleam. Hairy poppy buds hold crystalline mist while graceful trellises await their roses and clematis. Summer color will come from astilbes, obedience plant (*Physostegia* sp.), turtlehead (*Chelone* sp.), coneflowers, and a host of other old favorites. Comfortable benches invite restful contemplation of the beauty here.

These beds and borders, although planted and maintained by several different garden clubs of the Kalamazoo Garden Council, are unified by color and plant varieties. You'll find the plantings in this quiet neighborhood park attractive in any season.

For information contact the Parks and Recreation Department, City of Kalamazoo, 234 West Cedar Street, Kalamazoo MI 49007. (616) 337-8002.

From I-94 take Exit 76 and follow Westnedge Avenue north about 2 miles until traffic splits and the one-way north lanes shift to Park Street. Crane Park is just beyond this split; look for tennis courts on your right and the small Crane Park signs. Turn right into the park and follow the short road to the gardens on your left.

Heaven's Herbal Creations
8202 West ML Avenue
Kalamazoo MI 49009
(616) 375-2934

Commercial. Small display and theme gardens.

Shop. Many plants labeled. Picnic facilities. Plant sales. Workshops and other special events. Open Monday-Saturday 10am-6pm.

If you love nicely scented things, you'll love Heaven's Herbal Creations, where the emphasis is on essential oils, potpourri, and pure cosmetics. There are demonstration gardens and the herb product factory to visit, a children's garden and a petting zoo, free recipes and flyers, and other assorted treats. From May to October, you can choose from over 500 different herb plants and heritage roses in pots and planters. You'll also find an excellent book selection in the shop. Perhaps you want to treat yourself to a class on soap-making, perfumery, or another appealing topic. There are usually free herbal delights to sip and nibble or you can carry your own goodies to the picnic area . . . and enjoy.

Heaven's Herbal Creations is actually in Oshtemo, just west of Kalamazoo. There are Oshtemo exits from US Route 131 and from I-94.

Kalamazoo Nature Center
7000 North Westnedge
Kalamazoo MI 49007
(616) 381-1574

Many acres woods and meadows. Small hummingbird/butterfly garden. Nature education center.

Trails. Workshops and other activities.
Nature Center grounds open daily 9am-6pm. Buildings open Monday-Saturday 9am-5pm, Sunday and holidays 1-5pm.

If you're spending a little time around K'zoo, drive north on Business Route 131 to Westnedge, then north through an area of large greenhouses and nurseries where many of the *Flowerfest* plants originate. Further north on Westnedge you'll come to the Kalamazoo Nature Center, which offers a number of worthy exhibits and activities. The hummingbird and butterfly garden, a delightful pocket of red-flowered plants surrounded by lawn, is particularly pleasing. When we visit at dusk, only the flowers are there; hummingbirds and butterflies have settled down for the night. After a full day of garden-visiting, we'll soon do the same.

From Crane or Bronson parks, continue north on Park Street (BR MI 131) to Westnedge, just around a curve. Turn onto Westnedge and continue north to the Nature Center, on the east side of the road.

Lansing

Lansing, the capital of Michigan, and East Lansing, its twin city and the home of Michigan State University, offer a number and variety of gardens that could keep the garden-lover happily occupied for two or three days. For information on other civic and university offerings and activities contact the Convention and Visitors Bureau of Greater Lansing, Lansing Civic Arena, Suite 302, Lansing MI 48933, (517) 487-6800.

Cooley Garden
225 West Main

Nearly one and a half acres of perennial gardens.

 Turf paths.
Open daylight hours from the first Sunday in May through the second Sunday in October.

These rich perennial beds, planted in the late 1930s, are well-established compositions of mature, happy-in-their-site plants. The garden is colorful all season long but irises and a small collection of historic tree peonies add fragrance and special elegance to springtime here. This may be the garden you'd like to have at home.

For details contact the Horticulturist, Parks and Recreation, City of Lansing City Hall, 124 West Michigan Avenue, Lansing MI 48933. (517) 483-4277.

From eastbound I-496 take the Pine-Walnut Exit and follow Main Street east to the third traffic light, where the garden entrance will be on your right. From westbound I-496 take the Grand Avenue Exit and follow St. Joseph Highway west to the second traffic light (at the Capitol Building). Turn left at the light, then get into the righthand lane, which leads to the garden entrance.

Carl G. Fenner Arboretum
2020 East Mt. Hope
Lansing MI 48910
(517) 483-4224

125 acres. Native plants in varied natural habitats.

Nature Center is barrier-free. Many plants labeled. Shop and library in Nature Center. Trails. Picnic facilities. Workshops and other special events.
Arboretum open every day 8am-dark. Nature Center open Monday-Friday 9am-4pm, Saturday 10am-5pm, Sunday 11am-5pm. Shop open Saturday and Sunday only, variable hours.

On this September morning, washes of goldenrod glow across the foggy prairie. Take just a short walk through this prairie and escape the surrounding urban area; five miles of trails wind through Fenner's prairies, old orchards, maple groves, oak uplands, marshy thickets, and pine plantations.

Near the Nature Center, a small wild garden holds seed plants for birds but today the finches and chickadees are more interested in sunflower seeds on the feeding shelf. The garden's dry leaves quiver and rustle with steady bird traffic. Suet-filled pine cones hang in front of a viewing window to provide a food source that also breaks up reflections so the birds don't fly into the window. The Nature Center offers trail maps, interpretive displays, and a wide variety of nature-oriented activities.

This arboretum was established in 1959, thanks to admirable foresight and persistence by the Lansing Parks and Recreation Department; the lovely rolling land could just as easily have become a housing tract or yet another shopping mall. Although Fenner isn't a garden as such, it's a fine place to stretch your legs and enjoy plants. If you're tired of the highway or of cultivated gardens, you'll enjoy the rusticity and the space of Fenner.

From I-496/US 127 take the Trowbridge Road exit. Turn south onto Harrison and go a short distance to East Mount Hope. Go west on East Mt. Hope 1½ to the arboretum on the south side of the road.

Frances Park Memorial Garden
2600 Moores River Drive

Large city park. 2-acre All-American Rose Selections garden. Formal garden.

 Many plants labeled. Picnic facilities.
Open daily May 1-second Sunday of October dawn-dusk.

Today, carpets of coleus and marigolds glow in the light September fog and the luscious scent of late summer roses saturates the Rose Garden. Chickadees and migrating warblers move through the trees while gulls squabble on the river below, and it's delightful to be almost alone in this lovely park. Later in the day, the fog will clear, the heavily vined wisteria arbor will provide shade, and the hillside terrace will allow fine views up and down the river. I hope to return to appealing Frances Park when the wisteria blooms.

For information contact the Horticulturist, Parks and Recreation, City of Lansing City Hall, 124 West Michigan Avenue, Lansing MI 48933. (517) 483-4277.

From I-96 take Michigan Route 99/M. L. King Boulevard north to Moore's River Road just south of the Grand River. Turn west and follow the River Road a mile or more to Frances Park on your left.

Papa's Barn
22464 French Avenue
Mattawan MI 49071
(616) 668-4433

Commercial. Two acres. Herbs and everlastings.

♿ Catalog. Shop. Many plants labeled. Seasonal plant sales. Workshops and other special events. Group tours during Kalamazoo Flowerfest.
Open March 1-December 23 Monday-Saturday 10am-5pm, Sunday 1-5pm. Closed major holidays and during inclement weather.

These colorful fields and gardens yield herbs and everlastings by the armfuls, rich flowers and foliage that are dried to become attractive arrangements. Wreaths, centerpieces, and flower-filled baskets join books, fragrance products, and herb-themed pottery to fill the inviting shop. Perhaps you'll want to observe a demonstration or hear a lecture at Papa's Barn; their extensive schedule of activities, always "free of charge to all," stretches from early May to late December.

From I-94 take Exit 66 for Mattawan, County Road 652. Go north on CR 652 to 52nd Street (French Avenue) then go east to Papa's Barn on the north side of the road.

Fernwood
13988 Range Line Road
Niles MI 49120
(616) 695-6491 or (616) 683-8653

105 acres total grounds. 6 acres gardens. Japanese garden. 45-acre arboretum. Reconstructed tallgrass prairie.

💲 ♿ ☕ Catalog. Shop. Many plants labeled. Library. Trails. Seasonal plant sales. Workshops and other special events.
Grounds, visitor center, and gift shop open Monday-Saturday 9am-5pm, Sunday noon-5pm. Tea Room open Tuesday-Friday 11:30am-2pm. Fernwood closed Thanksgiving and Christmas days. ▶

"Fernwood" implies a wealth of ferns; we found them in the woods, scattered through the rock garden, against stone walls, in the handsome art exhibit, and in the two-story tropical conservatory. The visitor center balcony affords a bird's-eye-view of the conservatory, which encourages us to descend one level and enter this lush wonderland of ferns, bromeliads, and other tropical beauties. Fernwood became the home of Kay and Walter Boydston in 1941; Mrs. Boydston particularly loved ferns and the conservatory is a fine tribute to her.

A new dovecote/gazebo behind the visitor center overlooks the area that will become a formal herb and sensory garden. Today, the herbs are heeled into beds near the Art Studio while their future home is a sunhole of bare ground, construction materials, and partially completed structures. It will be a fine garden with theme beds, wattle fences, stone walls, and benches for resting, a garden just right for a party or for your personal pleasure.

Beyond the Daffodil Bowl (filled today with pink trumpets of autumn-blooming amaryllis), the rock and fern garden adorns a particularly pleasant hillside and the tiny spring-fed bog at its base. Ferns, dwarf conifers, and other rock garden jewels are accented by tall waterside irises. I treasure today's blooms of hardy cyclamen but I'm sorry we missed springtime here; wide patches of sturdy primrose foliage are evidence of a spectacular show.

Tall, dark rhododendrons along the path are almost oppressive in today's heat but I counter this by thinking of their spring glory. We've missed the best season of the Lilac Garden and the Azalea Allée but a graceful pond rimmed by delicate *Verbena bonariensis* holds blooming waterlilies, always a welcome sight. Meadows beyond the structured gardens hold an exaltation of late-summer wildflowers.

The Rector Pioneer Garden, limited to plants grown in the area during pioneer days, is an intimate reminder of earlier times. From this spot we admire blazing perennial borders and have a teasing view of the Terrace Garden, where a fine variety of buddleias are blooming and where we later admire the unusual fountain/pool that is a watery knot garden.

Beyond the bright perennials and the rustic pioneer garden, we come upon a stunning contrast and a subtle treasure, a serene and shady Japanese garden of carefully shaped evergreens above wavy patterns raked into the white gravel.

The visitor center shop offers a fine selection of garden-related items, a particularly good selection of nature-oriented books, and an impressive display of the Portmerion Collection, those joyous floral ceramics. Here, too, are flocks and coveys and tribes of almost irresistible bird sculptures in all sizes; we came close to adopting a life-sized hand-carved great blue heron.

Fernwood is a non-profit organization; nearly 200 volunteers work in the gardens, teach classes, and generally keep it going, for which we thank them. The variety of activities offered is most impressive and many are open to non-members for a fee.

I had anticipated our visit to Fernwood for several weeks and it surpassed my expectations. I can still see sprightly cyclamen flowers among tree roots in the rock garden, a vivid autumn image to carry with me.

From the west: at the intersection of Michigan Route 12 and Redbud Trail (stoplight), turn north toward Buchanan. Go through downtown Buchanan and turn right on River Road, which becomes Walton Road east of the St. Joseph River. Range Line Road is just a little further, on your left. The Fernwood sign is fairly small and easy to miss. Turn north onto Range Line and go a short distance to Fernwood on your right.
From Niles: west of Niles, take the US Route 31 Bypass north to Walton Road, then back southwest on Walton to Range Line Road and north on Range Line to Fernwood.

Fox Hill Farm
444 West Michigan Avenue
Parma MI 49269
(517) 531-3179

Commercial. Herbs and everlastings. 5 gardens of various sizes include 2500 sq.ft. basil maze and a circular garden 60 feet in diameter.

Brochures. Many plants labeled. Shops. Seasonal plant sales. Workshops and other special events.
Open April 15-October 15 Wednesday-Saturday 9am-5pm, Sunday noon-5pm. Other hours by appointment.

This is a long-established and well-known herb-growing business but, through an unfortunate combination of events, I was unable to visit Fox Hill or to gather written information about it. It's close to the Interstate and, from all accounts, is certainly worth a visit.

From I-94 take Exit 128 and go one mile to Fox Hill, just west of the village of Parma.

Braeloch Farm
9124 North 35th Street
Richland MI 49083
(616) 629-9884

Commercial. 60'x40' semi-formal herb/perennial garden. Shade gardens.

Many plants labeled. Shop. Seasonal plant sales.
Open all year Tuesday-Saturday 10am-5pm, Sunday 1-5pm. Closed Monday.

This lovely semi-formal garden usually holds perfumes of lavender and nicotiana but last night's light rain has activated the cocoa hull mulch. We wander through clouds of chocolate scent to be charmed by tidy clumps of cushion spurge (*Euphorbia polychroma*) around the central fountain and by the tiny pink trumpets of variegated calamint (*Calamintha grandiflora* 'Variegata'). Urns filled with scented and trailing geraniums add an elegant touch to the display, where later color will come from herbs, lilies, and other traditional garden favorites. Shady garden spots hold lungwort (*Pulmonaria* sp.), astilbes, and foamflower (*Tiarella* sp.) among their ferns and hostas, all united by the hairy hearts and blue forget-me-not flowers of Siberan bugloss (*Brunnera macrophylla*). Rhododendrons are brilliant rose and cerise against the chalk blue house, whose door is guarded today by an untidy pile of this year's kittens.

Do you want to put a rabbit in your garden rather than chase one away? The Braeloch shop has them in cast stone, plush, or lace, an entire herd of rabbits large and small, young and old, lop-eared or standard, rabbits running, reclining, sitting, standing. In the shop you'll find delightful flowery rain hats, an excellent selection of herb and garden books, dried flowers and herbs, and a year 'round Christmas corner. All seasons are pleasant at Braeloch.

From I-94 take Exit 80 and go north on Sprinkle Road to Michigan Route 43/ Gull Road. Turn right (northeast) and follow MI 43 through the center of Richland, then turn left at the stoplight in the center of town. Stay on MI 43 and go north about a mile from the stoplight to the Stagecoach Inn at C Avenue; look for the Braeloch sign at this corner. Turn east onto C Avenue and follow it to the "T" at 35th Street. Turn left at the "T"; Braeloch is the first driveway on the right.

St. Johns Mint Festival
St. Johns ▶

◀ Municipal and county-wide festival.

♿ ☕ Picnic facilities. Shops (festival souvenirs). Workshops and other activities.
Festival held in early August. For mint farm tours at other times, contact the address below.

St. Johns' festival celebrates mint farms and the mint oil industry; several hundred Clinton County acres hold peppermint (*Mentha piperita*) and spearmints (*M. spicata* and *M. cardiaca*) that are ultimately distilled into mint oils. Gardeners will be drawn to mint-oriented features although standard festival attractions (parade, flea market, stage shows, raffle) are here too. You can admire the mint pictorial display, study the history of mint, collect recipes that use fresh or dried mint, or refresh yourself with mint-flavored beverages and the ever-popular mint-chocolate-chip ice cream. Guided tours of mint farms and their oil distillation facilities are a festival highlight, although such a tour can be arranged at almost any time. But at festival time the harvest will probably be in process, most of the county will be mint-scented, and you can truly immerse yourself in this most popular of herbs.

For festival or mint farm information contact the St. Johns Chamber of Commerce, Box 61, St. Johns MI 48879. (517) 224-7248.

St Johns is on US Route 27 about 20 miles north of Lansing. Festival activities are centered in St. Johns City Park and at the Clinton County 4-H Fairground.

Dr. Liberty Hyde Bailey Birthsite Museum
903 Bailey Avenue
South Haven MI 49090

Nineteenth-century homesite.

Brochure.
Museum open Tuesday and Friday only, 2-4:30pm.

In 1858, Liberty Hyde Bailey, "The Father of American Horticulture," was born in this small white house. The museum, a registered Michigan and National Historic Site, contains a number of articles used by the Bailey family and an array of other nineteenth-century collections, tools, and furnishings. It may seem strange that there are no special gardens here but in 1858 this site was just a clearing in the woods, without even the smooth lawn it now has. You don't come here to admire gardens; you come to pay homage to Bailey and his nearly ninety-six years of learning, his prolific writing, his forward-looking ecological suggestions, and his never-ending efforts to share horticultural knowledge with non-professional gardeners.

For information contact the Southwestern Michigan Tourist Council, 2300 Pipestone Road, Benton Harbor MI 49022. (616) 925-6301.

Bailey Avenue stops and starts as it crosses South Haven; your best bet is to ask for directions when you get into town.

Minnesota: North

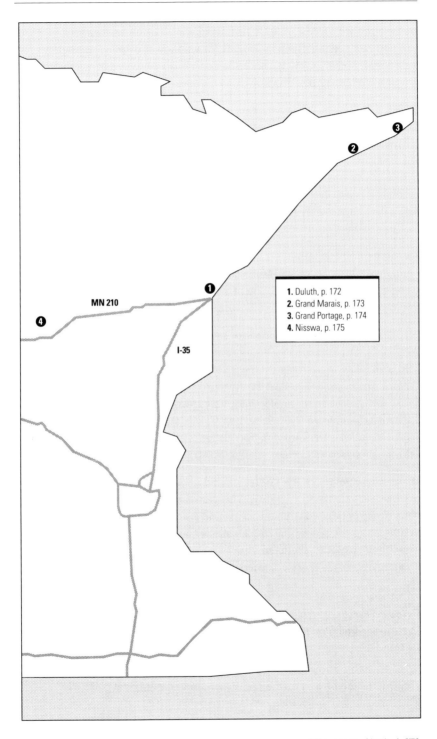

Minnesota: North

Nearly eighteen and a half *million* acres of Minnesota, 34% of the state's land, are covered with forest. Add thousands of acres of prairie, meadow, and bog and you can see that the possibilities for wildflower displays are nearly endless. Various state agencies sponsor special observances to celebrate Minnesota's wildflower resources.

Spring Wildflower Weekends include conducted wildflower hikes, photography workshops, movies, identification hunts, and other activities that promote awareness and appreciation of native plants. Wildflower Routes are highways whose flowering roadsides are especially attractive. In August, when prairie plants are at their peak, statewide Prairie Days offer a wide range of events. Sites for all these vary from year to year; the DNR will send you a free list of the year's events and their locations. Also, the DNR sells, for a nominal fee, an excellent guide to the Minnesota prairies.

For general information on Minnesota wildflower projects, contact The Wildflower Task Force, c/o Minnesota Beautiful, Minnesota Department of Trade and Economic Development, 900 American Center, 150 East Kellogg Boulevard, St. Paul MN 55101-1421, (612) 297-3190.

For specific sites and calendars of events for Prairie Days and Wildflower Weekends, the locations of Wildflower Routes, and a short list of nurseries who specialize in native plants, contact the Prairie Biologist, Department of Natural Resources, 1221 East Fir Avenue, Fergus Falls MN 56537, (218) 739-7576. You can acquire similar information from the Resource Management Specialist, Minnesota DNR, P. O. Box 6247, Rochester MN 55903, (507) 285-7432. Or, call the DNR Information Center: from within the Twin Cities, 296-6157, or Minnesota Toll Free: (800) 652-9747.

Many of us appreciate the virtues of wild geranium (*Geranium maculatum*), blazing star (*Liatris* sp.), and wild bergamot (*Monarda fistulosa*) in our gardens. We're entranced with the colors and grace of native grasses; my clumps of little bluestem please me in the summer and make me smile in the winter, when their rosy-gold seems to glow from within on even the grayest of days. It's gratifying to see these charmers in their natural haunts.

Enger Park
Skyline Parkway at 13th Avenue West
Duluth

Three acres theme and natural gardens in larger municipal park. ▶

◀ ♿ Many plants labeled. Picnic facilities.

Open daily April 1-November 1 daylight hours.

Aspens rattle in the breeze, late spring blossoms ornament the gardens, and I have the park to myself on this sunny June morning. Enger is on Duluth's highest bluff above Lake Superior and the plantings in this natural rock garden, where dianthus and other alpines bloom beside the chartreuse gleam of cushion spurge (*Euphorbia polychroma*), are delightful. Dwarf conifers thrive in their sunny home against a rock outcropping, with nearly 500 different alpines massed at their feet. It's still spring in Duluth but I've missed May's 4,000-plus daffodils. Peony buds are still tight little balls but hostas, ferns, and other shade-lovers are lush beneath mature trees. Azaleas and ground covers expand into the woodland gardens in naturalistic progression. Today, the small stone pavilion is reserved for an afternoon wedding reception; it will be the perfect event for this lovely site.

Lester River Park, just off Minnesota Route 61, is Skyline Parkway's northern entry. These woods, ravines, and high meadows are cool and refreshing in the evening of this unseasonably warm June day. Lupines, daisies, buttercups, and wild roses brighten meadows and roadsides and our leisurely excursion seems the perfect conclusion to a long day.

For information contact the City of Duluth, City Gardener, 208 City Hall, 411 West 1st Street, Duluth MN 55802. (218) 723-3337.

From I-35 take Exit 255 (21st Avenue West); this becomes US Route 53 North. Go north on US 53 to a five-way stop then take an immediate right onto Skyline Parkway. Go past Enger Park Golf Course and turn at the sign reading "Enger Tower."

Wild Flower Sanctuary
Along Gunflint Trail
Grand Marais

About one acre naturalized wildflower plantings. ▶

FYI Don't miss the spectacular Lake Superior view from the top of Enger Tower . . . it's worth the relatively easy climb.

Duluth's well-known Rose Garden, dismantled during I-35 tunnel construction, will be replanted in 1994. Contact the City Gardener for information and directions.

◀ Brochure. Many plants labeled.
Open daylight hours.

In late June, the Gunflint Trail is edged with yellow and orange hawkweed, tall buttercups, wild roses, and daisies. The wooded sanctuary is lively with blooming wildflowers: nodding trillium, white clintonia (*Clintonia umbellulata*), wild columbine, wild geranium, carpets of dwarf cornel (bunchberry, *Cornus canadensis*), and charming wild lily-of-the-valley (*Maianthemum canadense*). Woodland ferns have a good start on their summer's growth and buds on other plants show promise of later bloom.

This sanctuary was first developed in the early 1960s by the Grand Marais Garden Club, on land owned by the Hedstrom Lumber Company. It thrived for a few years, then fell into weedy decline and was little used. In 1979, inspired by the persistent yearly bloom of Showy Lady's-slippers (the Minnesota State Flower), the Garden Club determined to rehabilitate the sanctuary. Brush was cleared, paths redefined, new signs installed, and new plants and trees set in.

Ironically, the Showy Lady's-slipper population is now greatly reduced due to additional shade supplied by the growing trees and increased dust blown in from the mill across the river. Nevertheless, you'll enjoy a walk in this natural garden; the Gunflint Trail eventually leads to the International Boundary Waters Canoe Area but you don't have to go that far for a pleasant botanical experience.

For information contact the Tip of the Arrowhead Information Center, Box NSA, Grand Marais MN 55604. (800) 622-4014.

Take Gunflint Trail (County Road 12) north from Grand Marais. The sanctuary is about 5½ miles north of town, on the east side of the road just *before you reach the Devil Track River.*

Grand Portage National Monument
Grand Portage

 Brochure.
Open days and hours vary with the season.

When you visit this restored Northwest Fur Company facility, be sure to notice the small vegetable garden. It's planted with heritage seeds to grow those vegetables known by our ancestors, a practice initiated in 1990. And, perhaps more interesting and less common, are its raised beds, used not for improved drainage or soil conditioning but to protect possible archaeological remains in the unexcavated soil.

The site is well-marked from US Route 61 along Lake Superior, just south of the Canadian border.

Grand View Lodge
South 134 Nokomis
Nisswa MN 56468
(218) 963-2234. Minnesota only: (800) 432-3788

Extensive plantings around resort lodge.

 Brochure. Shops and snacks in lodge. Occasional special events. Gardens open daylight hours.

Colorful borders and lush flower beds thrive here on Gull Lake, surrounded by birch woods and others of Minnesota's 10,000 lakes. Flowers to suit every taste, including over 100 varieties of annuals, perennials, and shrubs, fill these masterful gardens.

In late July, Grandview is the site of the Nisswa Garden Club Flower Show, an annual exhibition that is over 50 years old. Take a break from woods and lakes to revel in "nature rearranged" at Grand View.

Winter address, October to May: Grand View Lodge, 5201 Eden Circle, Edina MN 55436. (612) 925-3109.

From Brainerd take Minnesota Route 371 north 14 miles to Interlachen Road. Turn left at the Grand View sign and go a mile to the lodge and gardens.

Minnesota: South

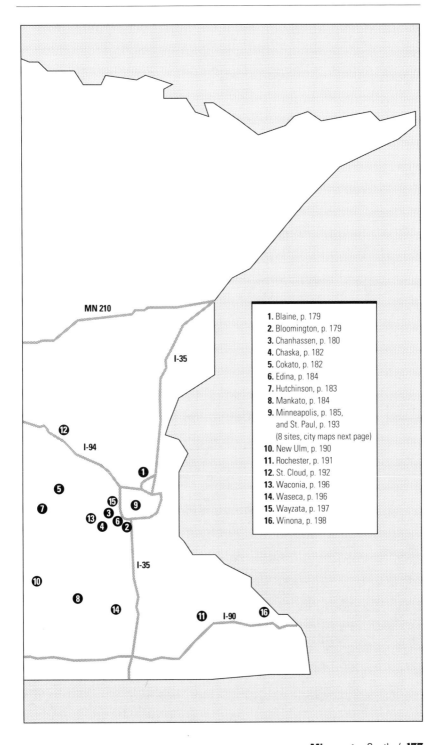

Minnesota: South / MINNEAPOLIS and ST. PAUL

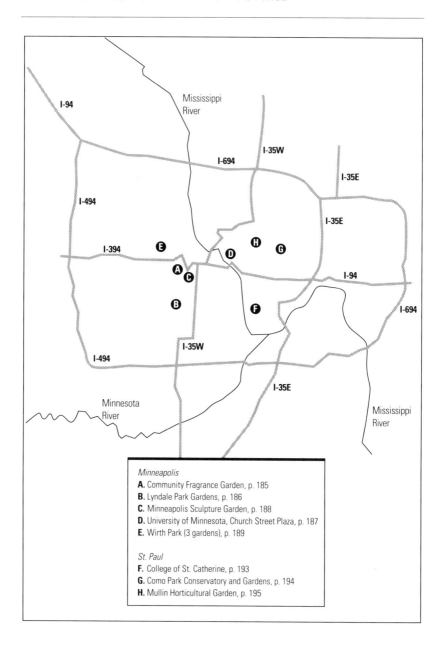

Minneapolis
A. Community Fragrance Garden, p. 185
B. Lyndale Park Gardens, p. 186
C. Minneapolis Sculpture Garden, p. 188
D. University of Minnesota, Church Street Plaza, p. 187
E. Wirth Park (3 gardens), p. 189

St. Paul
F. College of St. Catherine, p. 193
G. Como Park Conservatory and Gardens, p. 194
H. Mullin Horticultural Garden, p. 195

Rice Creek Gardens
11506 Highway 65
Blaine MN 55434
(612) 754-8090

Commercial grower of perennials. Homesite display gardens.

Turf paths. Most plants labeled. Plant sales. Group tours of display garden by appointment.
Sales area open May 1-November 1 Monday-Saturday 9am-5pm, closed Sunday.
Display garden open May 1-November 1, first and third Saturday of each month 9am-5pm.

Plants for all sorts of ecological niches live at Rice Creek Gardens: dwarfs and alpines for rock gardens, herbs and ornamental grasses, ferns and other shade-lovers, groundcovers and waterside plants, vines, conifers, and shrubs. Terraced gardens at the home of Rice Creek's owner display these plants in lush and inspiring combinations.

The sales area and the display gardens are 8-10 miles apart.
From I-694 take Minnesota Route 65 north 6-8 miles to Rice Creek Gardens sales grounds. Inquire here for directions to the display gardens.

The Japanese Garden at Normandale Community College
9700 France Avenue South
Bloomington MN 55431
(612) 832-6303

2-acre hill-type Japanese stroll garden.

Fee for guided group tours. Brochure. Some plants labeled. Group tours by prior arrangement. Food available in college cafeteria (summer hours Monday-Friday until 2:30pm, closed weekends).
Garden open daylight hours.

Yellow cinquefoil is blooming near the waterfall, tiny tadpoles make shifting black masses at the edge of the pond, and the distant Minneapolis skyline gleams with late afternoon sun. Vigorous growth in a nearby bog contrasts with the gently controlled forms and colors in the garden around us. The arched bridge makes a perfect circle with its reflection in the still pond.

This garden, sponsored by the Bloomington Minnesota Affiliated Garden Clubs, was dedicated in 1976; since then, its designer has come from Tokyo several times to visit it and to train garden volunteers in pruning and maintenance techniques. The arched bridge and the charming *bentendo* (a small six-sided building) are gifts from Japanese-American Veterans of World War II "to the people of the Twin Cities for the kind treatment (we) received while stationed here during World War II."

Spring's crabapple, azalea, and tree lilac blooms will be enchanting after a long Minnesota winter. But autumn's clear yellow ginkgoes and willows, shining against dark conifers and reflected in placid water, will be equally attractive. Although the garden is directly behind a college building and not far from busy roads, it is a sanctuary, a quiet place of restful spaces and textural contrasts . . . in short, a successful Japanese stroll garden.

From I-494 take France Avenue about two miles south to Normandale Community College. Parking and access to the garden are behind the main building.
From I-35W take either 98th or 90th Street west to France; the school is on the west side of France between these two streets.

Minnesota Landscape Arboretum
3675 Arboretum Drive
P. O. Box 39
Chanhassen MN 55317
(612) 443-2460

---

675 acres. Theme, display, and demonstration gardens. Plant collections. Woods, bogs, and meadows.

💲♿☕ Brochure. Shop. Many plants labeled. Library. Trails (including cross-country ski trails). Picnic facilities. Seasonal plant sales. Workshops and other special events.
Arboretum grounds open daily May-October 8am-9pm, November-April 8am-5pm. Snyder Building, including library, open weekdays 8am-4:30pm, weekends 11am-4:30pm. Gift shop and tea room hours are seasonal and variable.

You'll want more than just a quick stop here, where you can enjoy theme gardens, tree collections, scenic drives, walking trails, cloisters, ponds, ▶

FYI A booklet for self-guided garden visits is available at the College Center Desk adjacent to the garden. This desk closes at 2:30pm and the entire college is closed on summer weekends, so you may want to write ahead. Send $1.00 for the *Guide to Normandale Japanese Garden* to the Director of Community Relations and Development, Normandale Community College, 9700 France Avenue South, Bloomington MN 55431.

overlooks, and everything else a complete garden offers. Theme gardens, allowing no jarring transitions, flow one into another, up slopes, down hills, and around fountains. It's apparent that there will be masses of bloom all season, from early spring to frost. Strategically sited teak benches provide cozy garden views and long arboretum vistas. We appreciate those benches on this warm June evening.

The Woodland Azalea Garden highlights 'Northern Lights Azaleas', a series of particularly hardy azalea varieties that was developed here. Rhododendrons, goatsbeard (*Aruncus* sp.), and other shade-lovers join azaleas and the sculptural leaves of skunk cabbage around a small, still pond. Nearby, shady Hosta Glade presents over 250 varieties of hosta and is the national display garden of the American Hosta Society. The Home Demonstration Garden, full of ideas for home landscapers, contains a pavilion and pergolas surrounded by functional and ornamental plants. The informal herb garden is comprised of culinary, medicinal, fragrant, dye, and ornamental herb beds. From a small hillside overlook, you can look down upon the formal knot garden and see it the way knot gardens were meant to be viewed. In the perennial garden, trollius 'Golden Queen' glows against the gray softness of catmint (*Nepeta* sp.) and the glossy leaves of *Amsonia tabernaemontana*. The Rose Garden's charming gazebo, with its long view to a row of cedars, overlooks the excellent color and texture combination of roses interplanted with junipers and white verbena.

The gift shop in the Snyder Education and Research Building offers an exceptional variety of garden-related items and an excellent selection of books, greeting cards, stationery, and other paper goods; a handsome poster came home with us. The Andersen Horticultural Library, also in this building, holds special reference files, one of the country's largest collections of seed and nursery catalogs, and a Plant Locator Service. Deats Conservatory, another part of the Snyder Building, is ". . . designed to display plants commonly grown in homes and indoor public areas," and puts particular emphasis on bromeliads.

The Arboretum offers a wide variety of classes and garden events. To help plan your visit, write for the schedule, a seasonal calendar, and the timetable of expected bloom for various plant collections. Wouldn't it be lovely to be here when the crabapples on the ridge are at their most gorgeous or when the wild irises brighten their small boggy ponds? In truth, it would be lovely here at any time of year.

From I-494 take Minnesota Route 5 west. The Arboretum is west of Chanhassen, just beyond the intersection of MN 5 and MN 41.

Shady Acres Nursery
7815 Highway 212
Chaska MN 55318
(612) 466-3391

Commercial. Large herb display garden. Greenhouses.

♿ Catalog. Shop. Many plants labeled. Plant sales. Workshops and other events.
Open mid-April-mid-December Wednesday-Friday 10am-5pm, Saturday 10am-4pm, closed Sunday-Tuesday.

Seeds and plants for herbs, gourmet vegetables, and wildflowers are in the shop, in the greenhouse, and on outside tables at Shady Acres. Most of the plants sold here are propagated and grown on in Shady Acres' greenhouses. On this late June day, those greenhouses hold a wide variety of herbs, scented geraniums (*Pelargonium* spp.), and some less common eucalypti, including the striking sickle-leaved 'Snow Top'. A major display garden is under development; it will be most impressive when verdant herbs fill its raised beds.

Shady Acres was born in the basement of the small house that's now the Herb Shop. I love this shop; as a weaver, I identify with its centerpiece, an old family loom that had been kicked from barn to barn before it came to rest here. Among the potpourris, soaps, and oils, you'll find treasures that you may not see in other shops. There are posters, prints, and original watercolors of herbs, unusually attractive stoneware ceramics, and comely needlework pillows with herb-based designs. The selection of books and of dried herb arrangements is quite tempting.

Shady Acres offers a full schedule of gardening and cooking workshops and, with luck and good planning, you may be able to combine one of these with your visit.

From Chaska, take US Route 212 6 miles west to Shady Acres, on the south side of the road.

Busse Gardens
Route 2 Box 238
Cokato MN 55321-9426
(612) 286-2654

Commercial grower of perennials. 3 acres. 50 display beds. ▶

Catalog. Many plants labeled. Plant sales.
Open during growing season Monday-Friday 8:30am-4:30pm, Saturday 8:30am-noon, closed Sunday.

These colorful gardens boast nearly all the perennials you've ever heard of . . . and probably some that are new to you, such as the *kirengeshoma* and the six different *ligularias* that bring shades of yellow and gold to the late summer garden. Here is *heucherella*, that charming hybrid of *heuchera* and *tiarella* (coral bells and foamflower), whose delicate stems of pink and white stars will brighten your garden in early summer. There are *Rodgersia*, *sisyrinchium* (blue-eyed grass), and *tellima* (a saxifrage), fine plants with fine-sounding names. Native plants, including grasses, stand near hundreds of varieties of daylilies, hostas, peonies, and irises. You'll see many of the plants that are offered in Busse's extensive catalog and you may want them all. Busse Gardens is a mail-order business but an inviting collection of plants is potted up and ready to travel, so you won't have to go home empty-handed.

From US Route 12 at Cokato, take Wright County Route 3 north 5 miles to County Route 35. Go east on CR 35 a mile, then north 1 mile, then east another half mile to Busse Gardens. You'll see their signs along these roads.

Dooley Gardens
Route 1 Box 20
Hutchinson MN 55350
(612) 587-3050

Commercial. Grower of garden chrysanthemums. Display field. 2-acre production field.

 Catalog. Most plants labeled.
Display field open to the public mid-September-mid-October. Write or call for specific dates as they change from year to year depending on growing conditions.

Thousands of chrysanthemums in all their glorious hues and forms, the flowers of over 200 varieties, will delight you here in autumn. The "open season" at Dooley's is short but you'll be glad you fit these brilliant fields into your travel schedule.

At Hutchinson, take Minnesota Route 15 to North High Drive, then go east three blocks to Dooley's.

Minnesota: South / **183**

Savory's Gardens, Inc.
5300 Whiting Avenue
Edina MN 55434
(612) 941-8755

Commercial. Hosta specialist. Large show garden.

Catalog. Most plants labeled. Plant sales.
Spring hours (through early June) Monday-Saturday 9am-5pm, Sunday noon-5pm. Summer hours the same except Saturday hours variable (call first) and closed Sunday. Call to check on hours at beginning and end of season.

Over 900 varieties of hostas await you at Savory's. The cool and shady display garden, large enough to accommodate meetings of the American Hosta Society, also includes shade-loving ground covers and other perennials. Savory's hybridizes and propagates new hostas; many of the plants you see here are their own recent introductions. For your less shady garden spots, there are a few daylilies and other sunlovers here but it's the hostas that will charm you.

From I-494 take Minnesota Route 100 about a mile north to 70th Street. Exit for 70th east and immediately take the frontage road north to 66th Street. Go west on 66th to Wilryan Avenue, then north on Wilryan two blocks to 64th Street. Go west 5 blocks on 64th to Holborn, then north a short distance to Savory's at the corner of Holborn and Whiting.
From the Crosstown Highway (County Route 62) go south on MN 100 to 70th Street, then as above.

Hubbard House Gardens
500 block of Broad Street
Mankato

2½-acre estate grounds and gardens.

♿ Fee for house tours. Group tours by appointment.
Grounds and gardens open daily 6:30am-10:30pm. House open for tours Tuesday-Saturday.

These attractive grounds hold a garden feature that I've seen in only one other municipal garden in our area: an outdoor room designed specifically for weddings. In this idyllic space, *arborvitae* hedges enclose lush lawn, a living green altar, and charming borders of hostas, old-fashioned roses, and climbing vines. Other plantings around Hubbard House, the former home of the family that gave us Mother Hubbard's Bread Flour, include a sunken garden and an herb garden. Most of these installations are maintained by Mankato area garden clubs, although the house and grounds belong to the City of Mankato and the Blue Earth County Historical Society. A visit here, especially during peak bloom in July, will add a colorful touch to your day.

For information contact Mankato Parks and Forestry, 202 East Jackson Street, Mankato MN 56001. (507) 387-8650.

Hubbard House is near downtown Mankato, at the corner of Warren and Broad streets, and is clearly marked.

Minneapolis

For information on Minneapolis gardens, except for Church Street Plaza and the Community Fragrance Garden, contact the Horticulture Division, Minneapolis Park and Recreation Board Operations Center, 3800 Bryant Avenue South, Minneapolis MN 55409-1029. (612) 348-4448.

Community Fragrance Garden
19th Street and Aldrich Avenue South
Minneapolis

Two-thirds city block. Emphasis on fragrant plants.

 Picnics permitted.
Open daylight hours all year.

The Fragrance Garden, an oasis of flowers, scent, and greenery at the edge of downtown Minneapolis, is the result of determination and hard work on the part of the Men's Garden Club of Minneapolis, with the support of many plant and supply donors. Flowering trees and fragrant shrubs rise above aromatic plants on land that was, until 1971, a veritable boneyard of highway construction trash. Today, shrub roses fill one corner of this luscious triangle, modern roses perfume another corner, and lilies add dignity and scent throughout the grounds. Some plants reside in raised beds along the paved path, the better to entice you with their aroma and texture. A handsome handcrafted iron urn overflows with flowers and ivy and benches and tables invite you to relax, relish your surroundings, and admire the nearby Minneapolis skyline.

For information write to the Community Fragrance Garden, 1001 Hackman Circle, Fridley MN 55432-5759.

From I-94 take the Lyndale Avenue exit and go 1 block south to Franklin. Turn west on Franklin and go 1 block to Aldrich, then turn back north on Aldrich and go 1 block to Frontage Road. The garden is at the corner of 19th and Aldrich.

Lyndale Park Gardens
North shore of Lake Harriet
Minneapolis

61-acre municipal park. 2-acre All-American Rose Selection garden. 1-acre rock garden. Large annual/perennial flower gardens. Small arboretum. 13-acre Roberts Bird Sanctuary.

♿ Brochure. Many plants labeled. Trails. Picnic facilities.
Park and most gardens open daylight hours all year.
Rose garden open early April-early October.

There's something beautiful at the Lyndale Gardens from spring right through summer and winter and back into spring. The rock garden is perhaps at its loveliest in the spring, when most of the stronger-than-they-look alpines, adapted to short mountain summers, hurry to bloom and set seeds. This 60-year-old garden has a turbulent history. When it was planted in 1929-30, heavy boulders were simply tumbled down the slope to make a "garden of rocks." Weedy, woody vegetation grew in the crevices, took over the garden, and soon shaded it into oblivion; by 1946 the "garden" was an oak woods where only an occasional rock could be seen. A 1981 tornado felled the woods and revealed the garden's original skeleton. In 1983, high school crews removed 17 large trucksful of weedy brush and the site was ready for reincarnation. The east cliff was constructed and planted with mugho pines and by late 1989 the first acre of garden was fully installed. Another half-acre is evolving into a shady rockery of azaleas and rhododendrons, perennial flowers, and a water cascade. A Japanese-style bridge features stones found near ground zero of the 1945 atomic blasts over Hiroshima and Nagasaki; those cities presented the rocks to the City of Minneapolis as peace symbols. Each year, several peace-related activities take place among the alpines, dwarf conifers, and diminutive flowering trees of the rock garden.

◀ Lyndale Park holds one of the nation's oldest public rose gardens, two acres that should satisfy any rose-lover. Over 4,000 rose plants of all types, including the almost wild, perfume an area that was once a swampy slough. Numbered hybrids populate the AARS Test Garden, the northernmost such garden in the US. The bronze and marble Heffelfinger Fountain, flanked by tree roses, quietly surveys all this beauty.

Lyndale's large flower beds, accented by the Phelps Fountain, change every year but you'll always find a good variety of cannas, a Minneapolis favorite since the turn of the century. The nearby arboretum, a natural contrast to the manicured rose and flower gardens, includes some of the rarest and oldest trees in Minneapolis. In the same general area is the Roberts Bird Sanctuary, 13 acres of woodland and wetland and their botanic riches. Much of this area suffered severe losses in 1979 and 1981 storms. Extensive restoration includes an on-going search for appropriate methods of controlling the alien purple loosestrife, a beautiful but intensely aggressive plant import that displaces less vigorous natives.

Lyndale is inviting even in winter, when the skeletons of trees and gardens are apparent and cross-country skiers fill the trails.

From I-35W exit at 35-36th streets or 46th Street and go west to Bryant Avenue South. Take Bryant north from 46th Street or south from 35/36th to 40th Street West. Go 2 blocks west on 40th to King's Highway, then south 1 block to Roseway Road and west on Roseway to the visitor parking lot.

University of Minnesota, Minneapolis campus
Church Street Plaza
Minneapolis

1½-acre pedestrian plaza.

 No particular amenities.
Open daylight hours all year.

It's hard to believe this richly planted space is the roof of a telecommunications center and a parking facility. Mini-groves of dwarf Swiss mountain pine (*Pinus mugo mugo*) contrast with masses of airy Russian sage (*Perovskia atriplicifolia*) and sweeps of tall purple moor grass (*Molina arundinacea* 'Windspiel'). Silvery artemisias march before stately clumps of tufted hair grass (*Deschampsia caespitosa*) while thornless honeylocusts cast flickering shadows on ligularias and astilbes, benches and walkways. Spikenards

(*Aralia racemosa*) and sages and coreopsis will add flowers in their time. These plantings were designed by Oehme, van Sweden, an East Coast firm whose installations are planned for all-season interest. The prolific flowers of spring and early summer are dramatic but the subtle colors and textures of later weeks are equally rewarding. Autumn is worth waiting for when it brings luscious rose-violet sweeps of sedum 'Autumn Joy' and Joe-Pye weed (*Eupatorium purpureum*). A winter walk through the plaza presents skeletal trees and sturdy conifers, rosy-gold and silvery grasses, striking seedheads, and the persistent spikes of yucca.

Those lucky people who work in surrounding buildings are rewarded with bird's-eye views of the plaza, a delightful sort of garden-viewing that's not common in our relatively flat part of the country. The plaza offers respite from the trials of campus life . . . or from traveling around the city and on the highways.

For information contact the Office of the Vice President, Physical Planning, 340 Morrill Hall, 100 Church Street SE, Minneapolis MN 55455. (612) 625-7355.

From I-35W go east on University Avenue 8 blocks to Church Street. Turn south onto Church Street and go a block and a half to the plaza.
From I-94 take the Huron Boulevard exit and follow Huron northwest to 4th Street SE. Continue west to 17th Avenue SE, then turn south and go two and a half blocks to the plaza. Public parking is available in the structure beneath the plaza.

The Minneapolis Sculpture Garden
Vineland Place
Minneapolis MN 55403
(612) 375-7655

11-acre sculpture garden. 8,000 sq.ft. Cowles Conservatory. Major art museum and theater complex.

♿ ☕ Guide to sculpture. Museum shop. Restaurants in museum. Special events.
Sculpture Garden open every day from sunrise to midnight. Cowles Conservatory open all year Tuesday-Sunday 10am-9pm, sometimes later.

Contemporary sculpture grows here, in rooms defined by deciduous trees and clipped arborvitae hedge and furnished with plants selected for all-season interest, rooms that have the handsome Minneapolis skyline as a "borrowed view." These rather formal spaces, Phase One of the garden's plan, were designed as neutral backgrounds for sculpture; they've been joined recently by less-formal Phase Two. In this more relaxed design, curving paths carry you to the sculptures, through surroundings that more nearly fit our concept of "garden." The new block-long stainless steel arbor, itself an impressive sculpture, shelters masses of perennials at its feet. These plants were chosen to enhance the sculptures, rather than simply frame them. The sculpture garden, and the greenery within, will bear watching as they continue to develop.

Frank Gehry's *Standing Glass Fish*, surrounded by Washingtonia palms, dominates the conservatory's central room. The north wing features upright growing arches of creeping fig (*Ficus reptans*) in a bit of architectural topiary; both the north and south wings house seasonal floral displays. The conservatory is often open late into the night if there is a performance at the Guthrie Theater across the street; wouldn't it be gratifying to spend a day with the visual, performing, and horticultural arts at this excellent complex?

From I-94 westbound, take the Lyndale North exit. Get immediately into the left lane of Lyndale, as the Vineland Place access from Lyndale is on the left (west) side of the street.
From I-94 eastbound, exit at Wayzata Boulevard/Dunwoody and stay in the far right lane on Wayzata. Turn right at Hennepin/Lyndale avenues, go one block south and turn right onto Vineland Place.

Theodore Wirth Park
Around Wirth Lake
Minneapolis

743-acre municipal park. 13-acre Eloise Butler Wildflower Garden and Bird Sanctuary. J. D. Rivers' 4H Childrens' Garden. Wirth Daylily Garden.

♿ Wildflower garden brochure. Some plants labeled. Trails. Picnic facilities. Special events. Butler Wildflower Garden open April 1-October 31 7:30am-dusk. Childrens' and Daylily gardens open daylight hours during the growing season.

Note: Hilly natural terrain makes the Wildflower Garden very difficult for handicapped visitors. Also, the Park Board has issued a special caution against leaving valuables in your vehicle at this garden, which is not a good idea wherever you are.

In 1907, Eloise Butler's passion for wildflowers led her to create this haven, a botanical refuge that's believed to be the oldest of its kind in the nation. These acres shelter hundreds of common wildflower species and several that are seriously endangered. In spring, bold masses of white trillium carpet rich woodlands, more delicate wildflowers bloom among fresh new ferns, and sunny marshes are filled with the gold and green of marsh marigold (*Caltha palustris*). Wild orchids and orchises, those botanical jewels, can be found throughout the garden during spring and summer. Summer also brings intensely scarlet cardinal flowers (*Lobelia cardinalis*) to streamsides and yellow pond lilies (*Nuphar* sp.) to shallow ponds. In late summer, the swamps are purple with Joe-Pye weed (*Eupatorium purpurea*) and the prairies explode with blazing star (*Liatris* sp.), goldenrods, coneflowers, and asters. Prairie dock (*Silphium terebinthinaceum*), whose sand-papery leaves can be used as potscrubbers, lifts sunflower-like blossoms above big and little bluestem and other native grasses. Well-marked trails and boardwalks meander through the varying ecosystems and past numbered sites that are described in the excellent garden guide (available at the garden's entrance).

The 4H Childrens' Garden encourages city youngsters to plant, grow, weed, harvest, and share vegetable garden products. Weekly sessions during the growing season teach horticultural skills, provide gardening time, and often include field trips to informative sites nearby.

Just a half block from the Childrens' Garden, you'll find the Wirth Daylily Garden, extensive plantings that were installed to welcome the 1991 National Convention of the American Hemerocallis Society. Several hundred daylily cultivars and their companion perennials fill this spacious garden; thanks to thoughtful planning and careful plant selection, these beds are colorful from late June through early autumn.

Wirth, the largest park in the Minneapolis system, offers water sports and a host of other outdoor activities in addition to garden-viewing. You'll want far more than just a few hours amidst the pleasures of Wirth Park.

To Butler Wildflower Garden: Exit I-394 at Penn Avenue. Take the frontage road south of I-394 west to Wirth Parkway. Turn north onto Wirth and go a half mile to the garden's entrance.
To the Childrens' and the Daylily gardens: Exit I-394 at Penn Avenue and go north about a mile to Glenwood Avenue. Turn west and follow Glenwood into the park. The Childrens' Garden is at the intersection of Glenwood and Washburn, the Daylily Garden a half block away at Glenwood and Xerxes.

August Schell Brewing Company
Schell's Park
New Ulm MN 56073
(507) 354-5528

◀ Sizable corporate gardens.

Fee for brewery tours. Shop (brewery-related items). Special events.
Gardens open daily all year 7am-10pm. Museum and brewery tours Memorial Day-Labor Day. Tours in afternoons.

Follow a winding road through gentle woods to the historic Schell Brewery and its expansive gardens. In this quiet greenery, deer, peafowl, and ducks keep company with lush flowers and mature trees and shrubs. You can visit the Museum of Brewing and take a brewery tour or pick up a souvenir at the gift shop and, after all that exertion, take refuge in the gardens. You may even have the good fortune to arrive during one of the summer Sunday musicales; local newspapers list these and other special garden events. Even without the music, you'll find these gardens refreshing.

From Minnesota Route 15 (Broadway Street), turn onto 18th South Street and follow the signs to Schell Brewing Company.

Mayo Medical Center Gardens
200 West 1st Street
Rochester MN 55905
(507) 284-2511

10 acres landscaped flower beds.

 Restaurants and cafeterias in clinic facilities.
Gardens open all year 7am-6pm.

To the casual visitor, this amazing complex feels like a major hotel; public areas are spacious, a uniformed doorman summons cabs and greets shuttle vehicles, and the buildings are surrounded by gardens. Lacy sumacs ornament a terrace and its rock-floored fountain, while numerous benches and ledges encourage rest and quiet thought. Bright flowers are scattered among ground covers and masses of shrubs and trees in a landscape where 50% of the permanent plantings are evergreen. Over 6,000 bulbs bloomed here in the spring but, on this late June day, it's the annuals, over 10,000 of them, that brighten every corner of these award-winning grounds. Peak bloom is planned for early August but it's hard to imagine the gardens more colorful than they are today. You'll find few garden rarities here but these well-cared-for installations invite leisurely and appreciative perambulations. ▶

For further information contact the Grounds Supervisor at the address above or ask at information desks in the Mayo building.

The clinic and its gardens, just west of the center of Rochester, are very easy to find.

Riverside Park
13th Street and Riverside Drive Southeast
St. Cloud

Large municipal park. 15 acres of gardens (Munsinger Gardens, Clemens Gardens, and Virginia Clemens Rose Garden). 60,000 sq.ft. production greenhouses.

♿ Many plants labeled. Picnic facilities. Annual plant sale. Guided garden and/or greenhouse tours by appointment.
Gardens open April-October sunrise-sunset. Greenhouse open all year weekdays 7am-3:30pm.

Dramatic vistas, mature trees, and graceful shrubs enhance these lush gardens above the Mississippi River. Bloom progression begins in early spring with the bulbs and wildflowers that are followed, in early summer, by Showy Lady's-slipper orchids and other beauties. For all-season color and charm, 65,000 bedding plants surround hosta and daylily collections and other perennials in shade gardens, in sunny sites, and in the formal garden. Roses of many persuasions, 1,100 bushes in the Virginia Clemens Rose Garden, provide color and fragrance from spring until frost. An informative pamphlet for a self-guided garden tour is available in the gardens and will add to your enjoyment. Doesn't this sound like a perfect place for the September plant sale? What a delight it would be to shop for perennials, house plants, and dried flowers in such surroundings.   ▶

FYI Mayowood. The extensive estate gardens around Mayowood, former home of a founder of Mayo Clinic, were inspired by historic English gardens. You'll find flower beds and ponds, pergolas and pavilions, a tea house and a man-made lake, islands and Oriental-style bridges . . . and space to wander. These gardens are open during the growing season; the house is open for guided tours all year.

Mayowood is about four miles southwest of downtown Rochester. You can visit it *only* by making arrangements at the Olmsted County Historical Center at the corner of County Road 122 and Salem Road SW.

For information contact Mayowood, Box 6411, Rochester MN 55903-6411. (507) 282-9447.

◀ Although the Munsinger Gardens originated in the late 1930s and early 1940s, expansion and development are on-going. The garden's neighbors recently set up a sizable endowment that will encourage further improvement of existing gardens, initiation of herb and vegetable demonstration gardens, establishment of a horticultural library, and building an interpretative center and small conservatory. Enjoy the gardens now and, in years to come, keep your eye on ensuing improvements.

For information contact Saint Cloud Parks and Recreation, 400 South Second Street, St. Cloud MN 56301. (612) 255-7216 or (612) 255-7238 (Riverside Park greenhouse).

From I-94 take the St. Cloud/St. Augusta exit, go to the first stoplight, and turn right onto Clearwater Road, which becomes 9th Avenue South. Go to the next stoplight and turn right onto 10th Street South. Cross University Bridge and, at Kilian Boulevard, turn left. Follow Kilian to 13th Street SE. Turn left and take 13th Street SE to Riverside Drive and the park.

St. Paul

The College of St. Catherine
2004 Randolph Avenue
St. Paul MN 55105
(612) 690-6000 or (612) 690-6777

100-acre college campus. Extensive annual and perennial beds. Theme gardens. 2-acre pond. 1,000 sq.ft. greenhouse.

♿ ☕ Shop (general campus bookstore). College cafeteria and snack bars. Group tours by prior appointment. Dormitory-style lodging available for summer visitors.
Gardens open daylight hours during growing season.

This self-contained campus feels like a refuge in the middle of the city; woods, water, and gardens will do that for you. Open spaces and intimate nooks hold annual and perennial gardens, including an English garden, shade plantings, and a rock garden. I attended the Midwest Weavers' Conference here years ago, long before I was much aware of gardens; even then, it seemed a delightful green domain to me.

Entrance to the college is at the corner of Cleveland and Randolph Avenues. From I-94 take the Cretin Avenue exit and go south about two miles to ▶

◀ Randolph Avenue, then east a short distance to Cleveland Avenue.
From I-494 take Minnesota Route 5 toward St. Paul to Edgecumbe Road. Follow Edgecumbe/Fairview to Randolph, then go west about a half mile to Cleveland.

Como Park Conservatory
Midway Parkway at Kaufman Drive
St. Paul MN 55103
(612) 489-1740

Three acres. 21,000 sq.ft. conservatory. 1-acre Ordway Memorial Japanese Garden. McKnight Formal Garden.

Fee for conservatory in winter only. Shop. Many plants labeled. Picnic facilities. Food concessions at zoo.
Conservatory open daily all year 10am-6pm. Formal garden open daylight hours. Japanese Garden has limited, variable hours.

In the central dome of this "Crystal Palace," massive palms reach for the sun and tropical underplantings flaunt their grand variety of textures and colors. The conservatory's north wing houses plants that are particularly fragrant or that have economic value: bamboo, citrus, *Coffee arabica*, eucalpyti, camellias, the cinnamons *Cinnamomum camphora* and *C. cassia*, pomegranates, figs, and much more.

As with many public horticultural sites in our area, Como Park Conservatory is undergoing major reconstruction; if all goes according to plan, all areas of the 80-year-old conservatory will have been renewed or expanded by 1994. The Fern Room and the Sunken Gardens were closed when we visited but, even during reconstruction, the conservatory has continued to hold several annual plant shows and the yearly tropical fish show.

On this late June afternoon, the Victorian-style structure teems with enthusiastic children and their families; they've probably visited the adjacent Como Park Zoo, too. McKnight Formal Garden lies between the conservatory and the zoo. This small paved area of raised beds and carpet-bedded annuals may be a lovely site for an evening wedding or a midday eulogy but on this fine Friday, while the rest of the park churns with visitors, the formal garden sits deserted and somewhat forbidding, a lonely space watching the fun go by.

On the other side of the conservatory, the Japanese Garden speaks of quiet respite although it, too, is *full* of visitors today. The "snow-viewing lantern" at the entrance was a gift from the City of Nagasaki, Japan, St. Paul's Sister City; other lanterns came from the Japanese exhibit at the 1904 World's Fair in St. Louis. This large stroll garden was designed by a landscape architect from Nagasaki who, in 1984, visited the garden to instruct volunteers and staff members in traditional Japanese design and maintenance techniques. His instruction "took." The garden is beautiful today and was surely breath-taking earlier in the season, when all the azaleas bloomed. Plants here range in size from ground-huggers to soaring trees. You'll have a satisfying stroll through this artful garden of attractive greenery, water both active and placid, and carefully sited rocks.

For information contact St. Paul Parks and Recreation, 300 City Hall Annex, 25 West Fourth Street, St. Paul MN 55102.

From I-94 take Snelling Avenue four or five miles north to Midway Parkway, then go east on Midway to the Conservatory.

Mullin Horticultural Garden and Woodland
University of Minnesota, St. Paul campus

One and a half acres. Prairie, woodland, and ornamental gardens. All-America Selections garden.

Many plants labeled.
Open all year, daylight hours.

Here's a chance to compare and contrast native wildflowers with related horticultural varieties in test and display gardens; perhaps you'll identify wild relatives of your garden favorites. Between early spring and late autumn, from adjacent streets or the garden's wood-chip paths, you can savor the spectacular colors of over 350 cultivars that are being performance-tested for southeastern Minnesota.

For information contact the Department of Horticultural Science, 305 Alderman Hall, 1970 Folwell Avenue, St. Paul MN 55108. (612) 624-5300.

From I-35W or I-94, take Minnesota Route 280 to Larpenteur Avenue. Go east on Larpenteur a little over a mile then turn right onto Gortner Avenue and go south to Folwell Avenue. The garden is near the intersection of Folwell and Gortner.

Ambergate Gardens
8015 Krey Avenue
Waconia MN 55387
(612) 443-2248

Commercial. Two-thirds acre display gardens.

 Catalog. Plant sales. Call before visiting.
Open May 1-September 30 Tuesday-Sunday.

Ambergate specializes in ". . . uncommon and/or unusual herbaceous perennials hardy in USDA Zone 4." You'll find native and exotic plants here, with particular emphasis on martagon lilies. Although this is a mail-order nursery, there are always a few good plants potted up for on-site retail sales. Because this is a small, family-operated business, appointments for visits are greatly appreciated. The owners hope to expand and relocate Ambergate in the mid-1990s, which is another good reason to call before visiting; the business may have moved. But if uncommon plants intrigue you, it will be worth your while to find Ambergate.

From I-494 on the southwest side of Minneapolis, go west on Minnesota Route 5 to a mile west of Victoria (10 or 12 miles). Turn left onto Krey Avenue. The gardens surround the first home on the east side of Krey.

Shady Oaks Nursery
112 10th Avenue SE
Waseca MN 56093

Commercial. Emphasis on shade plants. Greenhouse. Production and display gardens.

 Catalog. Many plants labeled. Plant sales.
Open June 1 through summer, "business hours."

If your garden is more shade than sun, you'll love Shady Oaks. The 20'x60' display garden at the address above, and a much larger garden (12,000 sq.ft.) at the owner's home, may give you more ideas than you can handle. Here are hostas, epimediums, and ferns, woodland wildflowers, shrubs, trees, and vines. There are plants here, too, that may surprise you with their tolerance or preference for shade, such as the tall stonecrop sedums, evening primroses (*Oenothera* spp.), and several types of irises.

Shady Oaks' extensive catalog lists many, many hostas and other shade-loving perennials and these gardens allow you to admire them *in situ*. This is predominately a mail-order business but there are always some plants available on site. So your zinnias get too much shade? Never mind, there are far more interesting plants to be admired and adopted here.

Mailing address: Shady Oaks Nursery, 700 19th Avenue NE, Waseca MN 56093. (507) 835-5033.

From US Route 14 in Waseca, go about a mile south on US 13 to 112 10th Avenue SE. For directions and permission to visit the owner's extensive semi-private gardens, ask at, or phone, the 10th Avenue site.

Noerenberg Memorial County Park
2840 North Shore Drive
Wayzata MN

74-acre county park. Several acres formal estate gardens.

♿ Many plants labeled. Group tours weekdays only, by prior appointment.
Open daily May 1-September 30 9am-8pm.

These elegant gardens once supplied cut flowers to the Noerenberg mansion and to local hotels and hospitals. Today, they are a popular site for weddings and other delightful garden events. Every year, nearly 10,000 annuals join established perennials and bulbs here; some of those bulbs were brought from Europe when the Noerenberg family arrived in the 1880s. You may also see new introductions or unusual plants that were propagated in the Hennepin Parks greenhouses. The Hemerocallis Society of Minnesota helped establish the 1,000 daylily cultivars that add their color and grace to the gardens.

On summer Sundays, informal garden tours inform visitors about the Noerenberg family and their flowers. The mid-July Garden Party brings guests, music, and refreshments to the vibrant gardens. Lake breezes and expansive garden views are yours on the upper deck of the Noerenberg boathouse, an Oriental-type structure that has long been a Lake Minnetonka landmark. On hot summer days, when the gardens are most colorful, those breezes will be welcome indeed.

For information contact Hennepin Parks, 12615 County Road 9, P. O. Box 47320, Plymouth MN 55447-0320. (612) 476-4666.   ▶

From US Route 12 west of Minneapolis, go south on Old Crystal Bay Road to its junction with County Road 84. Continue south on CR 84 about a mile to the park.

Rohrer Rose Garden
On Lake Winona
Winona

Large municipal park. One-acre rose garden.

♿ ☕ Some plants labeled. Picnic facilities. Snacks available at park concessions. Open daylight hours.

The well-tended rose garden is pleasantly aromatic on this warm June evening. Luxuriant roses haven't gone into heat-induced summer doldrums yet, there is a slight breeze off Lake Winona, and it's a treat to be here. Most of this side of the lake is a large city park that offers swimming beaches, food concessions, picnic areas, and inviting walkways. On our next visit, we'll carry a picnic breakfast to the small gazebo among the roses and savor the morning scents and lakeside scenes.

From I-90 take Minnesota Route 43 toward Winona. This will take you around Lake Winona and to Lake Park Drive. Follow Lake Park Drive to the garden.

Ohio: North

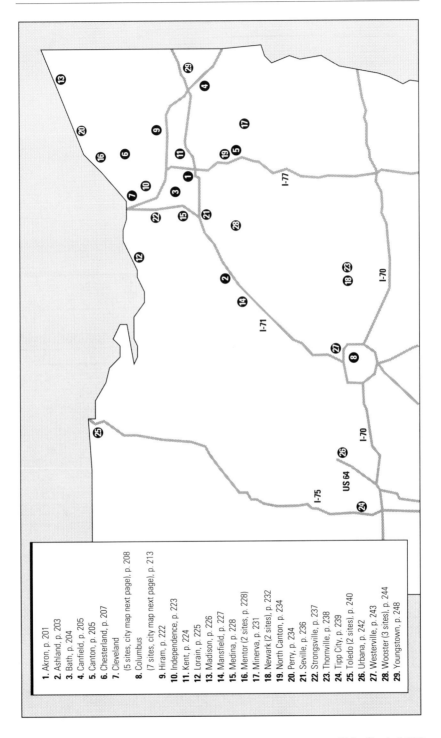

1. Akron, p. 201
2. Ashland, p. 203
3. Bath, p. 204
4. Canfield, p. 205
5. Canton, p. 205
6. Chesterland, p. 207
7. Cleveland
   (5 sites, city map next page), p. 208
8. Columbus
   (7 sites, city map next page), p. 213
9. Hiram, p. 222
10. Independence, p. 223
11. Kent, p. 224
12. Lorain, p. 225
13. Madison, p. 226
14. Mansfield, p. 227
15. Medina, p. 228
16. Mentor (2 sites), p. 228
17. Minerva, p. 231
18. Newark (2 sites), p. 232
19. North Canton, p. 234
20. Perry, p. 234
21. Seville, p. 236
22. Strongsville, p. 237
23. Thornville, p. 238
24. Tipp City, p. 239
25. Toledo (2 sites), p. 240
26. Urbana, p. 242
27. Westerville, p. 243
28. Wooster (3 sites), p. 244
29. Youngstown, p. 248

Ohio: North / CLEVELAND and COLUMBUS

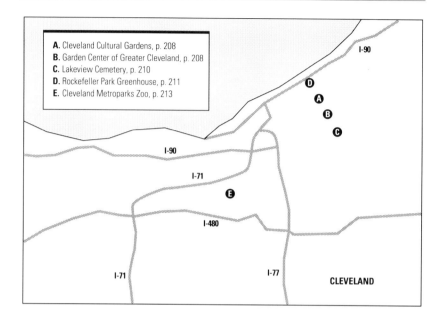

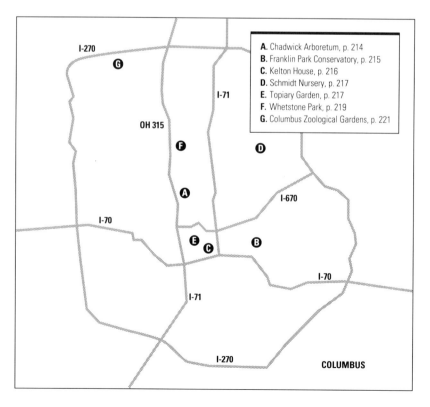

Ohio: North

As you travel the interstate highways and the state routes of Ohio, you'll see delightful patches of flowers in the median strips and along the roadsides. I'm told the Ohio State Police consider these a traffic hazard; too many people slow down to admire them and to park along the roadside for a closer look. It *is* difficult to identify plants at 65 mph. In mid-June, along I-70 not far east of Richmond IN, blue blossoms, vivid as blue jay feathers, float through a lively poppy "garden" in the median strip. Further along the road, a mass of traffic-sign yellow with the same blue highlights delights us. It's probably coreopsis accented with cornflowers but, being good road citizens, we don't stop to make sure. In August, coneflowers and black-eyed Susans blaze; by Halloween all the plantings are just patches of stubble, barely distinguishable from their surroundings. But my images of summer's colors persist.

Stan Hywet Hall and Gardens
714 North Portage Path
Akron OH 44303
(216) 836-5533 (Administrative Offices)
(216) 836-9075 (Recorded Information)

70-acre estate grounds. All-American Rose Selection garden. Japanese and walled English gardens. Conservatory. Naturalistic landscape.

$ ♿ Brochure. Gift shop. Some plants labeled. Trails. Light snacks in gift shop. Seasonal plant sales. Workshops and other special events. Tickets available for grounds and gardens only or for house and grounds. Group tours by appointment. No group rates on weekends or during special events.
Open all year. Closed Monday and major holidays.
Grounds open at 9am during summer, later in winter. Manor tours offered Tuesday-Saturday 10am-4pm, Sunday 1-4pm.

Stan Hywet's entrance drive, as it winds through the remnants of apple orchards, may feel pastoral but sophisticated gardens and well-designed naturalistic plantings lie ahead. Imagine the French-influenced Rhododendron Allée in spring, when rhododendrons and azaleas glow beneath tall London plane trees. Perhaps you'll fancy the woodsy Dell, a natural amphitheater that once saw staged entertainments and family weddings. When the Seiberlings and their four children lived at Stan Hywet (he was a co-founder of the Goodyear Tire and Rubber Company), the English Garden was Mrs. Seiberling's favorite garden refuge. Today this secluded, pool-centered space is an inviting shade garden. Another intimate space, the Breakfast Room Garden, is perhaps best appreciated as it's seen from inside the house; its blues, whites, and yellows echo the Breakfast Room colors and would provide cheerful beginnings to summer days.

Terraces, balustrades, and lush perennial borders add to the "Englishness" of Stan Hywet's Tudor estate. Formal terraces and lawns, designed for outdoor entertaining on a grand scale, provide enchanting vistas over rolling meadows and woodlands. Closer views feature the Japanese Garden and the lagoons that were the stone quarries for which the estate is named; "Stan Hywet" evidently means "stone quarry" in Old English.

There are gardens here for nearly every taste. Over a hundred rose bushes fill the enclosed cartwheel of the All-American Rose Selections garden, an especially romantic spot. The birch allée, a long path of light and shadow, leads to garden teahouses and an expansive view across the countryside. The Cutting Gardens remind us of those beds that yielded fresh flowers and vegetables to the Seiberlings and their guests. The ornamental shrub collection, not in the original garden plan, holds unusual specimens donated to Stan Hywet. Beds and baskets of annuals are another contemporary touch added for the pleasure of today's visitors. But the Seiberlings *did* enjoy their tropical conservatory. The original structure deteriorated over the years and the building you see today, with its waterfalls, fountains, and exotic plants, is of recent construction.

Although Stan Hywet was built for a private family, it fully exemplifies that family's motto, *Not For Us Alone*. It was shared through parties, entertainments, and other festivities from its very beginning. Even today, the visitor is considered in the three different garden tours (the comprehensive, the highlights, and the limited walking) structured for those with varying amounts of time and mobility. Stan Hywet welcomes visitors to over a dozen special events during the year, from antique shows to alfresco dramatics and, in winter, madrigal dinners. At the May Garden Mart, you can choose from all types of flower and herb plants as you munch on festival food; on this particular day, admission to the grounds is free. The manor's Music Room is the frequent site of concerts, flower shows, lectures, and travelogues. It's easy to see why the gardens and manor of Stan Hywet please today's visitors much as they delighted the Seiberlings and their guests.

Stan Hywet, on the northwest side of Akron, is accessible from all area freeways and interstate highways. It's near Sand Run Metro Park and is probably marked on the Akron enlargement of your road map. Write for two pages of ▶

> **FYI** If you have to ask for directions, sound like a native and call it "Stan Hee'-wet."

◀ *direct and scenic routings from all directions. You'll see brown and white Stan Hywet directional signs along most area highways, except for the interstates.*

The Parsley Pot
697 County Road 1302
R. D. 2
Ashland OH 44805
(419) 322-7514

Commercial. 30'x30' herb garden. Roadside display garden.

Gift shop. Some plants labeled. Seasonal plant sales.
Open all year Tuesday-Saturday 10am-5pm, Sunday 1-5pm.

A comely roadside bed of coneflowers, yarrows, and hibiscus marks this pleasant spot in the Ohio countryside. Walk down the hill and behind the buildings, where the radiant combination of hibiscus, black-eyed Susan, and magenta lythrum welcomes you to the herb garden. A half-barrel overflows with lush, crisp, and fragrant scented geraniums (*Pelargonium* spp.). Pots of curly parsley hang fresh and cool-looking from the shop's high deck while an elegant 6-foot bay tree (*Laurel nobilis*) dominates the shady area below. The sweet autumn clematis (*Clematis virginiana*) that's climbing vigorously on a deck support will be a dense and aromatic bower in the early fall. Sages, artemisias, coneflowers, and other heat-lovers thrive in this sunny space that feels like a courtyard, enclosed as it is by buildings on three sides.

In the large old barn that is the Parsley Pot shop, I'm entranced by the ancient and well-worn floor timbers, some of them 18 or 20 inches wide and very thick, evidence of the massive trees that once grew in this area. Above these timbers, interesting cabinets and shelves hold "country" items, teas, unique herb and spice blends, stationery, dried everlastings, herb-related books, and a wide assortment of other tempting items. Today, in mid-July, I'm surprised by a special collection of Christmas ornaments. Thoughts of Christmas and winter require a short period of adjustment, since I've just come in from the warm, sunny, and nicely growing garden. Obviously, the Parsley Pot offers something for all seasons.

From US Route 30 take Ohio Route 60 north to US 42. Go northeast on US 42 a short distance to County Road 1302 (Middle Rowsburg Road), then turn east and go a little over 1½ miles to the Parsley Pot.

The Goldsmith Garden at Hale Farm and Village
2686 Oak Hill Road
P. O. Box 296
Bath OH 44210-0296
(216) 575-9137 or (216) 666-3711

Facsimile of 1830s garden. Living history museum of the Western Reserve from 1825 to 1850.

$ ☕ Brochure. Shop. Library (Western Reserve history). Seasonal plant sales. Seminars, festivals, and other events. Group rates by reservation.
Open June 1-October 31 Wednesday-Saturday 10am-5pm, Sunday noon-5pm. Closed Monday, Tuesday, and the first two weeks of September.
No admittance after 4pm; it's suggested that you allow 2½ hours for the full experience.

Goldsmith Garden lies around a genteel home that was built at Willoughby, Ohio, in 1832 and moved to Hale Farm in 1973. The delightful gardens you see here reflect boundless enthusiasm and countless hours of research and fundraising by volunteers. Extensive research revealed landscape designs appropriate to a home of this age and quality. Lists of plants that were used in the area then, or that were at least available, were developed from agricultural society notes, the journals and diaries of early homeowners, newspaper advertisements, and gardening columns. The gardens continue to expand and develop as time and funds allow, as "new" heritage plants become available, and as knowledge increases.

Herb Thyme, an early June herb festival, is a major source of funds for Goldsmith Garden. Pioneer gardens were built by trading plants, cuttings, seeds, and information; Herb Thyme continues that tradition with lectures and demonstrations on herb and garden topics and with sales of unique plants.

Nearly every historic restoration or living history museum has a garden of some sort. These are often small herb and vegetable gardens or ornamental plantings that are not particularly appropriate to the time period portrayed. This site is an exception. Its handsome garden, true to nineteenth century horticulture and design, ". . . reflects the elegance and sophistication of the Goldsmith House." In this restoration, the gardens will truly take you back in time.

Hale Farm and Village is in the Cuyahoga Valley National Recreation Area between Cleveland and Akron, south of I-80 and I-271, west of I-77. It's easily reached from Akron or from the small towns of Bath on the west and Peninsula on the north. State and county roads in the area carry directional signs. Or, write for the brochure that gives 9 different routes from nearby interstate highways.

Backyard Herbs 'n' Things
4101 Canfield Road
Canfield OH 44406
(216) 793-8326

Commercial grower of herbs and everlastings. Several acres of production fields.

Shop. Many plants labeled. Seasonal plant sales. Workshops and other events.
Open May 1-June 30 Monday-Saturday 10am-5pm. Early October-December 24 same days and hours. July-September or other hours by appointment or by chance.

Globe amaranth, statice, love-in-a-mist, and a host of other herbs and everlastings march in the fields and, in their dried or drying forms, fill the barn/shop here. If you prefer to grow your own everlastings, "sample gardens" help you visualize these plants in your garden. The shop offers supplies for dried arrangements, the books that tell you how to make them, and bee skeps and sundials for your garden. Workshops inform you on herb-growing and other botanical arts. There's much to see and learn in this particular backyard.

From US Route 30/Ohio Route 11 on the southwest side of Youngstown, take US 224 to Canfield. From Canfield go northeast on US 62 (Canfield Road) to Backyard Herbs.

Canton Garden Center
1615 Stadium Park, NW
Canton OH 44718
(216) 455-6172

▶

FYI In 1662, Charles II of England granted this land to the colony of Connecticut. In 1786, the young state of Connecticut yielded claim to some of its other western lands but reserved this area for settlers, especially those who had lost their property in the Revolutionary War. Thus, *Western Reserve*. It became part of the Northwest Territory in 1800 and is now northeastern Ohio.

◀ Two acres within Stadium Park. Garden Center. Japanese garden.

♿ Shop. Many plants labeled. Library. Trails and picnic facilities in park. Classes and special events.
Park and Garden Center grounds open daily during daylight hours. Garden Center office and Arranger's Cupboard Gift Shop open Tuesday-Friday 10am-4pm.

In spite of a very early severe freeze, these gardens are still lively when we visit in early November. In the Garden of the Five Senses, bright berries decorate shrub hollies and creeping cotoneasters while waxy bayberries are glacial blue against bronze foliage. Thymes and catmint (*Nepeta mussinii*) and fernleaf tansy have held their color and pungent scents. A few hardy blooms join sturdy buds among leathery azalea leaves but, in the herb garden, only white alyssum survives. Raised beds, paved walks, comfortable benches, and braille and visual labels make this garden "user-friendly" for everyone.

A brick bell tower stands nearby, its openwork dramatic against the leafless trees. At its feet, rose bushes, junipers, red barberry, and red twig dogwood supply winter interest. In the woodland Japanese garden, an arched bridge spans the terraced stream and its ice-rimmed, rock-lined pools. Evergreens, azaleas, and masses of irises add texture to a carpet of russet oak leaves and evergreen ivy. This is a very small Japanese garden but, even in early winter, it gives me quiet joy.

In the Garden Center, the Arranger's Cupboard is in full Christmas mode today. Santa in myriad forms, theme trees, wreaths, and dried arrangements nearly overwhelm an appealing assortment of botany-themed gifts. Comfortable furniture in the adjacent library encourages research or browsing. Nearly 60 different garden clubs and horticultural societies use Garden Center facilities and support its programs. These groups' activities are often open to visitors.

A well-surfaced walking/jogging trail winds through this large city park, past streams and ponds, ducks and geese. Monument Park, an extension of Stadium Park, contains President William McKinley's burial place and monument. McKinley Museum, near the monument, offers a planetarium, science and industrial exhibits, period street scenes, and a research library. You'll also find the Football Hall of Fame not far from the Garden Center. One could bring a picnic lunch and spend a most pleasant and informative day in these parks.

Exit I-77 at Fulton Road, which will take you to Stadium Park Drive if you follow the signs for the Football Hall of Fame.

Sunnybrook Farms Nursery
9448 Mayfield Road
P. O. Box 6
Chesterland OH 44026
(216) 729-7232

Commercial. Three acres of shade, herb, and theme gardens. Seven greenhouses and shade houses.

♿ Catalog. Shop. Many plants labeled. Plant sales. Festivals, lectures, and other events. Group tours by appointment.
Open all year Monday-Saturday 9am-5pm, Sunday 10am-4pm. Extended hours in May and December.

If you're fond of hostas, this is the place for you; over 800 hosta species and cultivars live here. Hostas in all their permutations join other shade-lovers in plantings that are attractive from spring's foamy astilbes, through autumn's last colorful leaf, to the all-season grace of conifers.

Sunny theme gardens include a "working garden" of culinary herbs and a striking collection of grasses. The gray and silver garden, cool-seeming on a hot day, will glisten under the full moons of summer. Varied leaves and delicate flowers of scented geraniums (*Pelargonium* spp.) fill another bed; brush the leaves gently and be reminded of apples or nutmeg, pine woods or roses in the sun. Perennial flowers and sun-tolerant hostas fill other bright corners.

Sunnybrook welcomes spring with Springfest, a series of garden-related lectures and demonstrations. September's Herb and Garden Fair/Wool Hollow Festival brings continuous presentations on herbs, gardening, and crafts and is highlighted by garden tours and a fleece-to-shawl demonstration.

Greenhouses and shade structures here offer house plants, alpines for your rock garden, perennials for sun and shade, and a special selection of plants for wet areas. In the shop you'll find handcrafted wreaths and sachets, the bounty of the herb garden. Here, too, are thoughtful gifts for gardeners and a range of plant-related books.

If, like me, you're of the generation that equates Sunnybrook Farm with a girl named Rebecca, come enjoy these gardens while you look for her. ▶

FYI A "fleece-to-shawl" demonstration involves workers who card raw wool and spin it into yarn, then pass the yarn to knitters or weavers who make it into a shawl. More demanding demonstrations begin with sheep shearers and washed sheep. Some events feature contests wherein teams of shearers, spinners, and weavers, knitters, or crocheters work with a given amount of wool and within time limitations to produce a shawl of specific dimensions.

◀ *From I-271 take Exit 35, US Route 322, then go east on US 322 about 8 miles to Sunnybrook Farm.*

Cleveland

Cleveland Cultural Gardens
Rockefeller Park

Several acres of gardens and monuments.

Open daylight hours. Special ethnic and cultural events held throughout the year.

These assorted gardens tend to be semi-formal arrangements of lawn, sculpture, memorials, trees, and shrubs accented by a few flowers. The land was donated by the City of Cleveland in recognition of many national or ethnic groups' contributions to the life of the city. These groups have developed gardens to use for festivals, holiday observances, and other gatherings. The Shakespeare Garden, built in 1916, was the first installation; it later became the British Garden. The idea became a series of gardens that was dedicated as a unit in 1939. Today, twenty cultural gardens have been developed or are nearly complete. Some are more complex than others; the Italian Garden, dedicated in 1930, features a bi-level terrace, a variety of sculpture, and a stone from the Roman Forum. The British Garden is Elizabethan in mood while others are poignantly simple. Famous people and ethnic heroes have planted trees or performed in many of the gardens. Time spent among the range of moods and architectural styles here will be soothing and informative.

For more information and a map for a walking tour of the gardens contact City of Cleveland Greenhouse, 750 East 88th Street, Cleveland OH 44108-4100. (216) 664-3103.

This string of sedate gardens is bordered by Martin Luther King Drive on the west, East Boulevard on the east, and St. Clair Avenue and Superior Avenue on the north and south. They begin not far south of the Rockefeller Park City Greenhouse. The larger, more complete gardens lie along East Boulevard.

The Garden Center of Greater Cleveland
11030 East Boulevard
Cleveland OH 44106
(216) 721-1600

▶

◀ Eight acres. Major metropolitan garden center. Herb, rose, Japanese, and other specialty gardens.

♿ Shop. Many plants labeled. Library. Seasonal plant sales. Full range of educational activities and events.
Gardens open every day, daylight hours. Garden Center building (including Squire Library) open Monday-Friday 9am-5pm, Sunday 2-5pm. Closed Saturday and legal holidays. Trellis Shop open Monday-Friday 10am-4pm, Sunday 2-4:30.pm

---

A painter is trying to capture the lambent evening light, the air is rose-scented, and visitors are enjoying the riches of six different gardens. We move from garden room to garden room, from the open and sunny Western Reserve Herb Garden to the deep shade of rhododendron thickets. At one point, the path is guarded by a massive tree peony, a 10-foot beauty that is an omen for spring drama.

Herb Garden bees, clumsy with golden saddlebags, clamber over delicate white flower spikes of Culver's root (*Veronicastrum virginicum*). Circular millstones set into the paving give both unity and variety to this otherwise rectangular garden. Clematis climbs on hoops in front of a thicket of thorny, green, and fragrant heritage roses. Black-eyed Susans and lemon-yellow marigolds add their own afterglow to the evening dye garden.

A sibilant fountain graces the rose garden, where artfully trimmed domes of dwarf yews and trapezoids of Korean littleleaf box contrast with the shaggy roses. Nearby, a vigorous bayberry hedge, laden with waxy berries, accompanies rhododendrons, azaleas, dogwoods, and tree lilacs in a combination that seems to promise sweet candles for winter evenings and spring days filled with beauty.

In these gardens, as well as in the Japanese Garden and the Evans Reading Garden, you'll find gazebos, benches, and comfortable rocks for resting and admiring your surroundings.

The handsome Garden Center building houses the Eleanor Squire Library, an extensive reference library that includes the Corning Collection of Horticultural Classics. The Trellis Shop is filled with an assortment of things hard-to-resist . . . tropical plants, porcelain and terra cotta items, garden-theme wind socks, and books, books, books. Numerous classes and workshops are held here, including gardening activities for children and sessions of horticultural therapy. There are seasonal plant exhibits, flower shows, and plant sales; the three-day plant sale in late spring is surely heaven-on-earth for gardeners. ▶

◀ On even the hottest of days, garden fountains and the serene lily pond add the cool relief of water. And, on snowy winter days, these thoughtfully planned gardens will be inviting in other subtle ways. Spring bloom and autumn color will be spectacular . . . these are truly gardens for all seasons.

From I-90 take Martin Luther King, Jr. Drive southeast to East Boulevard. Continue southeast on East Boulevard to University Circle, Wade Oval, and the Garden Center.
NOTE: This can be a confusing area. There is limited access to Rockefeller Park, which also contains the City of Cleveland Greenhouse and the Cleveland Cultural Gardens. The park runs northwest/southeast and MLK Drive is a parkway along its west side; East Boulevard, along the park's east side, starts and stops. When MLK Drive ends near the bright blue Mt. Sinai Hospital, East Boulevard and access to Wade Oval are just across the street and a few hundred feet to your left. Considered the cultural center of Cleveland, University Circle also holds Case-Western Reserve University, the Fine Arts Museum, the Historical Society, and a number of other facilities.

The Lake View Cemetery Association
12316 Euclid Avenue
Cleveland OH 44106
(216) 421-2665

---

285 acres. Memorial architecture. Naturalized gardens. Woodlands.

♿ Brochures. Shop (in Garfield Monument). Many trees and plants labeled. Library. Grounds open daily 8am-5:30pm. Office and library open Monday-Saturday 8:30am-5pm. Garfield Monument open daily April 1-mid-November 9am-4pm.

Massive plantings of daffodils give particular punch to spring at Lakeview. Their beauty is followed by the flowers of azaleas, rhododendrons, crabapples, and other trees, shrubs, and perennials that bloom through summer into fall. As different varieties come into impressive bloom, floral auto routes are marked through the grounds. Nearly 500 trees and shrubs are identified by labels that can usually be read from your car. You may want to visit on Daffodil Sunday in mid-April or on Azalea Sunday in early May. In late summer the unusual flowers of castor aralia trees (*Kalopanax pictus*), Korean evodias (*Evodia daniellii*), and Japanese pagoda trees (*Sophora japonica*) will impress you. You'll see a bald cypress grove, a century-old weeping hemlock, and dramatic mature threadleaf maples (*Acer palmatum dissectum*) among the myriad of horticultural treats here. ▶

Lakeview holds so many significant plantings and so much Cleveland area history that it has become an active teaching resource. School classes and group tours come to visit and an educator's handbook has been prepared. The best-known memorial at Lakeview is the James A. Garfield Monument, a circular sandstone tower that includes mosaics, stained glass, sculpture, exterior friezes, and a gift/book shop. Jeptha Wade Memorial Chapel joins the Garfield Monument on the National Register of Historic Places. The entire interior of the classic-style Wade Chapel, including a large stained glass window, was designed by Louis Comfort Tiffany. If you ask at the cemetery office, near the main entry on Euclid Avenue, someone will take you to see this splendor. Maps and other information are available at the office too.

When Lakeview was established in 1869, this area was open countryside; now it's surrounded by city and suburbs. Whether you visit Lakeview for the botany or for its history, you'll find it a lovely refuge.

Take I-71 north to Chester Avenue. Go east on Chester to Euclid, then further east on Euclid to the main (office) entry near 123rd Street.
Or, take I-271 to the Mayfield exit. Go west on Mayfield to Kenilworth in Cleveland Heights. The cemetery's secondary entrance is near the junction of Mayfield and Kenilworth.

City of Cleveland Rockefeller Park Greenhouse
750 East 88th Street
Cleveland OH 44108-4100
(216) 664-3130

32,000 sq.ft. greenhouse/conservatory. 2½ acres of outdoor gardens include Latin American, Japanese, and other theme gardens. Talking Garden for the Blind.

 Many plants labeled.
Open every day, including weekends and holidays, 10am-4pm.

Here is an oasis, a parcel of beauty amidst freeways and crowded neighborhoods. An attractive gazebo is surrounded by numerous varieties of hibiscus and butterfly bush (*Buddleia* spp.), birch trees edge a sea of bright annuals and perennials, and irises will provide a sweep of color and fragrance in spring. All this is becoming the Peace Garden and it *is* peaceful this afternoon.

The formal Mall, whose flowering crabs promise springtime glory around a garden of lawn, clipped hedge, and sculpture lies in front of the greenhouse. ▶

◀ For striking contrast, stroll from the formal Mall into the naturalistic Japanese Garden. This courtyard, with its bamboo hut, traditional water basin, and small pond, is graced by a tree that looks much like a pine. It is, however, a dawn redwood (*Metasequoia glyptostroboides*), a deciduous tree that was believed extinct until living specimens were discovered in China in 1948. In the adjoining Latin American Garden, banana trees and lemon trees flourish among cacti, succulents, and exotic flowering plants.

Sighted and sight-impaired visitors alike will enjoy the Talking Garden for the Blind, where plants in raised beds (to encourage touching and smelling) are described in "talking books." Plant labels are in both Roman and braille type and a guide-wire system aids the sight-impaired. This garden was completed in 1965 and is still one of few such facilities in the country. Composed largely of perennials and woody plants, with annuals added for textural contrast and scent, it can be enjoyed in any season.

Indoors, the lush Tropical House is full of citrus, coffee, and cacao trees, ground covers, and stunning tropical flowers. A waterfall and stream add gentle movement and sound to please visitors . . . and humidity to please the plants. From January into April, orchids bloom in the adjacent Orchid Room. Later, when many of the orchids are dormant, lilies dominate the display. The Main Showhouse, in seven or eight changing presentations, flaunts seasonal brilliance. The Waterfall Showhouse highlights these exhibits with particularly dramatic displays, such as masses of poinsettias in winter and sweeps of white lilies, bright tulips, and daffodils in spring. In one corner, cacti and succulents bloom, a visual treat unexpected on the shores of Lake Erie. The verdant Fern House boasts, among the lush ferns and cycads, a sunken carpet of tiny baby's-tears, a trickling wall fountain, and a small pool where Japanese koi roam.

The remaining greenhouses, not open to the public, are used to propagate over 150,000 annuals for Cleveland's parks and urban flowerbeds. When you admire these plantings around the city, you'll know they had their beginnings in a lovely place. These greenhouses and gardens are on a portion of 270 acres given to the city by the first John D. Rockefeller, the founder of Sohio. They serve their city well.

Exit I-90 at Martin Luther King, Jr. Drive and almost immediately, just beyond the first traffic light, turn east onto East 88th Street. The greenhouse and gardens are at the top of the hill, on your right.
From the south, take MLK Drive through this long park. Just before the stoplight at the north end of the park, you'll see a sign for 88th Street and the greenhouses. Turn right to the greenhouse grounds and parking lot.

Cleveland Metroparks Zoo
3900 Brookside Drive
Cleveland OH 44109
(216) 661-6500

160-acre zoological park. 2,000 sq.ft. greenhouse. Naturalistic animal settings. Major RainForest and Chinese garden exhibits under development.

💲 ♿ ☕ Animal-oriented shop. Many plants labeled. Plant lists.
Grounds open daily 9am-5pm. Buildings open daily 10am-4:45pm. Sundays and holidays during Daylight Saving Time, grounds open 9am-7pm. Extended Friday hours during the summer. Closed Christmas and New Year's days.

These naturalistic settings replicate or mimic the animals' home habitat and include collections of ornamental grasses, magnolias, oaks, and birches. Come in the spring to enjoy the flowering bulb display . . . and the baby animals. Through spring into fall, annual and perennial plant displays brighten many areas of the zoo. Other areas, too, are becoming more and more attractive to those interested in gardens. The Chinese Plant Collection is being expanded and will be reborn as The China Pagoda and Gardens. The 80,000 square foot RainForest dome will feature plants and animals from rain forest ecosystems. Seasonal plant displays share greenhouse space with 1,800 permanent plant residents. Like many other major zoos, the Cleveland Zoo is increasing their emphasis on the park and garden aspect of their mission. Any time of year, there is something here to please plant-lovers and garden enthusiasts.

The zoo is between West 25th Street and Fulton Road and between I-71 and I-480. The route is clearly marked from the highways.

Columbus

Columbus is the largest city in the world named after Christopher Columbus. But there is much more to this city than that. *Colour Columbus*, a non-profit corporation, strives to brighten the city through community beautification with the cooperation of individuals, businesses, and neighborhoods. The corporation also supports research that deals with horticulture in the urban environment and long-term planning to improve usable open spaces. You'll see results of these on-going efforts in many corners of Columbus.

For more information contact Colour Columbus, 150 East Broad Street, Columbus OH 43215, (614) 221-0652

Chadwick Arboretum
The Ohio State University

35-acre arboretum developing on campus grounds.

♿ Pamphlet for walking tour. Plant lists. Many plants labeled. Seasonal plant sales. Open daylight hours.

Chadwick, an urban arboretum that will eventually encompass much of The Ohio State University grounds, is even now a fine place to wander on a summer evening. Current arboretum gardens are centered around Howlett Hall, the Horticulture and Food Industries Center. Some of the gardens are interspersed among greenhouses and other facilities that aren't open to the public so, for informed discovery, one should write for the Walking Tour guide ahead of time.

The area around Howlett Hall will be lovely in spring, when the flowering trees and shrubs perform. Mature linden trees will add their perfume and the low buzz of attendant bees. In autumn, abundant fruits will be joined by vivid foliage. A mélange of branch patterns, rich bark textures and colors, and somber evergreens will be winter's richness. Today, a large tree shelters a fine group of blooming hardy cyclamens, another protects a handsome stand of ferns. Behind the building, well-tended raised beds sport an assortment of thymes and lavenders, annual herbs, and several varieties of scented geraniums (*Pelargonium* spp.). Ornamental grasses of various sizes and characters are planted in several locations in the gardens; a comprehensive and informative list of these is available from the Arboretum Office.

The extensive Arboretum Master Plan calls for the addition of many gardens and other features. Current emphasis is on Lane Avenue in the Olentangy River Road area. Trees have been planted, with more to come, and Lane Avenue will become a tree-lined boulevard, a handsome western entrance to the campus. In the future, there will be a bog garden, an entomology cove, a children's garden, plantings that portray design history and experimental design, a lake, sensory gardens, and taxonomic gardens. Meadows will be filled with wildflowers and ornamental grasses. A retail nursery, a residential landscape design center, an arboretum center, and a library will add to the usefulness of the arboretum. These will surely delight and benefit garden-lovers and OSU students. This is truly a *long-range* plan, with near-completion planned for the year 2000; it will be interesting to watch the arboretum develop.   ▸

◀ For up-to-date information contact the Chadwick Arboretum Office, 2120 Fyffe Road, Columbus OH 43210-1099, (614) 292-3136; The Ohio State Visitor Information Center, Room 208 Ohio Union, 1739 North High Street, Columbus OH 43210, (614) 292-0428,; or the OSU College of Agriculture Development Office, (614) 292-0473.

From I-70 take Ohio Route 315 north to Lane Avenue. Go east on Lane a block or so to Fyffe Court. Turn south onto Fyffe, which ends at Howlett Hall. During class hours visitors can park in metered spaces on Fyffe.

Franklin Park Conservatory
1777 East Broad Street
Columbus OH 43203
(614) 645-3000

60,000 sq.ft. conservatory with 10 thematic zones. Associated exterior plantings. Large Japanese garden.

💲 ♿ ☕ Shop. Some plants labeled. Library. Picnic facilities in park. Plant sales. Special events.
Flexible hours; inquire by phone or letter.

This splendid new conservatory, dedicated in 1992 for Columbus' AmeriFlora celebration, still contains, deep within, bits of the 20,000 sq.ft. Victorian conservatory that graced Franklin Park for many years. During the expansion and new construction, 1,650 panes of glass were added to create new thematic and habitat zones. You can admire flora from the Himalayan mountains, plants that live in tropical rain forests, desert inhabitants from all over the world, and botanical residents of Pacific islands. The bonsai collection, with two dozen specimens grown from tropical plants and a dozen deciduous varieties, will entrance you. Those handsome boulders that anchor the conservatory's exhibits so naturally may surprise you; in the interest of weight conservation, they're plaster "rocks," cast in molds of the original stones. Outside, you can relax on the Succulent Patio, with its array of hardy cacti and succulents, or become acquainted with the assortment of hardy bamboos.

The conservatory shop features gardening and horticulture books, hard-to-find tools, and, for those of us who love to buy green and growing souvenirs, orchids and carnivorous plants. When you're tired from shopping and plant-viewing, relax and have a snack at the conservatory café. ▶

◀ Several installations in Franklin Park are remnants of AmeriFlora. The Grand Mallway is accented by Stephen Canneto's *Navistar*, three bronze sail-like forms that comprise Columbus' largest public sculpture. The sizable Japanese garden, with its lanterns and arched bridge, its water features and handsome perennials, will become even more beautiful and serene as years go by. Other AmeriFlora features have been removed and will be gradually replaced by permanent gardens. Various plantings and theme gardens have been undertaken by assorted local garden clubs; it will be interesting to watch these develop.

When AmeriFlora closed in October 1992, responsibility for the operation of Franklin Park Conservatory changed jurisdictions. As of this writing, schedules for public hours and special shows had not been solidified. But it will certainly be worth your effort to contact the conservatory and then to add these wonderful habitats to your time in Columbus.

From I-70 take Exit 102 and go north to Broad Street (US 62/OH 16). Go east a short distance to Franklin Park, on the south side of the road.
From I-270 take Exit 39 (Broad Street/OH 16) and go west a little over 4 miles to the park.

The Kelton House Museum and Garden
586 East Town Street
Columbus OH 43215
(614) 464-2022

Restored nineteenth-century home. 820 sq.ft. gardens.

💲 ♿ Museum shop.
Open Monday-Friday 10am-4pm.

The Kelton House gardens, small but restored to Victorian splendor, contain hedged garden "rooms." These rooms, in turn, contain the statuary, planted bowls, and urns so loved by nineteenth-century gardeners. You'll see unusual specimen plants large and small, lattice trellises, a promenade edged by flowering crabapple trees, and mixed perennial borders. Add the wildflower garden just west of the Carriage House and the parterre beds behind it and you have a full range of pleasing Victorian garden features.

Kelton House, just east of downtown Columbus, dates from a time when Columbus was *much* smaller and people lived close to downtown. The strong collection of antique furniture, costumes, and decorative objects in the house complements the gardens outside.

From I-70 exit at Fourth Street (US Route 23 north), go north a few blocks to Town Street, then turn east to Kelton House.

Schmidt Nursery
3001 Innis Road
Columbus OH 43224
(614) 471-1755

Commercial. 2,500 sq.ft. All-America Selections garden. 14,000 sq.ft. sun and shade displays.

♿ Catalog. Most plants labeled. Seasonal workshops and open houses.
Open all year Monday-Friday 9am-7pm, Saturday 8am-5pm, Sunday 10am-4pm.

Here are All-America Selections gardens in all their brightness, with thousands of individual plants blooming behind their numbered tags and under trial for their performance in central Ohio. Here, too, you'll see AAS winners from 1979 on, plants that have done particularly well in a variety of garden situations. Schmidt's award-winning sun and shade display gardens look like home gardens, except that their plants are labeled with common and botanical names and cultural information.

If you visit Schmidt's in the spring, you'll find the production greenhouses filled with colorful annuals. Spring and autumn workshops will help you plant water gardens, plan for fall garden color, choose and plant bulbs, and develop other garden skills. Winter fills the greenhouses with glowing poinsettias, elegant cyclamens, and the scents and textures of scented geraniums. There are truly fine things to do and see throughout the year at Schmidt's.

Exit I-270 at Morse Road on the northeast side of Columbus. Go west on Morse a little over a mile to Sunbury Road and turn south onto Sunbury. At the next main intersection, turn west onto Innis Road and you'll soon see Schmidt's on your left.

The Topiary Garden in Old Deaf School Park
Downtown, corner of East Town Street and Washington Avenue
Columbus   ▶

◀ Half-acre topiary garden, based on Seurat's *Sunday Afternoon on the Island of the Grande Jatte*, within 9-acre park.

♿ Limited picnic facilities. Special events.
Open dawn to dusk. Installation of lighting planned for 1994, when hours will extend to 11pm.

As far as is known, this is the only place in the entire *world* where you can walk through a living green "painting," where you can become part of Seine-side life as one artist saw it in 1884-6. This exciting and imaginative arrangement of topiary figures will do that for you.

Although there are a few other major topiary collections in this country, human forms are rare. Here, 46 lounging, sitting, and strolling figures from Seurat's painting are transformed into green sculptures, all grown of yews (*Taxus*, several varieties), shaped on bronze armatures, and surrounded by thyme ground covers. Here, too, in greenery, are the painting's dogs and monkeys and small boats. The Seine River, represented by a pond, holds water lilies and bog plants and topiary boats whose sails blossom white with sweet autumn clematis in the fall. In spring and summer, those boats provide perfect homes for mallards and their ducklings. Beds of spring-blooming bulbs and of summer-blooming perennials and annuals brighten the pond's edge and other choice spots. If you stand on the garden's easterly hill, the scene lies before you just as Seurat saw it, just as the painting portrays it. Attractive benches invite further appreciation of this panorama.

Special events planned for the park will be in keeping with Seurat's Paris of the late 1880s: hoop rolling and croquet tournaments, garden songs and music of the era, and ice cream socials. To add to the ambiance, costumed volunteers will recreate recognizable figures from the painting. A museum shop for the garden is planned; for the time being, volunteers in the garden will sell you postcards of Seurat's painting, so you can stand on the hill and admire the likeness.

For several years, this downtown site was merely a vacant lot, the former home of the Ohio School for the Deaf, which burned in 1980. In the late 1980s, creative individuals, generous donors, supportive administrators, enthusiastic gardeners, and a wealth of ideas came together to originate the Topiary Garden. The first yews were planted in 1988; bronze armatures were installed and plant-shaping began in 1989. Most figures were relatively "complete" in time for the garden's 1992 dedication, in conjunction with the Quincentenary of Columbus' arrival in America, although the tallest figures and their parasols may take a few more years to fill in. This is a very new park and various amenities are still being discussed and developed but it's already an impressive site, a park and greenery surrounded by downtown Columbus. Don't miss it.

For details contact the Topiary Project Manager, Cultural Arts Center, 139 West Main Street, Columbus OH 43215. (614) 645-7464 or (614) 299-7510.

From I-71 in downtown Columbus, take the Broad Street exit and go west on Broad three blocks to Ninth Street, then turn left and go one block to the park. Weekdays before 5pm, parking is on the street. After 5pm, and on weekends, visitors may park in the lots of adjacent businesses.
From I-70 take the Fourth Street exit and go north a few blocks to Town Street, then turn east onto Town and go a few blocks to the park, on the north side of Town Street. Note: The park is just a half block west of Kelton House.

Whetstone Park
Columbus Park of Roses
3923 North High (US Route 23)
Columbus OH 43214

---

13 acres of gardens within very large park. Extensive rose and daffodil collections. All-American Rose Selections garden. Rose Festival. Herb garden and perennial beds.

♿ Brochure. Many plants labeled. Seasonal plant sales. Picnic facilities in park.
(The gardens are quite level, with paved walks, but the ramp by the shelter is steep. There is easier access from the Senior Community Center on High Street, just north of the library.)
Open dawn to dusk all year.

On this summer evening, several ball games and tennis matches are underway in Whetstone Park, cyclists and walkers fill the trails, somewhere the local bagpipe club is practicing, visitors amble along the garden walks, and roses and petunias perfume the air. I've had the good fortune to arrive when volunteers are tending the gardens; to me, a garden is even more pleasing when those who love it are there. The area teems with workers clipping, deadheading, weeding, and generally nurturing the roses, the herb garden, and the perennial garden. ▶

FYI *Sunday Afternoon on the Island of the Grande Jatte,* the pointillist masterwork of Georges Seurat (1859-91) hangs in The Art Institute of Chicago, which is along the western edge of Grant Park. The Art Institute's large collection of Impressionist and Post-Impressionist works contains a number of other paintings that have particular appeal to gardeners, such as Monet's *Water Lilies.*

◀ The Columbus Park of Roses holds over 9,000 rose bushes of 319 varieties. Here are hybrid tea roses, miniature roses, and an assortment of climbers. Nearly 100 different heritage roses clamber along fences at the far end of the main rose garden, near the Community Center. Most of these sturdy individuals are lush, still blooming, richly thorned, and intensely perfumed. Indeed, heritage roses have unique character but *all* the park's roses are enchanting in the westering sun.

A Rose Festival is held here the second weekend of June, when many of the roses are in peak bloom. Festivities include music, drama, children's activities, refreshments, horticultural displays, and plant sales. The lovely rose arbor is often the site for weddings and Sunday evening concerts are held in the rose garden during the summer months.

The herb garden here is not your usual herb garden. The temptation to try plants in great diversity has been resisted; here, there are a limited number of plant varieties but the individuals or clumps of plants are large, scaled to fit the expanse of roses nearby. Mounded beds, in a pleasing rectangular layout, hold a rich assortment of textures.

Herb garden workers also maintain the perennial garden, where a tapestry of daylilies spreads before the deep green foliage and tasseled stalks of snakeroot (*Cimicifuga racemosa*). Impressive stands of phlox and clumps of ornamental grasses border the daylilies and the lawn. Beneath a nearby tree, yellow ligularia 'The Rocket' glows in the last of the evening light. (When I return to these gardens in early August, the ligularia and cimicifuga sport tall seed stalks, a few daylilies are still blooming, and plume poppies [*Macleaya cordata*] rule the scene.)

The daffodil garden holds over 1,000 varieties, some of them rare or particularly unusual; it's surely a visual extravaganza here in April. Grasses and seedheads will join rose hips for subtle interest and color in the winter gardens. This park deserves a visit any time of year.

For brochure and other information contact Columbus Parks and Recreation, 440 West Whittier Street, Columbus OH 43215. (614) 645-3300.

From I-70 take US Route 23 (High Street) north several miles, past the OSU campus, to Hollenbach Drive. There is a large park sign at the corner of High and Hollenbach, in front of the branch library. Follow Hollenbach down and around to the parking lot for the garden. The main gardens are behind the large shelter building.
From I-270 take US 23 south to Hollenbach Drive, then proceed as above.

Columbus Zoological Gardens
9990 Riverside Drive
P. O. Box 400
Powell OH 43065
(614) 766-3400

100-acre zoo grounds. 92 acres with plant collections.

💲 ♿ ☕ Brochure, plant guides, and schedules. Shops. Many plants labeled. Picnic facilities. Seasonal plant sales. Special events.
Memorial Day-Labor Day Monday-Friday 10am-6pm, weekends 10am-8pm. Off-season Monday-Friday 10am-4pm, weekends 10am-6pm.

This large, well-planted zoo is also an accredited botanic garden. Two acres of wildflowers, 50 varieties of daffodils and 20 other kinds of spring bloomers, 80,000 plants of 100 kinds of annuals, ornamental grasses, perennials, 200 species of tropical plants . . . all these green growers enrich the zoo grounds. The banana trees, cacti, and bromeliads here may surprise you but doesn't it seem the logical place for carnivorous plants?

The zoo's shrub inhabitants are chosen for seasonal color, fragrance, or fruits. They're used for barrier camouflage or decorative hedges and, in some cases, to provide food or shelter in bird or animal yards. Flowering dogwoods, plums, red buckeye (*Aesculus pavia*), and other beauties join charming animal babies in the spring. Informative printed guides are available for tree, shrub, and evergreen walks; you'll want to use these as you visit the animals.

In the safari-themed Sokoni Gift Shop there's a wide array of zoo-related gifts and souvenirs. During May, your souvenir can be annuals and bedding plants from the plant sale. Perhaps you'd enjoy an early April visit to the *Island of Tulipitan* or summer attendance at the Zoo Music Series. Fund-raising walks and runs wind through the grounds from time to time, late October brings *Boo at the Zoo!*, and *Wildlight Wonderland* makes the zoo even more special during December. You'll find this an active and lovely place at any time of year.

From I-270 use Exit 20 (Sawmill Road) on the northwest side of Columbus and follow signs to the zoo.

▶

FYI Most zoos have "Friends" or "Adopt-an-Animal" programs but Columbus' *Plant Parenthood* is unusual, I think. Members can choose to support zoo-wide projects such as seasonal displays or plant labeling, specific plant collections such as bamboos or water plants, or a single exhibit area such as the white tiger environment. This plan encourages increased feelings of ownership in the zoo gardens and, as the brochure states, makes it ". . . easy to play Father or Mother Nature."

The Village of Hiram

Six small public gardens.

Plants labeled in Century House garden only.
All gardens open daylight hours.

Six distinct public gardens grace this agreeable village. Hurd Memorial Garden, the showpiece of the Hiram gardens, lies at the corner of Bancroft and Hayden streets. This 85'x192' installation honors two doctors, father and son, who served the Hiram community for a total of almost 100 years. Various aspects of the garden are unveiled as you walk the winding gravel paths, making it all seem larger than it is. Mature spruce trees provide a stately background for daylilies and hostas while impressive stands of lamb's-ears and the sedum 'Autumn Joy' edge the path; sedum flower heads will be stunning with the autumn foliage of viburnums, fancy sumacs, and tall grasses. Spring color will come from lilacs, peonies, flowering trees, and bulbs of many sorts. Memorial benches encourage contemplation of this intriguing mix of plants. The handsome old streetlights that adorn the garden, a gift from the Hiram College Class of 1914, originally stood in front of Hinsdale Hall, an 1886 building that also contributed large stones to this gardenscape.

Across Bancroft Street and a half block west, small and shady Copper Beech Garden Park holds contemporary sculpture, benches, a small bed of old-fashioned perennials, and tidy lawns. One block north of Copper Beech Garden is Bonney Castle Inn, once a busy inn, now home to the college English Department. The inn's backyard garden, in lawn dominated by a maple tree, holds two 8'x40' beds filled with plants old-fashioned in character or history: garden phlox, daylilies, astilbes, yarrow, lavender, daisies, black-eyed Susans, and others of that ilk. A pair of rug-sized beds gain persistent summer color from pansies, snapdragons, and blue annual salvia.

Pendleton House, which houses the college History Department, sits a few doors west of Bonney Castle. Its deep city lot holds perennials and spring-blooming shrubs against a wooded background. Rosy cleome joins feathery golden celosia, annual sage, and the delicate tassels of tall grasses in an alleyside bed.

On your way into Hiram you've probably seen the village's only stoplight, at the corner of Ohio Route 82 and Garfield Street, not far south of these gardens. To enjoy additional small and colorful gardens, walk or drive to the church parking lot on that corner. The low fence at one side of the parking lot surrounds a private 20'x30' herb garden that invites public admiration; plant labels are legible from outside the fence. In this full-to-overflowing enclosure, rambunctious lemon balm (*Melissa officinalis*), artemisias, oreganos, and comfrey have burst their bounds and are growing through the fence. Calendulas and geraniums brighten soft herbal greens and thymes cushion the flagstone path. At the far end of the parking lot, tiny but colorful Missionary Garden honors missionaries of the adjoining church. Across the lawn and beyond the Municipal Building, you'll find Century House, an old home that houses the Hiram Township Historical Society. The octagonal herb garden here boasts Russian sage (*Perovskia atriplicifolia*), tansy, yarrow, and a persistent mint that is alive with bees on this warm, still afternoon.

Hiram, a quiet collection of small gardens and attractive nineteenth-century buildings, isn't on the way to anywhere else but if you have some unplanned time you can spend it very pleasantly here.

For further information contact the Hiram Gardens, P. O. Box 402, Hiram OH 44234 or the Clerk, Village Hall, Hiram OH 44234.

You'll probably come into Hiram on Ohio Route 82. Turn left at the stoplight at OH 82 and Garfield, go a block or so to Bancroft and turn left again to Hurd Memorial Garden. All the other gardens are within an easy walk from Hurd.

William Tricker, Inc.
7125 Tanglewood Drive
Independence OH 44131
(216) 524-3491 or (216) 524-3492

Commercial. Specialist in water gardens. Outdoor ponds. Greenhouses for tender water plants and fish.

Catalog. Shop. Many plants labeled. Plant sales.
Open Monday-Saturday 8am-6pm, Thursday 8am-8pm, Sunday noon-5pm.

Display ponds edged with bogbean (*Menyanthes trifoliata*), cattails, and blooming loosestrife (*Lythrum salicaria* 'Morden's Pink') tell me I have arrived at Tricker's, "America's Oldest Water Garden Specialists." Nervous frogs of many sizes jump into the water as I walk around the ponds; the less timid simply stay hidden and thrum lazily in the evening air. Healthy plants lift their leaves of many shapes above the still water and dragonflies patrol the ponds, pausing only momentarily to ornament the loosestrife.   ▶

◀ Concrete vats near the greenhouses hold tadpoles, so you can have your own frogs, and mussels, living filters for your pond. Small fish populate another tank. Wide, shallow vats inside the greenhouses host a rich variety of water lilies and other water plants. Some of the lilies are tropical and some are hardy in northern climates, some bloom in the daytime, some are night bloomers. Here are pygmy water lilies with 1-inch flowers and *Victoria trickerii*, an aquatic plant whose rimmed leaves can reach 6 feet in diameter. You'll see papyrus (*Cyperus* sp.) and lotus (*Nelumbo* sp.), evocations of ancient Egyptian tomb paintings. And Chinese water chestnut is growing here, proof that water chestnuts don't just come in cans at the Oriental grocery. It's really just a greenhouse, hot and humid on this July day, but there *is* a hint of magic here. Side windows are open for ventilation and a small blue jewel of a dragonfly drifts in and lands on my pen as I write. I pause and wait for him to leave, feeling as if I've been blessed somehow.

Tricker's is also a major source for home aquarium enthusiasts. One room is packed with tanks of ever-moving fish and gently waving aquarium plants. In the shop, shelves are filled with books that tell you how to set up and maintain your aquarium or your water garden or how to heal your fish if they're ailing. Here, too, are fountains, sculptures, pumps, and rocks for your pool. Tricker's offers sizable preformed pools but, for those of us with limited sunny garden space, they also supply miniature tubs or complete tub gardens that can sit on a deck or patio.

Give yourself an unusual garden treat with a visit to Tricker's. A hint: most day-blooming water lilies are at their best in the morning or early afternoon. However, Tricker's is an uncommon delight at any time of day.

From I-77 take the exit for Independence, onto Rockside Road. Go east a few blocks and look for the classy Georgian-style McDonald's at Brecksville Road, then turn right onto Brecksville. Go to the second street and turn left onto Tanglewood, which looks more like an alley than a street. You'll see Tricker's immediately.

Gateway Garden Center
1238 West Main Street (Route 59W)
Kent OH 44240
(216) 678-1660

Commercial nursery. One acre. 600 sq.ft display gardens. Heritage roses and other perennials. ▶

◀ Catalog. Garden shop. Turf and woodchip paths. Workshops.
Seasonal variations in open days and hours. Peak season: open at 9am daily except Sunday (10am). Close at 4pm Sunday, 5pm Monday, 8pm Wednesday and Thursday, 6pm other days.

At Gateway, where the emphasis is on perennial flowers and shrubs, these beauties fill the display garden and the firm's extensive catalog. Heritage roses add their perfume and rich color, their deep greens and abundant thorns, to the garden. The beehive tucked away in a corner is home to the bees who visit all these chemical-free plants. A garden guide, available at the site, helps you know which plants and combinations you're enjoying and "thinking stumps" encourage you to relax while you think about the plants and plant combinations you want to add to *your* garden.

From I-76 take Exit 33 (Kent-Hartville) and go north on Ohio Route 43 to OH 59. Then go west on OH 59 to Gateway, which is "nestled among car dealers." Look for the Gateway sign on the south side of the road.

Lakeview Rose Garden
Lorain

Major rose collection.

Picnic facilities in surrounding park. Snacks available at beach concessions.
Open daylight hours. Lighted at night.

Thousands of rose bushes stand in concentric circles here at Lakeview. Today, their leaves and blooms are sparse; the bushes are conserving vitality in this unusually hot and dry summer but they look as if they'll survive to fill another season with flowers and scent. Lighted at night, this park will be particularly pleasant on a June evening, when the early roses are in full bloom.

It seems strange to me that of all the roses here, roses of many forms and colors, not one bush is labeled. Visiting homeowners, potential rose purchasers, might like to know what they are admiring. Perhaps vandalism of labels is a problem; a heavily used Lake Erie swimming beach and its bath house are just across the parking lot.

Conversation with the garden's other visitors reveals that they've driven over 100 miles just to visit these roses. They grow few roses themselves but particularly enjoy this garden and try to make several visits during the season. That tells us something about the appeal of these lovely flowers and of this park. It's worth the drive. ▶

◀ For information contact the Lorain County Metroparks, 12882 Diagonal Road, LaGrange OH 44050, (800) LCM-PARK (526-7275), or the Lorain County Visitor's Bureau, P. O. Box 567, Lorain OH 44052. (800) 334-1673.

The park is west of downtown Lorain, on US Route 6 along Lake Erie. From I-90 take Ohio Route 57 about 5 miles north through town to US 6. Go west on US 6 less than a mile to the park.

Bluestone Perennials
7211 Middle Ridge Road
Madison OH 44057
(800) 852-5243

Commercial. Many acres. Production nursery specializing in perennials. Stock and trial fields. Greenhouses. Shadehouses. 50'x100' display garden.

Catalog. Many plants labeled. Seasonal plant sales on site.
Spring hours: Monday-Saturday 8am-8pm. Summer and winter hours: Monday-Friday 9am-5pm.

Bluestone ships field-grown plants all over the country; here's your chance to see them at their source. Fields of irises and mums, promising beauty for spring and fall, surround the entry road that leads to acres and acres of shadehouses and greenhouses. Butterflies drift through these open-sided buildings that are relatively empty on this mid-summer day. The greenhouse pace is leisurely, in contrast to the digging and dividing and packing and shipping of spring and autumn. Later, these houses will again be filled with seedlings and young plants. I feel I'm seeing the skeleton of the business without the distraction of thousands of plants, although it would be a treat to see these plant-growing units when they are full.

Production fields bake in the sun as a bulldozer strains against hard, dry soil, digging a pond that, it is hoped, will be irrigation insurance against the next dry summer. In the trial garden, yarrow, coneflowers, silvery blue globe thistle (*Echinops* sp.), Russian sage (*Perovskia atriplicifolia*), and white phlox stand in abundant summer bloom to prove their resistance to drought.

Bluestone says "People are always welcome to look around" and they mean it. At almost any time of year, the gardener will find interesting and admirable features here. ▶

◀ *From I-90, turn north on Ohio Route 528. Go through Madison and beyond to Middle Ridge Road. Turn east on Middle Ridge and go a mile further to Bluestone, on the north side of the road.*

Kingwood Center
900 Park Avenue West
Mansfield OH 44906
(419) 522-0211

47-acre estate includes 20 acres of gardens. Greenhouses. All-American Rose Selections garden. Herb garden.

♿ Museum shop. Most plants labeled. Library. Plant sales. Trails. Special events.
Grounds and greenhouses open daily 8am-sundown.
Kingwood Hall, library, and shop open Tuesday-Saturday (except holidays) 9am-5pm, Sunday (Easter-October) 1:30-4:30pm, closed Monday.

Kingwood Center is a mansion, lush perennial gardens, small trial gardens, cheeky birds, and plant-filled greenhouses. Those greenhouses, which hold a fine cactus/succulent collection, tables filled with blooming orchids, and hundreds of elegant tropical plants, make Kingwood worth visiting even in the dead of winter, when the outdoor gardens are dormant. We're intrigued by a collection of unusual ivy topiaries and the tiny jewel that's a complete knot garden in a 2-foot square box. This treasure is a little world unto itself, as appealing as a well-crafted bonsai.

Outdoors, on a totally different scale, vast sweeps of astilbes and evening primroses are glowing in the morning sun, accented by ornamental grasses, desert-candles (*Eremurus* sp.), and Japanese irises (*Iris ensata*). From a terrace near the house, the elegant walled herb garden overlooks an inviting shade garden. Chipmunks are chasing each other in the herb garden today, their noisy chipmunky ways adding considerable life to the semi-formal plantings. The shade garden just below offers a bench or two for quiet enjoyment of its hostas, ferns, and spring bulbs.

The birds of Kingwood will delight you. The pond is filled with dabbling, squabbling ducks, majestic peacocks patrol the lawns, guineas weed the gardens, and a lone pure-white peacock struts and preens. These sleek individuals, well-fed on the insects and weedlings they find in the gardens, snub the food pellets we buy for them.

We appreciate the complete labeling of virtually all the plants in these gardens but the labels at the backs of the beds, where some of the most interesting plants live, are the same size as those near the paths. Our "mature eyes" would have appreciated larger print in some cases; binoculars would have come in handy.

Kingwood Center, constructed in 1926, is the estate of the late Charles K. King, whose fortune was based on the streetcar industry and the Ohio Brass Company. Having no heirs, he established the Kingwood Center Trust which, upon his death, began developing the estate ". . . for the advancement of horticulture and other cultural activities." The Center and various horticultural societies sponsor a full schedule of plant shows and plant sales during the year. There are also on-going plant sales, with a limited but appealing selection, in the greenhouse. In July, the greenhouse courtyard hosts the drama of Shakespeare. At other times you may share the grounds with an art exhibit, craft demonstrations, a gem and mineral show, or a photography exhibit. Between the gardens, the greenhouses, and the activities of Kingwood, you'll find something to enjoy whenever you visit.

For more detailed information contact the Education Coordinator at the address above.

From Ohio Route 30 take the Trimble Road exit and go south less than a mile to Park Avenue West. Go east on Park Avenue a few hundred yards to the Kingwood entrance, on the north side of the road.
From I-90, turn north on Ohio Route 528. Go through Madison and beyond to Middle Ridge Road. Turn east on Middle Ridge and go a mile farther to Bluestone, on the north side of the road.

Falconskeape Gardens
7359 Branch Road
Medina OH 44256
(216) 723-4966

These spacious gardens include an extensive lilac collection (over 600 species and cultivars), bog plant and conifer collections, and a 20-acre lake. Here, too, are woodland gardens and other specialty plantings. There's much to explore and discover at Falconskeape.

The gardens are just off Ohio Route 18 at Medina.

A. Borlin Company
9885 Johnny Cake Ridge Road
Mentor OH 44060
(216) 354-8966

◀ Commercial. 30,000 sq.ft. orchid and tropical plant greenhouse.

💲 Fee for guided greenhouse tours, which must be pre-arranged. Shop. Many plants labeled. Plant sales.
Open all year Monday-Friday 9am-5pm, Saturday 9am-2pm.

For a tropical mini-vacation among thousands of orchids and other exotic plants, come to Borlin's. Changing exhibits in the show greenhouse feature orchids native to the US as well as denizens of the tropics, orchids in their many colors and forms. If you tour all the facilities here you'll see flasks of tiny plantlets in the propagating rooms, nursery houses of adolescent plants, and ranks of flowering adults. You'll receive information on home orchid care and, as a crowning touch, a souvenir orchid flower. If, like me, you find orchids nearly impossible to resist, the variety here will be most tempting.

From I-90 use either Exit 193 (Ohio Route 306) or Exit 200 (Ohio Route 44) and go north a short distance to OH 84, Johnny Cake Ridge Road. A. Borlin, on OH 84, is about six miles east of OH 306 and three miles west of OH 44.

Holden Arboretum
9500 Sperry Road
Mentor OH 44060
(216) 946-4400

3,100 acres of horticultural collections and natural areas. Rose Garden at Lantern Court.

💲 ♿ Brochures for arboretum and for rose garden. Shop. Many plants labeled. Trails. Seasonal plant sales. Workshops and other special events.
Open all year Tuesday-Sunday 10am-5pm.
Rose Garden at Lantern Court open only during peak rose bloom, Wednesday only, 1-3pm.

If you're in Lake County during the spring, don't miss this arboretum, where the early bloom season extends from mid-March to June. You may revel in the subtle beauty of witch hazel or the more flamboyant attractions of magnolias, wildflowers, crabapples, azaleas, lilacs, rhododendrons, hawthorns, and viburnums. Later, summertime wildflowers in bog and prairie will claim your attention; fall color is magnificent in the mixed woods. ▶

◀ On a warm day late in a drought summer, all is quiet in Holden's rolling high meadows and extensive woods. We watch a Canada goose guide her young across the road toward water, then *we* head for the air-conditioned Corning Building, the visitor and education center. Here, in addition to general information and brochures, the small shop offers an extensive selection of gardening and natural history books, many of them for children. There is also jewelry, stationery, and a variety of "Wings-on-Strings," those charming bird and butterfly mobiles.

Does a seminar on Horticultural Hand Tools appeal to you? Would you like to spend A Day in Stebbins Gulch or to Get To Know the Native Ferns? Perhaps you want to know more about Backyard Meadows or Birds, Butterflies, and Beasts in Rare Books. Holden hosts a myriad of classes and events that focus on horticulture, natural history, children's interests, and art and nature, with nominal fees for most activities. Time your visit to enjoy spectacular natural beauty *and* an educational experience.

Along Kirtland-Chardon Road, on your way to the arboretum, you'll see the entrance to Lantern Court, a Georgian Colonial home and 25-acre estate that is owned by the arboretum. Plantings here include formal rose beds and naturalistic sweeps of roses intermingled with azaleas and other handsome perennials. Here are modern roses as well as heritage roses, pastel blooms and bright flowers, roses all chosen for their performance in this climate. Here, too, are benches and walls and carefully trimmed evergreens. Lantern Court and its gardens are open only at selected times for special occasions, most often during peak rose-blooming season, but you'll find your visit worth the planning.

For information contact the Lantern Court Committee at the arboretum.

From I-90 take Exit 193 at Ohio Route 306. Go south on OH 306 to the bottom of the hill and Kirtland-Chardon Road. Go east on Kirtland-Chardon 3½ miles to Sperry Road. Turn north on Sperry Road and go a short distance to the arboretum entrance.
A helpful map of the area is available at the Corning Building desk if you ask for it.

FYI Along Kirtland-Chardon Road, you'll pass the recently acquired headquarters of the Herb Society of America. This nineteenth-century stone cottage, currently under renovation and revision, is used for meetings and to house the group's library, archives, and business office. It stands on arboretum land, on the north side of the road. Visitors are welcome.

Lily of the Valley Herb Farm
3969 Fox Avenue
Minerva OH 44657
(216) 862-3920

Commercial. Small herb display gardens. Production fields.

 Catalog. Most plants labeled. Shop. Plant sales.
Shop open all year Monday-Saturday 10am-5pm. Closed Sunday. Greenhouses open mid-April-July 4 Monday-Saturday 10am-6pm, Sunday 2-5pm. Greenhouse operation continues on a limited basis after July 4. Call to be sure someone is there or take your chances.

African wormwood, Syrian rue, East Indian basil, Thai peppers, French sorrel, Mitsuba parsley, Mexican oregano, Japanese hops . . . if you want a cosmopolitan garden, make a stop at Lily of the Valley. You'll see plants you didn't know you needed, plants you didn't know existed. Even in mid-June, after the spring plant-buying frenzy, the greenhouses still contain a rich mix of common and uncommon herbs. These plants are propagated here, with emphasis on material *not* found in your neighborhood garden center. Large specimens winter in the greenhouse and emerge in spring to decorate the sales area; a full and healthy lavender, 4 feet tall, towers over a splendid array of pleasantly scented geraniums. The sales area also offers a fascinating selection of terra cotta plant containers in unusual shapes, many of them planted with tiny herb gardens.

Large display gardens are being developed here. If the current small gardens in front of the shop are any indication, the new ones will be beautifully designed, rich in color and texture, and worthy of anticipation.

A jaunty medicine show wagon welcomes us to the Herb Shop, which offers dried everlastings, floral arrangements, potpourri, and materials for making your own treasures. Here, too, are Lily of the Valley's own herbal healing products; Ivy All Lotion for poison ivy, Mother's Mender Salve, and others. When the show wagon visits regional festivals, the owner of Lily of the Valley, clad in appropriate costume, presents an old-fashioned medicine show and dispenses bits of information about herbs and herbal products.

Lily of the Valley offers intriguing workshops, an informative catalog and reference guide, pleasing gardens, thriving plants, and all the other elements required for a delightful visit.

Lily of the Valley is just off Ohio Route 153, a few miles east of Canton and I-77, 5 miles south of Alliance, a mile west of OH 183. Turn south at the large sign on the south side of OH 153.

The Dawes Arboretum
7770 Jacksontown Road SE
Newark OH 43055
(614) 323-2355

Total grounds 1149 acres. Japanese garden. Tree collections. Bonsai collection. Daweswood House Museum.

♿ Brochures. Many plants labeled. Picnic facilities. Shop. Library. Hiking trails. 2½ auto tour route. Fee for house museum tours.
Arboretum grounds open daily dawn to dusk except Thanksgiving, Christmas, and New Year's days. Visitor Center and Gift Shop open weekdays 8-11:30am and 12:30-5pm, Saturday 9-11:30am and 12:30-5pm, Sunday and holidays 1-5pm. Nature Center open weekdays 8am-4:30pm, Saturday 9am-5pm, Sunday 1-5pm, closed Saturday and Sunday November through April. Guided tours of Daweswood House daily at 3pm, no weekend tours November through April.

Our first glimpse of the glowing rose-pink beech tree near Dawes' Visitor Center suggests that we've come to a special place; we *know* we're in a special place when we see Dawes' bonsai collection. This exquisite wonderland of tiny forests, waterfalls, rockscapes, and minute mosses makes me feel like an awkward giant but the beech and the bonsai are well worth a short excursion off the Interstate . . . and there's more.

Dawes' sizable Japanese Garden, currently undergoing long-term renovation, is going to be very impressive, with mature trees, a large pond, running water, and a thousand subtle details. Tree collections, such as holly, oak, magnolia, or maple, are sometimes interplanted with dwarf conifers and other unusual plants. The special Rare Tree Collection holds a fascinating variety of barks and leaves and branch and tree forms. The fern and wildflower garden, beneath a leafy canopy, is a refreshing place to walk on this warm June day. We stroll from the fern garden to a very small swamp, "one of the northernmost outposts of southern native bald cypress." The swamp boardwalk, edged with flag iris just past prime bloom, is an unexpected treat. Not far away, the luscious All Seasons Garden displays woody and herbaceous plants that will provide year-round interest in home landscapes.

An observation tower overlooks Dawes Lake and the famous hedge lettering but only from an airplane could you clearly read DAWES ARBORETUM as it is spelled out in 145-foot letters of Eastern arborvitae. The Park Woods, an expansive area of majestic trees, lawns, azaleas, paths, and footbridges near Daweswood House, was designed for the strolling pleasure of the Dawes family and their guests.

▶

◀ Dawes Arboretum was created in 1929 by Beman and Bertie Dawes. Mr. Dawes had been in the US House of Representatives and, in 1920, founded the Pure Oil Company, which provided assets for arboretum endowment. Mr. Dawes' brother, Gen. C. G. Dawes, a former US Vice-President (1925-29) and a 1925 Nobel Prize winner, also contributed to the initial endowment. Today the arboretum offers a full schedule of shows, plant and seed sales, workshops, lectures, and short courses. You may want to plan your visit for one of the special public events; we've just missed the annual Bonsai Show but we're delighted that we came Dawes.

From I-70 or US 40 between Columbus and Zanesville, take Ohio Route 13 north a few miles, through Jacksontown and beyond. The arboretum is on the west side of the road just past a wide curve.

Wilson's Garden Center/Hillview Display Gardens
10923 Lambs Lane NE
Newark OH 43055
(614) 763-2873

Commercial. Two acres. Water, rock, and flower display gardens. All-America Selections garden.

♿ Turf paths. Shop. Many plants labeled. Plant sales. Workshops and other special events. Open all year, with seasonal variations. Summer hours Monday-Saturday 9am-6pm, Sunday noon-5pm.

Every town should have a place like Wilson's/Hillview, a place of verdant plantings that you can duplicate in *your* garden. Over 400 varieties of perennial flowers and an interesting assortment of ornamental grasses inhabit the gardens and fill the saleyard here. Three display ponds add the gentle sound of water and the beauty of water plants for summer ambiance. Water gardening is a developing vogue in the US and Wilson's offers a wide range of appropriate equipment and plants. For garden accents there is sculpture, furniture, and an unusual collection of dwarf, grafted, weeping, and topiary evergreens.

Beginning in 1993, Hillview will have trial grounds for the All-America Selections program; you'll have a chance to meet new plants here before they're available commercially. Wilson's offers occasional garden-related workshops and seminars; open houses in early autumn include garden demonstrations and tours. These gardens have hosted weddings and have even been the site of radio remote broadcasts. I admire a gardening business that dedicates land and staff to display gardens and public relations. I repeat, every town should have a place like Wilson's/Hillview. ▶

◀ *From I-70 take Exit 132 and go north on Ohio Route 13 to Newark. In Newark go east on OH 16 to the flashing light that's between Dayton Road on the west and OH 668 on the east. Turn northeast at the light, go a short distance to Marne Road, and turn back west to Wilson's/Hillview.*

Hoover Historical Center, Gardens of the Herb Society
2225 Easton NW
North Canton OH 44720
(216) 499-0287

Three-quarters acre. Period theme gardens.

 Library. Workshops and other special events.
Open all year, every day but Monday, 1-5pm. Other hours and group tours by appointment.

Old-fashioned flowers and gardens add their charm to this 1870 home, the birthplace of W. H. Hoover, a developer of the Hoover Suction Sweeper. The fragrance garden and the formal herb garden are particularly compatible with the home's style and period. The cutting garden is an abundant source of fresh flowers and everlastings while another installation holds plants useful to dyers and weavers. Storytellers hold court in Tales in Thyme, a delightful spot designed specifically for that purpose.

Special events at the Center range from harness-making demonstrations to puppet plays; the herb garden is the frequent site of informative programs about herbs. Costumed guides add a special touch to July garden tours. Changing exhibits in the Center focus on Victoriana, on rug making and cleaning, and on Hoover history. The Center's Research Library emphasizes Hoover family and business history and "all things Victorian," including herb growing and use. Here is a very pleasant respite from too much time in your car and on the highways.

From I-77 take Exit 111 and go east on Portage Street. Portage becomes East Maple, which becomes Easton. The Center is on Easton near its intersection with Ohio Route 43.
From OH 43 or 44 go west on Easton to the Center.

Lake County Nursery
5052 South Ridge Road (Ohio Route 84)
P. O. Box 122
Perry OH 44081-0122
(216) 259-5571

▶

◀ Commercial. 100'x250' display garden.

♿ Catalog. Many plants labeled. Plant sales (retail site only).
Mary Elizabeth's Garden open Monday-Friday business hours.
Champion Garden Towne open weekdays 9am-6pm, Saturday and Sunday 9am-5pm. Closed Christmas and New Year's days.

A tunnel of grafted flowering crabapple trees, a spectacular self-supporting arbor, leads you into Mary Elizabeth's Garden . . . you'll feel like royalty making a grand entrance. This comely hillside garden honors Mary Elizabeth Zampini, "a woman who loved little children and plants" and progenitor of the second- and third-generation Zampinis now associated with this nursery. It's an effective tribute.

Espaliered flowering crabs recline on rail fences while euonymus and privet stand erect in topiaries and standards. You'll see striking variegated liriope and an ophiopogon whose satiny dark blades are neither green nor brown nor black. Lake County Nursery is known for its introductions of new plant hybrids and cultivars; this registered ophiopogon, 'Black Knight', is one of them.

We've missed the springtime splendor of the flowering crabs but are delighted with the garden's mid-summer riches. An impressive display of *Astilbe taqueti* 'Superba' provides subtle color on this July day, its congregation of tall bronze seedheads lavender-pink at their tips. Airy stems and delicate flowers of white gaura (*Gaura lindheimeri*) quiver beside sturdy silver-blue globe thistle (*Echinops ritro*). One terrace presents exuberant daylilies in all their colors while prim ranks of golden pygmy barberry march nearby. Variegated azaleas and dwarf evergreens accent sweeping flower beds and will help this handsome garden remain attractive all through its winter. For more informed viewing, use the visitor's guide that is available in the garden or at the office. ▶

FYI Lake County, Ohio, is a nurseryman's dream. Geologic history has given it many different soil types, variations in *ph*, and differing drainages. Well-drained sandy ridges separate old swales and their pockets of loamy, acid soil. Temperature-moderating aspects of nearby Lake Erie supply varying rates of "lake effect" snow and rain. All this combines to allow economically feasible nurseries on as little as 5 acres. In times past there have been as many as 500 different nurseries in the county. Today, nearly 120 nurseries occupy over 10,000 acres between Willoughby and Madison. These operations make the county one of the nation's leading sources of nursery/greenhouse materials. Most likely, some of the plants in your garden originated in Lake County, Ohio.

◀ Lake County Nursery is developing or redesigning other test and display gardens; inquire about them at the office. This is LCN's wholesale site; their retail location is a few miles north at Champion Garden Towne. You'll want to visit Champion to carry home some of the beauty you saw in Mary Elizabeth's Garden.

Lake County Nursery is very active in local, regional, and national preservation/beautification programs. For information on conferences and other activities, contact the Director of Marketing at the nursery.

From I-90 take Exit 212 (Ohio Route 528) and go north about a mile to OH 84 (South Ridge Road), then west on OH 84 to the nursery.
Retail site: Champion Garden Towne, 3717 North Ridge Road, Perry OH 44081-0122. (216) 259-2811.

Go north on OH 528 to US Route 20 (North Ridge Road), then west to Champion.

Bittersweet Farm
6294 Seville Road
Seville OH 44273
(216) 887-5293

Commercial. One-half acre cutting gardens. 100'x100' display gardens.

Catalog. Shop. Many plants labeled. Plant sales.
Open Tuesday-Saturday 10am-5pm, Sunday 1-5pm. Closed January and February.

Bittersweet Farm lies in a sunny woodland clearing at the end of a gravel road, just beyond bright beds of everlastings. Tall bronze fennel, graceful in the gentle breeze, guards display gardens where autumn anemones boast heavy buds and feverfew is in its second blooming. On this late July morning, cicadas maintain a steady chatter as butterflies patrol the garden. Giant sunflowers bend heavy heads above statice and lungwort (*Pulmonaria* spp.), appearing to pray for rain in this very dry summer. Nearby, a rustic wattle fence surrounds the luxuriant herb garden. Wrens fuss among tempting plants in the shade house, tidying the place and snatching juicy morsels for their nestlings.

Small garden sculptures huddle in the shade of a weathered bench near the Country Barn shop. Inside, dried flowers and herbs hang from every available beam while walls, shelves, and tables hold beautiful dried arrangements and other inviting objects. Bittersweet's own potpourri scents the air. A pleasant deck, the perfect perch for woods-watching, overlooks a wooded ravine and provides shady respite from the sunny gardens. You'll find much to please you at Bittersweet Farm.

Seville is on Ohio Route 3 just south of I-76 west of Akron. From the center of Seville, take Main Street (Seville Road/County Road 46) west about 2½ miles to Bittersweet Farm.

Gardenview Horticultural Park
16711 Pearl Road (US Route 42)
Strongsville OH 44136
(216) 238-6653

Total grounds 16 acres. 6 acres cottage-style gardens. 10-acre arboretum.

💲 Library. Many plants labeled. Group tours at any time, by appointment only. Open to non-members April 1-November 1, weekends only, noon-6pm.

These lush gardens are made primarily of rare, uncommon, or unusual plants from all over the world, with special emphasis on variegated, golden-leaved, and silver-leaved varieties. For many of the plants, these are the only live specimens in this country.

Gardenview grew from one man's dream and his lifetime of dawn-to-midnight work days and 7-day weeks. In 1949, these acres were swampy clay overgrown with brambles and weeds; Henry Ross' persistent vision and enthusiasm (and thousands of tons of horse manure and compost) have given us today's verdant plantings.

Cottage gardens require many plants, in a wide variety of forms and colors, informally massed in beds and borders. Some years ago, Ross estimated that Gardenview held over 10,000 varieties of plants. Today, even more varieties inhabit the 30-plus distinct installations that blend into one luscious greenery.

The entry garden is at its peak in spring, when tulips, daffodils, and azaleas bloom beneath flowering crabapple trees. In summer, it sings with bright annuals and perennials. Winding paths lead through all-season gardens to arrays of hostas and other shade plants and past the 500 different varieties of flowering crabs that live here. Plant-filled nooks present themselves at every turn. Small, unexpected gardens may surprise you with variegated plant rarities or with a carefully sited and nurtured plant that is not usually expected to be hardy in this climate. Lily ponds and water gardens await you and, just before you reach the arboretum, you'll discover the glorious English Garden, as nearly a bit of floriferous England as horticulture, elbow grease, and adequate rain can make it.

The "super fine horticultural library" at Gardenview contains over 4,000 volumes, including the very best garden books from this country and all the British classics. These are, of course, available for on-site use and enjoyment only.

Because Gardenview has been, and continues to be, the love and the project of one man, keeping it beautiful and keeping it open have been an on-going struggle. Take time to visit, to marvel at the beauty Henry Ross has created, and to supply your admiring support.

From I-80 exit at US Route 42 and go south to Strongsville. Continue on US 42 a mile and a half south of Strongsville to Gardenview.
From I-71 exit at Ohio Route 82, go west to Strongsville, then south on US 42 to the gardens.

Herb N' Ewe
11755 National Road S.E.
Thornville OH 43076
(616) 323-2264

Commercial. Small herb theme gardens.

♿ Shop. Many plants labeled. Seasonal plant sales. Workshops and special events (small fee for food and/or materials).

Concrete sheep and a picturesque old watering can, hints of the pleasures to come, welcome you to this ". . . herbal farm for gardeners and shepherds." Small, well-tended theme gardens include dye plants, culinary herbs, a silver garden, and plants for teas. We enjoy iced tea from some of those plants as we browse through the shop's collection of unusual herb-and sheep-related items. You'll see a fine selection of books, seeds, herb blends, dried everlastings, linens, teapots and mugs, soaps, botanicals for dyeing, and on and on. We love the large aprons printed with flocks of grazing sheep. The ultimate tea cozy, a handsome fleecy sheep, called to me from the shelf so I took him home.

Herb N' Ewe's pleasant tea room, which overlooks a wooded hillside and the sheep pasture below, is used for lectures, workshops, and other events (by reservation only). Such functions include a tussy-mussy workshop, the salad lecture that features edible flowers, topiary workshops, and other appealing activities. In the spring, Herb N' Ewe offers a wide variety of herb plants, seeds, and scented geraniums. The workshops and the gardens help you know what to do with them.

From I-70 go north on Ohio Route 13 to Jacksontown, then east on US Route 40, the Old National Road. Herb N' Ewe is a few miles east of Jacksontown; check the numbers on the mailboxes and you'll eventually see their sign. Turn north off the highway, then immediately back left for Herbs N' Ewe.

Spring Hill Nurseries
110 West Elm Street
Tipp City OH 45371
(513) 667-2491

Commercial. 5-acre demonstration garden. Extensive shade houses. All-American Rose Selections garden.

♿ Catalog. Garden shop. Most plants labeled. Plant sales.
Open every day, all year, 9am-6pm, except Christmas and New Year's days.

Spring Hill's thriving demonstration gardens are quite varied. On this mid-June day, opuntias (prickly pear cacti) are budded and ready to bloom in a bed that's accented by glowing Japanese blood grass and the delicate creamy spires of goatsbeard (*Aruncus dioicus*). Variegated houttynia, a colorful ground cover, gleams in the late afternoon sun. Nearby, a shaded swing suggests relaxation while we admire the surrounding ferns and hostas. In the rose beds and the All-American Rose Selections garden, I consider the heavily blooming miniatures most pleasing of all.

Spring Hill does a large mail-order business, as evidenced by the UPS semi-trailer trucks lined up at the loading dock like pigs at a trough. Extensive shade houses protect a wide range of unusual shrubs and evergreens, as well as the more common varieties; their colors and textures are a delightful mosaic. Today there are vast empty spaces on the greenhouse shelves but I found, among the standard offerings, blooming edelweiss and a few unusual vines. There's just basic garden center fare in the extensive shop but Spring Hill offers interesting, healthy plants to appreciate and fine gardens to enjoy.

From I-75 not far north of I-70, take Exit 68. Go east on Main Street 3 traffic lights to Hyatt, then turn south and go several blocks to the blinking light. You'll see Spring Hill's large sign; turn left into the parking lot.

Toledo Botanical Garden (formerly Crosby Gardens)
5403 Elmer Drive
Toledo OH 43615
(419) 536-8365

---

58 acres total, not all in gardens. Extensive shade and herb gardens. Garden Village.

♿ ☕ Shops. Many plants labeled. Seasonal plant sales. Special events.
Gardens open daily, daylight hours. Garden Emporium Gift Shop open Monday-Saturday 10am-5pm, Sunday 1pm-5pm. Garden Café open daily 11am-5pm May-first week in October.

Come to the Toledo Botanical Garden for the shade. A winding path carries you through rhododendron thickets, past azalea masses, and in and out of fern and hosta banks. Here are admirable clumps of unusual hostas; at a curve in the path, the dark-edged chartreuse leaves of one variety stand in stunning contrast to the chartreuse-edged dark blue leaves of its neighbor. On this late July day, pale yellow mayapple fruits (*Podophyllum peltatum*) litter the ground beneath tall oaks that are alive with chattering chickadees. Astilbes line the poolward path and, at the pool's rim, *Ligularia przewalskii* thrusts its yellow blossoms toward the sun. A comely gazebo overlooks water plants and lazy goldfish in the small pond.

Come to these gardens for the light. The sun-drenched herb garden is alive with butterflies today. Espaliered apple and juniper trees add interest to bright expanses of brick wall and a stately fountain made of granite cubes murmurs as I stroll the wide brick walks. This tasteful garden is a project of the Maumee Valley Herb Society. They've established an appetizing collection of basil varieties, a handsome knot garden, and other very attractive spots. A good-looking bay bush (*Laurel nobilis*) erupts from the center of a boxwood and lavender carpet. Elsewhere, many colors of everlasting statice and globe amaranth surround a Japanese stone lantern. The multitude of dogwood trees here will add grace and beauty to spring bulb color.

A major installation of perennial plants is under development on the far side of small Crosby Lake; the current perennial garden, the one I relish, is a pocket of color surrounded by the Garden Village buildings. Today, in late July, few blooms remain on the lush wisteria arbor but the garden is a riot of daylilies, *Hemerocallis* of many heights, daylily colors from pale lemon yellow through apricot and coral to glowing rusty red. Pink and white phlox, spires of blue-green juniper, and massive clumps of a clear green grass add softer colors. I admire the view from a shaded bench, watching a little tractor-type sprinkler creep across the lawn, adding gentle sound and motion to the scene as it goes.

Near the main entrance to the gardens, the Garden Village is home to 18 different art, environmental, and horticultural groups; you may find individual artists, classes, workshops, or meetings in some of the studios during your visit. The Visitor Center, which consists of folders and maps in a rack, is in the Garden Gallery, a gallery that emphasizes the work of Ohio craftsmen and that offers a small selection of excellent gardening books. The Garden Café supplies carry-out food that you can enjoy on the shaded terrace. Toledo Botanical Garden hosts two major festivals each year; imagine fine arts and crafts, lively dance and music, craft demonstrations, and ethnic foods surrounded by these admirable gardens. Come and enjoy.

From I-475 on the west side of Toledo, take the Central Avenue/US Route 20 exit. Follow US 20 east about a mile until it curves south and becomes Reynolds Road. Go about a half mile south on Reynolds to Elmer Drive and turn west. Elmer Drive is not a major street; *look for the used car lot on the corner of Reynolds and Elmer. Go west on Elmer to the gardens, on your left. From I-80/90 take Exit 4 for Reynolds Avenue/US 20. Go north several miles to Elmer and turn west to the gardens.*

Toledo Zoological Gardens
2700 Broadway
Toledo OH 43609
(419) 385-5721

50-acre zoo grounds. 800 sq.ft. conservatory. Rose garden.

💲♿☕ Brochure. Shops. Many plants labeled. Picnic facilities. Food at zoo concessions. Open every day except Thanksgiving, Christmas, and New Year's days. April 1-September 30 10am-5pm, October 1-March 31 10am-4pm.

Bromeliads are the specialty of the house in the Toledo zoo's Victorian (1900) conservatory. This charming structure sits among perennial gardens, the rose garden, and naturalized plantings in the animal exhibits. Many varieties of aquatic plants inhabit the zoo's aquariums and scattered ponds, while annuals supply summer color throughout the grounds. Special botanic/geographic representations here include Chinese woodland, African savanna, and South American rain forest. You'll undoubtedly find some plants here that are new and exciting to you. ▶

◀ *From I-75 take Exit 201A and go south on US 25 (Broadway) a short distance to the zoo.*
From I-80/90 take Exit 4 and go north on Reynolds Road to Glendale Avenue. Go east on Glendale to US 25/Broadway, then north to the zoo.

Swisher Hill Herbs
4089 Swisher Road
Urbana OH 43078
(513) 653-8730

Commercial. Two acres. Small greenhouse. Theme gardens.

♿ Catalog and brochures. Seasonal plant sales. Shop. Workshops and special events. Garden tours by arrangement.
Open April 1-December 20 Tuesday-Saturday 10am-6pm. Shop *may* be open during late winter-early spring; call ahead.

The raised beds in front of Swisher Hill's shop are abundant sources of materials for classes and seminars and for the herbal items sold in the shop. Lavenders, thymes, and other useful favorites are segregated, each in its own bed, to simplify cultivating and harvesting. I never tire of the sight and scent of lavender and a whole bed of it seems like a little piece of heaven to me. Other plants, those that are inclined to look a little ragged after harvest or that have different growing needs, fill production gardens behind the shop and in other areas of the farm.

On this late July day, yarrows (*Achillea* var.) in pink, red, magenta, salmon, and shades in between blaze in the partially depleted cutting bed. In the three-year-old hillside rock garden, sturdy heathers, pygmy barberries, and dwarf conifers make a handsome display that looks as if it has been there for years. Fields of clover provide a gentle backdrop for the gardens, where blooming plants and rich scents abound.

Do you want to grow and *control* several different mints, rather than having them pop up where they're not wanted? Plant them in a strawberry jar as the gardeners at Swisher Hill have done. In late summer, take cuttings, root them in water, then heel them into the garden to wait for their spring repotting. Comfortable benches, the mint jar, and thriving plants in containers and in pocket gardens make Swisher Hill's pleasant shop-side patio very inviting. We accept the invitation to relax in the late afternoon shade and to admire the bluebirds that have returned to Swisher Hill. ▶

◀ Today, the shop overflows with everlastings and dried herbs in potpourri, on stems, and in made-to-order arrangements. You'll find a rich selection of potpourri supplies, a small collection of excellent books on herbs and everlastings, and a variety of herb products. Hanging bunches and bundles of drying plants adorn the workshop behind the shop, the home of classes and seminars that cover a wide range of herbal topics, such as basic herb harvesting and preservation, making novelty wreaths, and designing theme gardens. Seasonal festivals and open houses add to the fun at Swisher Hill but the gardens and the shop are appealing at any time.

From I-70 take US Route 68 north to Ohio Route 36 in Urbana. Go east on OH 36 about 5 miles to OH 814, then north on OH 814 about 1½ miles to Swisher Road. Look for the Swisher Hill Herbs sign at this corner. Turn east and go about a half mile to the farm, on your right.

Inniswood Metro Gardens
940 Hempstead Road
Westerville OH 43081
(614) 895-6216

Ninety-one acre estate. Rose garden. Herb garden. Woodland and meadow gardens.

♿ Brochure. Many plants labeled. Library. Seasonal plant sales. Workshops and seminars. Picnicking is specifically *not* allowed at Inniswood.
Gardens open daily 7am-dark. Innis House open Tuesday-Friday 8am-4:30pm.

A fine pergola and its extensive rose garden will probably be the first thing you see at Inniswood. This morning, dewy roses are shining in the August sun. At Innis House, nestled under trees near the Rose Garden, volunteers are cataloging journals in the cozy library. The library is available for on-site use, so I *could* settle in for a little research, surrounded by Oriental rugs and over 1,000 books and countless journals. But the gardens are calling.

The shady hillside rock garden is masses of astilbe, perilla (*Perilla frutescens*), hostas, and other shade lovers. Recently renovated to please Ameri-Flora visitors, it's a lovely garden, perfect for its site.

The "crown jewel" of Inniswood, the garden most mentioned by Inniswood admirers, is the herb garden. It was designed and planted by the Ohio Unit of the Herb Society of America, whose volunteers now maintain it. Today, one of those volunteers weeds and prunes in the medicinal garden while her children curl up with books on nearby benches. The inviting entrance and the traditional knot garden are formal, symmetrical designs but most installations are richly textured clumps and masses of plants, many in hip-high raised beds. You'll enjoy the subtleties of the blue-gray garden and the mints, basils, oreganos, and other appetizing plants in the culinary plantings. In the Bible Garden, an antique handhewn watering trough is filled with miniature thymes and dwarf conifers. One planting is especially rich in nectar-producing plants, another displays traditional medicinal plants, and yet another showcases shade-tolerant herbs and ground covers. A special thyme collection, alive with bees today, enriches several of the raised beds. The Fragrance Garden surrounds a tiny pool and a small gazebo. This is a garden for strolling or for enjoying the strategically placed benches, a garden whose intriguing textures, fine perfumes, sunny spots, and shady nooks offer nearly everything you could wish for in an herb garden.

Beyond the sunny meadow and its small bog, a boardwalk leads into the extensive woodland nature preserve. Today's deep shade affords a restful walk and subtle attractions, with little evidence of spring's wildflower riot.

The 37-acre estate of Grace and Mary Innis is the nucleus of Inniswood; the Metro Parks System added 54 acres of woodland and meadow. Grace Innis was strongly interested in horticulture and Mary in ornithology, so the combination of gardens and natural areas here is particularly fitting. Inniswood offers a variety of lectures and workshops throughout the year, all focusing on some aspect of the natural sciences. Add these educational events to the gardens and the renowned plant collections that reside here and you'll begin to understand why Inniswood is so popular.

For additional information contact the address above or the Metropolitan Park District of Columbus and Franklin County, P. O. Box 29169, Columbus OH 43229. (614) 891-0700.

From I-270 go north on Westerville Pike/Ohio Route 3 (called State Road in Westerville). Turn right at the third stoplight, Schrock Road. Follow Schrock as it winds through a residential area and ends at Hempstead, then turn right onto Hempstead. You'll soon come to the Inniswood entrance on your left.

Ohio Agricultural Research and Development Center (OARDC)
Dover Road (Ohio Route 250)
Wooster

Arboretum of several acres. Three-acre rose garden. Conifer, shrub, and flowering crabapple collections.

◄ Brochure and garden map available by mail or in the garden. Many plants labeled. Open daylight hours all year.

The Garden of Roses of Legend and Romance is an array of colorful arcs and circles and rectangles of roses on this July day. Roses that were known in pre-Christian times grow near twentieth-century introductions and you'll see roses that originated in China, in the Middle East, in Europe, and in the United States, especially in this part of Ohio. We're entranced by a shining bed of Peace roses and by the bright coral blooms of 'McGregor Sunset', a sturdy plant particularly rich with buds and flowers. At the back of the garden, vigorous ramblers and climbers cover the rail fence and the shade arbor.

This slightly rolling open space, where ornamental trees and shrubs and the conifer collection offer color and texture for all seasons, is an arboretum and a research facility. The road to the rose garden is lined with crabapple trees that are part of the National Crabapple Evaluation Program. Today the trees are decorated by muted red eggs, deep red globes, and rose-tinged yellow marbles, fruits that are evidence of a flamboyant spring. The fields and open plantings at OARDC are unlike most arboreta but they hold luscious roses and many other woody plants that will interest you.

For information contact The Ohio State University, Ohio Agricultural Research and Development Center, 1680 Madison Avenue, Wooster OH 44691. (216) 263-3700.

From US 30 on the south side of Wooster take Ohio Route 250 (Dover Road) a short distance to OARDC. (US 30, the Wooster Bypass, is clearly marked for OARDC.) Once you're on the small campus, follow Gerlach Street to Williams then go past the greenhouses to the Rose Garden and the tree collections.

The Ohio State University/Agricultural Technical Institute (OSU/ATI)
1328 Dover Road
Wooster OH 44691
(216) 264-3911, Ext. 243, Horticulture Division
(In Ohio only, [800] 647-8283, Ext. 243)

Over one acre. Display, trial, and theme gardens. Small Victorian conservatory. ►

◀ ♿☕ Fee for Spring Garden Preview. Many plants labeled. Picnic facilities. Food at college cafeteria (limited hours). Workshops and other special events.
Gardens open daylight hours all year. Conservatory hours vary.

In one of this year's flower beds, the rich blues and violets of ageratum, heliotrope, salvia, and bachelor's button are seasoned by touches of dusty miller, 'White Porcelain' salvia, and the red-violet seed spikes of cinnamon basil. Elsewhere, touches of violet enrich masses of yellow dahlias, golden zinnias, and flowers of all shades between. These bright beds surround the Black Conservatory, a Victorian structure that originally stood near Mansfield, Ohio, and was moved here in 1976 by OSU/ATI students. Today it's nearly overflowing with brilliant crotons, various palms, and blooming bromeliads and arums.

Nearby, in a woodsy garden, yellowed mayapple remnants languish among more colorful coleus and caladium and other shade-lovers. Water lilies bloom lavender and coral in a small rock garden pool, a pool fed by a water "trickle" too small to be a water*fall*. Weathered bricks are a particularly pleasing floor beneath greens and grays in the terraced herb garden. Flowering crabs and tall pines are a handsome backdrop for low herbs and graceful grasses in the perennial garden, where round, dry heads of drumstick allium (*Allium sphaerocephalum*) hover in striking counterpoint to the grasses.

Because this garden is a learning laboratory for OSU/ATI students and staff *and* an All-America Selections display garden, color themes and annual plant varieties change from year to year. You'll also see landscaping materials, such as various bricks, stones, and timbers, being tested in permanent structures. Energetic clematis and roses adorn the handsome pergola and, on this warm day, the breezy gazebo is a perfect picnic site.

The annual Spring Garden Preview occurs in late February, just when a gardener's blue moods are deepest. Come see artful gardens, new plant varieties, and student projects. Attend a bridal show, a garden lecture, or a symposium. Prepare yourself for the gardening season . . . then return to OSU/ATI later to enjoy these small but gratifying gardens.

Follow the directions for OARDC. The OSU/ATI is about ½ mile further east on Ohio Route 250/Dover Road, near the intersection of OH 83 and 3 with OH 250. The gardens are behind the main college buildings.

Quailcrest Farm
2810 Armstrong Road
Wooster OH 44691
(216) 345-6722

▶

◀ Commercial. Several acres. Theme gardens. Emphasis on herbs and perennials.

♿ Fee for autumn herb fair. Shops. Many plants labeled. Trails. Picnic facilities. Plant sales. Workshops and other special events.
Open mid-March-January 1 Tuesday-Saturday 10am-5pm. Special additional hours for winter holidays and spring planting season.

If it will grow in this part of Ohio, or in other parts of the midwest, you'll find it in the gardens and sale houses of Quailcrest. No matter what your gardening itch, you can probably scratch it here. Small herb gardens are tucked into all appropriate spaces while more ambitious plantings adorn shady spots and break up expanses of sunny meadow. You'll see an English border garden, old-fashioned roses, a cutting garden of everlastings, and water features designed to remind Quailcrest's owner of childhood days near Lake Erie.

For many visitors, the strength and jewel of Quailcrest is the plant sales barn. You may find it hard to choose among the sturdy perennials and the many, many herbs. There's a reason why small wagons are available; we filled one with plants we really, really needed . . . gaura, tritoma, tradescantia . . . lovely names and lovely plants.

A few years ago, Quailcrest lost several structures, including greenhouses, to a fire and, although the gardens weren't touched, plant production was impeded. Rebuilding has entailed garden revision and expansion. Quailcrest is being reinvented with love, knowledge, and enthusiasm. The Phoenix Shop has risen from the ashes to offer up-scale country items, gourmet seasonings and cookbooks, handcrafted tableware and linens and baskets, and a splendid assortment of travel, herb, and gardening books. The Gallery Shop holds additional fine stoneware, designer garments, fancy paper goods, and handsome jewelry. An intriguing group of small glass vases will give new dimension to single stems or tiny bouquets. The Garden Shop contains benches and tables, pots and planters, fountains and baskets and "authentic English garden statuary direct from Oxfordshire" . . . almost everything your garden could want.

You can wander the meadows and woods of Quailcrest, shop to your heart's content, then enjoy your picnic and a glass of herbal lemonade in the new pavilion. Perhaps you'll take part in one of the many workshops offered throughout the year. You might prefer to come for Kite Day in April, September's Annual Herb Festival, or another of the annual events. Whenever you come to Quailcrest, you'll agree it's a treat you deserve. ▶

◂ *From Wooster, take Ohio Route 83 to Armstrong Road, about 8 or 10 miles. Turn west on Armstrong and follow the Quailcrest signs.*
From I-71 take the OH 83 exit (Wooster/Lodi) and go south 7 miles to Armstrong Road. Turn west to Quailcrest, which is about a mile west of OH 83.

Fellows Riverside Gardens
Mill Creek Park
816 Glenwood Avenue
Youngstown OH 44502
(216) 740-7116 or (216) 743-PARK (7275)

Eleven-acre garden within 2,600 acre municipal park. Rose, shade, herb, Victorian, rock, and formal gardens.

♿ Shop. Many plants labeled. Library. Hiking trails. Seasonal plant sales. Workshops, concerts, and other special events.
Gardens open every day 10am-dark.
Garden Center open all year Monday-Friday 10am-4:30pm. Additional Garden Center hours April-mid-December Saturday noon-4pm, Sunday 1-5pm.

Wonderful garden treats await you beyond the verdant wall of Riverside Gardens' parking lot. You'll feel like "Alice Through the Looking Glass" as you step through the tall hedge and into the garden's Long Mall. Shrub roses and thousands of pastel wax begonias add color to this grassy, gracious mall that is bordered by conifers and flowering trees. Beyond the mall, the full glory of the gardens spreads before you and it's hard to decide which way to walk first. Verdant sweeps of rolling lawn are framed by shrub collections, ornamental trees, and luxuriant flower beds. The unusually large and striking gazebo, a lacy and graceful structure that suggests string quartets and gentlefolk in Victorian dress, stands out against mature trees and dark hedges. This evening, white nicotiana perfumes the cool air and the perfect garden scene.

The south end of the garden offers a stunning vista of Lake Glacier. Here you can stroll through an extensive and colorful rose collection, accompanied by the pleasant sounds of the K. Calvin Sommer Fountain. The nearby Perennial Border Walk is spectacular with old and new favorites; brilliant scarlet crocosima 'Lucifer' and distinctive blue cardoon (*Cynara cardunculus*) are especially dramatic in the evening light. A startling black pansy lies at their feet, a somber and sturdy plant whose velvety flowers are brightened by tiny golden-yellow throats and occasional royal purple petals. Another treat awaits you in the formal garden, near the Garden Center. Here, red sage and blue lobelia rise above a lush carpet of crisp, densely planted curly parsley in a most attractive use of this common herb.

The Schmidt Rhododendron Collection lies along the edge of the bluff, sheltered by tall trees, while other rhododendrons and azaleas are scattered through the park. Can you imagine the glory of springtime here, when the park's thousands and thousands of spring bulbs are also blooming? A handsome rock garden of splendid grasses, dwarf conifers, yuccas, sedums, and rock cresses climbs a hillock further along the bluff. I'm stunned, nearly overwhelmed, by the stately tree that guards one entrance to the rock garden, a tree whose floral fireworks of knobby, creamy, two-foot-wide flower clusters explode above deep green palmate leaves. This is castor-aralia (*Kalopanax pictus*), a native of the Far East. It was worth the trip to Fellows just to see this tree's midsummer bloom.

At the north end of the garden, a small and inviting grove of comely beech trees stands just in front of the Great Terrace. The Terrace provides a long view over a hillside of daylilies to the hills of residential and industrial Youngstown. In the nearby Four Seasons Garden, where you'll find rigidly planted flower beds, one spread of tightly packed satiny green and ruby plants looks good enough to eat. It *is* good enough to eat; this luscious carpet is made of radicchio 'Rossa Di Treviso' in another uncommon use of an edible plant, another example of "edible landscaping." A slightly raised garden is covered with the intricate floral patterns of Victorian "mosaiculture" in honor of Mill Creek Park's 1991 centennial celebration.

All through the gardens you'll notice the pyramidal European hornbeam (*Carpinus betulus* 'Fastigiata'), a tree that's particularly attractive in form and foliage. Picture its exuberant branches flaring against the winter sky. Add to your image smooth gray beeches and the massed greens of rhododendrons, hollies, and a wealth of conifers, their forms no longer hidden by summer's deciduous verdure. You're seeing Fellows' lovely winter garden.

At the Fred W. Green Memorial Garden Center, garden devotees can take part in seasonal plant sales, floral and gardening workshops, and field trips. Perhaps you can time your visit to coincide with one of the summer Sunday afternoon concerts. There's always something pleasing in these gardens high above I-680, Mill Creek, and Lake Glacier.

From I-680 take the Glenwood/Mahoning Avenue exit and follow the signs to Mill Creek Park. The gardens are in the northwest corner of the park, on the bluffs above Mill Creek.

Ohio: South

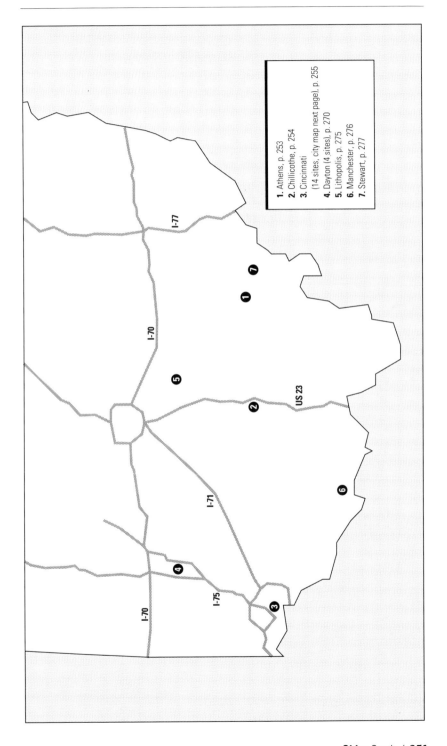

Ohio: South / CINCINNATI

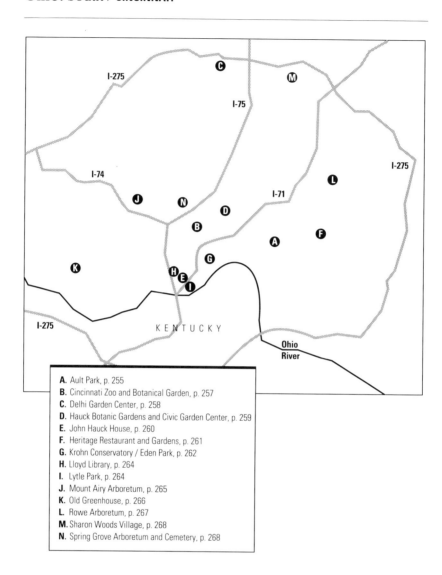

A. Ault Park, p. 255
B. Cincinnati Zoo and Botanical Garden, p. 257
C. Delhi Garden Center, p. 258
D. Hauck Botanic Gardens and Civic Garden Center, p. 259
E. John Hauck House, p. 260
F. Heritage Restaurant and Gardens, p. 261
G. Krohn Conservatory / Eden Park, p. 262
H. Lloyd Library, p. 264
I. Lytle Park, p. 264
J. Mount Airy Arboretum, p. 265
K. Old Greenhouse, p. 266
L. Rowe Arboretum, p. 267
M. Sharon Woods Village, p. 268
N. Spring Grove Arboretum and Cemetery, p. 268

Companion Plants
7247 North Coolville Ridge
Athens OH 45701
(614) 592-4643

Commercial. Over two acres. Emphasis on herbs, hard-to-find annuals and perennials. Greenhouses.

Catalog. Many plants labeled. Plant sales.
Open March 1-mid-November Thursday-Sunday 10am-5pm. Closed major holidays and the first two weeks of August. No telephone hours on Wednesday.

These hilltop gardens and fields are proof that the owners of Companion Plants love collecting, breeding, propagating, planting, and tending plants. Greenhouses, terraced gardens, and stock fields work their way down slopes below the owners' home. It's a delicious place to wander, a showcase for many plants you've seen only in catalogs and for some of your old favorites.

Hops (*Humulus lupulus*) climb and beautify a utility pole, a practical use for this good-looking but invasive vine, and thymes on a sunny hillside quiver with laboring bees. Tiny creeping ground covers, especially *Thymus serpyllum* 'Elfin' and the equally minute dwarf English pennyroyal, suggest the scale of bonsai creations. If you're a basil lover, this is the place to be. The basil bed holds familiar varieties and some dandy lesser-known variations; dwarf opal basil and African blue basil are uncommonly handsome. In the hillside stock field, swamp rose mallow (*Hibiscus moscheutos*) and Joe-Pye weed (*Eupatorium purpureum*) bloom luxuriantly in a small depression that holds just enough moisture to keep them happy.

Near the main greenhouse, bloodflower, the tropical milkweed *Asclepias curassavica*, flaunts its bold red and orange flower heads. Now, in late July, the greenhouses hold only progapation stock and a few remaining perennials; in the spring, when they're filled with the plants offered in the catalog, they must be a plant-lover's heaven.

The gardeners here have added small surprises to their plantings; like many of us, they find a new plant or variety an irresistible challenge. Hardy cacti thrive beneath tall ornamental grasses and other sun lovers, a tiny woodland garden hides beneath the pines, and you're sure to find other treasures.

Companion Plants' catalog, with thorough and concise information on each variety of the 500 plants and seeds they offer, is an excellent reference. For most plants, it provides history, uses, a verbal description, and cultural information; you'll know what you're getting. If you can't visit these sunny hillside gardens, having the catalog in hand is the next best thing.

◀ *From either US 50 or US 33 exit for Stimson Avenue/County Road 25. Go under the overpass then turn left almost immediately onto CR 25 (watch carefully; the sign for CR 25 was nearly illegible when I was there). Follow CR 25 up the hill for 1½ miles and bear left at the top of the hill. When you reach the stop sign in another half mile, go straight onto CR 90. Stay on CR 90 for 1¼ miles, until you reach a big red barn. Go to the right of the barn onto Canaan Township Road 92 (which is not always marked). Companion Plants is another ⅕ of a mile, at the crest of a hill. Park beyond the house, by the greenhouses.*

Adena State Memorial
Adena Road
Chillicothe OH 45601
(614) 772-1500

Restored 1807 stone mansion and grounds. 100′x200′ formal garden. Small herb garden.

💲 Brochure. Museum shop. Group visits by reservation only.

Open Memorial Day-Labor Day Wednesday-Saturday, Sunday afternoon. September and October, open Saturday and Sunday only. Closed November-late May. Open days and seasonal events subject to change.

These terraced gardens were the pride and joy of Thomas Worthington, an early governor of Ohio, from 1807, when he built Adena, until his death in 1827. Then, as now, the gardens brimmed with local native species and "imports" from the east coast, tickseed and spiderwort among the peonies. Daylilies and other traditional perennials join time-honored flowering shrubs, such as lilacs, mock orange, and snowball (*Viburnum opulus*). Trees with ornamental flowers and varieties with especially appealing foliage or seedpods provide shady refuge in the garden; Worthington undoubtedly *needed* that refuge, as his busy life included the governorship of Ohio, service in the US Senate, several active businesses, and the clamor of his ten children.

Adena, including its gardens, roads, fences, and outbuildings, has been restored as nearly as possible to its early nineteenth-century state. In most years, occasional weekend festivities bring early Ohio back to life; June often brings a special garden event. Come to Adena to enjoy its gardens . . . and for the distant view of Mount Logan and the Scioto River Valley, a view so entrancing that it inspired the design for the State Seal of Ohio.

For further information contact the Curator, Adena, P. O. Box 831-A, Chillicothe OH 45601.   ▶

From US Route 23 take US 35 west to Ohio Route 104 (High Street). Go north on OH 104 to Pleasant Valley Road, then west on Pleasant Valley to Adena Road. Follow Adena Road to its end at the mansion.

Cincinnati

Cincinnati is a city of hills, parks, gardens, winding streets, and ethnic neighborhoods, as well as the ubiquitous shopping centers and strip malls. It's also an easy city in which to get lost or, as we call it in our family, "temporarily misplaced." If you plan to look for some of its smaller attractions, arm yourself with a good map of Cincinnati; have your bookstore order one or buy one when you get there because the insert on your road map *won't* be sufficient. The Convention and Visitors Bureau can supply a map of downtown Cincinnati which is, at least, a start.

Many of the Cincinnati Park Board properties are included in a long-range master plan that focuses on redefining gardens, improving accessibility, and extending program development. You may find the Cincinnati gardens quite different, and presumably even better, than I found them.

The Park Board will send a number of helpful booklets and brochures about the various parks. A particulary good booklet, *Cincinnati Parks*, was published in 1988. The pocket map *Cincinnati . . . Horticulturally Alive!* is a guide to downtown garden areas. Also ask them for information on specific parks and, perhaps, a calendar of events.

For information contact the Cincinnati Board of Park Commissioners, 950 Eden Park Drive, Cincinnati OH 45202, (513) 352-4080, or the Cincinnati Convention and Visitors Bureau, 300 West Sixth, Cincinnati OH 45202, (513) 621-2142.

Ault Park
Observatory Drive
Cincinnati

224-acre park. 4 acres of theme gardens. Herb gardens. Rose collection. Dahlia Society garden. Small arboretum.

♿ Many plants labeled. Foot trails. Picnic facilities. Major garden show every spring. Park and gardens open daylight hours.

◀ Something wonderful happens at Ault Park, on the crest of Mt. Lookout. It's a garden party or, to be more accurate, a party of gardens. Here are over 30 different theme gardens, each one planned, planted, and maintained by a different individual or group; to visit these small plantings is like meeting 30 gardeners who have varying interests. In yew-bordered pockets, each about 8'x15', there are herb gardens, a plot of food plants, and a bed of edible flowers. One spread features bulbs for spring, summer, and fall color. Others stretch the limits of one particular color or color combination. The "accessible garden" features a tiny water garden in a plastic-lined barrel and holds other plants in raised tubs and tiles or on trellises. Its neighbor, just across the walk, is a handsome rock garden of varied colors and textures. The Victorian cutting garden features plants chosen for their "language of flowers" connotations while the cactus and succulent bed endorses the values of xeriscaping. A garden "to delight the senses" is sponsored and maintained by the owner of an area restaurant. Shady walks lead us through these gardens to a delightful shade garden that affords an expansive view of Ault Park.

"Trees for Your Yard," a small arboretum that surrounds the main garden area, is sponsored by the Tree Council and continues the theme of civic involvement in Ault Park. Here are trees you might choose for their size or shape, their attractive flowers or fruits, or their interesting foliage. On this August afternoon, the creamy panicles of pagoda tree (*Sophora japonica*) are especially pleasing.

Between the two main groups of theme gardens, The Mall stretches its expanse of lawn. A circular bed of modern roses marks one entry to The Mall and, near another entry, a grand collection of heritage roses surrounds Dahlia Society display beds. Today, in early August, most of the roses are fading but the dahlias are coming on strong. Scattered blooms of many sizes and forms, in all the lovely dahlia colors, promise an admirable display in weeks to come.

Ault's impressive Italianate pavilion, former home of "ten-cents-a-dance" events, will probably be the first thing you see as you come up the hill toward the gardens. Now, the pavilion is often used for weddings and receptions. When we visit Ault a second time, floral arrangements float in the pavilion's terraced pools and there is indeed a wedding reception in progress. Consequently, we have to forego our visit to the pavilion's roof and do without the pleasant breeze and stunning views it provides.

Several years ago, when the Park Board felt they could no longer afford the Municipal Rose Garden, the volunteer-run Adopt-A-Plot program was born. Now there are, where roses once ruled, those delightful individual gardens. ▶

◀ Add to these The Mall, the pavilion and its terraced waterfall, the arboretum, and striking vistas . . . and you'll understand the appeal of Ault Park.

For information on the spring garden festival and other Ault Park activities contact the Cincinnati Park Board.

From I-71 take the Dana Avenue Exit. Go east on Dana across Madison Road, where Dana becomes Observatory Road, then follow Observatory Road to its end at Ault Park.

Cincinnati Zoo and Botanical Garden
3400 Vine Street
Cincinnati OH 45220
(513) 281-4701

65 acres, including animal enclosures. Prize-winning landscape. Theme gardens and plant collections. Butterfly Rainforest. Botanical Center.

$ ♿ ☕ Shops. Many plants labeled. Library. Picnic facilities. Seasonal plant sales. Special events.
Zoo open at 9am daily. Closed at 6pm Memorial Day-Labor Day, at 5pm the rest of the year.

Tropical palms, elephant ear plants, bamboos, and bananas, temperate zone perennials, annual flowers, roses, and summer bulbs . . . this is the zoo's botanical garden in summer. Fall brings late-flowering perennials, the showy plumes of ornamental grasses, and bright fruits and berries that will last into the winter. Winter's subtle beauty includes evergreens, the persistent grasses, and handsome bare trees. Come spring, the glory of 250,000 spring bulbs joins that of ornamental flowering trees, shrubs, vines, and early-blooming perennials.

Wherever possible, an animal exhibit at this zoo includes plants native to that animal's home habitat. You'll see Indian yellow-groove bamboo, Himalayan white pine, threadleaf Japanese maple, and a fine collection of other plants not commonly seen in this country. Orchids and bromeliads tempt exotic hummingbirds and tropical butterflies in the enclosed Butterfly Rainforest, while the outside butterfly garden is designed specifically to attract native butterflies. Native wildflowers, trees, and shrubs surround the Passenger Pigeon Memorial. The Dinosaur Garden, near the Reptile House, holds plants of ancient lineage, such as dawn redwood, cycads, ferns, and horsetails (*Equisetum* spp.). The winter garden emphasizes witchhazels, red twig dogwoods, maples with decorative bark, and other plants with "off-season" beauty. ▶

◀ The Cincinnati Zoo and Botanical Garden, founded in 1875, is the nation's second oldest zoo (after Philadelphia's) and one of our oldest public gardens. Since 1979, it has won four national awards for landscaping and grounds maintenance.

The Botanical Center houses bonsai exhibits, interpretative displays, and occasional workshops and demonstrations. Spring Floral Festival, mid-April to mid-May, makes the zoo "one of the greatest spring gardens in the country." I think it rates as a great garden any time of year.

For information on classes, tours, and special events call the zoo's Education Center (513) 559-7715. At the entry gate, ask for the pamphlets *Self-Guided Tour of the Gardens* and *History of the Zoo's Gardens*.

From I-75 take Exit 6 (Mitchell) and go east on Mitchell to Vine, then south on Vine almost a mile to Forest. Go east on Forest to Dury, then south on Dury to the zoo's main gate.

Delhi Garden Center
135 Northland Boulevard
Cincinnati OH 45246
(513) 771-7117

Commercial. 7½ acres includes 25,000 sq.ft. greenhouse. All-America Selections display. Water garden.

 Garden shop. Most plants labeled. Plant sales. Seminars and special events.

Lush plants in large containers, All-America Selections winners, and a landscaped hillside enhance the parking lot at Delhi; this isn't your ordinary garden center. The fence-enclosed nursery and the large shadehouse, filled with particularly attractive ornamental grasses and dwarf conifers, are lively with mockingbirds and goldfinches on this summer evening.   ▶

FYI The last passenger pigeon (*Ectopistes migratorius*) on earth died at the Cincinnati Zoo in 1914. That must have been a mournful day for those who were paying attention. It's estimated that, in 1500 AD, there were 3 to 5 *billion* passenger pigeons in eastern North America. In 1840, John James Audubon reported a mile-wide flock that took 3 hours to pass. Even those billions couldn't survive vast habitat destruction and uncontrolled market slaughter; only the Passenger Pigeon Memorial remains.

In Delhi's main building, they offer a wide range of public seminars on garden-related topics, and local botanical societies, notably the orchid, hosta, and daylily groups, hold their exhibits here. In the garden shop, next to 10,000 sq.ft. of "hard goods" (everything *but* plants), you may find 3,000 sq.ft. of seasonal plants, such as poinsettias, tender azaleas, or Easter lilies, or another special display. Here, too, you can admire Delhi's attractive water garden. I need to go back to Delhi; all those treasures behind the fences and in the shop are calling me.

From I-275 on the north side of Cincinnati, take Ohio Route 747 south a short distance to Kemper, where Tri-County Mall will be on your left. Turn west onto Kemper and go to the second stoplight, Northland Boulevard. Turn south onto Northland and Delhi will immediately appear on your left.

Hauck Botanic Gardens and The Civic Garden Center of Greater Cincinnati
2715 Reading Road
Cincinnati OH 45206
(513) 221-0981

12 acres total grounds. Naturalistic estate gardens. Dahlia Garden. Herb garden. Education Center.

Shop. Many plants labeled. Library. Intermittent plant sales. Workshops and special events. Hauck Gardens open daylight hours. Civic Garden Center open Tuesday-Friday 9am-4pm, Saturday 9am-3pm. Gift shop open Tuesday-Saturday 10am-3pm. Garden Center and shop closed December 22-third week of January.

This former estate, now a public garden with mature trees and shady nooks, is a mid-city oasis that still *feels* like a private garden. On this summer Sunday afternoon, neighborhood residents amble through the flower-filled shade or sit on scattered benches and chairs to read their Sunday papers. Vast colonies of autumn-blooming anemones wave stalks heavy with sculptured buds. Blossoms of *Lycoris squamigera*, commonly known as magic lilies, naked ladies, or hardy amaryllis, float above the lawn and in the shady spots like pink sprites. Brilliant beds of phlox front a splendid tri-color beech and majestic oaks tower above the garden. True to its genteel history, this garden-park, designed for strolling, is a delightful site for an alfresco breakfast or a picnic lunch.

In spring, vast sweeps of naturalized bulbs embellish the garden's lawns. Later in the season, color arrives in the wildflower garden, the daylily collection, the hosta beds, and the All-American Dahlia Trial Garden.

Early in this century, Cornelious Hauck created this estate, "Sooty Acres," in a residential area where soot and ash from nearby industries fell freely and heavily onto his gardens. During this time, Mr. Hauck, an early president of the Cincinnati Park Board, saved many fine plant specimens from areas that were under urban development; those salvaged plants became the nucleus of today's Hauck Gardens. Most of the trees and shrubs on the property are Mr. Hauck's original plantings and retaining walls from those early gardens have become multi-leveled green terraces.

On the hill at one side of Hauck Gardens, the Civic Garden Center features perennials and annuals, shade plants, and an herb garden with theme beds. I especially enjoy the white hibiscus that have been trained into lollipop-shaped standards and are surrounded by masses of brilliant impatiens. On this warm afternoon, hillside thymes vibrate with bee activity and, in herb garden paths, creeping thyme and santolina release their heady aromas as I walk on them. Below a terrace filled with small conifers, sunny gardens descend the hillside to merge with the shady Hauck Gardens.

The main building of the Garden Center includes meeting rooms, a library/reading room, changing art exhibits, and a sizable potting shed/greenhouse. The nearby garden shop offers a large selection of gardening books, dried materials, and handsome garden sculpture. The Center offers a variety of lectures, workshops, festivals, and plant sales throughout the year; there's much to see, to learn, and to enjoy here at "Sooty Acres."

For more information contact the Cincinnati Park Board.

From downtown Cincinnati, go north on I-71 to the Dorchester/Reading Road exit, then north on Reading Road to its intersection with W. H. Taft Road. The park entrance is just north of this intersection, on the west side of Reading. From the north, take I-71 south to the Taft Road exit. Go one block on Taft and turn north onto Reading Road, then proceed as above.

John Hauck House
812 Dayton Street
Cincinnati

Small Victorian garden. Restored nineteenth-century home.

 Special events.

Open Thursday and Friday 10am-4pm, Sunday noon-4pm. Call for calendar and hours for special events.

◀ Here is a bit of Victorian richness surrounded by the twentieth century. You'll enjoy the small garden behind Hauck House, which is close to downtown Cincinnati. Currently undergoing restoration, this elegant Italianate house was the home of John Hauck, a prominent early Cincinnati brewer. His son, Cornelius J. Hauck, developed "Sooty Acres," which became Hauck Botanical Gardens. The Hauck tradition survives; Hauck descendents continue to serve on the Cincinnati Park Board and on the board of Historic Southwest Ohio, Inc. Special events and exhibits at Hauck House tend to focus on Victorian arts and history of the Cincinnati area.

For more information contact Historic Southwest Ohio, Inc., John Hauck House, P. O. Box 41475, Cincinnati OH 45241-0475. (513) 563-9484.

From I-75 going north, take Exit 1-G to Linn Street, then go north on Linn to Dayton.
From I-75 going south, take Exit 2-A. Take Western Avenue south to Liberty Street, go east on Liberty to Linn, then north on Linn to Dayton.

The Heritage Restaurant and Gardens
7664 Wooster Pike
Cincinnati OH 45227
(513) 561-9300
Gardens and shop: (513) 561-2504

Commercial. Restaurant. Herb gardens. Historic landmark.

♿ ☕ Shop. Many plants labeled. Plant sales. Workshops, classes, and other special events. Shop open Monday-Saturday 10am-5pm. Closed January and February except by appointment. Restaurant open for lunch Monday-Friday, dinner every day, Sunday 4-9pm.

Wander through gardens "created for your enhanced dining and visual pleasure" around this historic restaurant and sharpen your appetite for lunch, dinner, or a workshop. Theme gardens include culinary herbs, ornamental herbs, edible flowers, kitchen, fragrance, and perennial herbs . . . and "not-a-knot" garden. The restaurant's regional American menu makes good use of the bounty from these gardens. The Cottage Workshop, nestled into the gardens, houses a wide variety of gourmet and herbal gifts and is home to a series of workshops, cooking classes, and open houses. Holiday-oriented workshops teach you how to make tabletop trees from herbs and everlastings, gifts from your kitchen, and herbal wreaths and centerpieces. ▶

◀ The buildings and site that are now The Heritage have been an 1827 farm, a fashionable turn-of-the-century restaurant, a roadhouse complete with slot machines, and a Prohibition-era watering hole equipped with trap doors and hiding places. Now it's an agreeable place to spend an hour or a day, to have a stroll or a meal, to consider days gone by or gardens to come.

From I-275 on the east side of Cincinnati, take US 50 (Wooster Pike) west. The Heritage is on US 50, a mile east of the Village of Mariemont.

Irwin M. Krohn Conservatory
In Eden Park
Martin Street and Eden Park Drive
Cincinnati

22,000 sq.ft. under glass. Desert, palm, and tropical houses. Floral display house for seasonal shows.

💲♿ Shop. Most plants labeled. Plant sales. Trails and picnic facilities in park.
Krohn Conservatory open daily 10am-5pm. Special evening hours during Christmas and Easter shows. Eden Park open during daylight hours.

I hardly know which way to turn in the spacious glass-roofed lobby of Krohn Conservatory. To my left, the gift shop and the thousand greens of the Tropical House are inviting. Straight ahead, water is falling somewhere in the lush Palm House. To the right, the Desert Garden beckons through temporary summer gardens in the Floral Show House.

I choose the Desert Garden and find that it holds a delightful surprise. A small orchid house back in the corner is filled with blooms that seem less exotic than usual when compared to some of the cactus flowers. The juxtaposition of these two habitats and their plants is intriguing; I see succulent, needle-pointed agave leaves about 6 inches wide and an inch and a half thick and tiny bright orange orchids that are less than an inch across. A plumeria (frangipani), perhaps an escapee from the Tropical House, thrusts its fragrant, waxy blossoms above a mass of euphorbias. The crested blue candle cactus (*Myrtillocactus geometricans*) is the most impressive specimen of its kind I've ever seen.

The Palm House waterfall feeds a goldfish stream and ponds that lie below lush "rain forest" foliage; you *can* walk behind the waterfall for the experience but it hides only wet rock. This forest holds many varieties of palms and tropical shrubs, vigorous ground covers and, overhead, epiphytic ferns, bromeliads, and orchids. Several examples of plants with economic value, such as bananas, bamboo, coffee, ginger, screw pine (*Pandanus odoratissimus*, a source of fiber for cordage), and taro, are tucked in here and there.

The Tropical House, even more warm and humid than my central Illinois home in August, contains a staggering assortment of vines, ferns, cycads, and bromeliads. The clear yellow bracts of lollipop plant (*Pachystachys lutea*) hover above a small pond. Pomegranate fruits of many sizes and degrees of maturity hang over the path, while small black ants travel around the nearby cacao tree and its pods. An admirable clump of lobster-claw (*Heliconia humilis*), huddles near another pond, its shiny red bracts looking *just* like their eponymic animal parts. Vanilla vine, the orchid *Vanilla planifolia*, climbs overhead and the colorful bracts of bromeliads shine nearly everywhere I look. Bromeliads even decorate the conservatory lobby, where the gift shop offers an appealing selection of unusual plants as well as the usual assortment of garden-related items.

Eden Park, fourth largest of Cincinnati's fine parks, includes the Hinkle Garden Magnolia Collection, just south of the conservatory. In spring, hundreds of ornamental trees and shrubs, 50,000 naturalized daffodils, and a multitude of other spring bulbs decorate the park. April and May must be heavenly here, Eden indeed. The Park Board has a special *Spring Floral Guide* for Eden Park. Here, too, you can admire a floral clock that tells the *right* time and Mirror Lake, a shallow reflecting pond that is actually the roof of a major city reservoir. You can visit the Cincinnati Art Museum or the the Cincinnati Museum of Natural History. Take a walk in the President's Garden, where an appropriate tree commemorates each of our national presidents; a sapling from George Washington's Mount Vernon was one of the first trees planted here.

Conservatories are usually winter haunts for me, because I'd rather be outside in spring, summer, and autumn, but Krohn Conservatory and Eden Park deserve a visit at any time of the year.

For additional information contact the Cincinnati Park Board.

From I-71 take the Reading Road/Dorchester exit. Turn right at the stoplight and go a short distance to Gilbert Avenue. Turn left onto Gilbert, then soon turn right into Eden Park. Follow Eden Park Drive and the signs to the Conservatory.
From I-75 take Columbia Parkway (Route 50) east and exit on Martin Drive ▶

FYI *Vanilla planifolia* is one of the orchid species whose seed pods (vanilla "beans") yield the vanilla extract we use in our kitchens.

(Martin Drive is easy to miss; it's right after the Newport sign.) Follow Martin Drive to Eden Park Drive.

From downtown Cincinnati take Gilbert Avenue to Eden Park Drive.

The Lloyd Library and Museum
917 Plum Street
Cincinnati OH 45202
(513) 721-3707

Extensive collection of rare botanical works.

Closed stacks, non-circulating.
Open Monday-Friday 8:30am-4pm, plus the first and third Saturday of each month 9am-4pm.

The Lloyd Library is a treasure for those who love books, gardens, and particular types of research. You need to prepare yourself, to know what you want to see; few materials are exposed for casual browsing. The closed stacks protect rare Linnean literature, illustrated folios, floras, and treatises on medical botany. There are first editions of Linnaeus, Darwin, and others, herbals from the 16th century to the present, complete sets of old botanical serials, magazines, and journals. For a fine change of pace from roads and gardens, treat yourself to a purposeful visit to the Lloyd Library.

Lloyd Library is at the corner of Court and Plum streets; it's northwest of, but not far from, downtown Cincinnati. There is a parking lot behind the library.

Lytle Park
Above Fort Washington Parkway and I-71
Downtown Cincinnati

2 acres. Formal gardens. Flag allée.

Summer band concerts.
Open daylight hours.

In spring, flowering bulbs and ornamental trees decorate Lytle Park, to be followed by summer's perennials and annuals and autumn's vivid chrysanthemums. Historic monuments accent the park, banners in the flag allée trace the history of our nation's flag, and the Michael Mullen bandstand is the frequent site of free band concerts.

◀ This rather formal garden represents one of the country's first *garden* uses of air rights. (At least two other such gardens are proposed or under development: the Duluth Rose Garden above a tunnel along I-35 and a tea garden in the Phoenix, Arizona, area.) Lytle Garden celebrates General William Henry Lytle, who was the first Surveyor-General of the Northwest Territory and of the State of Ohio. Lytle established his homestead on this site in 1809.

While you're at Lytle Park, take the footbridge to Yeatman's Cove, Cincinnati's very popular riverside park that features the handsome Serpentine Wall and a wide variety of community activities.

For further information contact the Cincinnati Park Board.

Lytle Park, at the eastern edge of Cincinnati's central business district, is bordered by East Fourth and Lawrence streets.

Mount Airy Arboretum in Mt. Airy Forest
5083 Colerain Avenue
Cincinnati

1466 acres. Woody plant collections. Theme gardens. All-America Selections garden.

♿ Many plants labeled. Picnic facilities. Seasonal plant sales. Foot and bridle trails. Classes and special events.
Grounds open daily during daylight hours. Arboretum Center hours vary, depending on the season and the programs offered.

Soon after you enter this park and turn onto Arboretum Road, you'll be greeted by the Meyer Lake and Raraflora Garden, a collection of unusual landscape plants on the terraced edge of a spring-fed lake. A small gazebo overlooks the lake, its fountains, and its flock of militant white geese. On this hot August day, an afternoon rain has left mist that's rising from the low areas of Mt. Airy Forest. The geese and songbirds are delighted with the rain, and the trees, hills, and gardens are especially inviting in the mist.

Arboretum Road ends at the Arboretum Center, the focus of several hillside display gardens and woody plant collections. The small herb garden has been neglected in this particular year, possibly because of ambitious renovations taking place in the Raraflora Garden. Healthy weeds and borage wildlings surround a lonely clump of chives, reminding me that any garden quickly reverts to nature. The clematis collection covers its hillside trellises and a gentle trail leads to shade gardens and the fern and hosta collections. Another trail leads to the Braam Memorial Garden of rhododendrons and azaleas and the Wilson Wild Flower Trail. Hawthorns, dogwoods, redbuds, golden rain trees, and other spring-flowering ornamentals, scattered across the hills, will be spectacular in spring. The arboretum also includes a ground cover garden, lilac, magnolia, and viburnum collections, and an All-America Selections garden. All through the arboretum, benches provide pleasant overlooks of gardens, hillsides, and ravines.

When you see Mt. Airy's lush forest, it's hard to believe this was waste land such a relatively short time ago. In 1911, when the first 168 acres were purchased by the Park Board, this land had suffered decades of poor agricultural practices and unrestricted grazing. By the early 1920s, another 1,000 acres had been acquired and conservation and reforestation had begun. Because the arboretum was started from "scratch," tree placement in the forest was *planned* and, actually, the whole forest is an arboretum. Many trees, even in the picnic and play areas, are labeled.

If you return to the entrance and take the *other* road, you'll be in the park area of Mt. Airy. Here are shelters, picnic tables, playing fields, and miles of hiking and riding trails, all surrounded by deep woods not far from downtown Cincinnati.

For information contact the Cincinnati Park Board or call the Arboretum Center, (513) 541-8176.

From downtown Cincinnati, take I-75 north to I-74 West and I-74 west to the Colerain Avenue exit. Turn left at the stoplight and follow Colerain a little over a mile to the park entrance. Take the right fork at the entrance and turn onto Arboretum Road. This is all well-marked from I-74.

The Old Greenhouse
1415 Devils Backbone Road
Cincinnati OH 45233
(513) 941-0337

Commercial. Greenhouses. Display gardens.

♿ Shop. Most plants labeled. Plant sales. Workshops and other special events. Guided garden tours by prior request.
Open daily April 1-July 15 9am-5pm; July 16-March 31 Tuesday-Saturday 10am-4pm. Extended hours in December.

Delightful gardens, a greenhouse filled with lush plants, the musical chatter of exotic birds, and impressive begonia towers are some of the treats you'll find here. In the spring, Old Greenhouse sells bedding plants, fine plant-filled hanging baskets, those begonia towers, and herb plants. All these are shown at their best in the extensive display gardens.

A variety of gardening and plant-craft workshops and special events fill the Old Greenhouse calendar. There's much to enjoy here.

From downtown Cincinnati go west on 8th Street as it becomes Glenway Avenue, then follow Glenway 4 or 5 miles to Cleves-Warsaw Pike. Veer left onto Cleves-Warsaw and follow it for 2 miles until you see the Western Hill Country Club on your right. The first street on the right after the Country Club is Devils Backbone. Turn here and look for the large Old Greenhouse sign.

Stanley M. Rowe Arboretum
c/o Village of Indian Hill
4600 Muchmore Road
Indian Hill OH 45243
(513) 561-5151

Nine and three-quarter acres.

 Many plants labeled. Trails.
Open all year dawn to dusk.

Rowe Arboretum will enchant you in spring, when the flowering crabapple and lilac collections bloom. Other aggregations emphasize ornamental trees and shrubs that flower in late summer and early autumn. Between those seasons, you can admire dwarf and standard conifers and a broad assortment of variegated plants. The arboretum, which originated in 1926 as one person's hobby, now holds 900 different species, each labeled by its common and botanic names. Stone and turf paths encourage leisurely strolls among the 1,200-plus specimens, through surrroundings that are inviting all year.

For further information contact the Horticulturist, The Village of Indian Hill, 6525 Drake Road, Cincinnati OH 45243.

From I-71 exit for Redbank Road and go south to US 50, then east on US 50 to Walton Creek Road. Go north on Walton Creek three or four blocks to Muchmore Road, turn west onto Muchmore and go about a half mile further to the arboretum, on your right.

Sharon Woods Village
11450 Lebanon Pike
Sharonville OH 45262

Commercial. Historic village restoration within 750-acre county park. 75'x75' herb garden.

💲♿ Brochure and garden information. Shops. Many plants labeled. Special events (history-oriented). Trails and picnic facilities in park.
Sharon Woods Village open May-October Wednesday-Friday 10am-4pm, Saturday and Sunday 1-5pm. Special hours for Thanksgiving and Christmas celebrations. Park open daylight hours all year.

Along the streets and in the yards of Sharon Woods Village you'll see plants and flowers that were favorites in the nineteenth century but the main garden of interest here is the 75'x75' herb garden behind Hayner House. This bordered symmetrical garden features medicinal, culinary, and dye plants known to have been grown and used by area residents in the mid-nineteenth century. The helpful page *Uses of Herbs in the Hayner Garden* tells you exactly how these plants were used. Did you know, for instance, that monarda (bee balm) served both to attract honey-making bees *and* to sooth bee stings? Or that the smoke of garlic and dried hyssop was used as a medicinal inhalant for ailing poultry? These and many other useful and/or ornamental plants thrive in the Hayner House herb garden.

Sharon Woods hosts several exhibits and special events during its season; many of these include herb-oriented or garden-related activities that you'll particularly enjoy.

For a calendar of events and other information contact Historic Southwest Ohio, Sharon Woods Village, P. O. Box 41475, Cincinnati OH 45241. (513) 563-9484.

From I-275 on the north side of Cincinnati, take Exit 46 for US 42. Go south one mile to Hamilton County Park and Sharon Woods Village.

Spring Grove Cemetery and Arboretum
4521 Spring Grove Avenue
Cincinnati OH 45232
(513) 681-6680

▶

◀ Total 733 acres, 400 developed. Rose garden. Perennial and annual flower beds. Championship trees. Fourteen small lakes. Victorian sculpture and architecture.

♿ Brochures, maps, and plant bloom calendar. Many plants, particularly trees, labeled. Guided tours by prior arrangement.
Grounds open every day 8am-5pm. Office open Monday-Friday 8am-4:30pm, Saturday 8am-noon.

Spring Grove is a cemetery and an arboretum; it's also a sculpture and architecture garden and a good place to be on this summer Sunday morning. A carillon sings nearby and a few walkers are enjoying the shade, the hills, and the peace at Spring Grove, a peace guarded by a veritable forest of memorial obelisks. These hills hold an amazing richness of memorial and architectural styles; the little bit of Notre Dame Cathedral at the cemetery's entrance is particularly engaging.

Spring Grove Arboretum holds 25 State Champion trees, 4 National Champion trees, and over 1,100 labeled trees and smaller woody plants. A small rose garden and well-maintained beds of daylilies and tradescantia fill sunny spots and shade plants brighten plantings beneath mature trees. The arboretum includes many specimens of spring-flowering ornamental trees and shrubs; other varieties are chosen for winter interest. On this August day, feathery tamarix 'Summer Glow' (*Tamarix ramosissima* var.) is a pink haze against a dark iron fence. Small lakes nestle among the cemetery's hills and, today, the road through the undeveloped woodland is shady, cool, and bordered with late-blooming wildflowers.

Spring Grove, chartered in 1845, met the need for a rural cemetery when Cincinnati's growth restricted the expansion of in-town church cemeteries. At that time, the land held many mature groves of trees; consequently, some of the remaining trees are well over 150 years old. Now, of course, the city has grown around and beyond Spring Grove and its elegant acres.

From I-75 take Mitchell Avenue west to Spring Grove Avenue. Turn left onto Spring Grove then go about 1½ miles to the cemetery's main gate on your left.

FYI An Ohio State Champion Tree is the largest tree in Ohio of its species, as determined by the Ohio Forestry Association through a combination of measurements. Hamilton County, which includes Cincinnati, has 21 such trees; 16 of these are at Spring Grove, including the bald cypress and cedar of Lebanon champions. National Champions have been subjected to similar measurements by the American Forestry Association. Spring Grove's National Champions include yellow-wood and two-wing silverbell.

Aullwood Gardens
Englewood Reserve
Dayton

32 acres woodland and gardens.

Brochure. Trails and picnic facilities in Englewood Reserve.
Aullwood Gardens open March-December Tuesday-Sunday 8am-7pm. Closed January and February. Englewood Reserve open daily 8am-dusk, closed Christmas and New Year's days.

A pleasant riverside trail, edged on this August day by daylilies and spiderwort, leads you to the lawns and gardens of Aullwood. Since the Aulls began developing this property in 1920, the focus has been on natural, harmonious charm, gardens that merge imperceptibly into woods, wildflowers that mingle with greenhouse cultivars. Garden beds, filled today with blooming monardas, globe thistles, and cleomes, meld with woodland beds of hostas, ferns, and the frail remnants of spring wildflowers. For a short distance, the garden trail follows the quintessential babbling brook, delightful company on a warm day. Years ago, Mr. Aull dammed this spring-fed brook to create a swimming pond that's now a serene woodland pool surrounded by water-loving plants. As I admire the pool, a shaft of sunlight strikes a small scarlet-spangled tree near the dam and transforms it into a glowing watcher at the pond.

Farther along the trail, near the Aull home, another lawn lies below ferny hillsides where meadow rue (*Thalictrum* sp.) and other native woodland plants are interplanted with impatiens. In the occasional breezes, lush tuberous begonia leaves move flirtaciously, revealing their scarlet undersides and reminding me of cancan dancers lifting their skirts on cue. Comfortable benches encourage restful appreciation of the woods, lawn, gardens, and river. But other gardens will draw you onward, up the hill to a bright wide meadow, rich today with the coneflowers, Queen Anne's lace, and native grasses of August. A bulletin board near the meadow's mowed path holds announcements, prayers, and pertinent quotations: "Long ago in ancient Greece a wise man said, 'The gates of excellence are surrounded by a sea of sweat.'" Take heart, sweaty summer gardeners who strive for excellence.

These gardens *feel* like private gardens, as some of them still are, and the occasional DO NOT ENTER signs are the only slightly jarring notes. Few plants are labeled, which adds to the private garden mood, so carry your wildflower field guide along for the fullest enjoyment of every aspect of Aullwood Gardens.

For further information contact the Park District of Dayton-Montgomery County, 1375 East Siebenthaler Avenue, Dayton OH 45414. (513) 278-8231.

▶

◀ *From I-70 just west of I-75, take Ohio Route 48 north a short distance to US 40. Turn east onto US 40 and cross a long, high bridge; you'll see the picnic grounds and playing fields of Englewood Reserve below. Turn south at the east end of the bridge, to Aullwood Road. Aullwood Road passes Aullwood Nature Center and ends in a large parking lot; follow the signs. Near the river, by the parking lot, a small gate opens onto the path to Aullwood Gardens.*

The Cox Arboretum
6733 Springboro Pike
Dayton OH 45449
(513) 434-9005

---

160 acres. 64 acres in cultivated gardens. Greenhouses. Edible Landscaping Garden. Herb gardens. Woody plant collections.

♿ Brochure and trail guides. Shop. Many plants labeled. Library. Seasonal plant sales. Trails. Visitor Center. Workshops and special events.
Grounds open daily 8am-dusk. Visitor Center open weekdays 8am-4pm, Sunday 1-4pm. Greenhouse open weekdays 8am-4:30pm. Grounds and facilities closed Christmas and New Year's days.

The Cox entry road winds around handsome plantings and ends at the Visitor Center, where there are nearly always an attractive exhibit of botanical paintings or photographs on the lobby walls and garden and trail guides on the desk. Just off the lobby, Linden Tree Gift Shop offers a fine assortment of gardening and wildflower books, stationery, and home and personal products. The Visitor Center is open less often than the arboretum but you can enjoy the arboretum even if the center is closed.

In the cozy herb garden near the Visitor Center barn, masses of vigorous herbs surround a tidy knot garden; the thyme garden is particularly entrancing. Everlastings and flowers for cutting thrive near one corner of the barn. Nearby, sturdy scented geraniums (*Pelargonium* spp.) exhibit their variety of plant and leaf forms and invite you to caress their leaves and sample their scents. Herb garden volunteers usually work on Wednesday mornings during the summer; you'll be doubly fortunate if you visit Cox when those knowledgeable gardeners are here.

Cox greenhouses display their extensive collection of cacti and succulents on benches and shelves. Just outside the greenhouse, the delightful, intimate rock garden, tucked into stone terraces and among evergreens, will be captivating when its alpines bloom. ▶

You'll find attractive and fascinating ideas for your home grounds in the Edible Landscaping Garden. Espaliered dwarf apple trees are becoming a "Belgian fence," a fence of small trees firmly grafted to each other that will be stunning when those trees bloom or when they're loaded with apples of many colors. Scarlet runner beans cover the wooden trellis that welcomes you to the garden and, just beyond the trellis, tall corn makes a green screen that could shade windows in summer before it dies down to admit winter sun. A large raised bed contains other edible plants that have been carefully selected for their admirable flowers, foliage, or fruits, proving that a vegetable garden can be a subtly attractive and fruitful challenge to displays of annual flowers.

Nearby, a wattle fence surrounds "Time in Paradise," an herb garden that was inspired by medieval garden enclosures. You'll find theme beds of culinary herbs, tea plants, dye plants, and housewives' herbs, those plants women once grew to help with housekeeping or to keep their families healthy. And you'll find features you might not expect, such as the Garden of the Four Seasons, whose design and plant colors were chosen to dramatize seasonal changes. Here, too, you can become the gnomon of the analemmatic sundial that's set into the ground. ("Analemmatic," according to the Oxford English Dictionary, translates simply to "a sort of sundial." The designer of the herb garden says it means a "human sundial," one that employs the human as the vertical, shadow-casting gnomon.) Stand by the correct month-stone and if the sun is shining and if we're near a seasonal equinox and if you've been a good person all year, your shadow will fall upon an hour-stone to indicate the approximate time of day.

In the nearby Synoptic Shrub Garden, trees and shrubs arranged alphabetically by Latin name surround a small lake and its gazebo. "Synoptic" is related to "synopsis," a summary; therefore, the Synoptic Shrub Garden is a summary of the shrubs that will grow well in southwestern Ohio. Here the homeowner can easily identify the woody plants that will fit his landscaping needs. From this garden, too, a nature trail winds back into over 90 acres of native woodland.

At Cox, you can also enjoy a crabapple allée, a rock wall garden, woodland and shade plant collections, a clematis arbor, a water garden, spring bulbs, fall color, or winter's more subtle beauties. Cox Arboretum hosts or sponsors an amazing range of workshops, lectures, tours, plant shows, classes, and other events. Could you resist classes about Water Gardening for Beginners, Attracting Butterflies to the Garden, or Tough Plants for Tough Times? The three-day Spring Plant Festival includes plant sales and an art fair; the June Rose Fair offers workshops, a Rose Tea Party, and rose gardening demonstrations and lectures. Almost all of these are open to the public, although some require prior registration.

◀ I've been to Cox in mid-June and in early August, in early morning and at dusk, and it's never failed to please me. Most recently, on a cool and breezy gray morning, with my carry-out breakfast in hand, I joined grazing ducks and geese by the lake and had a splendid beginning to my summer day. This arboretum offers countless gardening and outdoor pleasures; in my next life I want to live near Cox Arboretum.

From I-75 take the Miamisburg-Centerville Exit (Ohio Route 725 East), on the south side of Dayton. Take OH 725E a short distance to OH 741 North (Springboro Pike), then turn north and go 1½ miles to Cox, on the west side of OH 741 North.

Smith Memorial Gardens
Oakwood Avenue and Walnut Lane
Oakwood (Dayton)

One acre. Mixed gardens.

Some plants labeled. Picnic facilities. Seasonal plant sales. Special events.
Open during daylight hours all year.

This small jewel of a garden, well-designed for strolling, feels larger than it really is. Today, in early August, it's alive with butterflies dining at the sturdy phlox. Giant hibiscus and clumps of coneflowers accent late-blooming daylilies. Flowing beds of annuals, masses of vibrant color, meander under the trees and through the rock gardens. A tiny stream runs to a small water lily pond that's framed by stone and loosestrife. There's a genteel birthday celebration on the gardenhouse patio and all the shaded benches have been claimed by other visitors and their sack lunches. On this particular day, this acre of gardens must be Dayton's most delightful place for lunch.

The Smith Gardens were planned and developed by donor Carlton Smith, with the help of only one part-time gardener; in the mid-1970s, Mr. and Mrs. Smith gave their home and gardens to the City of Oakwood. The Friends of Smith Gardens conduct seasonal plant sales in support of the gardens. Every fall, over 8,000 spring-blooming bulbs go into the ground here; the flowers of those bulbs and the spring-flowering trees and shrubs must be magnificent in their season. Over 20,000 annuals are added in the spring to embellish the extensive collection of perennial plants and deciduous and coniferous trees. Mr. Smith stipulated that a certain percentage of the garden must always contain evergreens so that his cozy piece of rolling land, with its carefully placed rock outcroppings, would be attractive in all seasons. The selection of annuals and their planting design changes from year to year; this year's Smith Gardens won't be the same as last year's Smith Gardens, nor the same as next year's.

In summer, concerts and poetry and fiction readings grace the gardens. I'm sure *everything* sounds better when you're surrounded by rock gardens, graceful trees, and beds of luscious flowers. Your sack lunch will taste better, and your day will look brighter, if you make time to visit Smith Gardens.

For information contact the City Horticulturist, City of Oakwood, 36 Park Avenue, Dayton OH 45419. (513) 298-0600.

Smith Memorial Gardens is at the north edge of Oakwood, immediately south of Dayton. Take Far Hills Drive (Ohio Route 48, known as South Main in Dayton). If you're going south from Dayton, you'll see a small group of commercial buildings on the left at a stoplight. At the next stoplight, Oakwood Avenue comes into Far Hills Drive at an angle; turn west onto Oakwood. In a very few blocks, look for the iron fence with Mediterranean-style gateposts on your right; that's the entrance to Smith Gardens.

Wegerzyn Horticultural Center and Stillwater Gardens
Riverbend Cultural Arts Complex
1301 East Siebenthaler Avenue
Dayton OH 45414
(513) 277-6545

---

60 acres. Rose garden. Other gardens developing.

♿ Brochures and maps. Shop. Many plants labeled. Library. Seasonal plant sales. Trails. Workshops and special events. Major plant sale in early May.
Grounds and gardens open daylight hours all year. Wegerzyn Center offices and shop open Monday-Friday 10am-5pm, Saturday 10am-4pm. Closed Sunday.

A sunny, open space surrounded by riverine woods is gradually becoming Stillwater Gardens. On this August afternoon, workers fight heat and humidity as they level terraces and install perennials but massive raised beds of marigolds, salvias, and moss roses (portulaca) are at their late-summer, heat-proof best. At one side of Wegerzyn Center, newly planted rose beds, looking a little sparse still, are backed by a long, curved arbor. This garden will be lovely when the roses bloom in future Junes, a perfect site for weddings and parties.   ▶

◀ Dedicated in 1973, Wegerzyn Horticultural Center is part of a complex that includes the Dayton Playhouse Community Theater and Riverbend Arts Center. Original funding was provided by Benjamin Wegerzyn; Dayton area garden clubs contributed another $100,000. When complete, Stillwater Gardens will have fountains, sculpture, and extensive plantings. There are plans for international exhibits, a Japanese garden, historic theme gardens, a comprehensive rose collection, a fully developed shade environment, and other special collections and experimental gardens. It will be fascinating to watch these gardens develop and mature.

The Wegerzyn Center building houses a number of horticultural activities, including the highly successful Grow With Your Neighbor program, which serves as advisor to neighborhood-based garden projects. You'll find an extensive horticultural reference library and a fine gift shop filled with nature-related art, ceramics, jewelry, and a small selection of appealing garden books, some of which I hadn't seen elsewhere. It's easy to leave a few dollars here in support of Wegerzyn.

The Center sponsors a busy schedule of workshops, lectures, festivals, nature-oriented activities, flower shows, and markets. At "MayFair," Wegerzyn's major plant sale, the emphasis is on hard-to-find plants; recent offerings included 39 varieties of geraniums, 61 different perennials, 47 kinds of less-common annuals, miniature roses, culinary herbs, space-saving vegetables, and a broad selection of unique seeds. The 60-acre complex also contains the Marie Aull Nature Trail, Wetland Woods, and the scenic Stillwater River. There's something for almost everyone, no matter what their horticultural bent, at Wegerzyn Center and Stillwater Gardens.

From I-70, go southeast on Ohio Route 48 a few miles to Siebenthaler Avenue, then east on Siebenthaler through commercial and residential neighborhoods and just across the Stillwater River to the Riverbend Cultural Arts Complex.
From I-75 take Exit 57B and go north on North Dixie a short distance to Siebenthaler, then west on Siebenthaler to the Riverbend Complex.

The Wagnalls Memorial
150 East Columbus Street
Lithopolis OH 43136
(614) 837-4765

One-quarter acre mixed gardens. Public library. ▶

◀ Library. Tours of the non-public parts of the house/library available. Garden open daylight hours.

This intimate, well-tended public garden retains a sense of privacy. Lush annuals and perennials, sedums and ferns, herbs, shrubs, and roses hold morning dew, children wait for the library to open, and it's very satisfying to lounge on the stone sofa and consider the morning-fresh garden. There *is* some bizarre stone-work among these plants; the sofa is my favorite. Lithopolis would translate to "stone city" so these pebbled follies seem appropriate.

Lithopolis is a one-stoplight town, a place where the skyline of Columbus gleams in the distance like the Emerald City of Oz. A town of small cottages, it holds in its midst the Wagnalls Memorial, a solid stone structure that looks like a church. This former home of Mabel Wagnalls, who was the only child of the Wagnalls of publishing fame, now houses a public library, an auditorium, meeting rooms, and a banquet hall.

You won't find anything overwhelming or on a grand scale at the Wagnalls Memorial. It's just a short, pleasant drive from Columbus or I-270, and its cozy plantings may remind you of the garden you left at home.

From US 33 southeast of Columbus, take Ohio Route 674 to Lithopolis. The road that leads into town becomes Columbus Street, where sits the Wagnalls Memorial.

Lewis Mountain Herbs and Everlastings
2345 State Route 247
Manchester OH 45144
(513) 549-2484

Commercial. Herb and everlasting gardens.

♿ Shop. Many plants labeled. Plant sales. Workshops and special events. Open Monday-Saturday 9am-4pm.

At delightful Lewis Mountain, you can wander through the garden of vigorous herbs, the busy greenhouses, and the shop, where you'll find items made from herbs and everlastings and books about herb gardening and plant crafts. Perhaps you've planned ahead and enrolled in a class to make an herbal wreath or swag, to learn more about gardening, or to cook with a well-known Cincinnati chef. ▶

◄ In October, Lewis Mountain hosts Harvest Festival, an event that features workshops and demonstrations, presentations by herb specialists, and a wide array of herbal products, including tasty herb snacks and herb jellies.

Remember that in Ohio there are *two* towns called Manchester; the one you want for herbal pleasures is in southern Ohio, not far from the Ohio River.

Lewis Mountain is on Ohio Route 247, about 60 miles east of Cincinnati. It's two miles north of the Ohio River, just off US 52, or 15 miles south of OH 32. The modest village of Manchester may not be shown on your road map; it's south of West Union OH.

Glasshouse Works
Church Street
Stewart OH 45778-0097
(614) 662-2142

Commercial. Specialist in unusual plants. Tropical conservatory.

 Catalog. Most plants labeled. Picnic facilities. Plant sales.

At Glasshouse Works you're surrounded by plants that, until now, you may have seen only in major conservatories: hard-to-find tropicals, unusual hardy plants, uncommon variegated plants, starters for tropical bonsai, unique peperomias and sansevierias, and rare ferns. You can see all these in GW's tropical conservatory and large saleshouse or read about them in the extensive and informative Glasshouse Works catalog. Uncommon plants and imaginative planting ideas fill outdoor displays. Comfortable benches invite you to relax and appreciate the view, perhaps while savoring your picnic lunch. This hilly and wooded part of Ohio is very inviting; the amazing array of exceptional plants at Glasshouse Works makes it even more attractive.

Stewart is on Ohio Route 329, about 3 miles northeast of US 50, 12 miles east of Athens OH. Glasshouse Works is a half block from the intersection of OH 144 and OH 329; the owner claims that Stewart is such a small town, you'll end up where you want to be even if you take a wrong turn.

Wisconsin: North

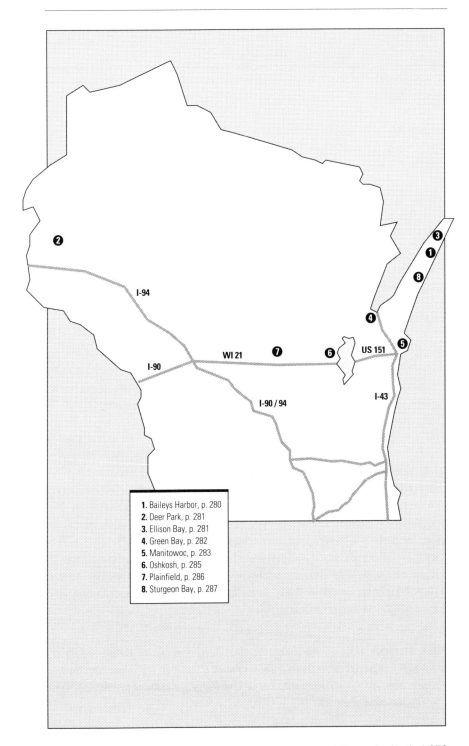

1. Baileys Harbor, p. 280
2. Deer Park, p. 281
3. Ellison Bay, p. 281
4. Green Bay, p. 282
5. Manitowoc, p. 283
6. Oshkosh, p. 285
7. Plainfield, p. 286
8. Sturgeon Bay, p. 287

The Ridges Sanctuary
Box 152
Baileys Harbor WI 54202
(414) 839-2802

Over 900 acres. Wooded bogs, sandy swales and ridges, Lake Michigan beach. Refuge for orchids and other wildflowers.

Brochure. Fee for special events; donation requested from hikers. Trails. Workshops and other special events. Group tours by prior arrangement only.
Open daylight hours all year; winter hours limited.

A garden is "a rich, well-cultivated region," according to Webster's *Ninth New Collegiate Dictionary*. The Ridges is no longer cultivated but it is certainly rich. I remember waxy marsh marigolds (*Caltha palustris*) reflected in dark pondlets, lady's-slipper orchids and orchid-like gaywings (*Polygala paucifolia*) in sun-spattered woods, bird song above the sound of waves, and a cool Lake Michigan breeze on sweat-salted faces . . . heady sensations all, for this girl from corn country.

Hiking trails and boardwalks wind across spongy bogs and along the dry ridges that are the remnants of ancient beaches. Bright and sandy patches, boggy swales, moist woods, and the sunny edges of woods provide homes for an amazing abundance and diversity of plant and animal life here.

This sanctuary for plants and people and other animals was established in 1937 by a small group of foresighted individuals, including the well-known landscape designer, Jens Jensen. Its mission is to provide a positive future for this botanically rich area and, especially, to protect the large population of native orchids. On-going research investigates the effects of browsing by deer and snowshoe hares, the life history of several species of lady's-slipper orchids, and other topics vital to understanding and preserving The Ridges. The sanctuary offers classes for adults and children and, in the summer, a weekly lecture series. Guided tours are scheduled daily from May to October but self-guided tours may be taken at any time. Take time from your Door County days for a fascinating and rejuvenating visit to The Ridges.

From Sturgeon Bay, go north on Wisconsin Routes 42/57. When the routes separate, follow WI 57 to its intersection with County Road Q north of Baileys Harbor, then turn northeast onto CR Q. The Ridges is a short distance beyond this intersection.

Capability's Books
2379 Highway 46
Deer Park WI 54007
(800) 247-8154 (All US states)
(715) 269-5346 (Outside the US)

Specialist in garden-related books.

 Catalog.
Open Monday-Friday 8am-4:30pm. Often, but not regularly, open on Saturday; call ahead.

This is paradise for those who love books and gardening. Capability Brown, the eighteenth-century English landscape gardener for whom the shop is named, might willingly have sold his soul to spend a few hours here. Over a thousand titles cover nearly everything you'll ever want to know about gardens and gardening, including garden history, landscape and garden design, and gardening with children. Numerous volumes about specific plants, such as roses and clematis, inhabit Capability's shelves and catalog; a recent catalog listed 10 different books on irises alone. Do you want a romantic garden, plantings that will attract hummingbirds, or a topiary collection? The books to help you are here, as are informative videos and useful computer software programs. Wildflowers and native plants have not been neglected, nor have trees, shrubs, and vines. If it's related to gardening and it's in print, you'll most likely find it at Capability's.

Although this is primarily a mail-order business, the owners ". . . always delight in meeting (their) customers, both new and established" and they even provide comfy chairs and benches that encourage browsing. Be sure there's room in your car for the irresistible treasures you'll find at Capability's, the books that will enrich your life and your garden.

Capability's Books is on WI 46, not far north of the small town of Deer Park.

The Clearing
Ellison Bay

128-acre grounds. Jens Jensen landscape around school.

Catalog (class schedule) and brochure. Trails. Workshops.
Grounds open to non-enrolled visitors June-mid-October Saturday and Sunday only 1-4pm. ▶

◀ Woods and clearings, lakes, high bluffs and rustic buildings, shrubs and vines and wildflowers, dreams and vision . . . to paraphrase Shakespeare's Prospero, "This is such stuff as The Clearing is made of." Jens Jensen's highly naturalistic landscape manipulates space, mass, and texture on a grand scale, so you'll find no cultivated flower gardens here. Instead, native trees, shrubs, and wildflowers, placed for the fullest impact of their best characteristics, surround pleasing spaces.

When he founded The Clearing in 1935, at the age of 75, Jensen was internationally known for his work with public parks, especially those in Racine, Wisconsin, and in Chicago. He had developed landscape plans for the private estates of industrial magnates and was instrumental in establishing the Illinois State Park system and the Chicago Forest Preserve District. In Door County, he helped form The Ridges Sanctuary and the county and township parks. He created The Clearing as a place for development of sound values and a temporary refuge from city life, a place for clearing the head. Over fifty years later, course offerings still focus on personal development, traditional skills, and awareness of nature. Recent courses with particular appeal for gardeners have included such as Gardening with Herbs, Identification and Natural History of Flowering Plants, and The Beauty of the Earth. If you're not participating in a class, come to The Clearing on a weekend afternoon to absorb the beauty and serenity that Jensen has left us.

For details and further information contact the Resident Manager at The Clearing, P. O. Box 65, Ellison Bay WI 54210 or call (414) 854-4088 during office hours, Monday-Friday 8am-4pm.

Take Wisconsin Route 42 to Ellison Bay and, in Ellison Bay, turn left onto Garrett Bay Road. Go a quarter mile on Garrett Bay Road to The Clearing, on your left.

Joanne's Garden
In Joanne's Park
Green Bay

One-third acre. Old-fashioned garden within a large city park.

 Some plants labeled. Picnic facilities in park.
Open daylight hours.

On this gray and cool summer day, cleomes and impatiens shine brightly in the mist but heat-loving marigolds and zinnias look soggy and disgruntled. Tall fir trees, dark and dripping with rain, guard this fence-enclosed garden of old-fashioned perennials and annuals. These plantings are charming in spite of the inclement weather; on a dry and sunny day they'll be even more colorful and appealing.

Note that "Joanne's" is pronounced "Jo-ann-ee's" here in Green Bay. For other information contact Green Bay Parks, Recreation, and Forestry, 100 North Jefferson, Green Bay WI 54301. (414) 436-3677.

On the east side of the Fox River in Green Bay, take Wisconsin Route 57 to Walnut Street. Go east on Walnut 8 or 9 blocks to Baird Street, then turn south on Baird to the park. Joanne's Garden faces Baird just south of Walnut.

West of the Lake Gardens
On Wisconsin Route 42 between Manitowoc and Two Rivers

5-acre estate gardens.

Brochure. No pets, picnics, or smoking permitted on the grounds. To protect the gardens and because the shoreline here can be hazardous, children must be closely supervised. Low-heeled shoes are requested. The house remains a private residence; please respect this privacy. Open daylight hours during the growing season.

These admirable gardens, just *barely* west of Lake Michigan, reflect over 50 years of the former owners' garden enthusiasm and expertise; their name was West so the gardens' name is doubly descriptive. In 1934, this was a stretch of ▶

FYI In the future, a 60-acre site behind the Northeast Wisconsin Technical College will become the Green Bay Botanical Garden; development and construction are expected to begin in 1994. The rose, all-seasons, children's, and entry gardens will be installed first, to be followed by other display areas, educational facilities, and research areas that focus on plant varieties adapted to northern climates. For a brochure or information on the gardens' location and progress, write to Green Bay Botanical Garden, Inc., P. O. Box 1913, Green Bay WI 54305-1913, or call the Brown County Extension Office, (414) 497-3216.

FYI If you're traveling along Wisconsin Route 57 between Green Bay and Sturgeon Bay, you can treat yourself to a wonderful array of "yard art" by stopping at Spude's, on the east side of Route 57, just north of Dyckesville. If you don't want gulls on posts or amorous Dutch children in your garden, have patience. Along Spude's drive and behind the barn you'll find a wealth of other sculptures, such as convincing tortoises, small but imposing lions, and refined Japanese lanterns. All these cast concrete treasures are produced here. Spude's maintains a rather flexible schedule; they appear to be open most daylight hours during the "tourist season," from late spring through late autumn.

quackgrass and thistle; today, thanks to the Wests, flowering trees, spruce windbreaks, luxuriant lawn, and graceful flower borders surround a modern steel and cement house.

On this late June day, the rich blue flowers of agapanthus shine against the white home, and echo the blue-green lake and the wide sky. A graceful border behind the house is bright and fresh with red and white; red barberries, white irises, and mostly-white hostas anchor red begonias and salvias, red roses, white calla lilies and alyssum, and red geraniums with white-edged leaves. Across the garden, rich rose and soft purple lupines float above pale yellow marigolds in another good-looking combination of colors. Thirty thousand bulbs bloomed here in the early spring; later there will be astilbes and lilies and irises bearded, Siberian, and Japanese (*Iris ensata*). Still later in the summer, banks of daylilies will sway in the lake breezes. Today, I'm entranced by a bird bath whose upper rim overflows with a rich variety of green and bronze succulents.

Black pots and planters, filled with agaves, aeoniums, and jade trees are striking against the stark white of the home's lakeward side. Bright hibiscus and camellias bloom on the glassed-enclosed terrace, protected against lake winds that can be frosty even in midsummer.

The greenhouses here provide winter protection for tender plants and are propagation houses for the garden's annuals, so they are relatively empty on this June day. But in a pebbled nook near the greenhouse, bonsais and dwarf conifers surround a lively "spouting fish" fountain and a small collection of cacti and succulents basks on sun-warmed river stones.

You may find it frustrating that there are no plant labels in these gardens, as there are some unusual varieties you'll want to know. But that seems unimportant when you can lounge in a pale blue poolside chair, or upon a sunny bench, and savor the beautiful lake, its wide skies, and sumptuous West of the Lake Gardens.

For details contact the Manitowoc-Two Rivers Chamber of Commerce at (414) 682-5575.

From I-43 take Wisconsin Route 42 through Manitowoc toward Two Rivers. West of the Lake Gardens is on the east side of the highway, across from Lakeview Center shopping mall. Look for the small sign. Use the parking area at the gardens or park across the road at the mall.

Festival of Flowers
Manitowoc County

◀ This is a season-long, county-wide beautification program, similar to Flowerfest in Kalamazoo, Michigan. Special features include a Fair and Flower Sale in early June, mid-July garden tours and lectures, and wildflower and bird walks in woodlands, dunes, and prairies. I'm intrigued by Art in Bloom, held in mid-July at the Rahr-West Museum in Manitowoc, when flower arrangers replicate the floral arrangements portrayed in some of the museum's paintings. Tickets are required for lectures and garden tours.

For festival schedules, maps, and other information contact the Manitowoc-Two Rivers Chamber of Commerce at (414) 682-5575.

Paine Art Center and Arboretum
1410 Algoma Boulevard
Oshkosh WI 54901
(414) 235-4530

10-acre arboretum and gardens. Tudor Revival mansion/art center/museum. Rose garden. Specialty gardens. Prairie woodland.

♿ Fee for Art Center. Museum shop. Many plants labeled. Library. Seasonal plant sales. Workshops and other special events.
Arboretum and Art Center open Tuesday-Saturday 10am-4:30 pm, Sunday 1-4:30pm. Art Center Library open Monday, Wednesday, and Friday 9am-noon. All above closed Monday and national holidays. Prairie Woodland open daylight hours all year.

A half-timbered masterpiece of golden stone and leaded windows, a mansion surrounded by well-groomed European-style gardens, lies behind the handsome wrought iron fence of Paine Art Center. Masses of caryopteris 'Blue Spires' and the sedum 'Autumn Joy' bring color to garden sweeps of white annual salvia while feathery celosias add their brilliance to the mansion's sunny terrace. Phlox and hardy amaryllis bloom among ferns and Solomon's seal and white birches in a small woodland behind the house. Nearby, clipped germander encircles the comely rose garden, where a gentle fountain plays amidst water lilies.

The jewel of Paine Arboretum is the formal garden, which is modeled after the Pond Garden at Hampton Court in England. This sunken area, centered upon a tiered fountain, is surrounded by limestone walls, carefully trimmed box hedges, and banks of delicate blue and white ageratum. In less formal beds against the enclosing walls, masses of gray-green lavender, lambs' ears

(*Stachys byzantina*), and spiky yucca play against low campanula, tall zebra grass (*Miscanthus sinensis* var.), and clumps of blue fescue. Peonies, irises, plume poppies (*Macleya cordata*), and climbing roses add their own richness. Magenta buds and lavender-blue blossoms of the ageratum 'Royal Delft' mix with the rich reds of dwarf barberry 'Crimson Pygmy' in a stunning color combination near another wall.

The herb garden in its brick-paved courtyard reminds me of cozy European gardens. Scented geraniums and lovely lisianthus surround the central sundial . . . but a century plant (*Agave americana*) dominates the scene. Seven feet tall and 10 or 11 feet wide, this imposing specimen is flanked by severely trimmed Cornelian cherry trees (*Cornus mas*). Handsome teak benches in *all* the gardens encourage relaxed admiration of your surroundings.

The Art Center's small shop holds an appealing selection of garden books, garden-theme stationery, and small gifts. You may want to use the Art Center's library, which specializes in horticulture and the decorative arts, or to plan your visit around one of the arboretum's semi-annual plant sales (the Saturday before Mother's Day and the two weekends following Labor Day).

The Paine Arboretum Prairie Woodland is about a half block west of the Art Center. Today it's truly a natural garden of sunflowers and goldenrods in bright bloom among the grasses and sumac. Woodchip paths wind among trees and shrubs, across patches of low grass, and through stands of native plants in this bit of wildness that's a provocative contrast to the Art Center's formal gardens. You'll find much to please you in the variety of gardens and plantings at Paine.

From US 41 go east on Wisconsin Route 21 (Congress Avenue) across the Fox River to Algoma Boulevard. The Art Center and Arboretum is near the corner of Algoma and Congress.

Waushara Gardens
R. R. 2 Box 570
Plainfield WI 54966
(713) 335-4462

Commercial. 45-50 acres. Gladiolus grower.

♿ Catalog. Many plants labeled.
Peak bloom time August 1-September 10.

◀ This is where you want to be in late summer if gladiolus are a special love of yours. When the fields are dry you're welcome to walk or drive on the field roadways and immerse yourself in all the glorious gladiolus colors.

Because Waushara's growing locations change from year to year, stop at the Amoco Truck Stop near Plainfield, at the intersection of US 51 and Wisconsin Route 73, and request the current map for Waushara's fields.

Peninsula Agricultural Research Station
University of Wisconsin
4312 Highway 42
Sturgeon Bay WI 54235-9620
(414) 743-5406

Over one acre. Field tests of shrubs and annual flowers.

♿ Most plants labeled. Turf paths.
Open daylight hours during the growing season.

Tidy plots of flowers and shrubs lie behind utilitarian buildings on this land that was the site of Door County's first commercial orchard. Pick up the Annual Flower Key in the garden for a more informed visit; each plant variety is numbered and keyed to the guide, so you can choose the flowers you want to add to *your* garden when they become available commercially. In this particular year, 178 varieties of annuals are being tested for performance in this climate; among them, I count 54 different petunia cultivars, 30 different zinnias, 21 varieties of geraniums, and 16 kinds of pansies. This summer has been cooler and wetter than usual and the heat-loving flowers aren't doing well but I'm charmed by #88 pansy, 'Characters Blue', its luminous bits of sky blue lifted in today's mist.

Among the on-going shrub tests here, you'll find several varieties of spirea, potentillas of various shapes and sizes and bloom color, a wide range of dwarf conifers, and assorted other shrubs. Potentilla golds, yellows, and whites are particularly pleasing on this gray day. In Door County, as in most resort areas, poor weather days during the growing (and tourist) season are uncommon but these flower plots, certainly striking on fine days, are inviting and informative even on wet, gray days.

Take Wisconsin Route 42 past Sturgeon Bay; don't *take the Business Route. The Agricultural Research Station is about 4 miles north of Sturgeon Bay, on the east side of WI 42.*

Wisconsin: South

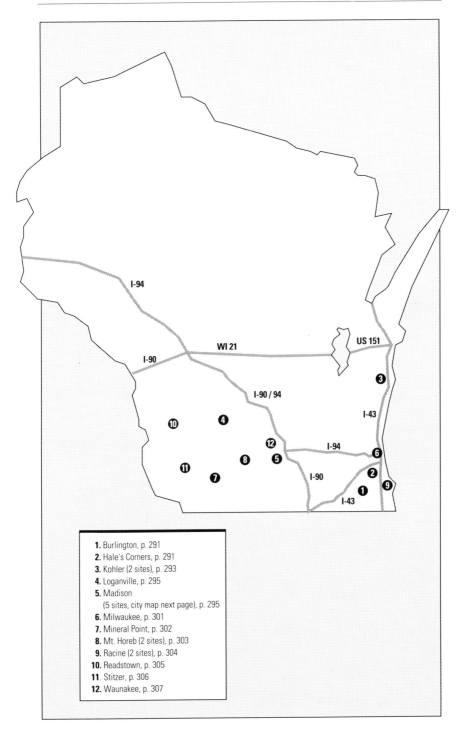

1. Burlington, p. 291
2. Hale's Corners, p. 291
3. Kohler (2 sites), p. 293
4. Loganville, p. 295
5. Madison
   (5 sites, city map next page), p. 295
6. Milwaukee, p. 301
7. Mineral Point, p. 302
8. Mt. Horeb (2 sites), p. 303
9. Racine (2 sites), p. 304
10. Readstown, p. 305
11. Stitzer, p. 306
12. Waunakee, p. 307

Wisconsin: South / MADISON

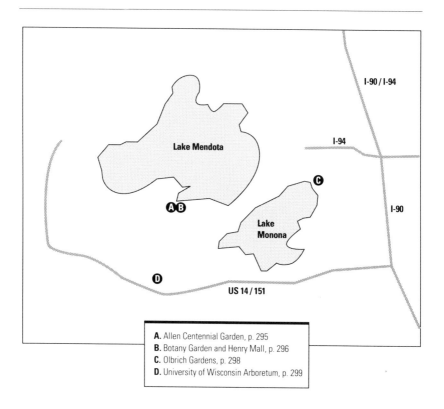

A. Allen Centennial Garden, p. 295
B. Botany Garden and Henry Mall, p. 296
C. Olbrich Gardens, p. 298
D. University of Wisconsin Arboretum, p. 299

St. Francis Friary and Retreat Center
503 South Browns Lake Road
P. O. Box 368
Burlington WI 53105
(414) 763-3600

One acre. Shade gardens, grottoes, waterfalls.

&♿ Church-oriented book store. Seasonal plant sales. Dinner available in monastery dining room by prior arrangement.
Gardens open daylight hours from spring to fall. Retreat office open 9am-4:30pm, closed over the noon hour.

These peaceful gardens, with plentiful benches and walls to sit upon, encourage contemplation and meditation. A blacktop path winds through the deep shade, and it will be cool here on even the hottest day. Hillside grottoes are complete with waterfalls and pools; carpets of begonias, caladiums, hostas, and impatiens thrive in this, their perfect environment. Floral borders, ribbons of color and texture, twine among the grottoes in the sunken garden while other inviting grottoes and small chapels nestle into the nearby landscape. On this mid-August day, the sunny hillside Fatima Grotto is a rich jumble of bright daylilies, dahlias, snapdragons, and celosias.

You can request a map of the Retreat grounds and gardens at the Friary office but it supplies little detail and isn't required for your enjoyment of the gardens, which are along the blacktop path to your right as you face the front of the church. The Friary holds intermittent plant sales during the growing season but the main plant sale is at the Harvest Festival, on the third Sunday of August. It's possible to have dinner in the monastery dining room, which would be a fitting conclusion to your time in these serene gardens.

From I-94 take Wisconsin Route 11 west to Burlington. At the east edge of town, turn north onto County Road W (Browns Lake Road). The Friary and Retreat Center is on the east side of County W less than three miles north of its intersection with WI 11.

Boerner Botanical Gardens and Arboretum
Whitnall Park
5879 South 92nd Street
Hales Corners WI 53130
(414) 425-1130

◀ 1,000-acre arboretum. 40 acres of gardens. Herb, rose, and rock gardens. Other theme plantings and collections. All-America Selection and All-American Rose Selection trial and display gardens.

♿ Brochures. Shop. Many plants labeled. Library. Trails. Seasonal plant sales. Classes and other special events.
There is a fee for parking on weekends and during special events. To arrange an individual or group tour, call the Garden Friends at (414) 529-1870.
Gardens open daily April-October 8am-dusk, closed November-March. Garden House open same hours in season, winter weekdays 8am-4pm, closed winter weekends.

The sun is shining, irises and peonies are blooming, workers are tidying the herb gardens, and Boerner Gardens is particularly appealing on this late May day. Showy fern-leaved peonies (*Paeonia tenuifolia*) add elegance to hostas in semi-shaded beds. Dwarf and intermediate irises in delicious colors lead us along the Shrub Mall to a commanding view of Whitnall Park and the arboretum. The Rock Garden, where buttercups gleam against the waterfall, provides another stunning vista. Boerner Gardens occupies high ground in a rolling landscape and these semi-aerial views are a specialty here.

There are trees and flowers here to suit most tastes and to fill most landscaping needs. The trial gardens contain dahlia and sod displays, and hedge, tulip, lilac, and dwarf shrub collections in addition to roses, annuals, and vegetables. Elsewhere in the gardens, you'll find a water lily pool, collections of shrub roses, dwarf fruit trees, and a host of other trees, shrubs, and perennials. Among all these plants and gardens you'll see statuary, ponds, walks, trails, and, just when you need them most, comfortable benches.

The arboretum, which tests woody plants from all over the world for hardiness and esthetic appeal, also contains many native trees and shrubs, including a few oaks and maples that are believed to date from before 1750. Here, too, is a noteworthy collection of flowering crabapple trees (over 1,000 trees of 250 species and cultivars) and a broad collection of nut trees.

The stone Garden House holds, in addition to Boerner Garden offices and meeting rooms, the Garden Gift Shop, where you'll find attractive window ornaments, a strong collection of garden-related books, and other botany-oriented items.

Boerner's Calendar of Events is a full one. A recent year offered 22 different activities in May alone, with topics as varied as the popular Plant Doctor Clinics, a forest walk, and the Iris Society show. June finds the Milwaukee Journal Rose Festival in the gardens, a celebration that encompasses nine days of lectures and seminars, garden walks, demonstrations and workshops, and musical performances. There are nearly always rewarding things to see and do at Boerner Gardens; don't miss the opportunity to enjoy them.

From I-894 exit for Wisconsin Route 24 West (West Forest Home Avenue). Take Forest Home southwest to 92nd Street, then go south on 92nd a short distance, through a residential area, to the gardens on the west side of the road.

The American Club
Highland Drive
Kohler WI 53044
(414) 457-8000 or (800) 344-2838

Sizable courtyard garden.

♿ ☕ Some plants labeled. Sandwich shop and other dining rooms in hotel. Courtyard open most daylight hours during warm weather.

The striking berm at the entry to the American Club, with its masses of cannas, grasses, and nicotianas, is just hint of the garden gems in the club's courtyard, a greenery that is just what a courtyard should be. It's intimate but not too small, lush with an intriguing variety of plants, and elegantly paved in flagstone and brick. Elevated semi-formal gardens boast ornamental grasses, nicotianas, and a variety of roses while comely pots house handsome topiaries and cunning succulents. Curly parsley and gray santolina surround flower beds where the summer's second generation of forget-me-nots blooms beneath taller plants. Dogwoods and flowering crab trees hover over banks of white-flowered hosta as cleome and plume poppies (*Macleaya cordata*) stand erect nearby. The view from the hotel rooms around this courtyard will be delightful even in early spring, because these plantings hold thousands of spring-flowering bulbs. A shade ramada and a graceful fountain adorn one end of the courtyard while a cozy gazebo inhabits the other end. The courtyard's Greenhouse, a small ice cream shop, is the ideal spot for a quick treat before you move on to Kohler's Blackwolf Run, where highly successful plantings of a different style contrast vividly with the continental charm of the courtyard. ▶

FYI The American Club was built in 1918 as housing for the Kohler Company's immigrant employees. Today it's a fine public hotel that seems more like a private estate. For information on the history of Kohler Village and on other Kohler attractions, such as The Design Center and Waelderhaus ("a house in the woods"), stop at the Visitor Center not far south of The American Club or write to The American Club.

◀ From I-43 near Sheboygan, take Exit 126 for Wisconsin Route 23 West. Go west ⅔ mile to County Road Y/Highland Drive, then go south on Highland to the American Club.
From the south, exit I-43 at WI 28 and go west to Highland/Riverside. Go north on Highland to the club.

Blackwolf Run Golf Course
Riverside Drive
Kohler

Expansive naturalistic plantings around golf course.

Open daylight hours during the growing (and golfing) season.

We've arrived on the first day of a regional golf tournament so we've been asked to park in a field across from the golf course. So much the better, as that means we *walk*, rather than drive, along the winding entry road to Blackwolf Run, along a quarter-mile or so of compelling vistas and stunning plants in all the hues of August. Masses of sunflowers and golden coneflowers glow on this overcast day; they might be almost blinding on a sunny day. Tangles of a white prairie rose shelter the mounds of pale yellow coreopsis (*Coreopsis verticillata* 'Moonbeam') that sit at their feet. Deep purple asters accent blue clouds of Russian sage (*Perovskia atriplicifolia*) and throngs of daylilies mingle in colorful abandon with magenta liatris. Rosy-purple Joe-Pye-weed enriches coves of dark alder and feathery larch while delicate tamarisk blooms pink against sturdy purple smokebushes. Conifers of many kinds and sizes, from regal white pines to humble creeping junipers, are scattered across slopes and swales and elegant grasses add gentle movement in today's breeze.

As we walk, roadside hillocks recede to reveal the sculptured golf course and the riverine woods beyond. There's nothing fussy here, just sweeps and washes and masses of healthy plants under open sky, doing what they do best. As I write this on a cold and gray day in February, I recall Blackwolf Run's entry ▶

FYI Handsome plantings abound on the golf course but, unless you're playing golf, stay near the entry road and the club house, where there is much to admire. Blackwolf Run is part of a private 800-acre wildlife sanctuary. Use of hiking trails and the golf course is limited to members or guests of the American Club, although one can walk freely along the roadways.

drive and I smile. Rarely does one see plantings with the visual impact of those that grace Blackwolf Run.

For details about Blackwolf Run Golf Course, contact the American Club (see above).

From I-43 near Sheboygan, exit at Wisconsin Route 28 and go west to Highland Drive/Riverside Drive West. Turn south onto Riverside and follow the signs for Blackwolf Run.

Spring Valley Gardens
S. 6143 Spring Valley Road
Loganville WI 53943
(608) 727-5397

Commercial. Small herb demonstration garden and greenhouse.

Most plants labeled. Seasonal plant sales. Workshops. Small business, suggested that you call before visiting.
Open May 1-December 24 Tuesday-Saturday 10am-5:30pm.

Over 300 varieties of herbs and everlastings await you in Spring Valley's sales room from early May through July, while specimens in the greenhouse and in the demonstration garden forecast those plants' development. Many of these plants, in dried form, compose the bouquets, wreaths, and other arrangements you'll find in Spring Valley's shop. At the shop, too, occasional workshops on a number of garden topics, such as plant harvesting and drying techniques or arranging dried flowers, can add to your pleasure here.

From Wisconsin Route 23 at the south edge of Loganville, go a mile west on Spring Valley Road to Spring Valley Gardens.

Allen Centennial Gardens
University of Wisconsin campus
Madison

One acre. Rock garden, water garden, English garden, and other theme gardens.

♿ Many plants labeled.
Gardens open 7am-dusk all year.

◀ A wonderful gathering of gardens is developing around Allen House, the nineteenth-century house that's been home to 5 different deans of the University of Wisconsin College of Agriculture. Today, tall grasses and native coneflowers brighten one entry to the gardens and a winding gravel walkway draws us toward the rock garden and the water garden. Limestone walls and terraces provide visual unity now; they will become less dominant but no less handsome as the garden matures. In the hillside rock garden, brilliant scarlet penstemon flowers (*Penstemon barbatus praecox* 'Nana') accent gray-leaved creeping thymes and veronicas and a rich assortment of dwarf conifers. Delectable ruby-colored pasqueflowers (*Anemone pulsatilla rubra*) will announce springtime on this hill; for now, their lacy gray-green foliage is soft against the garden's rocks.

Beyond a handsome pergola, young borders in the English Garden surround a patch of lawn; a sculptural backdrop of dark castor bean plants separates these plantings from the edible-plant gardens that are nearer the house. The deep-orange blossoms of Mexican sunflower (*Tithonia rotundifolia*), stunning against the brownstone house, also bring life to the light shade under high-trimmed evergreens.

This garden, designed for "teaching and as a service to the lay community," is funded by gifts to the university, so it will grow as gift funds increase. Eventually, there will be over 25 different garden components, including a Renaissance Terrace with mosaiculture floral beds, a Medicinal and Herbal Garden, and a Victorian Garden. The fortunate "lay community" of Madison can watch these gardens develop, as I intend to do whenever I'm in the area.

For details or an update on the gardens' progress, contact the Outreach Specialist, Horticulture/Allen Centennial Gardens, 341 Plant Science Building, 1575 Linden Drive, Madison WI 53706. (608) 262-1549.

From US 12/14 on the south side of Madison, take US 151 (Park Street) north almost to Lake Mendota. (Stay on Park Street when US 151 turns east.) The last stop sign before the lake is at Observatory Drive; you'll see the lake ahead. Turn left here and follow Observatory Drive up the hill, past a scenic overlook, and across the campus to the stop sign at Babcock. Allen House and its gardens are behind the wrought iron fence on the northwest corner of Babcock and Observatory Drive.

The Botany Garden
University of Wisconsin campus
Madison

▶

◀ One-fifth acre. Plant species arranged by families and orders. 10,000 sq.ft. greenhouse.

♿ Garden guide. Turf paths. Most plants labeled.
Garden open daylight hours every day mid-May to mid-September. Greenhouse open Monday-Friday 8am-4pm when school is in session.

Here is an attractive garden that's a teaching-research facility, a compact trove of common and less-common plants thriving in the middle of a busy campus. Behind the rose hedge and the daylilies you'll find well-labeled, well-tended garden beds accented by restful flagstone patios and inviting benches. The orange glow of Mexican sunflower (*Tithonia rotundifolia*) draws me to the large Aster Family collection, where I discover narrow-leafed zinnia (*Zinnia angustifolia*), a white-flowered zinnia that looks more like a thread-leafed coreopsis, a charming annual that I want to grow. Also attractive is small pool with water lilies and lotus. Garden guide in hand, we wander from one collection to another, delighting in the plants and learning as we go.

The Botany Department greenhouses, where the garden's tender plants spend their winters, are just up the hill from the gardens and are often open to the public. Here, too, are various botanical research experiments and, in season, seedlings for the annuals that will go into the garden.

Your enjoyment and learning here will be greatly enhanced by the guide available in the garden (or write ahead); there is a wealth of interesting plants here and I find it particularly rewarding to know what I'm seeing.

For information contact the Director, Botany Department Greenhouses and Garden, University of Wisconsin, 144 Birge Hall, 430 Lincoln Drive, Madison WI 53706. (608) 262-2235 (Botany Department) or (608) 263-2033 (Greenhouse).

See directions for Allen Centennial Gardens. Take Park Street north to just beyond the stop light at University Avenue. Look for Lathrop on your left; it looks like a parking lot but is a short street. Turn left and follow it up a hill to its dead end almost at the garden. Metered "loading space" is sometimes available for parking in this area. Pedestrian access is from University Avenue; the garden lies between University Avenue and Birge Hall.

Henry Mall
University of Wisconsin Agriculture campus
Madison

◀ 5'x100' ornamental plantings.

♿ Some plants labeled.
Open daylight hours all year.

These handsome plantings of annual and perennial flowers, accented by graceful grasses, are just a short walk west of the Botany Garden. They're between buildings on the north side of University Avenue, just east of the "Y" where University Avenue and Campus Drive come together.

Olbrich Botanical Gardens
3330 Atwood Avenue
Madison WI 53704
(608) 246-4551

14 acres. 10,000 sq. ft. conservatory. All-American Rose Selections garden. All-American Selections garden. Rock garden. Herb garden. Butterfly garden and other theme gardens.

♿ Brochure. Shop. Many plants labeled. Library. Seasonal plant sales. Classes and special events. Guided garden tours on Sundays, mid-May to through mid-September 2-3pm. Gardens open daily all year. Botanical Center, including library, open mid-May to mid-September every day 9am-5pm; mid-September to mid-May Monday-Friday 9am-5pm. Gift shop daily 10am-4pm.

Olbrich's rose garden, with its particularly appealing variety of miniature roses, is rich with bloom on this June day but the late-blooming dahlia garden is just beginning to assert itself. Tall, lush delphiniums in the nearby perennial garden guard a multitude of brightly blooming plants, including the stunning globeflower 'Golden Queen' (*Trollius ledebourii* Hort.). Greens and grays, a wealth of textures, and rich scents make the tidy herb garden a pleasant retreat. Beyond the herb garden and a small woods filled with ferns, hostas, azaleas, and rhododendrons, we come upon the rock garden, a "mountain slope" vivid in the sun. Tiny plant jewels bloom in crevices, broader colors and textures play against each other and against the rocks, sunlight floods the garden and heats the soil, and the plants are joyfully thriving. Shade gardens have long been my favorites but this sunny treasure could cause me to adjust that prejudice. ▶

◀ Olbrich Gardens, established in 1950 to commemorate Michael Olbrich, a founder of the Madison Parks System, continues to develop; recent additions or those planned include the conservatory, "a tropical paradise of lush plants, beautiful flowers, meandering walkways, and waterfalls," and a gift shop that will also sell plants.

Public involvement in these gardens is high; local horticulture societies maintain some of the specialty gardens and the Annual Garden is supported by Olds Seed Company. In the summer there are free concerts, guided garden tours, an art fair and an herb fair, a plant sale, and, in their season, iris, rose, and dahlia shows. There's a full schedule of lectures, workshops, and horticulture society meetings throughout the year. Most activities are free and open to the public.

Admirable gardens, the rich, plant-filled conservatory, and an abundance of inviting activities make me wish I lived near Olbrich Gardens. They deserve frequent visits and admiration.

From I-90 go west on US 12/18 (West Broadway) to Monona Drive. Turn north and follow Monona to the northeast corner of Lake Monona. Monona Drive becomes Atwood Avenue but the route to the gardens is clearly marked. Total distance from I-90 is about 4 miles.

University of Wisconsin Arboretum
1207 Seminole Highway
Madison WI 53711
(608) 263-7888

1,280 acres. 60-acre prairie restoration. Lilac, viburnum, and other woody plant collections.

♿ Shop. Some plants labeled. Library. Seasonal plant sale. Trails. Workshops and other activities.
Arboretum trails and landscaped areas open daily 7am-10pm. McKay Visitor Center open 9am-4pm weekdays, 12:30-4pm weekends. Closed holidays.

We drive past the arboretum's Curtis Prairie, up a small hill, . . . and are transfixed by medium-sized trees heavy with large creamy panicles, whose scent mingles with the early evening breeze. The flowers look like lilacs, smell like lilacs, and *are* lilacs. These trees are *Syringa amurensis japonica*, Japanese tree lilacs, the last-blooming of the arboretum's large collection of lilacs. Imagine the sights and scents at the peak of lilac time here. ▶

Curtis Prairie is reputedly the world's oldest restored tallgrass prairie. In late June, its 60 acres are starred with purple-stemmed spikes of a creamy white wild baptisia and narrow paths lead us around and through patches of other intriguing prairie plants. In addition to this prairie, the arboretum includes tracts of deciduous woods that are famous for their spring wildflowers, coniferous woods, wetlands, a viburnum garden, and a 50-acre garden of ornamental flowering trees and shrubs. Hiking trails traverse all these areas.

We've arrived too late in the day to enjoy McKay Visitor Center, a stone building that overlooks Curtis Prairie. The Center, host to a number of activities throughout the year, includes a small bookstore, exhibits, slide programs, and a nature reference library. Binoculars can be rented, if you've forgotten yours. Workshops here focus on natural landscaping; a spring plant sale features native Wisconsin plants. Many of the Center's events are free and available to the public.

The arboretum stresses plant and animal communities that represent Wisconsin and the upper midwest, rather than exotic and ecologically unrelated species. But our most vivid memory is of the Japanese tree lilacs.

From the westbound Beltline (Highways 12, 14, 18, and 151), exit for Seminole Highway north. The arboretum's clearly marked entrance road is about three-tenths of a mile north of the Beltline.
From the eastbound Beltline, exit right onto Todd Drive and make a sharp right turn (uphill) to the stop sign at Seminole Highway. Turn north onto Seminole and go three-tenths of a mile to the arboretum.

Wood Violet Books
3814 Sunhill Drive
Madison WI 53704
(608) 837-7207

Specialist in herb and gardening books.

Catalog. Semi-annual open houses.
Open by appointment only.

If you can't visit Wood Violet, look for this mail-order seller of horticultural books at herb and garden fairs across the midwest, where they display part of their stock of over 500 new titles. They also handle older and out-of-print titles, conduct book searches, and will happily order a special volume for you if it's not on their shelves. Future plans include a demonstration herb garden, workshops, demonstrations, and teas. The two annual open houses at Wood Violet feature all those appealing books and, perhaps, herbal refreshments; what better way would there be to spend an afternoon?

To visit Wood Violet, call for an appointment and for directions.

Mitchell Park Domes
524 South Layton Boulevard
Milwaukee WI 53215
(414) 649-9800

Three conservatory domes, each 15,000 sq.ft., in 63-acre park. Tropical, Arid, and Show domes. Exterior sunken garden.

💲 ♿ Brochures. Shop. Many plants labeled. Picnic facilities in park. Plant sales. Seminars and special events. Group discounts and tours by appointment.
Open every day, including holidays, 9am-5pm.
Houseplant horticulturist available Monday-Friday 9am-3pm, weekends and holidays 10am-3pm.

As you approach Milwaukee from the west or the south, Mitchell Park's massive domes hover in the distance like Unidentified Flying Objects. But they're definitely attached to terra firma, although they *do* hold "other worlds" of greenery. You can travel the world's deserts in the Arid Dome and walk among aloes and stapelias and mountain cereus and a host of other cacti and succulents. The strange-looking "trees" you see may be dragon trees (*Dracaena draco*), Joshua trees (*Yucca brevifolia*), or boojum (*Idria columnaris*). You can visit an oasis, where pampas grass stands above a placid pool and the surrounding palms reach for the ceiling 85 feet above.

If deserts don't appeal to you, visit the lush Tropical Dome, with its 500 varieties of orchids and enthusiastic tropical growth. You'll see plants here that you may only know from your kitchen, such as guava, chocolate (cacao), black pepper, and a variety of citruses. Follow the path to luxuriant bougainvillea, curtain vine, and Rangoon creeper (*Quisqualis indica*), admire bananas and tropical palms near the waterfall, and spy on the tropical birds that sing and nest in this Wisconsin rainforest.

The Show Dome hosts five seasonal flower shows that are complete with imaginative themes and appropriate architecture; recent displays included such delights as "The English Woodlands" and "Arabian Nights." In the lobby gift shop you can buy trendy gifts, garden-related souvenirs, and exotic plants that will be your living reminder of the Domes.

From 1898 to 1955, a Victorian-style conservatory occupied this site; the outdoor sunken gardens, alive in summer with bright annuals and a water lily pond, remain from those days. Today's domes often host displays by local horticulture societies, houseplant courses and demonstrations, and daily houseplant consultation. These Domes may not have come from another galaxy but you can see a multitude of beautiful plants and learn a great deal about *our* planet here.

From I-94 take the 26th/27th Street exit and proceed to the Domes.

Shake Rag Valley Homes and Gardens
18 Shake Rag Street
Mineral Point WI 53565
(608) 987-2808
Madison phone: (608) 241-1242 (Felly's Flowers and Greenhouses)

Commercial. Several acres gardens and restored nineteenth-century buildings. All-America Selections gardens.

💲♿ Brochures. Shops. Many plants labeled. Seasonal plant sales. Group tours by reservation.
Open daily May-October 9am-5pm.

Bright flowers, handsome foliage, and 150-year-old buildings populate Shake Rag Valley. Mineral Point was one of the first settlements in Wisconsin and Shake Rag Valley was one of the earliest sections of Mineral Point. The gardens around these buildings, however, are a mix of the old-fashioned and the very-much-up-to-date because All-America Selections gardens performance-test new plant varieties prior to commercial release. A host of recent AAS winners, and new cultivars undergoing tests, are joined by traditional flowers and abundant foliage plants on Shake Rag's grounds. Take a leisurely self-guided tour through the buildings and the gardens for an overview of social and horticultural history and change.

Shake Rag Valley is off Shake Rag Street just northeast of its intersection with Wisconsin Routes 23/39 in Mineral Point. There are public parking lots on Shake Rag Street and two or three blocks south along High Street and Jail Alley.

Prairie Ridge Nursery / CRM Ecosystems, Inc.
9738 Overland Road
Mount Horeb WI 53572
(608) 437-5245

Commercial. Specialists in native plants. 4 acres open to the public.

Catalog. Many plants labeled. Plant sales. Tours at Open House or by appointment. Nursery open late April-late October Monday-Saturday 9am-5pm. Office open all year Monday-Friday 9am-5pm. Open House second Saturday in July 2pm-dusk.

The prairie is the garden at Prairie Ridge, an establishment that focuses on the restoration of natural areas. Prairie demonstrations are glorious parcels of delicate ground-huggers, graceful grasses, knee-high forbs, and tall herbaceous perennials. All the thriving native plants you see here were propagated from seeds, not transplanted from their homes in the wild.

An Open House in mid-July features the plants that early settlers knew, fought, and used, those natives that can be so intriguing in our gardens. If you, like many of us, derive special joy and satisfaction from the native plants in your garden, you'll find new favorites in the demonstration prairie and in the nurseries. Containerized plants let you carry a bit of native prairie or woodland home to your own gardens.

From Business Route US 18/151 in Mt. Horeb, go south three blocks on Wisconsin Route 92, then go straight ahead on County Highway JG. Follow County JG a little over 4 miles to Overland Road, then turn right onto Overland and go about a mile to Prairie Ridge Nursery.

The Mount Horeb Mustard Museum
109 East Main Street
Mount Horeb WI 53572
(608) 437-3086

Commercial celebration of mustard.

 Brochure and newsletter. Shop.
Open daily May 1-Labor Day 10am-5pm.

Although it's not an herb garden, there's something quirky and appealing about a museum devoted to useful, homely mustard. Here are over 1,250 mustards from all over the world, including some with such exotic ingredients as pineapple or nettles, and an array of mustard memorabilia. A video in the museum explains the cultivation and processing of mustard. You can donate a jar of a mustard that's not represented in the collection and become a Friend of the Museum. The adjoining Fancy Food Emporium sells over 100 different mustards, choice chocolates, and other gustatory treats.

You'll have no difficulty finding the museum, on the main street of Mount Horeb.

Milaeger's Garden Mart, Inc.
4838 Douglas Avenue
Racine WI 53402-4298
(414) 639-2371

Commercial. 50 greenhouses of annuals and perennials.

♿ Catalog. Shops. Most plants labeled. Picnic facilities. Plant sales. Seminars and other special events.
Open every day except Christmas and New Year's days: January-March Monday-Saturday 8am-5pm, Sunday 9am-5pm; April-December Monday-Friday 8am-8pm, Saturday 8am-5pm, Sunday 9am-5pm.

In early April, mammoth greenhouses are Milaeger's "display gardens." One such building holds tens of thousands of geraniums, a myriad of leaf shapes, patterns, and scents. They aren't blooming yet but the flowers will be equally varied and inviting. Other houses hold subtle herbs, brilliant ranunculus, heavy-budded Easter lilies, a total of nearly 800 varieties of perennials, and multitudes of annuals. When I expressed my appreciation for public access to most of Milaeger's greenhouses, the response was, "We don't hide our greenhouses." They shouldn't be hidden; these greenhouses are spotless, the workers are helpful, and the flourishing plants are irresistible. Later in the season, large shade houses protect a vast collection of perennials and roses. What a joy it is, to roam those aisles on a fine spring day and fill the shopping cart with plants my garden *needs*.

The garden shop offers tropical plants, cacti and succulents, bird houses and feeders, seeds and bulbs, and a small collection of helpful gardening books. The gift shop, in another building, houses more "country" items and silk flowers than I ever want to see again. A small play-yard gives kids a chance to stretch travel-weary legs and you can enjoy a picnic at a shaded picnic table. ▶

◀ Milaeger's conducts free gardening seminars at both their locations, any of which would be a worthy accent to your visit. Wouldn't you like to know more about planning your herb garden, hardy flowers for the cottage garden, or establishing a water garden? I've been told that "It's worth the trip" to visit Milaeger's between Thanksgiving and Christmas, when decorated trees fill the shops and the greenhouses nearly overflow with poinsettias, cyclamens, and other holiday plants. I consider a visit to Milaeger's worth the trip at *any* time.

Milaeger's secondary location is at 8717 Highway 11, Sturtevant WI 53177, (414) 886-2117. The hours are the same as at the Douglas Avenue site and some of the seminars take place here but largest greenhouses are on Douglas Avenue.

For the easiest route to the Racine location, take I-94 to Wisconsin Route 100 north of Racine, then go east on WI 100 about 6 miles to WI 32. Turn south onto WI 32 and go another 5 or 6 miles to Milaeger's, on the west side of the road. If you want to see more of Racine, its Scandinavian pastry shops, and its lakefront and riverside, take any of the Racine exits from I-94 and go east to WI 32, then north through town to Milaeger's.
For the Sturtevant location, exit I-94 for WI 11 and go east on WI 11. Milaeger's is on the south side of the road in the village of Sturtevant.

Jones Arboretum and Botanical Gardens
Route 1
Readstown WI 54652
(608) 629-5553

128-acre arboretum. 2 acres gardens. Theme gardens and garden center. Japanese garden. Rose garden.

♿ Shop. Many plants labeled. Plant sales.
Open every day April 15-October 15 8am-8pm.

The gently rolling acres of Jones Arboretum hold "... all the trees, shrubs, and perennials that are hardy in the area and (that) are of landscape value." Theme gardens display the plants in home-garden settings; you'll see familiar garden species and meet some unusual and exotic varieties. Treat yourself to a stroll through the Japanese garden, relish the scents and textures of the herb garden, and revel in the colors and fragrance of the rose garden. Bask in the sunny rock garden. Admire the lush fern collection and the array of shapes and hues in the succulent collection.

When you've decided which plants you can no longer live without, visit the garden center, where examples of the garden's hardy plants are sold; you can leave Jones Arboretum with healthy green souvenirs as well as pleasant memories.

Jones Arboretum is on US Route 14, 3 miles north of Readstown and 7 miles south of Viroqua.

Alpine Gardens
12446 County Highway F
Stitzer WI 53825
(608) 822-6382

Commercial. Specialist in rock garden plants.

Plant list. Many plants labeled. Plant sales. Guided tours for individuals or groups by appointment.
Open business hours during the growing season (call for specifics).

Sturdy succulents and fragile-looking alpines form green, bronze, and burgundy tapestries at Alpine Gardens, where over 400 varieties of these hardy plants populate rockeries, rock gardens, wall gardens, and borders. Imagine 90 different sempervivums ("hens and chicks"), from the cobwebby *arachnoideum* cultivars, through purple, red, and blue forms, to a plant simply called "Weirdo." Wouldn't you love to have a Weirdo in your garden? Here, too, intriguing forms of *orostachys* sprawl or stand among nearly 50 varieties of sedums and a myriad of tiny ground huggers and flowering alpines. Those alpines aren't as delicate as they appear; some of these varieties originated in the wilds of Siberia; all the plants grown and sold here are hardy in Wisconsin winters.

Some authors define a *rockery* as a site of strategically placed stones that contains any plants you choose and a *rock garden* as one that holds plants specific to only one ecosystem, such as high desert, sunny mountainside, or shady limestone hill. Whether you tend a rockery or a rock garden, the plantings you want to see and the plants you want to own are at Alpine Gardens.

From Fennimore, go east on US 18 a little over a mile to County Road F. Go south on CR F about a mile and a quarter to Alpine Gardens.

FYI Another aspect of Alpine Gardens is The Calico Shop, a source of quilting supplies and quilt appraisals. The owner of both the gardens and the shop, a certified quilt lecturer and teacher, feels that rock gardening and quilting have much in common, in that both allow her to manipulate small units into a larger thing of beauty.

Orchids by Ackers
Skolaski's Glads and Field Flowers
4821 County Highway Q
Waunakee WI 53597
(608) 836-4822

Commercial. 30,000 sq.ft. orchid greenhouses. Several acres gladiolus and perennial flowers.

♿ Catalog (Skolaski's Glads only). Many plants labeled. Plant sales.
Orchids by Ackers: "Standard business hours" all year.
Skolaski's Glads and Field Flowers: Fields open during bloom season only.

Acker's orchid greenhouse is a tropical joy in the middle of farmland near urban Madison. In the "show house," large orchids remind me of Dorothy Lamour and sarongs, while tiny orchids hang from their pots like jewels on a string, all amidst the colors and intricate forms of yet other orchid varieties. Additional greenhouses are filled with lush houseplants but, at Ackers, orchids are the prize.

During the growing season the fields that surround Ackers are filled with gladiolus, daylilies, and "field flowers," meaning sturdy perennials such as liatris and yarrow, baby's breath, and statice. These fields of Skolaski's Glads and Field Flowers can be visited during the flowering season, when the plants are at their most beautiful. At the right time of year, tender gladiolus, hardy perennials, and greenhouse orchids, all at the same site, make for fascinating contrasts and comparisons. But even if you visit in the winter, when the flower fields are dormant, Ackers' splendid orchids will welcome you.

From US 12 on the west side of Madison, go east on County K to County Q (about 2 miles), then south to Ackers/Skolaski's.
On the north side of Madison, from Wisconsin Route 113 take County M west to County K. Follow County K to County Q, then south on County Q to Ackers/Skolaski's.

Index

(H) at the end of a heading indicates that this site, or at least some part of it, is accessible to the handicapped.

A. Borlin Company, 228-29
Adena State Memorial, 254-55
Adopt-A-Plot gardens, Cincinnati (H), 256
African violets, 3
Air rights, garden use of, 265
All-America City Rose Garden (Richmond, IN), 104
All-America Selections (AAS) Trial and Display Gardens:
  in Illinois, 8, 33
  in Indiana, 81, 88-89, 106-7
  in Michigan, 137, 146
  in Minnesota, 195
  in Ohio, 217, 233, 245-46, 258, 265-66
  in Wisconsin, 292, 298, 302
All-American Dahlia Trial Gardens, 259
All-American Rose Selections (AARS) Trial and Display Gardens. *See also* Rose gardens, non-AARS
  in Illinois, 21, 46, 71
  in Indiana, 79, 103
  in Michigan, 153-54, 163
  in Minnesota, 186-87
  in Ohio, 202, 219-20, 227, 239
  in Wisconsin, 292, 298
Allen Centennial Gardens (H), 295-96
Allerton, Robert, 58
Allerton Park (H), 57-58
Alpine Gardens (Stitzer, WI), 306
Alpine plants, 306
Alwerdt's Pheasant Farm and Gardens (H), 54-55
Ambergate Gardens (H), 196
American Botanist, Booksellers, 42
American Club (Kohler, WI) (H), 293-94
American Hemerocallis Society, 190
American Hosta Society, 181, 184
American Iris Society, 71
Ameri-Can Pedigreed Seed Company, 62
AmeriFlora, 215-16
Ann Arbor Flower and Garden Show (H), 126
Anna Scripps Whitcomb Conservatory and Gardens (H), 130-31
Annual International Horseradish Festival (H), 64-65

Arboretums:
  in Illinois, 8-9, 18-19, 20, 26-28,45, 49, 63-64
  in Indiana, 103-4
  in Michigan, 126-27, 146-47, 150-51, 162-63
  in Minnesota, 187
  in Ohio, 214-15, 229-30, 232-33, 237-38, 244-45, 255-56, 265-66,267, 268-69, 271-73
  in Wisconsin, 285-86, 291-93, 299-300, 305-6
Aromatherapy, 143
Art Association of Indianapolis, 101-2
Art in Bloom, festival, 285
August Schell Brewing Company, 190-91
Aullwood Gardens, 270-71
Ault Park (H), 255-57
Azalea and rhododendron collections, 63, 64, 165, 181, 209, 210, 240, 249, 266. *See also* Arboretums

Backyard Herbs 'n' Things, 205
Bailey, Liberty Hyde, 168-69
Beal Botanical Garden (H), 152-53
Beautification programs, countywide, 158, 284-85
Bed and breakfast establishments, 55, 68-69
Belle Isle (Detroit) (H), 130-31
Bellwether Garden (H), 118-19
Belnap Creek Herb Farm (H), 120-21
Biblical gardens, 52, 111, 115, 119, 134, 138, 156, 244
Bio-dynamic farming and gardening, 110
Bittersweet Farm, 236-37
Blackwolf Run Golf Course (H), 294-95
Bloomington (MN) Affiliated Garden Clubs, 179
Blue Earth County (MN) Historical Society, 185
Bluestone Perennials, 226-27
Boerner Botanical Gardens and Arboretum (H), 291-93
Bonds Herb Farm (H), 56
Bonsai Center (Mt. Clemens, MI) (H), 139
Bonsai collections, 139, 146, 215, 232, 258. *See also* Arboretums; Conservatories
Booksellers, mail-order, 42, 281, 300-301

Index / **309**

Booth, Ellen Scripps, 128
Booth, George, 128
Boydston, Kay, 165
Boydston, Walter, 165
Braeloch Farm, 167
Bri-Lea Greenhouses (H), 3
Bronson Park (H), 159
Brookville Gardens (H), 141-42
Brown, Lancelot "Capability," 281
Brown County (IN), 108
Busha's Brae, 119-20
Busse Gardens, 182-83
Butler University at Indianapolis:
    Friesner Herbarium (H), 100
    James Irving Holcomb Woods and
Butler Wildflower Garden (Minneapolis), 189-90
Butterflies, gardens designed to
    attract, 24, 90, 95, 111, 161, 257, 298
Butterworth, Katherine Deere, 43
Butterworth Center (H), 43-44

Cactus and succulent collections:
    in Illinois, 11, 15, 17, 23, 32, 51
    in Indiana, 76, 96
    in Michigan, 130
    in Ohio, 212, 215, 227, 262, 271
    in Wisconsin, 301
Calhoun County (IL), 69
Canola (*Brassica napus* L.), 62
Cantigny Farms, 12
Cantigny Gardens (H), 37-39
Cantigny Military Museum (H), 37-38
Canton (OH) Garden Center (H), 205-6
Capability's Books (H), 281
Carl and Lois Klehm Arboretum, 49
Carl G. Fenner Arboretum, 162-63
Central Illinois Rose Society, 71
Century of Progress World's Fair (1934), 14
Chadwick Arboretum (H), 214-15
Champaign-Urbana (IL) Herb Society, 6, 8
Champion Garden Towne, 236
Champion trees, national and state, 269
Chapman, John ("Johnny Appleseed"), 78
Chicago Botanic Garden (H), 22-24
Chicago Park District:
    gardens maintained by, 9-13, 14-17
    publications available from, 9
Children:
    gardens designed for, 153-54, 160, 234
    gardens maintained by, 106, 189-90
Chinese garden, 213
Christy Woods, 80-81
Church Street Plaza, University of
    Minnesota, Minneapolis (H), 187-88
Cincinnati, OH, 255-69
Cincinnati Board of Park Commissioners:
    gardens maintained by, 255-57, 259-60, 262-66
    publications available from, 255

Cincinnati Zoo and Botanical Garden (H), 257-58
Circle Herb Farm, 115-16
City of Cleveland Rockefeller Park
    Greenhouse (H), 211-12
Civic Garden Center of Greater
    Cincinnati (H), 259-60
Clark's Greenhouse and Herbal Country, 52
Clearing, The (Ellison Bay, WI), 27, 281-82
Cleveland, OH, 208-13
Cleveland Cultural Gardens, 208
Cleveland Metroparks Zoo (H), 213
College of St. Catherine (H), 193-94
Columbus, IN, 94
Columbus, OH, 213-21
Columbus (OH) Park of Roses (H), 219-20
Columbus (OH) Zoological Gardens (H), 221
Commercial growers, specialty. *See*
    Specialty commercial growers
Commercial herb growers:
    in Illinois, 31, 52, 59-60, 65-66, 67-68
    in Indiana, 82, 83-84, 94-96
    in northern Michigan, 115-16, 117-21
    in Ohio, 205, 231, 246-48, 253-54
    in southern Michigan, 127, 132-33, 138-39, 140-43, 155-56, 164
Community Fragrance Garden (H), 185-86
Como Park Conservatory (H), 194
Companion Plants (Athens, OH), 253-54
Conifer collections, 24, 25, 30, 101, 173, 233, 245, 267. *See also* Arboretums
Conservatories:
    in Illinois, 10-12, 15-16, 19, 32-33, 35, 51, 71
    in Indiana, 75-76, 96-97, 98-99, 101
    in Michigan, 126, 130-31, 146, 165
    in Minnesota, 188-89
    in Ohio, 202, 211-12, 213, 215-16, 227, 241, 245-46, 262-64, 277
    in Wisconsin, 298-99, 301-2
Consumer Horticulture Extension Program
    of Purdue University, 89
Cooley Garden (H), 162
Cottage Garden (Piasa, IL) (H), 69-70
Cox Arboretum (H), 271-73
Cranbrook House and Gardens, 127-29
Crane Park (H), 159-60
CRM Ecosystems, Inc. (H), 303
Crosby Gardens (H), 240-41
Cuneo, John F., 36
Cuneo Museum and Gardens (H), 35-36

D. A. Hoerr and Sons (H), 45-46
Daffodil collections, 89, 106, 107, 108, 165, 210, 219-20
Dahlia gardens, 66, 130, 259, 292, 298
Danville (IL) Garden Club herb study
    groups, 18
Dawes, Beman, 233

Dawes, Bertie, 233
Dawes, Gen. C. G., 233
Dawes Arboretum (H), 232-33
Daylily collections, 89, 106, 190, 192, 197
Deep River County Park (H), 88
Deere family, 44
Deere-Wiman House (H), 44-45
Delhi Garden Center (H), 258-59
Detroit Garden Center (H), 131-32
Dr. Liberty Hyde Bailey Birthsite Museum, 168-69
Dooley Gardens (H), 183
Douglas Park Formal Garden (Chicago), 9-10
Dow Gardens (H), 137-38
Duluth Rose Garden, 173
Dye gardens, 7, 52, 142, 181, 238

E. G. Hill Memorial Rose Garden, 104
Early American Garden (Mahomet, IL) (H), 29-31
Earth Shelter (Oak Park, IL), 32
Ecology Center (Evanston, IL), 20
Economic plant collections, 11, 15, 23, 71, 126, 146, 212, 263, 301. *See also* Conservatories
Edible landscaping, 272
Edsel and Eleanor Ford House (H), 134-36
Einerlei, 114
Eli Lilly Botanical Gardens (H), 101-2
Elmhurst College Arboretum (H), 18-19
Eloise Butler Wildflower Garden, 189-90
Enchanted Crest, 55
Enger Park (H), 172-73
Englearth Gardens (H), 158
English-style gardens, 22-23, 193, 201-2, 238, 247, 285, 295
Ensata Gardens (Galesburg, MI) (H), 154-55
Euonymus collection, 38
Evergreen Garden (Glencoe, IL), 25

Fair Lane (Dearborn, MI) (H), 129-30
Falconskeape Gardens, 228
Fellows Riverside Gardens (H), 248-49
Fenner Arboretum, 162-63
Fern collections, 15, 32, 103, 130, 164-66, 194, 212
Fernwood (H), 164-66
Festival of Flowers (Manitowoc, WI), 284-85
Field Museum of Natural History, Library at (H), 10
Fithian, Dr. William, 18
Fleece-to-shawl demonstration, 207
Floral calendar, 51
Floral clocks, 49, 130, 263
Flowerfest, Inc. (Kalamazoo, MI), 158-59
Foellinger-Freimann Botanical Conservatory (H), 75-76
Ford, Henry, 129-30
Formal gardens:
    in Illinois, 9, 12, 16, 17, 22, 35, 38, 57-58
    in Indiana, 97
    in Michigan, 127-29, 130, 145, 154
    in Minnesota, 181, 192
    in Ohio, 211, 248-49, 264
    in Wisconsin, 285
Fort Wayne, IN, 75-79
Foster Gardens (H), 76-77
4H Children's Garden, 190
Fox Hill Farm (H), 166
Fragrance gardens, 18, 52, 111, 132, 134, 142-43, 181, 185-86, 234, 244, 261
Fragrant Fields (Dongola, IL) (H), 67-68
Frances Park Memorial Garden (H), 163-64
Franklin Park Conservatory (Columbus, OH) (H), 215-16
Fred W. Green Memorial Garden Center (H), 249
Freimann Square Civic Garden (H), 77-78
Friesner Herbarium, Butler University (H), 100

Garden Center of Greater Cleveland (H), 208-10
Garden Club of Evanston (IL), 22
Garden Club of Illinois, 70
Garden restorations, 108-9, 143-44, 204-5
Garden Village (Toledo, OH), 241
Gardenview Horticultural Park, 237-38
Garfield Monument (Cleveland), 211
Garfield Park Conservatory (Chicago) (H), 10-12
Garfield Park Conservatory and Formal Garden (Indianapolis) (H), 96-97
Garfield Park Formal Garden (Chicago), 12
Gateway Garden Center, 224-25
Gathered Herb, 140-41
Gene Stratton Porter State Historic Site, 82-83
George A. Luthy Memorial Botanical Garden (H), 46-47
Glasshouse Works (H), 277
Glencoe (IL) downtown parks (H), 24-25
Glenn Miller Park, 104
Goldsmith Garden at Hale Farm and Village, 204-5
Gordon F. Moore Community Park (H), 62-63
Grand Hotel Gardens (Mackinac Island) (H), 116-17
Grand Marais Garden Club, 174
Grand Oak Herb Farm, 127
Grand Portage National Monument (H), 174-75
Grand View Lodge (H), 175
Grandma's Garden (Lincoln Park, Chicago), 16
Grant Park (Chicago) (H), 12-13
Grass Roots Nursery (H), 140
Green Bay Botanical Garden, 283
Green Memorial Garden (H), 163-64
Greenfield Herb Garden (H), 83-84
Greenhouses:
    municipal, 25, 131, 211-12

Index / **311**

at universities, 80-81, 107, 297
Grosse Pointe Garden Center, Inc., 133-34
Grosse Pointe War Memorial Center, 134
Grow with Your Neighbor (Dayton, OH), 275

Hale Farm and Village, 204-5
Hamilton County (IN) Master Gardener Association (H), 81
Hampton Court (England), 285
Hauberg, Susanne Denkman, 50
Hauberg Civic Center (H), 50-51
Hauck, Cornelius, 260
Hauck, John, 261
Hauck Botanic Gardens and The Civic Garden Center of Greater Cincinnati (H), 259-60
Hauck House, 260-61
Hawthorn-Mellody Farms, 36
Hayes, Stanley W., 104
Hayes Regional Arboretum, 103-4
Heavenly Scent Herb Farm, 132-33
Heaven's Herbal Creations, 160-61
Hemerocallis Society of Minnesota, 197
Henry Mall, at University of Wisconsin (H), 297-98
Herb Barn (H), 151-52
Herb gardens:
  in Indiana, 82, 83-84, 88-90, 94-96, 102, 110, 111-12
  in Minnesota, 181, 182, 185
  in northeastern Illinois, 6-8, 17, 18, 24, 30, 32
  in northern Michigan, 114, 116, 117-21
  in northern Ohio, 203, 207, 209, 219-20, 227, 231, 234, 238-39, 240, 242-44
  in northwestern Illinois, 47-48
  in southeastern Illinois, 55-57, 59-60
  in southeastern Michigan, 125, 128, 131-34, 138-39, 140-42
  in southern Ohio, 253-56, 261-62, 268, 271-72, 276-77
  in southwestern Illinois, 65-66, 67-68, 70
  in southwestern Michigan, 150, 151-52, 156, 160, 164-67
  in Wisconsin, 286, 292, 295, 298, 305
Herb N' Ewe (H), 238-39
Herb product factory (Kalamazoo, MI), 160
Herb Society of America (Mentor, OH), 230
Herbal Endeavors, 142-43
Herbs of Grace Garden, 59
Herbs of Grace Workshop (H), 59-60
Heritage Restaurant and Gardens (H), 261-62
Hidden Lake Gardens (H), 145-47
Hill Memorial Rose Garden, 104
Hillsdale Gardens, 97
Hilltop Garden and Nature Center (H), 106-7
Hillview Display Gardens, 233-34
Hiram (OH), Village of, 222-23
Historic buildings with gardens:
  Adena State Memorial (Chillicothe, OH), 254-55
  American Club (Kohler, WI), 293-94
  Butterworth Center (Moline, IL), 43-44
  Clearing, The (Ellison Bay, WI), 27, 281-82
  Cranbrook House and Gardens (Bloomfield Hills, MI), 127-29
  Daweswood House Museum (Newark, OH), 232-33
  Deere-Wiman House (Moline, IL), 44-45
  Edsel and Eleanor Ford House (Grosse Pointe Shores, MI), 134-36
  Enchanted Crest (Belle Rive, IL), 55
  Fair Lane (Dearborn, MI), 129-30
  Gene Stratton Porter State Historic Site (Rome City, IN), 82-83
  Hauberg Civic Center (Rock Island, IL), 50-51
  Heritage Restaurant and Gardens (Cincinnati, OH), 261-62
  Hoover Historical Center (North Canton, OH), 234
  Hubbard House (Mankato, MN), 184-85
  John Hauck House (Cincinnati), 260-61
  Kelton House Museum and Garden (Columbus, OH), 216-17
  Kingwood Center (Mansfield, OH), 227-28
  Lantern Court (Mentor, OH), 230
  Mayowood (Rochester, MN), 192
  Moross House (Detroit), 131-32
  Paine Art Center and Arboretum (Oshkosh, WI), 285-86
  Robert Allerton Park and Conference Center (Monticello, IL), 57-58
  Saginaw (MI) Art Museum, 143-44
  Stan Hywet Hall and Gardens (Akron, OH), 201-3
  T. C. Steele State Historic Site (Nashville, IN), 108-9
  Vermilion (IL) County Museum, 17-18
  Wagnalls Memorial (Lithopolis, OH), 275-76
Historic homes (no gardens):
  Dr. Liberty Hyde Bailey Birthsite Museum, 168-69
  Herb Society of America headquarters (Mentor, OH), 230
Historic village restorations:
  Hale Farm and Village (Bath, OH), 204-5
  New Harmony, IN, 109-11
  Shake Rag Valley Homes and Gardens (Mineral Point, WI), 302
  Sharon Woods Village (Cincinnati), 268
Hoerr and Sons (H), 45-46
Holcomb Woods and Gardens, 99-100
Holden Arboretum (H), 229-30
Hoover, W. H., 234
Hoover Historical Society, Gardens of the Herb Society (H), 234
Horseradish Festival (H), 64-65
Horticultural libraries and archives:
  Andersen Horticultural Library

(Chanhassen, MN), 181
Bio-dynamics Lending Library (New Harmony, IN), 110
Canton (OH) Garden Center, 205-6
Chicago Botanic Garden, 24
Corning Collection of Horticultural Classics (Cleveland), 209
Dow Gardens (Midland, MI), 137-38
Eleanor Squire Library (Cleveland), 209
Gardenview Horticultural Park (Strongsville, OH), 237-38
Inniswood (Westerville, OH), 243
Jens Jensen archives (Lisle, IL), 27-28
Lloyd Library and Museum (Cincinnati), 264
Moross House (Detroit), 131
New Indianapolis Zoo, 99
Sterling Morton Library (Lisle, IL), 27-28
Wegerzyn Horticultural Center (Dayton, OH), 275
Horticultural therapy, 33
Hosta collections, 117, 181, 192. *See also* Arboretums; Specialty commercial growers
Houseplant clinics and hotlines, 11, 32, 131, 292
Hubbard House Gardens (H), 184-85
Humboldt Park Flower Garden, 13
Hummingbirds, gardens designed to attract, 90, 111, 161, 257, 298
Hunter's Creek Perennial Gardens (H), 136-37
Hurd Memorial Garden, 222

Illinois Herb Association, 54
Illinois Native Plant Society, 70
Indiana Department of Natural Resources, 106
Indiana University at Bloomington:
    Hilltop Garden and Nature Center, 106-7
    University Greenhouses, 107
Indianapolis, IN, 96-102
Indianapolis Museum of Art, 101-2
Innis, Grace, 244
Innis, Mary, 244
Inniswood Metro Gardens (H), 243-44
Insull, Samuel, 36
International Carillon Festival, 71
Iris Acres (Winamac, IN) (H), 91
Iris collections, 89, 106, 292. *See also* Specialty commercial growers
Irwin Gardens and Greenhouse, 94
Irwin M. Krohn Conservatory, 262-64
Italianate gardens, 94, 144, 208

Jackson Park (Chicago), 13-15
Jackson Park Perennial Garden, 14-15
Jaenicke Garden, 78-79
James A. Garfield Monument, 211
James Irving Holcomb Woods and Botanical Garden (H), 99-100

Japanese Garden at Normandale Community College (H), 179-80
Japanese Garden on Wooded Island, 9, 13-14
Japanese gardens:
    in Illinois, 9, 13-14, 23
    in Indiana, 90
    in Michigan, 144-45, 165
    in Minnesota, 179-80, 194-95
    in Ohio, 201-2, 206, 209, 211-12, 215-16, 232
    in Wisconsin, 305
Japanese maple collection, 64
Jaques House Garden (H), 6-7
Jensen, Jens:
    archives of, 27-28
    Chicago Forest Preserve District, creation of, 282
    Chicago Park System, work in, 27
    The Clearing, founding of, 281-82
    gardens and landscape designs by, 21-22, 27-29, 70-71, 129-30, 134-36, 281-82
    Illinois State Park System, creation of, 282
    The Ridges Sanctuary, participation in, 280
Jeptha Wade Memorial Chapel, 211
Joanne's Garden (H), 282-83
John Hauck House, 260-61
Johnny Appleseed legend, 78
Jones Arboretum and Botanical Gardens (H), 305-6

Kalamazoo, MI, 158-61
Kalamazoo Garden Council, 160
Kalamazoo Nature Center, 161
Kalamazoo Valley Plant Growers Co-op, 158
Kellogg Center, 153
Kelton House Museum and Garden (H), 216-17
Kent County Harvest Tours, 156
King, Charles K., 228
Kingwood Center (H), 227-28
Klehm Arboretum, 49
Klehm's Nursery, 4-5
Kohler Company, 293
Krohn Conservatory (H), 262-64

Ladd Arboretum (H), 20
Lake County, OH, 235
Lake County Nursery (H), 234-36
Lake Forest Symphony, 36
Lake View Cemetery Association (H), 210-11
Lakeside Rose Garden (H), 79
Lakeview Rose Garden, 225-26
Lansing, MI, 161-64
Lantern Court (Mentor, OH), 229-30
Latin American garden, 211-212
Lawn ornaments, 283
Leigh's Bloomers, 111-12
Leila Arboretum (H), 150-51
Leila Arboretum Society, 151
Lewis Mountain Herbs and Everlastings (H), 276-77

Library at the Field Museum of Natural
    History (H), 10
Lilac collections, 28-29, 100, 116,
    165, 228, 266, 267, 292, 299. *See also*
    Arboretums
Lilac festivals, 29, 116
Lilacia Park (H), 28-29
Lilly, J. K., 101
Lily of the Valley Herb Farm (H), 231
Limberlost State Historic Site, 79-80
Lincoln, Abraham:
    Abraham Lincoln Memorial Garden (H),
        70-71
    election of, 38
    St. Gaudens's sculpture of, 13
Lincoln Park Conservatory and Gardens
    (Chicago) (H), 15-16
Lindsay Tennis Center Garden (H), 5-6
Link, Mrs. Helen, 108
Link Memorial Daffodil Garden, 107-8
Little Farm Herb Shop (H), 150
Lloyd Library and Museum, 264
Longview Park and Gardens (H), 51-52
Luthy Memorial Botanical Garden (H), 46-47
Lyndale Park Gardens (H), 186-87
Lytle, Gen. William Henry, 265
Lytle Park, 264-65

Mackinac Island, 116-17
Madison in Bloom (Madison, IN) (H), 102-3
Maple Spring (Grant, MI) (H), 155
Marberry, William, 64
Marberry Arboretum, 63-64
Mari-Mann Herb Company, 65-66
Marquette Park Rose Garden and Trial
    Garden (Chicago), 16-17
Master Gardener Association of Hamilton
    County, IN, 81
Master Gardener Association of
    Tippecanoe County, IN, 89
Matthei Botanical Gardens (H), 125-26
Maumee (OH) Valley Herb Society, 240
Mayo Medical Center Gardens (H), 191-92
Mayowood, 192
McCormick, Col. Robert R., 38
Meadowbrook Herb Garden, 7-8
Medicinal plants:
    in Illinois, 7, 18, 33, 52, 57
    in Michigan, 115, 126
    in Minnesota, 181
    in Ohio, 243-244, 268
Medill, Joseph, 38
Memorial architecture, 210-11, 269
Menno-Hof Visitor Center, 84-85
Men's Garden Club of Minneapolis, 185
Merrick Rose Garden (H), 20-21
Michigan State University at East Lansing:
    Beal Botanical Garden (H), 152-53
    Hidden Lake Gardens (at Tipton) (H),
        146-47
    Horticultural Demonstration Gardens
        (H), 153-54
Midway Plaisance (Chicago), 14, 17
Milaeger's Garden Mart, Inc. (H), 304-5
Minneapolis, MN, 185-90
Minneapolis Sculpture Garden (H), 188-89
Minnesota Department of Natural
    Resources, 172
Minnesota Landscape Arboretum (H), 180-81
Mitchell Park Domes (H), 301-2
Moore Community Park (Alton, IL) (H),
    62-63
Moross House, 131-32
Morton, J. Sterling, 28
Morton, Joy, 28
Morton Arboretum (H), 26-28, 64
Mt. Airy Arboretum in Mt. Airy Forest (H),
    265-66
Mount Horeb Mustard Museum (H), 303-4
Mullin Horticultural Garden and Woodland,
    195
Munsinger Gardens, 192-93

Nan Elliot Memorial Rose Garden (H), 62-63
National Crabapple Evaluation Program, 245
Native plants. *See also* Prairie restorations;
    Prairie-type plantings; Wildflower
    gardens and sanctuaries; Woodland
    gardens
    medicinal plant collection, 57
    Prairie Days (MN), 172
    sources for, 34-35, 57, 68-69, 103, 182,
        183, 196, 303
    Wildflower Forays, IN, 106
    Wildflower Task Force, 172
    Wildflower Weekends, 172
    Wilson Wildflower Trail
        (Cincinnati, OH), 266
Natural Garden (St. Charles, IL), 34-35
New American Garden style, 5-6
New Harmony, IN (H), 109-11
New Hope Herb Farm (H), 111
New Indianapolis Zoo (H), 98-99
Newburgh Country Store (H), 109
Nichols and Dimes Antiques and Herbs
    (Elizabethtown, IN), 95-96
Nichols Arboretum (Ann Arbor, MI), 126
Noel Garden (Champaign, IL), 8
Noerenberg Memorial County Park (H), 197-98

Oak Hill Gardens, 37
Oak Park (IL) Conservatory (H), 32-33
Oak Park (IL) Visitor Center, 33
Oakdale Herb Farm, 56-57
OARDC, 244-45
Oehme, van Sweden and Associates, 5, 188
Ohio Agricultural Research and
    Development Center (OARDC), 244-45
Ohio State University at Columbus:
    Agricultural Technical Institute
        (OSU/ATI) (at Wooster) (H), 245-46
    Chadwick Arboretum (H), 214-15

Ohio Unit of the Herb Society of
    America, 243
Olbrich, Michael, 299
Olbrich Botanical Gardens (H), 298-99
Old Greenhouse (Cincinnati) (H), 266-67
Olds Seed Company, 299
Olmstead, Frederick Law, 131
Orchid collections. *See also* Conservatories;
    Specialty greenhouses
  in Illinois, 15, 23, 30, 35, 46, 49
  in Indiana, 80-81, 101, 110
  in Michigan, 126
  in Ohio, 212, 227
  in Wisconsin, 301
Orchids by Ackers (H), 307
Orchids by Hausserman, 36-37
Ordway Memorial Japanese Garden, 194-95
Oriental gardens, 63, 66-67, 128. *See also*
    Chinese garden; Japanese gardens
Ornamental flowering trees,
    collections of, 63, 237, 245, 263, 266,
    267, 272, 292. *See also* Arboretums
OSU/ATI, 245-46
Owen, Robert, 110

Paine Art Center and Arboretum (H), 285-86
Papa's Barn (Mattawan, MI) (H), 164
Parsley Pot, 203
Passenger pigeons, 258
Peninsula Agricultural Research Station
    (Door County, WI), 287
Peony collections, 89, 117
Peony growers, commercial, 4-5
Pioneer gardens, 102, 165
Plant Doctor Clinics, 11, 32, 131, 292
Plant Locator Service, 181
Planter's Palette (H), 39-40
Plantlife Resources Project, 25-26
Porter, Gene Stratton, 80
Prairie Days (MN), 172
Prairie restorations, 69, 126, 162-63,
    299-300
Prairie Ridge Nursery / CRM Ecosystems,
    Inc. (H), 303
Prairie-type plantings, 20, 24, 30, 32, 195
President's Garden (Cincinnati), 263
Purdue University at Lafayette:
    Consumer Horticulture Extension
      Program, 89
    Horticulture Gardens (H), 88-89

Quail Ridge Farm (H), 90-91
Quailcrest Farm (H), 246-48

Rahr-West Museum (Manitowoc, WI), 285
Reading, gardens for, 28, 209
Rice Creek Gardens (H), 179
Ridges Sanctuary, 280
Rivergreenway (Fort Wayne), 76, 77, 78
Riverside Park (H), 192-93
Robert Allerton Park and Conference
    Center (H), 57-58

Rock gardens:
  in Illinois, 16, 17, 38, 45
  in Indiana, 101
  in Michigan, 125, 133, 136, 138, 165
  in Minnesota, 173, 186, 193
  in Ohio, 233, 242, 243, 246, 249, 256,
    271, 273-74
  in Wisconsin, 292, 295-96, 298, 305, 306
Rock Island Women's Club, Garden
    Department, 50
Rockefeller, John D., 212
Rockefeller Park Greenhouse, 211-12
Rohrer Rose Garden (H), 198
Roman Cultural Garden (Springfield, IL), 71
Rose gardens, AARS. *See* All-American Rose
    Selections (AARS) Trial and Display
    Gardens
Rose gardens, non-AARS:
  in Indiana, 97-98, 104
  in Michigan, 116, 127, 129, 134-35, 159
  in Minnesota, 173, 181, 185-86, 192, 198
  in northeastern Illinois, 12, 16-17,
    22, 24, 26, 35, 38
  in northern Ohio, 209, 219-20, 225-26,
    229-30, 239, 241, 243, 248
  in northwestern Illinois, 44, 49
  in southeastern Illinois, 55-56
  in southern Ohio, 255-56, 269, 274-75
  in southwestern Illinois, 62-63, 66
  in Wisconsin, 285, 305
Rosenfeld, Dr. Ingrid J., 25
Ross, Henry, 237-38
Rotary International Friendship Garden
    (Evanston, IL), 20

Sacred (biblical) gardens, 52, 115, 119,
    134, 138, 156, 244
Saginaw (MI) Art Museum, 143-44
Saginaw (MI) Rose Garden, 145
Saginaw-Tokushima Friendship Garden (H),
    144-45
St. Francis Friary and Retreat Center, 291
St. Johns Mint Festival (H), 167-68
St. Paul, MN, 193-95
Sassafras Hutch, 156
Save the Prairie Society, 32
Savory's Gardens, Inc., 184
Scented geranium collections, 96, 214.
    See also Specialty commercial growers
Schmidt Nursery (H), 217
Scovill Park Gardens (H), 66-67
Sculpture gardens, 188-89
Seiberling family, 201-2
Senior Garden Club of Triton College, 33
Shady Acres Nursery (Chaska, MN) (H), 182
Shady Hill Gardens (Batavia, IL), 4
Shady Oaks Nursery (Wauseca, MN) (H),
    196-97
Shake Rag Valley Homes and Gardens (H), 302
Shakespeare Garden (Evanston, IL) (H), 21-22
Shakespeare gardens, 7, 21-22, 33, 90, 115,
    119, 138, 208

Sharon Woods Village (H), 268
Sinnissippi Greenhouse and Gardens (H), 49-50
Skolaski's Glads and Field Flowers, 307
Smith, Carlton, 273
Smith Memorial Gardens, 273-74
Smith's Greenhouse and Supply, 42-43
"Sooty Acres," 260
Specialty commercial growers:
    for bonsai plants, 139
    for chrysanthemums, 183
    for daylilies, 4-5, 158
    for edible flowers, 155
    for geraniums, 4
    for gladiolus, 31, 286-87, 307
    for gourmet vegetables, 155
    for herbs. *See* Commercial herb growers
    for hostas, 158, 184, 207-8
    for irises, 91, 154-55, 158
    for Japanese and Siberian irises, 154-55
    for mints, 167-68
    for native plants, 34-35, 68-69, 303
    for pansies, 42-43
    for peonies, 4-5
    for rock garden plants, 306
    for shade-loving plants, 196-97, 207-8
    for water plants, 140, 223-24, 233-34
Specialty greenhouses:
    for African violets, 3
    for bonsai, 139
    for geraniums, 4
    for orchids, 36-37, 228-29, 307
    for uncommon plants, 277
Spring Grove Cemetery and Arboretum (H), 268-69
Spring Hill Nurseries (H), 239
Spring Valley Gardens, 295
Springfield (IL) Roman Cultural Society, 71
Spude's, 283
Stan Hywet Hall and Gardens (H), 201-3
Stanley M. Rowe Arboretum (H), 267
Stillwater Gardens (Dayton, OH), 274-75
Stone Well at the Walnut Street Warehouse (H), 47-48
Stone Well Herbs (H), 47-48
Stream Cliff Herb Farm (H), 94-95
Succulents. *See* Cactus and succulent collections
Summer House (North Manchester, IN), 82
Sunnybrook Farms Nursery (H), 207-8
Sunshine Farm and Garden (H), 138-39
Swisher Hill Herbs (H), 242-43
Synoptic Shrub Garden (Dayton, OH), 272

T. C. Steele State Historic Site (H), 108-9
Theodore Wirth Park (H), 189-90
Tiffany, Louis Comfort, 211
Tokushima, Japan, 145
Toledo Botanical Garden (H), 240-41
Toledo Zoological Gardens (H), 241-42

Topiaries:
    in Illinois, 17, 23, 69-70
    in Michigan, 132, 138, 159
    in Minnesota, 189
    in Ohio, 217-19, 227, 233, 235
Topiary Garden in Old Deaf School Park (H), 217-19
Tree and shrub collections, 45, 55, 202, 248-49, 287, 292. *See also* Arboretums
Trial gardens, AARS. *See* All-American Rose Selections (AARS) Trial and Display Gardens
Trial gardens, AAS. *See* All-America Selections (AAS) Trial and Display Gardens
Trial gardens, non-AAS, 16-17, 134, 287
Tricker, Inc., 223-24
Triton College Botanical Garden (H), 33-34
Triton Horticulture Club, 33
Tropical plant collections, 30, 35, 49, 58, 202, 227, 241, 277. *See also* Conservatories; Specialty commercial growers

University of Illinois at Urbana-Champaign:
    Arboretum and Hartley Garden, 8-9
    campus gardens, 8
    Plant Sciences Laboratory conservatory, 8
    Robert Allerton Park and Conference Center (at Monticello), 57-58
University of Michigan at Ann Arbor:
    Fair Lane (at Dearborn), 129-30
    Matthei Botanical Gardens, 125-26
    Nichols Arboretum, 126-27
University of Minnesota at Minneapolis:
    Church Street Plaza (H), 187-88
    Minnesota Landscape Arboretum (at Chanhassen) (H), 180-81
University of Wisconsin at Madison:
    Arboretum (H), 299-300
    Botany Garden (H), 296-97
    Henry Mall (H), 297-98

Van Drunen Farm (H), 31
Veldheer/DeKlomp Tulip Gardens (H), 157
Vermilion (IL) County Museum, 17-18
Virginia Clemens Rose Garden, 192
Visually impaired visitors, gardens for, 18, 63, 206, 211-12

Wagnalls, Mabel, 276
Wagnalls Memorial, 275-76
Washington National Cherry Tree Walk (Evanston, IL), 20
Washington Park Botanical Garden (Springfield, IL) (H), 71-72
Washington Park Formal Garden (Chicago), 17
Water gardens. *See also* Water lily pools
    in Michigan, 136, 140

in Ohio, 223-24, 233, 237, 241, 256, 258-59, 272
in Wisconsin, 295
Water lilies, sales of, 140, 223-24
Water lily pools. *See also* Water gardens
in Illinois, 9-10, 12
in Michigan, 130
in Ohio, 210, 237
in Wisconsin, 292, 302
Watts, May Theilgaard, 28
Waushara Gardens, 286-87
Wedding gardens, 22, 46, 77, 96, 184-85
Weed collection, 153
Wegerzyn, Benjamin, 275
Wegerzyn Horticultural Center and Stillwater Gardens (H), 274-75
West Michigan Botanic Garden, 155
West Michigan Horticultural Society, 155
West of the Lake Gardens (Manitowoc, WI), 283-84
Western Reserve Herb Garden (H), 209
Wheeler Orchid Collection and Species Bank, 80-81
Whetstone Park (H), 219-20
Whitcomb Conservatory and Gardens (H), 130-31
Wilder Park Conservatory (H), 19
Wildflower Farm (Grafton, IL) (H), 68-69
Wildflower gardens and sanctuaries:
in Illinois, 20, 24, 32
in Indiana, 108
in Michigan, 128, 131
in Minnesota, 173-74, 189-90, 195
in Ohio, 216, 221, 259
in Wisconsin, 280
Wildflower Sanctuary (Grand Marais, MN), 173-74

William Marberry Arboretum, 63-64
William Tricker, Inc., 223-24
Wilson's Garden Center/Hillview Display Gardens (H), 233
Windmill Island Municipal Park (H), 157-58
Windy Pines Natural Farm, 57
Wintergreen Herbs and Potpourri (Charlevoix, MI), 115
Wirth Daylily Garden, 190
Wirth Park, 189-90
Witches' gardens, 48, 52, 142
Women's National Farm and Garden Association, 130
Wood Violet Books (Madison, WI), 300-301
Woodland gardens:
in Illinois, 34, 50, 70-71
in Michigan, 125
in Minnesota, 173-74, 180-81
in Ohio, 228, 243, 253, 272, 275
in Wisconsin, 286
Woodland Herbs (Northport, MI) (H), 117-18
World's Columbian Exposition (1893), 9, 10, 14, 17
Worthington, Thomas, 254
Wright, Frank Lloyd, 27, 33, 48

Xeriscaping, 131, 256

Yard art, 283

Zoological gardens:
in Cincinnati, 257-58
in Cleveland, 213
in Columbus (OH), 221
in Indianapolis, 98-99
in Toledo, 241-42